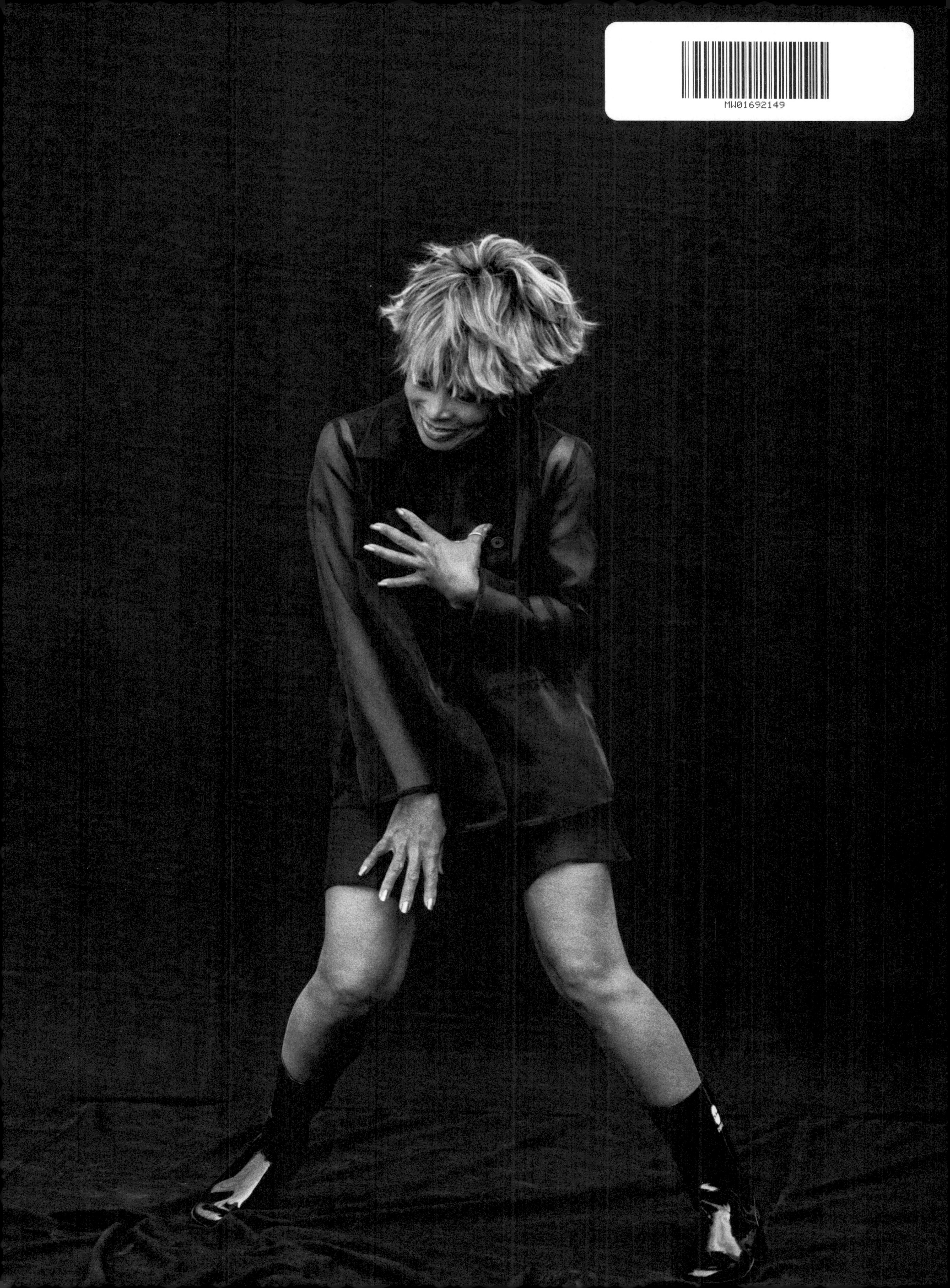

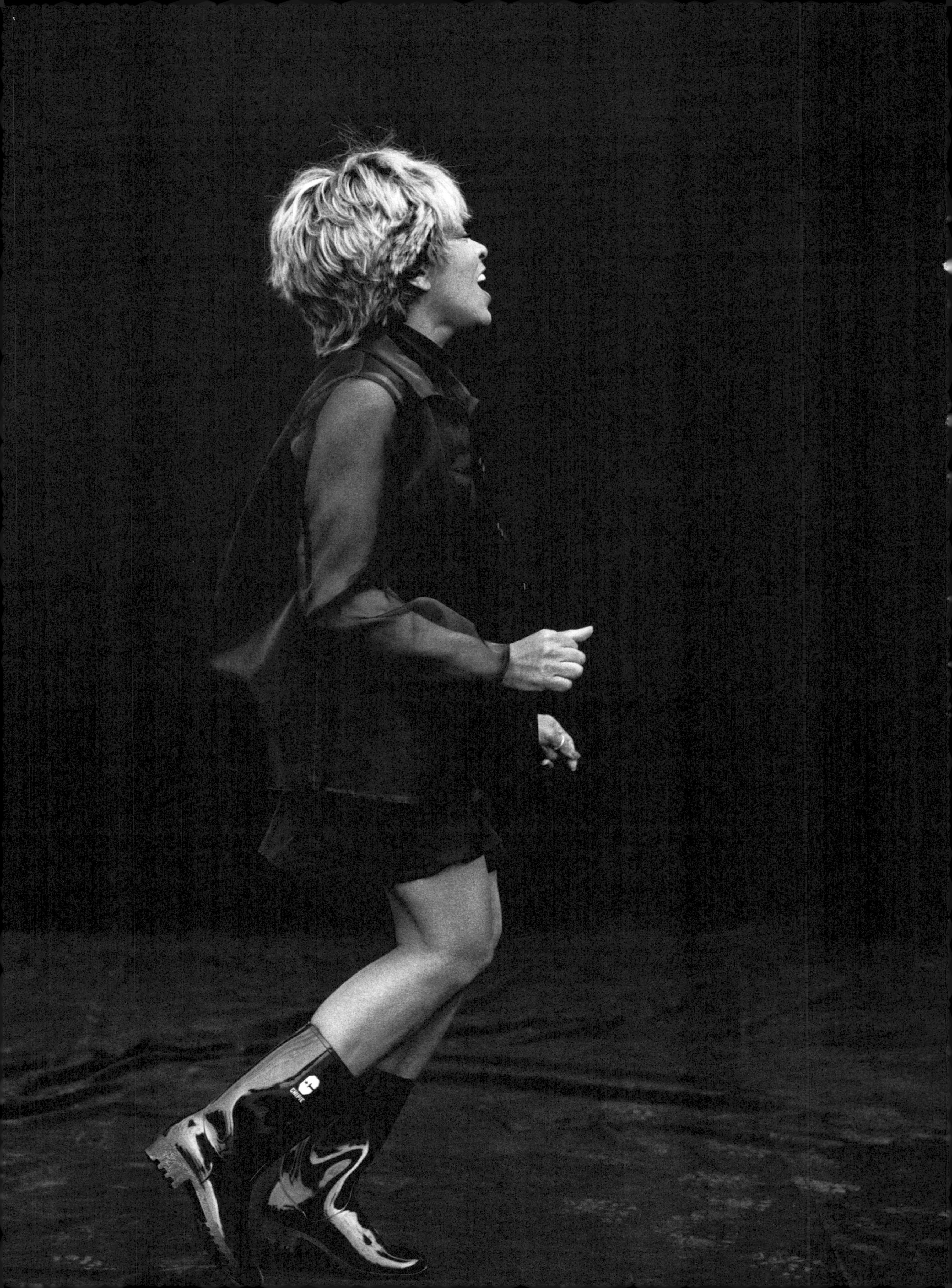
CHIPIE

Tina Turner

by Peter Lindbergh

TINA TURNER
BY PETER LINDBERGH

TASCHEN

Tina and Peter
Foreword by Erwin Bach

If I want to see vibrant images of Tina—the *real* Tina—I just have to look at Peter Lindbergh's extraordinary photographs. There she is, her head thrown back as she perches daringly on the Eiffel Tower with all of Paris at her feet. In another shot, she lowers her sunglasses to reveal a sultry look that says, "I know everything." And in yet another, only her hands and knees are visible—but her hands and knees are so expressive they could belong to only Tina. Peter saw her as a work of art, a fashion and beauty icon, and, more importantly, a joyous, powerful, and deeply spiritual woman.

Peter, who photographed a pantheon of remarkable subjects, had strong feelings about Tina. He said, "There is nobody in the world like Tina—an unbelievable woman. The most energetic woman I know and the most quiet woman I know." Whether he photographed her on the beach in Deauville for the *Foreign Affair* album (in one shot, she wears an Alaïa ball gown and carries a hat case and a boom box as she walks across the sand to the ocean, and somehow the improbable juxtaposition seems *exactly* right), or filmed her strutting exuberantly on the Paramount backlot for the "Missing You" music video and the Hanes advertising campaign, he always found the essence of Tina.

Tina marveled at Peter's talent and vision. She said, "Sometimes I felt he could see into my soul—Peter had a unique ability to capture all sides of me—the woman, the child, the prankster, the seeker, the true believer." He was an eclectic artist who found inspiration everywhere—his mind was always working. Seen through his transformative lens, even an image of Tina applying eyeliner becomes a meditation on timeless beauty. Tina trusted Peter because they had a true exchange of thoughts. When he said, "Give me *this*," during a photo session, she knew exactly what he wanted and immediately brought his idea to life.

What I loved about Peter was his complete lack of pretense. Despite being a great artist and a consummate professional, he was a casual, down-to-earth man who was happiest wearing jeans and a baseball cap. Fame meant nothing to him. He was more interested in the person behind the image. I felt the same way. We were both very grounded and forthright and appreciated that about each other. We also had similar backgrounds: we both grew up in the Rhineland in western Germany, only about a hundred kilometers apart, and spoke the same language. There was an immediate bond between us that was special in the circus of celebrity, where relationships can be superficial. In German, we call it *innige Freundschaft*—when you're happy to see someone because you share a real connection.

Tina and I were so comfortable with Peter that whenever one of us wanted or needed anything from the other, the automatic answer was yes, no questions asked.

In 2016, we attended the opening of his retrospective, *A Different Vision on Fashion Photography*, at the Kunsthal Rotterdam, where his friends from all over the world gathered to celebrate his life's work. Later that year, he visited us at our home in Switzerland when *Blau* magazine sent him to photograph the Giacometti sculptures at the Alberto Giacometti Foundation in Zurich—a brilliant pairing because Peter could make anything, even an inanimate object, come to life.

During his visit, we had dinner on the terrace and entertained each other with stories about the old days. Tina and Peter rubbed shoulders as we talked and laughed—good friends, enjoying each other's company, as we always did. Tina and I were both touched when Peter once said that we were "the best example of what two people can do with what is called love." He always knew what was real—in life and in art—and prized it above all else.

That was the last time we saw Peter.

I'll give Tina the final word here because she had a wonderful way of describing their relationship: "We were partners in crime. He was willing to try anything—and so was I! Together, we made magic!"

The magic they made together lives on in Peter's photographs. This book—a collection of images created during their long professional collaboration and enduring friendship—tells their special story.

Tina und Peter
Vorwort von Erwin Bach

Wenn ich lebendige Bilder von Tina sehen möchte – der *wahren* Tina – dann muss ich mir nur die außergewöhnlichen Fotografien von Peter Lindbergh ansehen. Da sieht man sie mit zurückgeworfenem Kopf, wie sie kühn auf dem Eiffelturm balanciert, während ihr ganz Paris zu Füßen liegt. In einer anderen Aufnahme senkt sie ihre Sonnenbrille und offenbart einen verführerischen Blick, der sagt: „Ich durchschaue dich." Und in einer wieder anderen sind nur ihre Hände und Knie zu sehen – aber was für welche! Hände und Knie so ausdrucksstark, dass sie nur Tina gehören können. Peter sah in ihr ein Kunstwerk, eine Mode- und Schönheitsikone und, was noch wichtiger ist, eine fröhliche, kraftvolle und zutiefst spirituelle Frau.

Peter, der ein ganzes Pantheon voll bemerkenswerter Personen fotografiert hat, hegte große Gefühle für Tina. Er sagte einmal: „Es gibt niemanden auf der Welt, der mit ihr vergleichbar ist – Tina ist eine unglaubliche Frau. Die energiegeladenste Frau, die ich kenne, und die ruhigste zugleich." Ob er sie am Strand von Deauville für das Album *Foreign Affair* fotografierte (in einer Aufnahme trägt sie ein Ballkleid von Alaïa, während sie mit einem Hutkoffer und einem Ghettoblaster in der Hand über den Sand zum Meer läuft, und doch erscheint diese unwahrscheinliche Szenerie auf absurde Weise *völlig* glaubhaft) oder sie beim ausgelassenen Stolzieren auf dem Studiogelände von Paramount für das Musikvideo „Missing You" und die Hanes-Werbekampagne filmte – er schaffte es stets, Tinas besonderes Wesen einzufangen.

Tina bewunderte Peters Talent und Weitblick. Sie sagte einmal: „Manchmal hatte ich das Gefühl, dass er in meine Seele blicken konnte. Peter hatte die einzigartige Fähigkeit, alle meine Facetten einzufangen

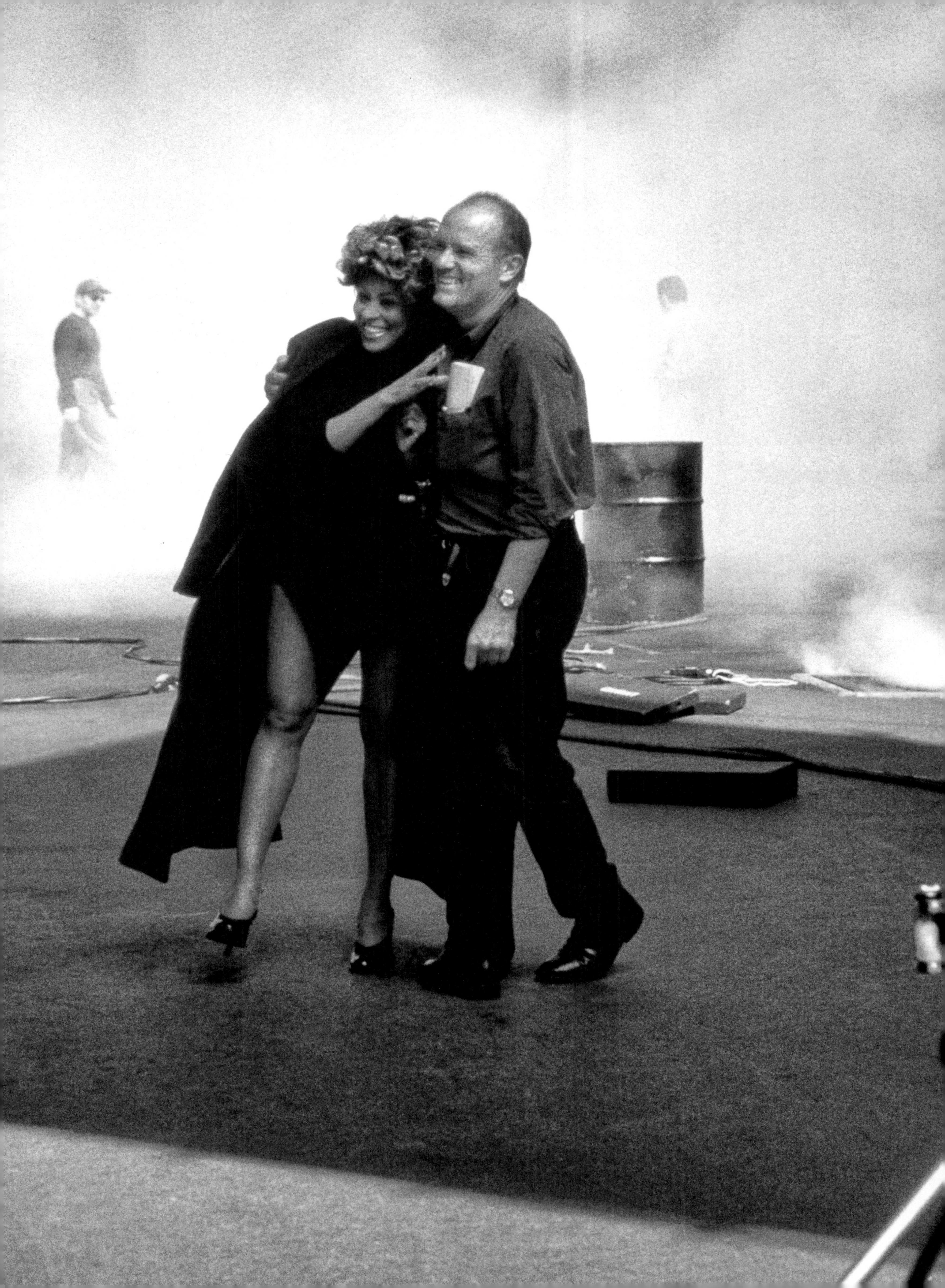

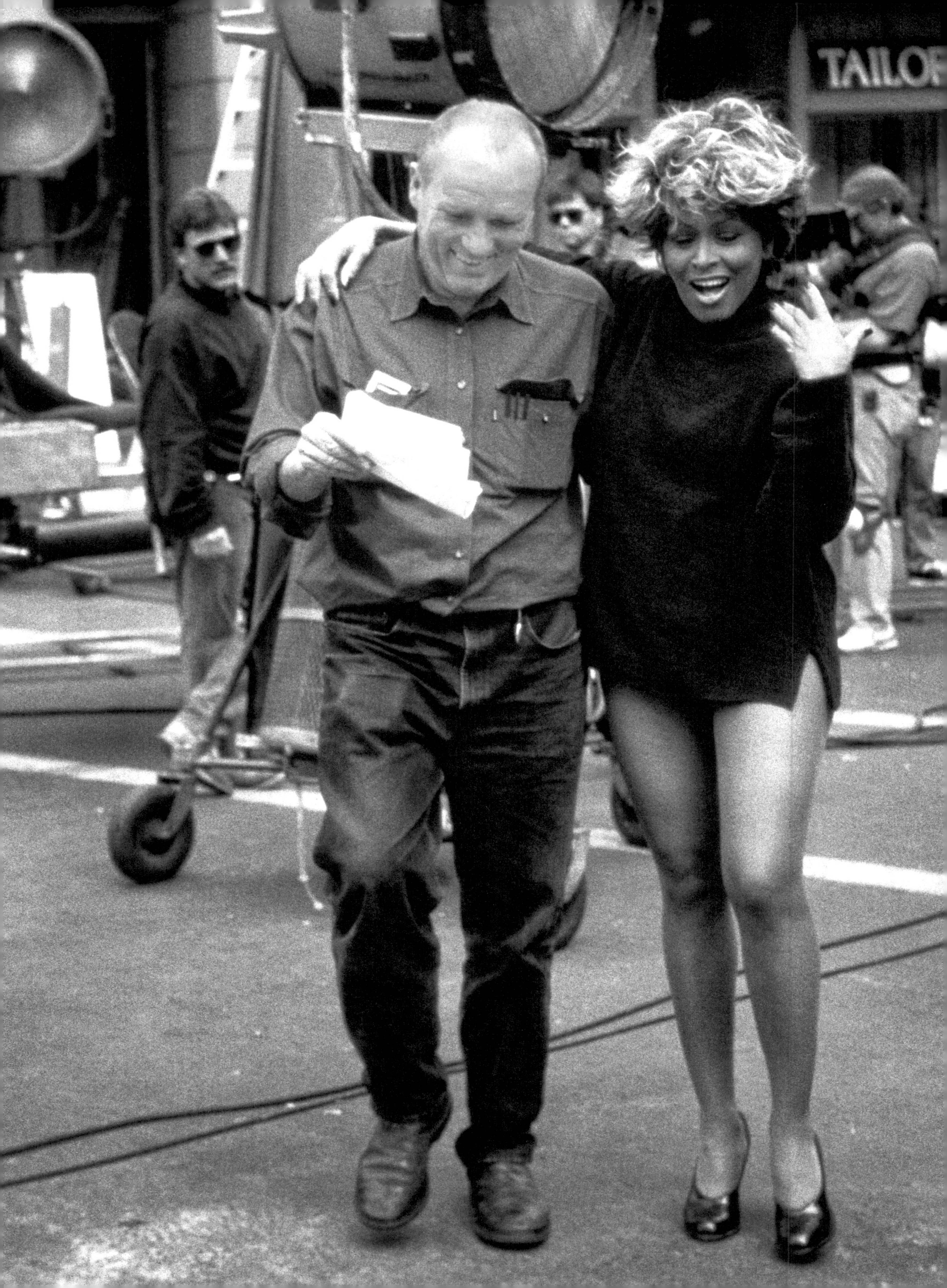
TAILOR

die Frau, das Kind, die Spaßmacherin, die Suchende und die wahrhaf
Gläubige.“ Er war ein vielseitiger Künstler, der in allem eine Inspiration fand – sein Geist war immer in Bewegung. Durch seine magische Linse betrachtet, erscheint selbst ein Bild von Tina, wie sie Eyeliner aufträgt, ein Sinnbild zeitloser Schönheit. Tina vertraute Peter, weil beide Seelenverwandte waren. Wenn er während einer Fotosession sagte: „Mach mal so“, dann wusste sie genau, was er meinte, und hauchte seiner Idee sofort Leben ein.

Was ich an Peter liebte, war seine Unfähigkeit, sich zu verstellen. Denn obwohl er ein großartiger Künstler und ein absoluter Profi war, blieb er stets ein umgänglicher, bodenständiger Mann, der am liebsten Jeans und Baseballkappe trug. Ruhm bedeutete ihm nichts. Er interessierte sich mehr für die Person hinter der Fassade. Mir ging es stets genauso. Wir waren beide sehr bodenständig und direkt, und das schätzten wir am jeweils anderen. Hinzu kam der Umstand, dass wir beide einen ähnlichen Hintergrund hatten: Wir wuchsen beide im Rheinland auf, nur etwa 100 Kilometer voneinander entfernt, und sprachen die gleiche Sprache. Zwischen uns gab es diese unmittelbare Verbundenheit, die im Promi-Zirkus, wo Beziehungen oft oberflächlich sind, etwas Besonderes ist. Ja, ich würde so weit gehen und sagen, uns verband eine innige Freundschaft!

Tina und ich fühlten uns Peter so verbunden, dass wir immer, wenn einer von uns etwas vom anderen wollte oder brauchte, automatisch mit Ja antworteten, ohne weitere Fragen zu stellen.

2016 besuchten wir die Eröffnung seiner Retrospektive *A Different Vision on Fashion Photography* in der Kunsthalle Rotterdam, wo seine Freunde aus aller Welt zusammenkamen, um sein Lebenswerk zu feiern. Später im selben Jahr besuchte er uns zu Hause in der Schweiz, als das Kunstmagazin *Blau* ihn einlud, die Giacometti-Skulpturen in der Alberto Giacometti Foundation in Zürich zu fotografieren – eine brillante Idee, denn Peter konnte alles zum Leben erwecken, selbst einen leblosen Gegenstand.

Während seines Besuchs aßen wir auf der Terrasse zu Abend und erzählten uns Geschichten über die guten alten Zeiten. Tina und Peter steckten ihre Köpfe zusammen, während wir redeten und lachten – gute Freunde, die die Gesellschaft des anderen genossen, so wie wir es immer taten, wenn wir uns trafen. Tina und ich waren beide gerührt, als Peter einmal sagte, wir seien „das beste Beispiel dafür, was zwei Menschen aus dem, was man Liebe nennt, machen können“. Er wusste stets, was wirklich zählte – im Leben wie in der Kunst – und schätzte es über alles.

Das war das letzte Mal, dass wir Peter sahen.

Ich überlasse Tina das Schlusswort, denn sie hat ihre Beziehung in einer wunderbaren Weise beschrieben: „Wir waren Komplizen. Er war bereit, das Unmögliche zu wagen – genau wie ich! Zusammen haben wir Magisches geschaffen!“

Der Zauber, den die beiden entfacht haben, lebt in Peters Fotografien weiter. Dieses Buch – eine Sammlung von Bildern, die während ihrer langen beruflichen Zusammenarbeit und innigen Freundschaft entstanden sind – erzählt ihre außergewöhnliche Geschichte.

Tina et Peter
Préface par Erwin Bach

Si je veux retrouver des images de la vitalité de Tina – de la *vraie* Tina – je n'ai qu'à regarder les extraordinaires photos de Peter Lindbergh. La voilà, tête rejetée en arrière, perchée au sommet de la tour Eiffel avec tout Paris à ses pieds. Dans une autre, elle baisse ses lunettes de soleil pour nous jeter un regard sensuel qui dit : « Je sais tout. » Dans une autre encore, seuls sont visibles ses mains et ses genoux, mais ses mains et ses genoux sont si expressifs qu'ils ne peuvent appartenir qu'à elle. Peter voyait en elle une œuvre d'art, une icône de la mode et de la beauté et, plus important encore, une femme puissante, joyeuse et profondément spirituelle.

Peter, qui a photographié tout un panthéon de personnalités remarquables, était très enthousiaste à son égard. Il disait par exemple : « Personne au monde ne ressemble à Tina, elle est incroyable. C'est la femme la plus énergique que je connaisse et la femme la plus détendue que j'ai rencontrée. » Qu'il l'ait photographiée sur la plage de Deauville pour l'album *Foreign Affair* (en robe de soirée d'Alaïa, une boîte à chapeaux et un radio-cassette à la main, elle déambule sur le sable, se dirige vers l'océan et cette improbable juxtaposition semble *absolument* juste), ou quand il la filme arpentant avec une énergie exubérante les décors de la Paramount dans le clip vidéo de « Missing You » et le spot publicitaire pour Hanes, il trouve toujours, à chaque fois, l'essence même de Tina.

Tina s'émerveillait du talent et de la vision de Peter. Elle disait : « Parfois, j'avais l'impression qu'il pouvait voir au tréfonds de mon âme. Peter avait le don unique de capter toutes mes facettes : la femme, l'enfant, celle qui aime blaguer, celle qui se cherche, l'authentique croyante. »

Peter était un artiste éclectique qui trouvait son inspiration partout. Son esprit travaillait en permanence. Vue à travers son objectif magique, même une image de Tina se mettant de l'eyeliner devenait une méditation sur l'intemporalité de la beauté. Tina lui faisait confiance parce qu'il y avait entre eux un véritable échange de pensées. Lorsqu'il lui disait « Donne-moi *ça* » au cours d'une prise de vue, elle savait exactement ce qu'il voulait et immédiatement donnait vie à son idée.

Ce que j'aimais chez Peter, c'était son absence totale de prétention. Bien qu'il ait été un grand artiste et un professionnel incontesté, il était resté un homme simple, les pieds sur terre, parfaitement heureux de vivre en jeans et casquette de baseball. La gloire ne signifiait rien pour lui. Il était plus intéressé par la personne qui se trouvait derrière l'image. Nous étions tous les deux très terre-à-terre et directs et nous appréciions cela l'un chez l'autre. Nous étions aussi d'origine similaire.

Nous avions grandi en Rhénanie en Allemagne de l'Ouest, à une centaine de kilomètres l'un de l'autre seulement, et parlions la même langue. Un lien immédiat s'était créé entre nous, ce qui est rare dans le grand cirque de la célébrité où les relations peuvent être superficielles. En allemand, on parle de *innige Freundschaft* – amitié intime –, lorsque

PETER LINDBERGH
4 AV. D'EPREMESNIL 78290 CROISSY/S. SEINE
34.80.16.76

Fax to Roger Davies!

Dear Roger,

I heard from Azzedine Alaia and also from my agent Marion de Beaupré that you tried to contact me concerning a shooting with Tina Turner.

I ~~be~~ back in Paris now and ready to answer your questions.

My fax number is: Paris 34801539

I see forward to hear from you —

truly yours

Peter Lindbergh.

P.S. – I would be more than happy to photograph Tina ...—

Paris May 2' 1989

ROGER DAVIES MANAGEMENT, INC.

VIA FAX

May 9, 1989

Att: Peter Lindbergh
Paris

Dear Peter:

I tried calling you today in Paris, as I hadn't received any response from you regarding my FAX to you on May 1, 1989.

I urgently need to know if you are available to shoot Tina in Paris between June 2 through 16th.

Please call me in Los Angeles, (office) (213) 850-0662, or at home, (818) 789-6708.

I look forward to hearing from you.

Kind regards,

Roger

Roger Davies

Marion
bitte anrufen + Ja sagen...

3575 Cahuenga Blvd. W. Los Angeles California 90068 USA Telephone (213) 850 0662 Telex 662520 RDM LSA Fax (213) 850 7019 vous êtes heureux de voir quelqu'un parce que vous partagez avec lui un lien profond.

Tina et moi nous entendions tellement bien avec Peter qu'à chaque fois que l'un de nous souhaitait ou avait besoin de quelque chose de l'autre, la réponse était automatiquement oui, sans poser d'autre question.

En 2016, nous avons assisté au vernissage de sa rétrospective *A Different Vision on Fashion Photography* au Kunsthal de Rotterdam, où ses amis du monde entier s'étaient retrouvés pour célébrer son œuvre et sa vie. Plus tard, la même année, il nous rendit visite en Suisse alors que le magazine *Blau* l'avait envoyé photographier les sculptures de Giacometti à la Fondation Alberto Giacometti de Zurich, une brillante idée car Peter pouvait donner vie à tout, y compris à un objet inanimé.

Au cours de cette visite, nous avons dîné sur notre terrasse et nous nous avons raconté des histoires du bon vieux temps. Tina et Peter se donnaient des coups d'épaule en parlant et riant, en bons amis heureux d'être ensemble, comme nous le faisions toujours. Tina et moi avions été très touchés que Peter nous dise que nous étions « le meilleur exemple de ce que deux personnes peuvent faire de ce que l'on appelle l'amour. » Il savait toujours identifier un amour réel – dans la vie comme dans l'art – et l'appréciait par-dessus tout.

C'est la dernière fois que nous avons vu Peter.

Je vais laisser à Tina le dernier mot car elle avait une merveilleuse façon de décrire leur relation : « Nous étions partenaires dans le crime. Il voulait tout essayer, et moi aussi ! Ensemble, nous avons créé une magie ! »

Cette magie vit encore dans les photographies de Peter. Ce livre – collection d'images nées de leur longue collaboration professionnelle et de leur amitié constante – nous raconte cette relation si particulière

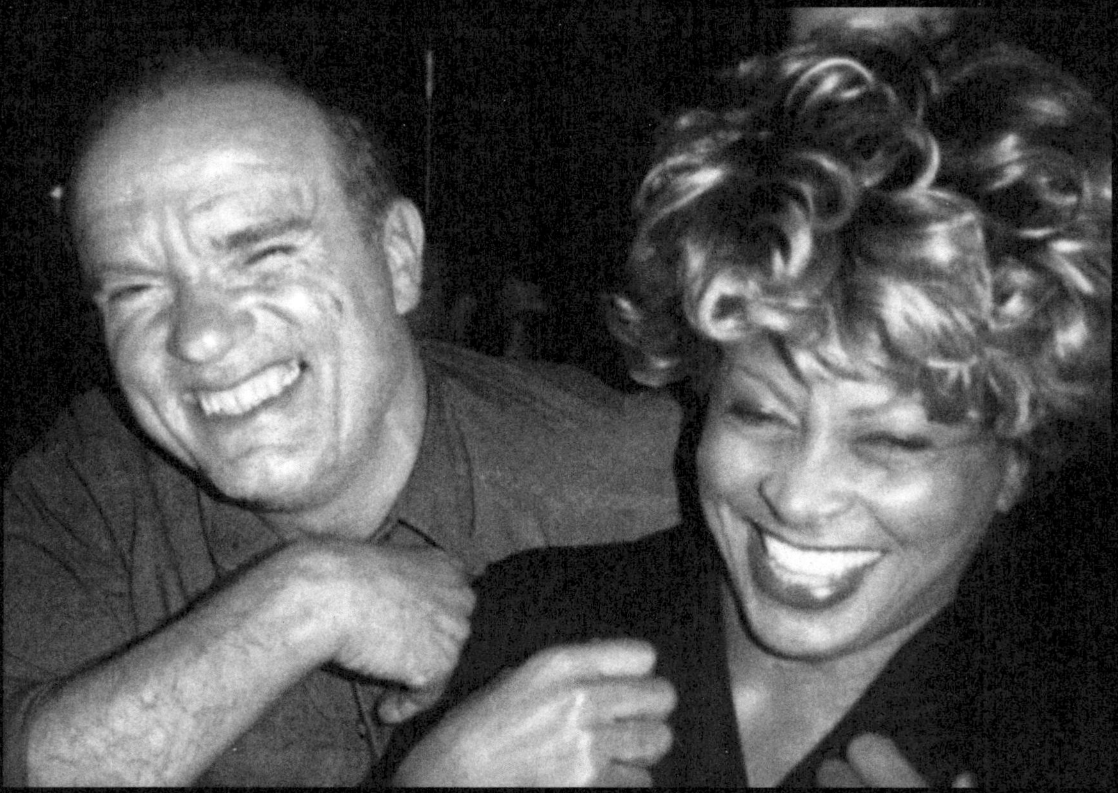

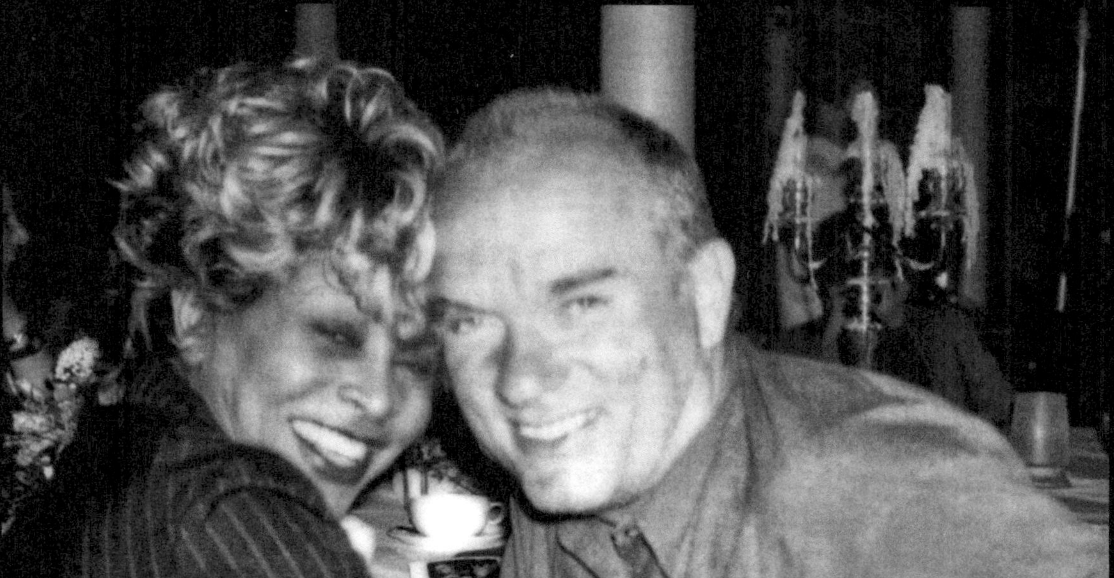

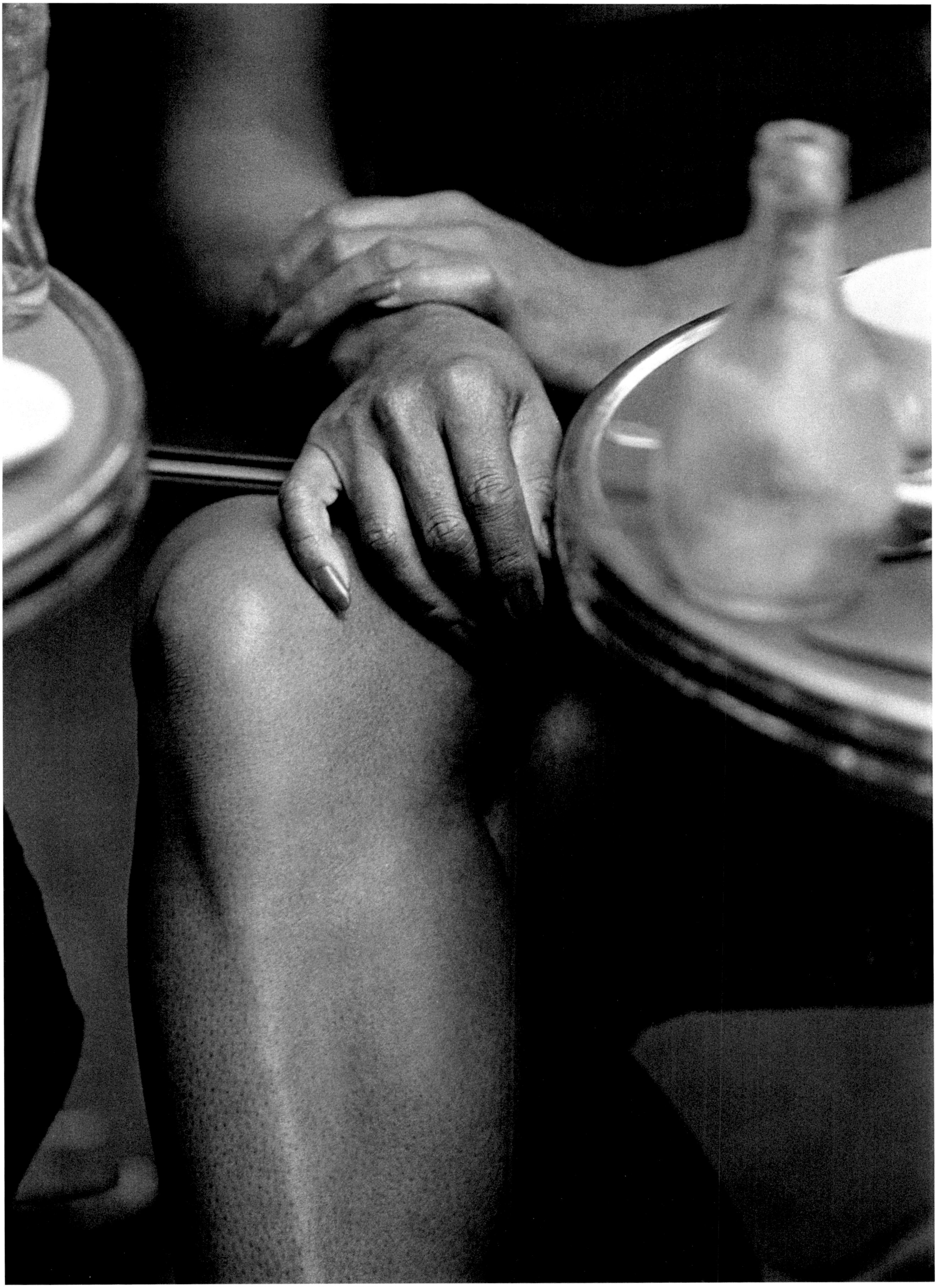

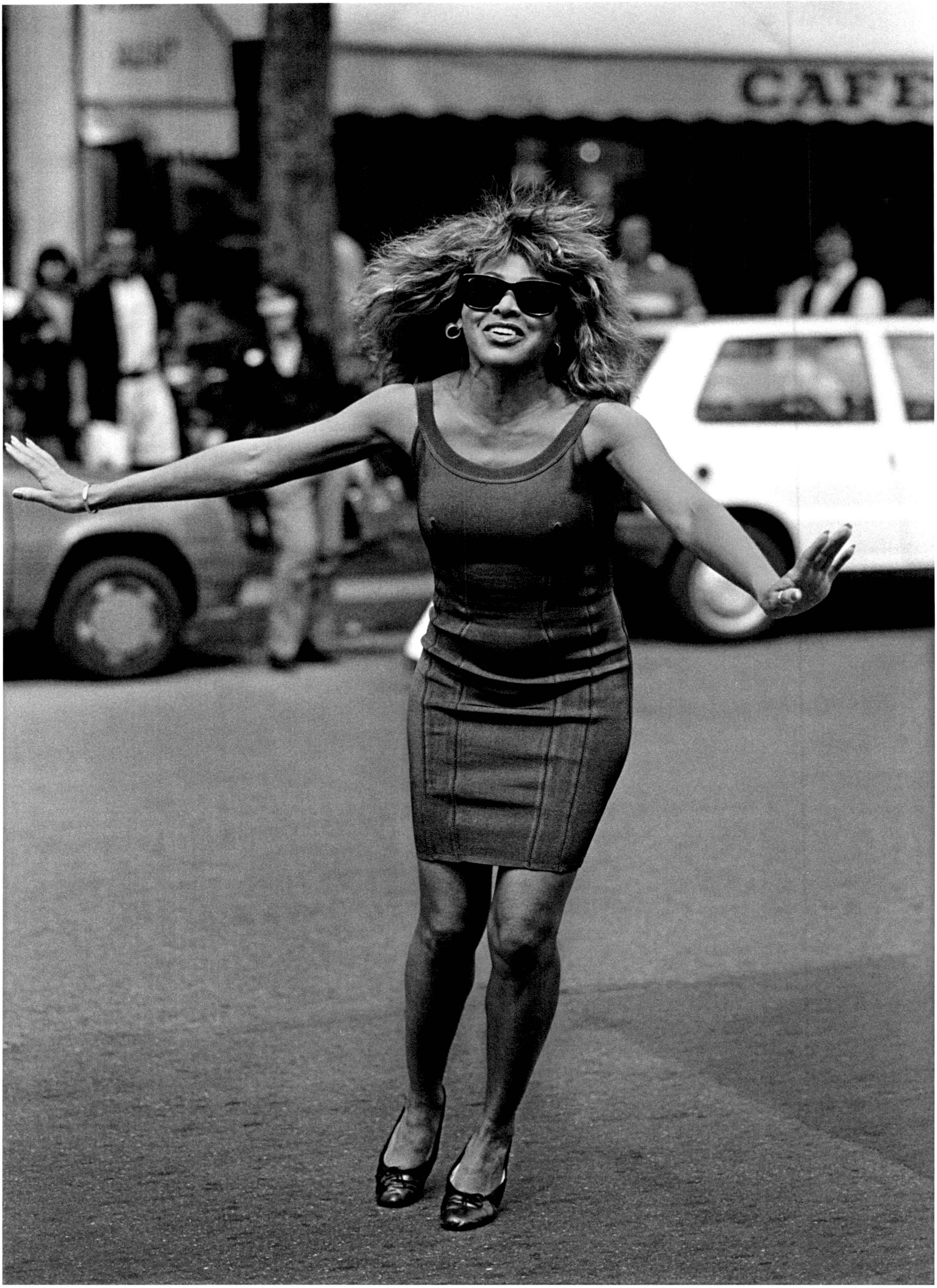
CAFE

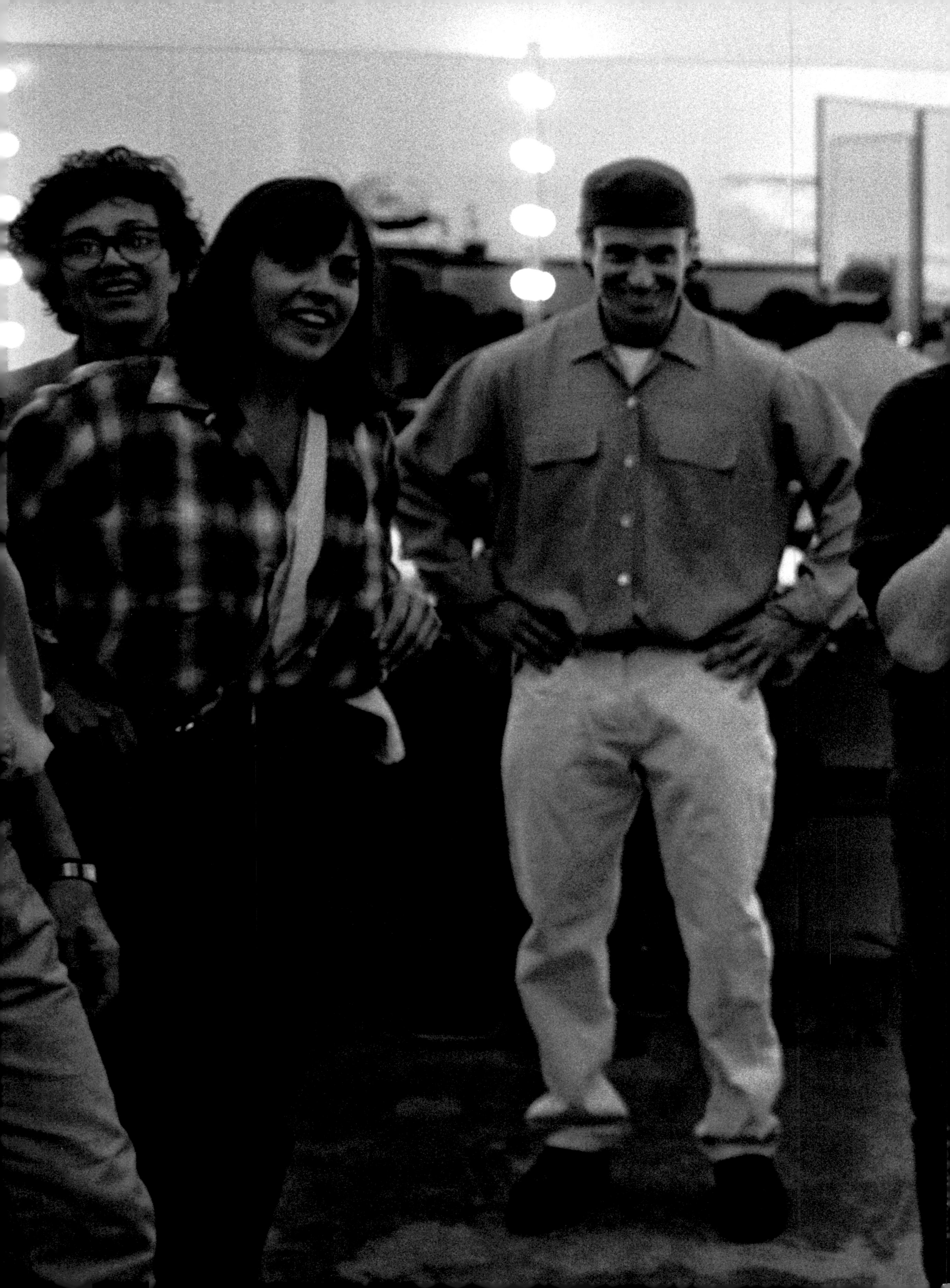

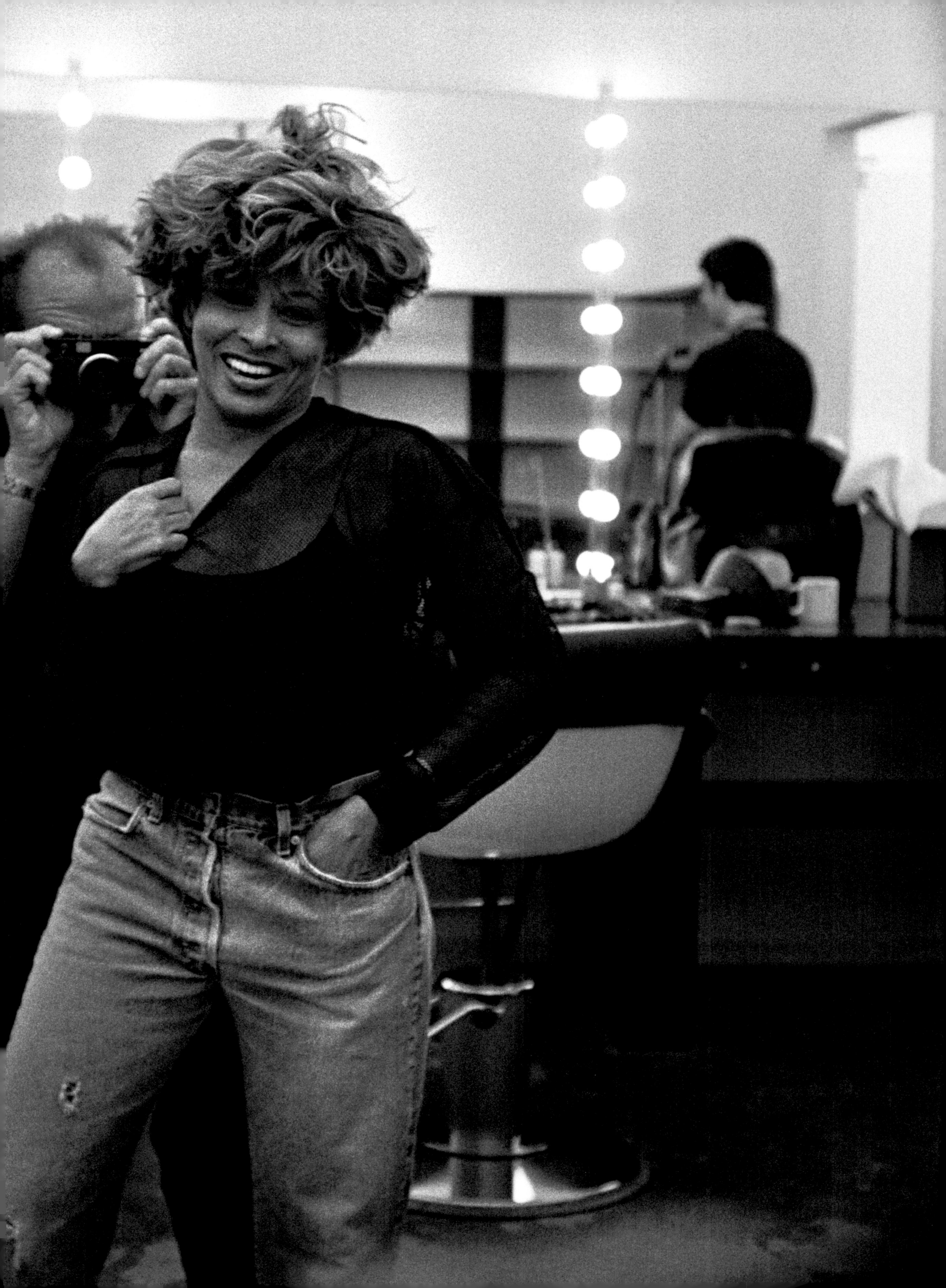

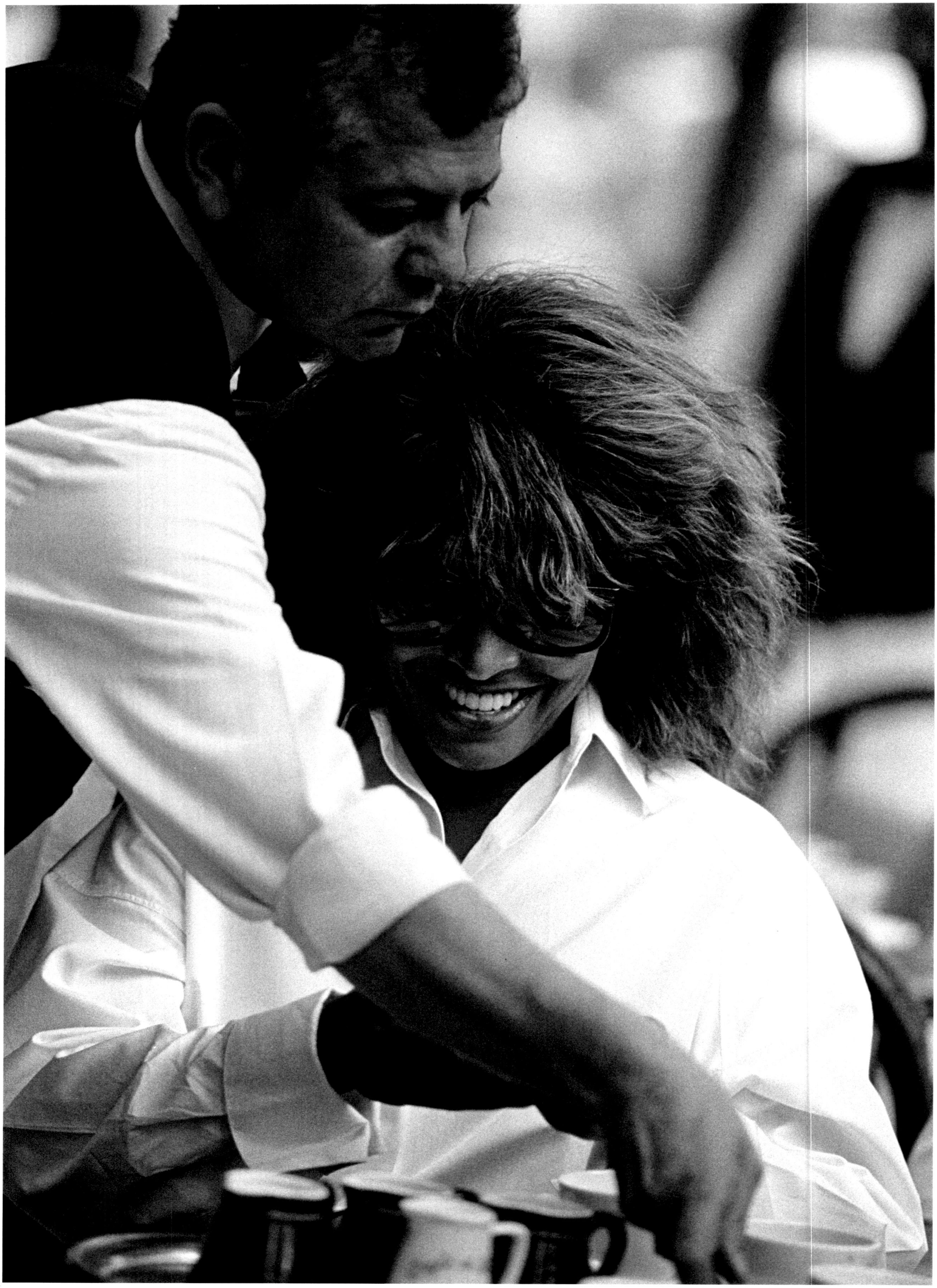

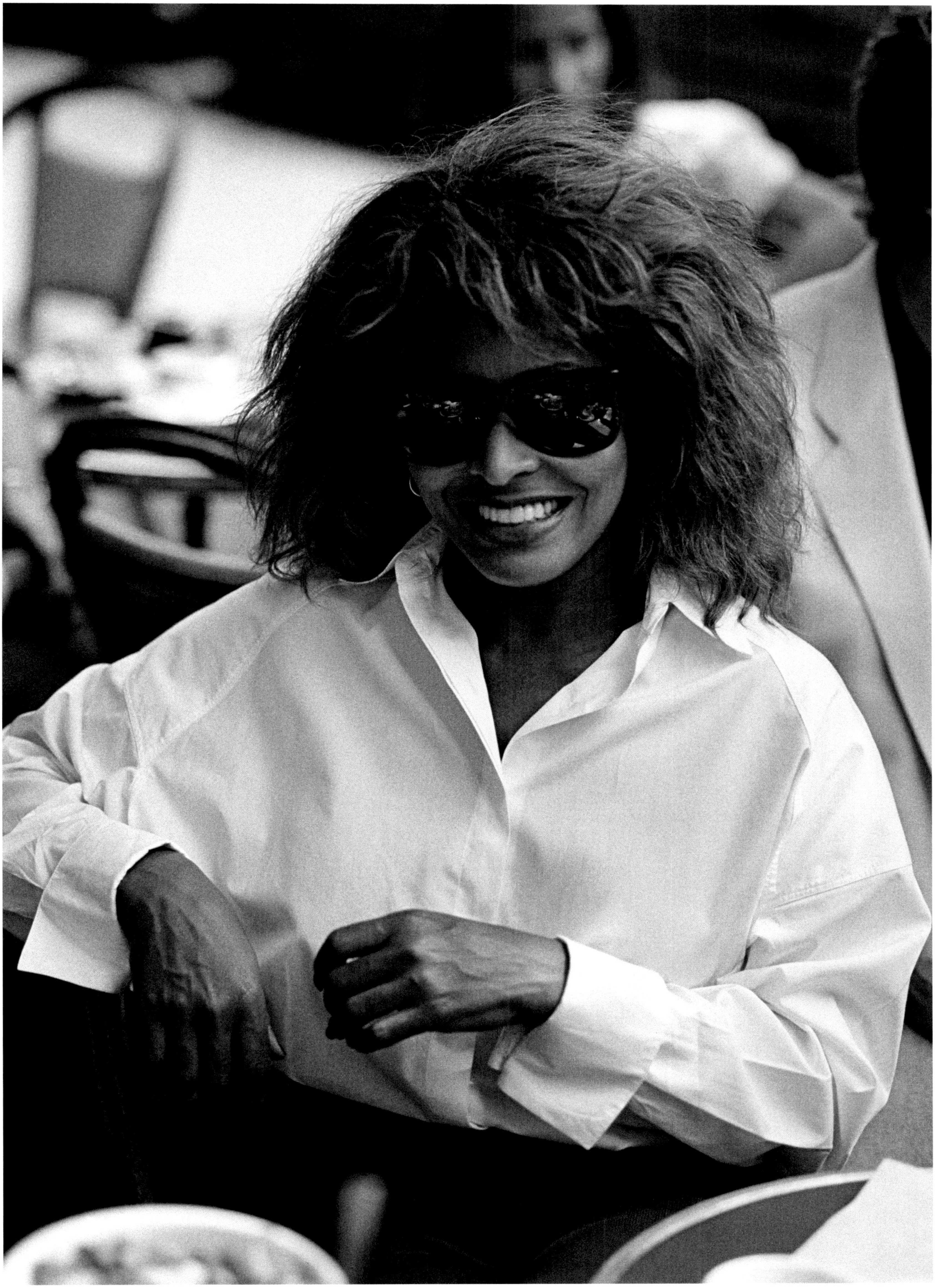

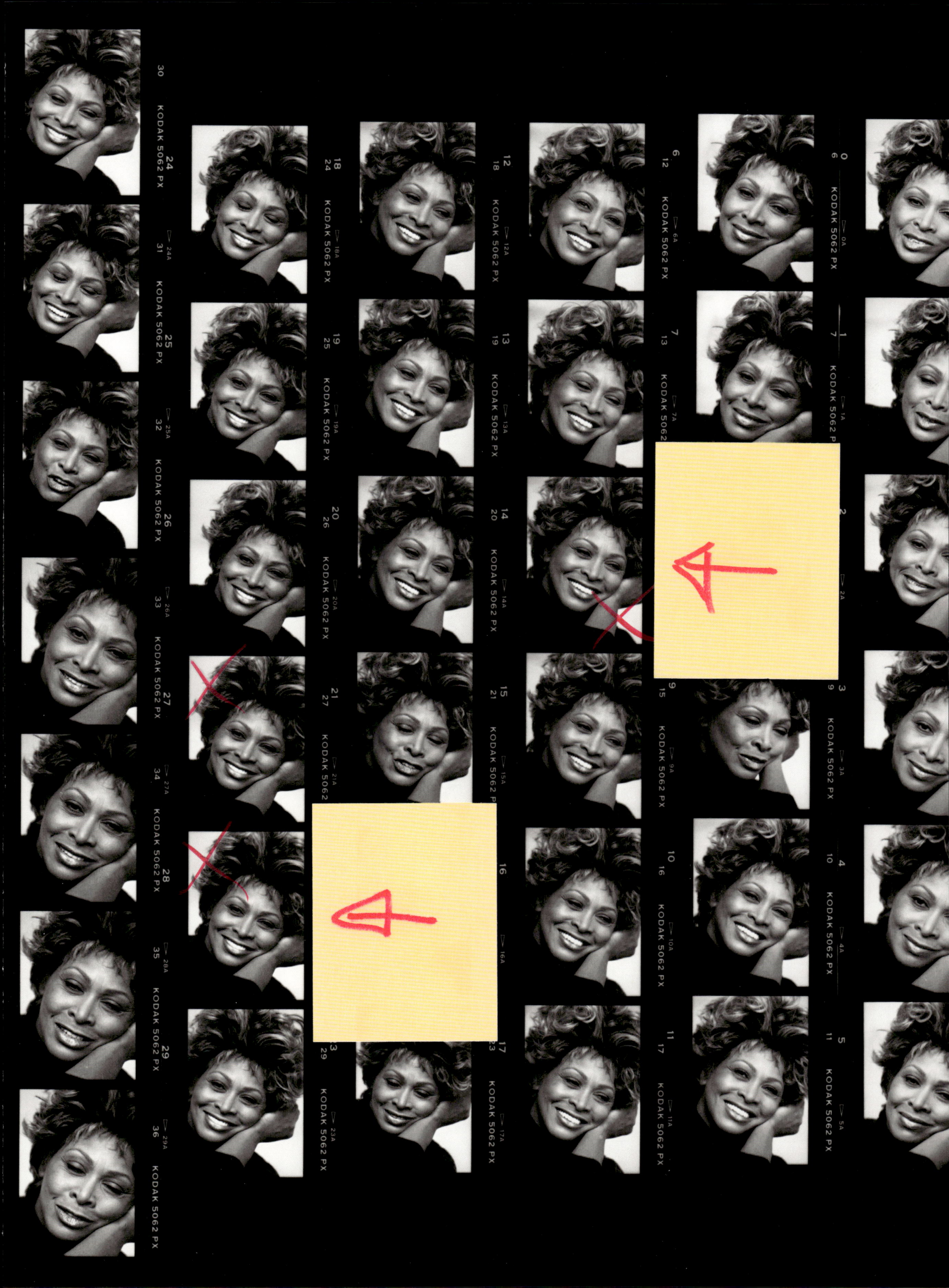
KODAK 5062 PX

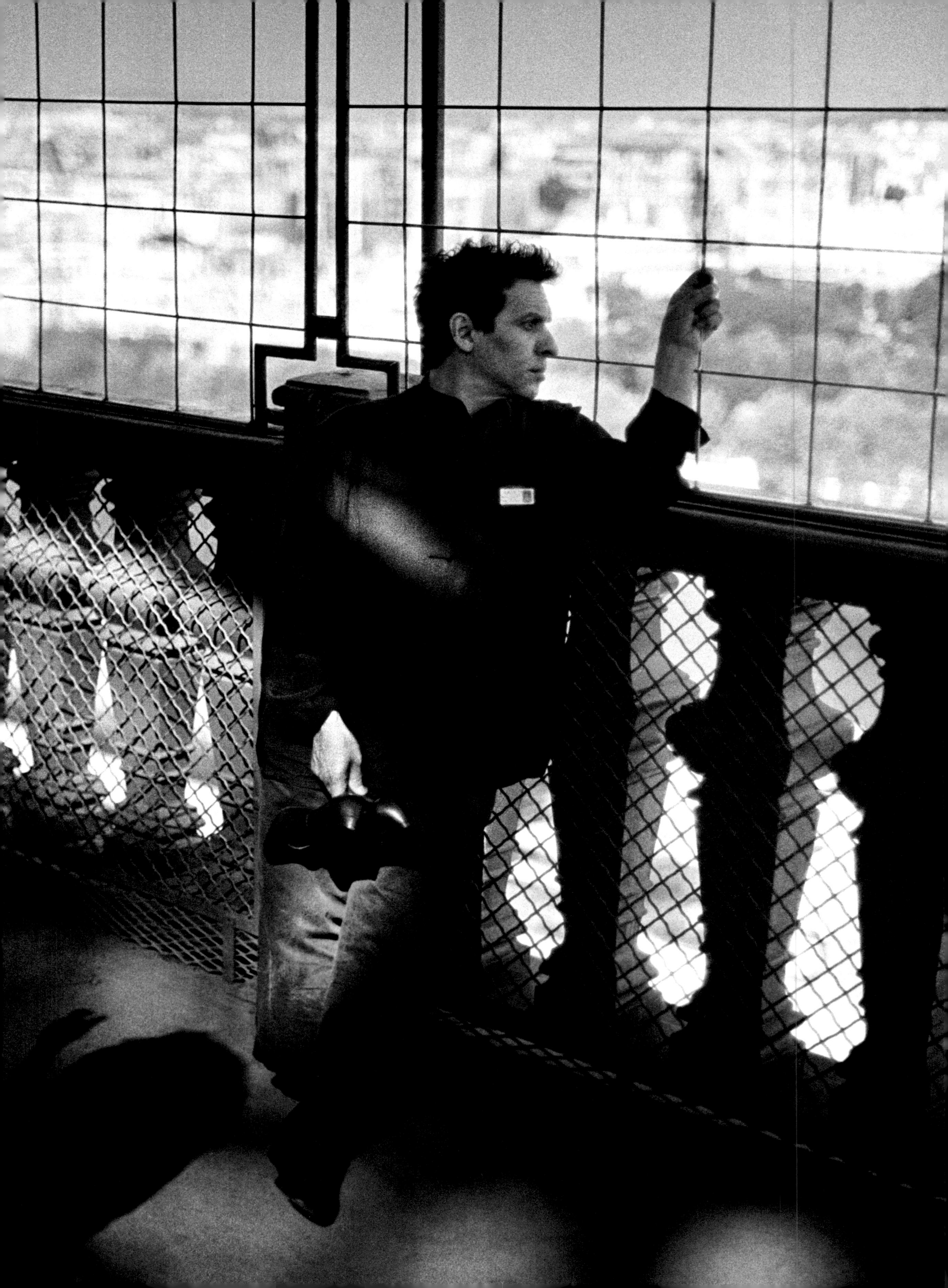

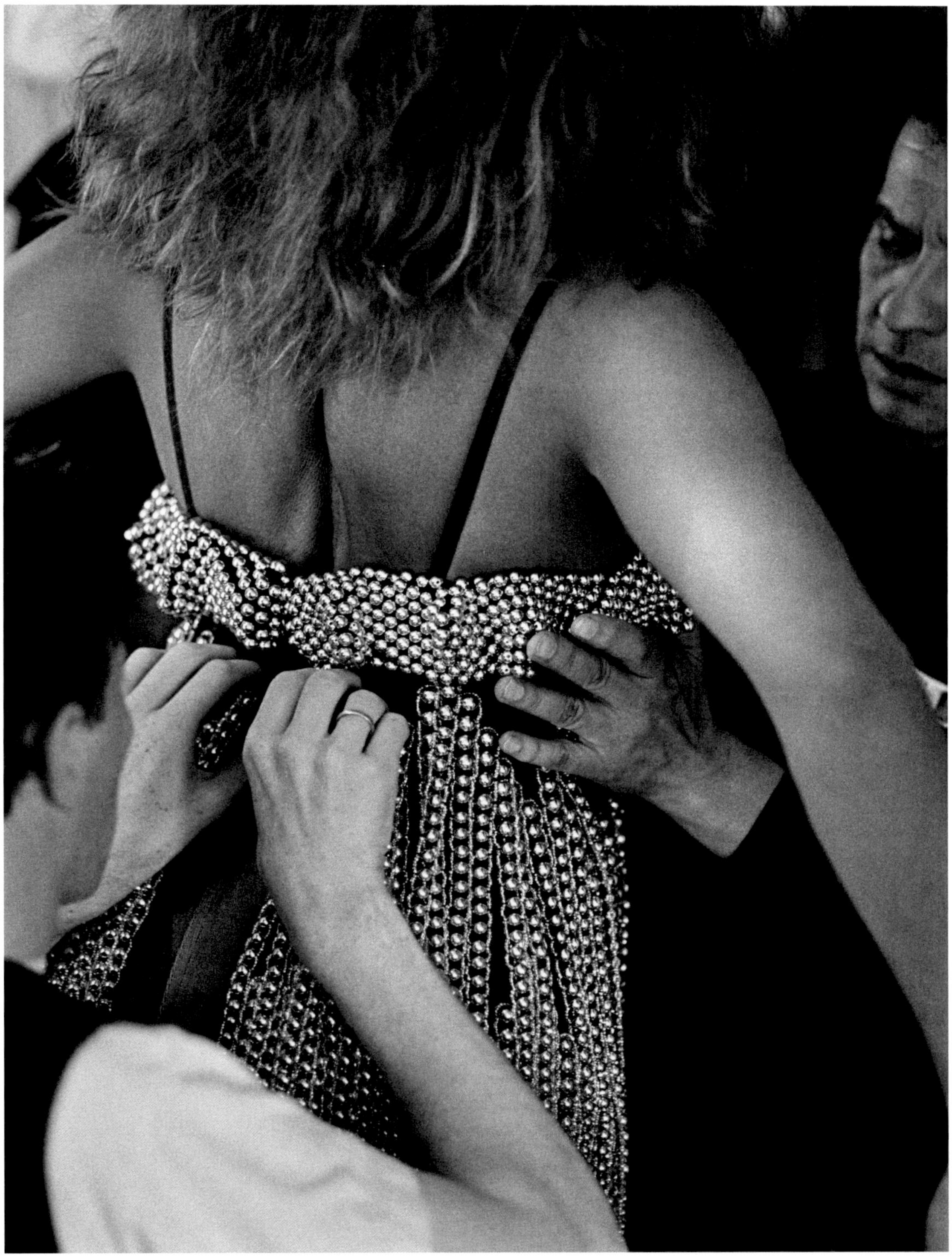

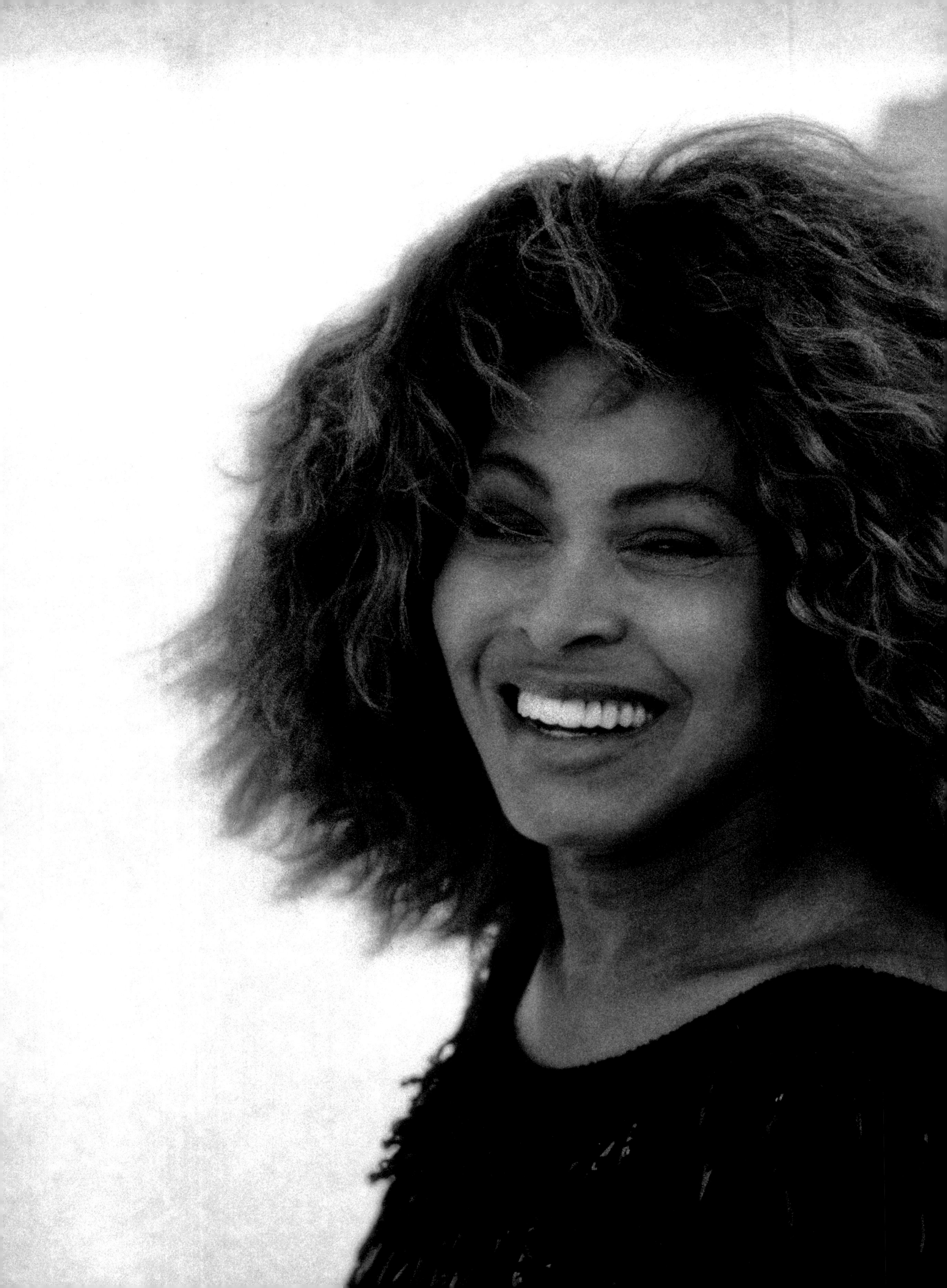

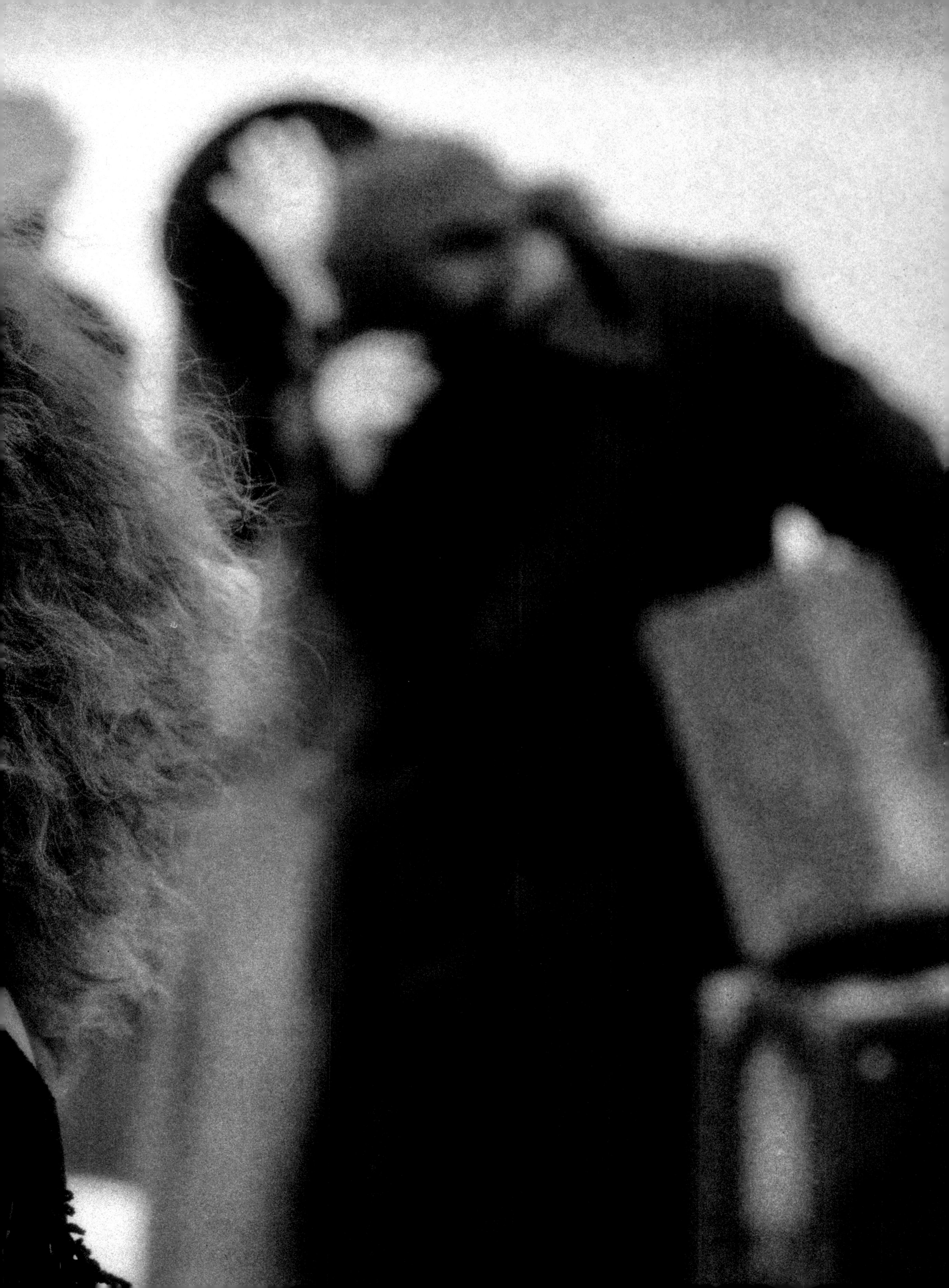

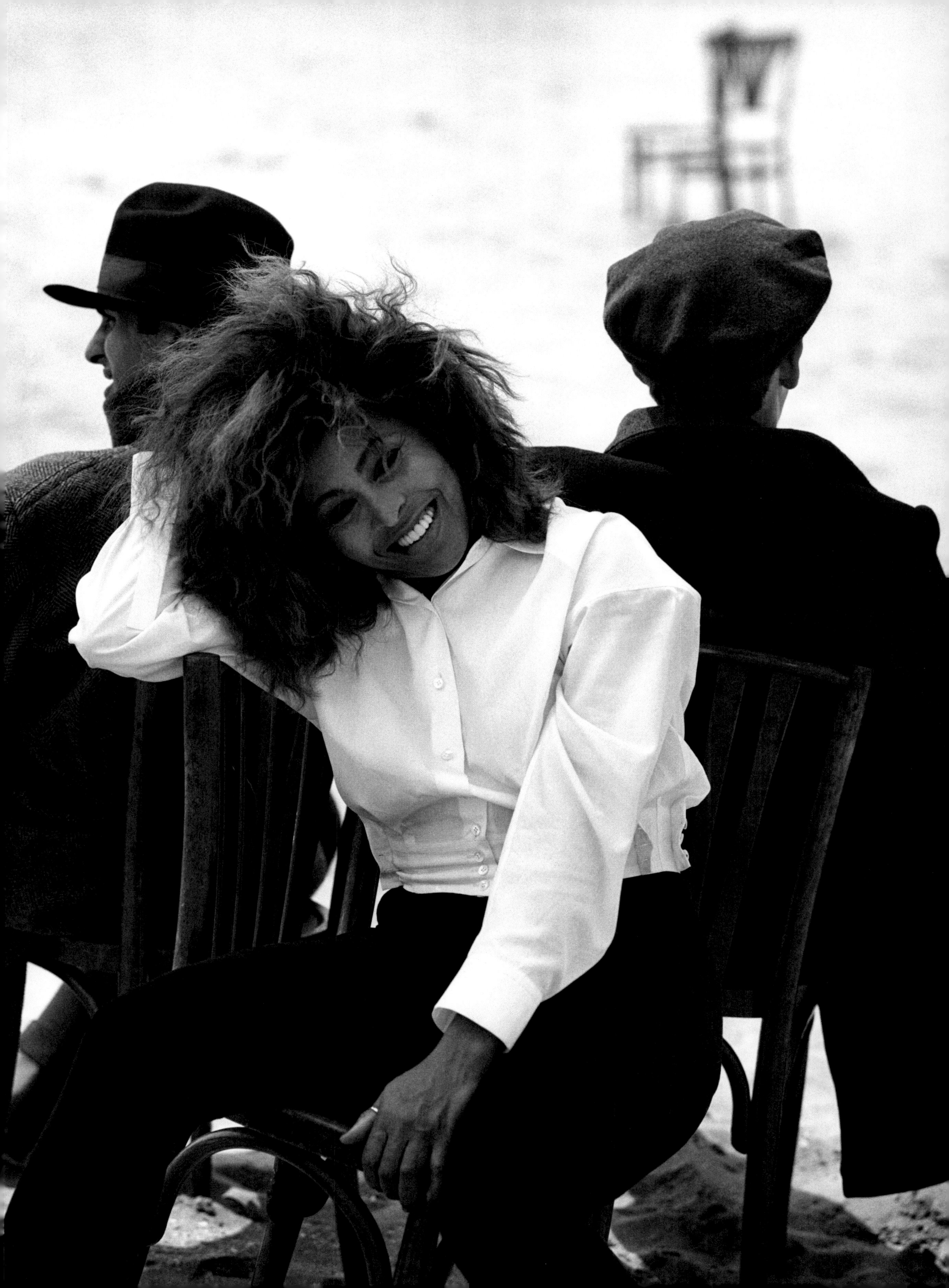

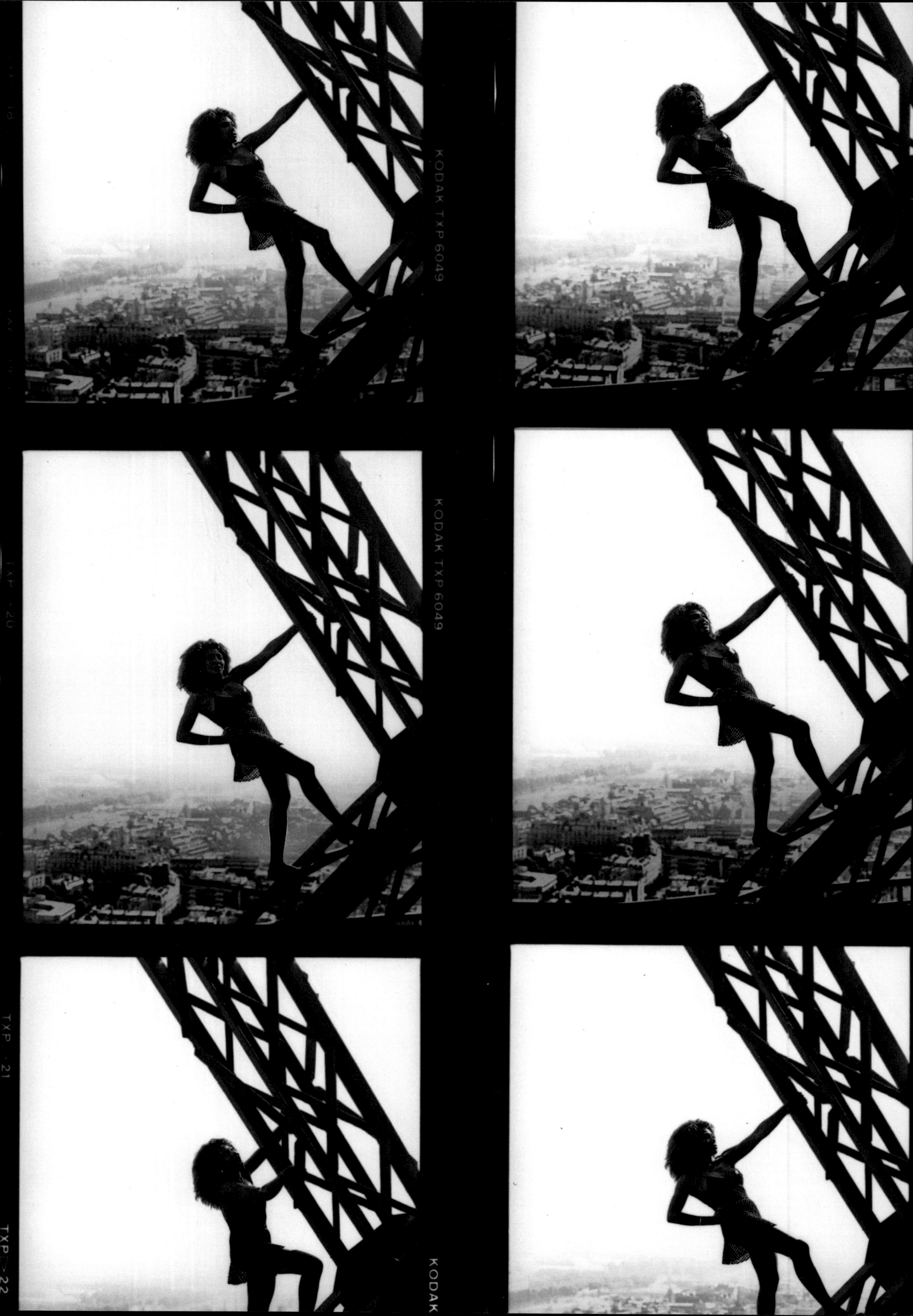
KODAK TXP 6049
KODAK TXP 6049
KODAK

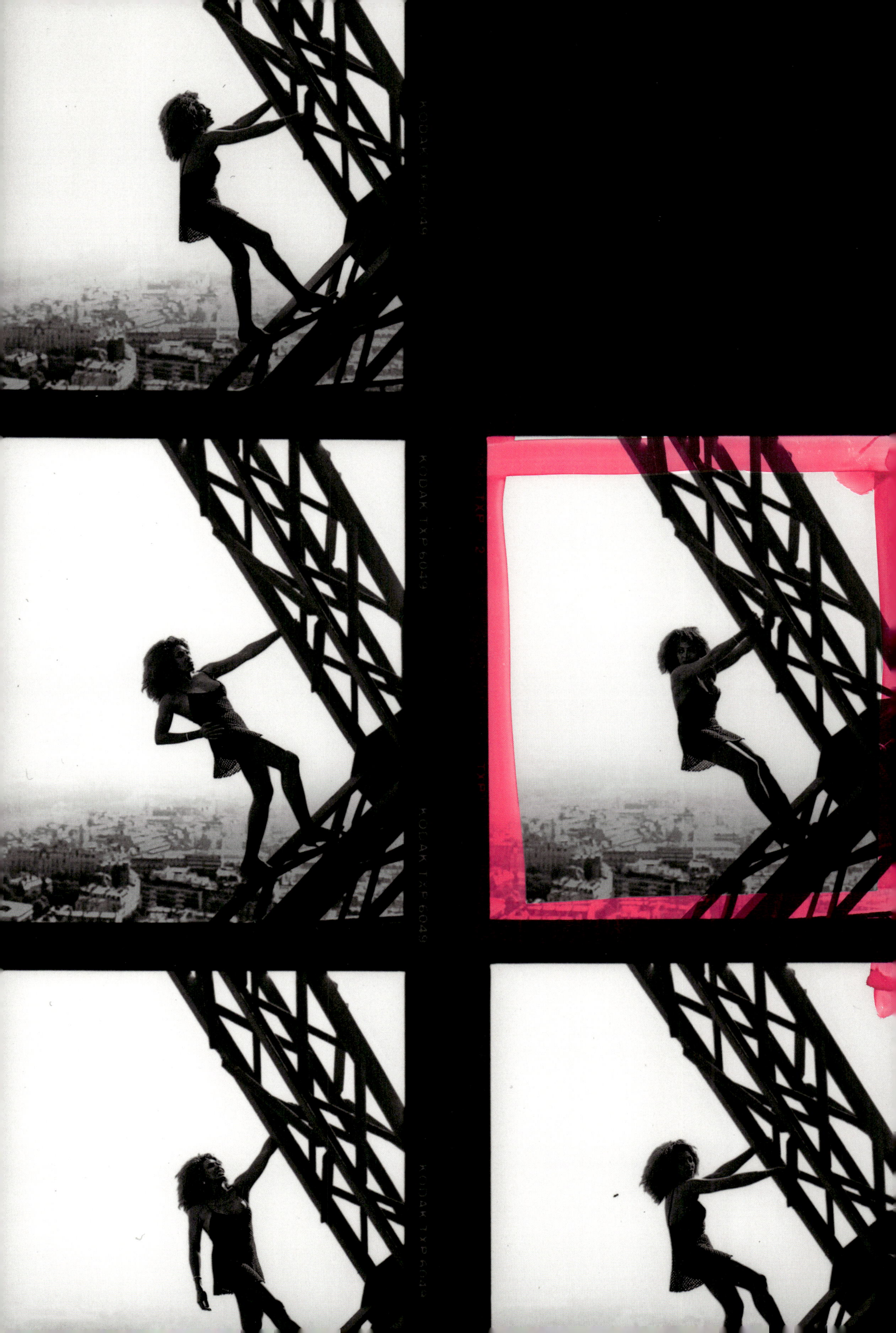
KODAK TXP 6049

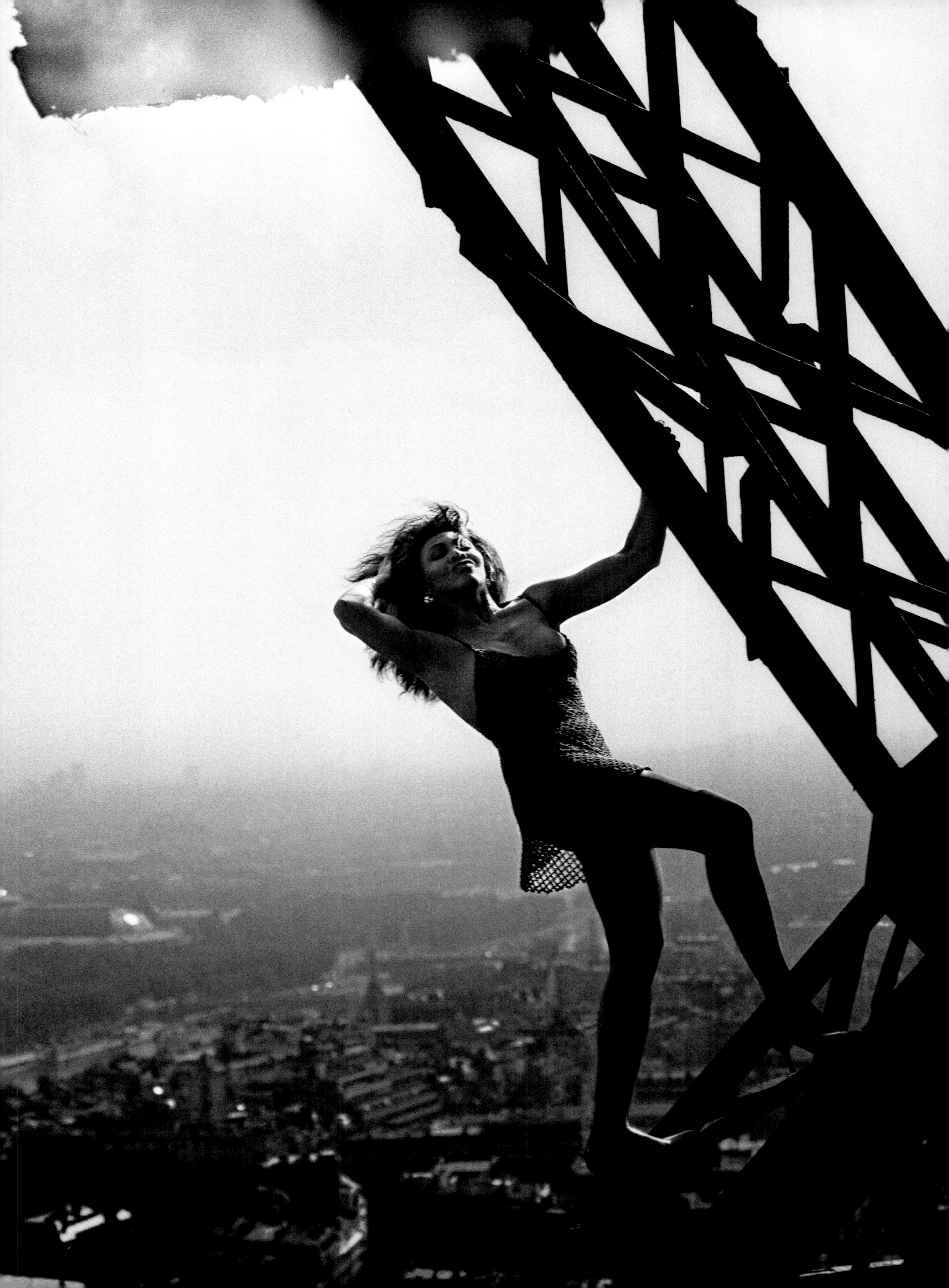

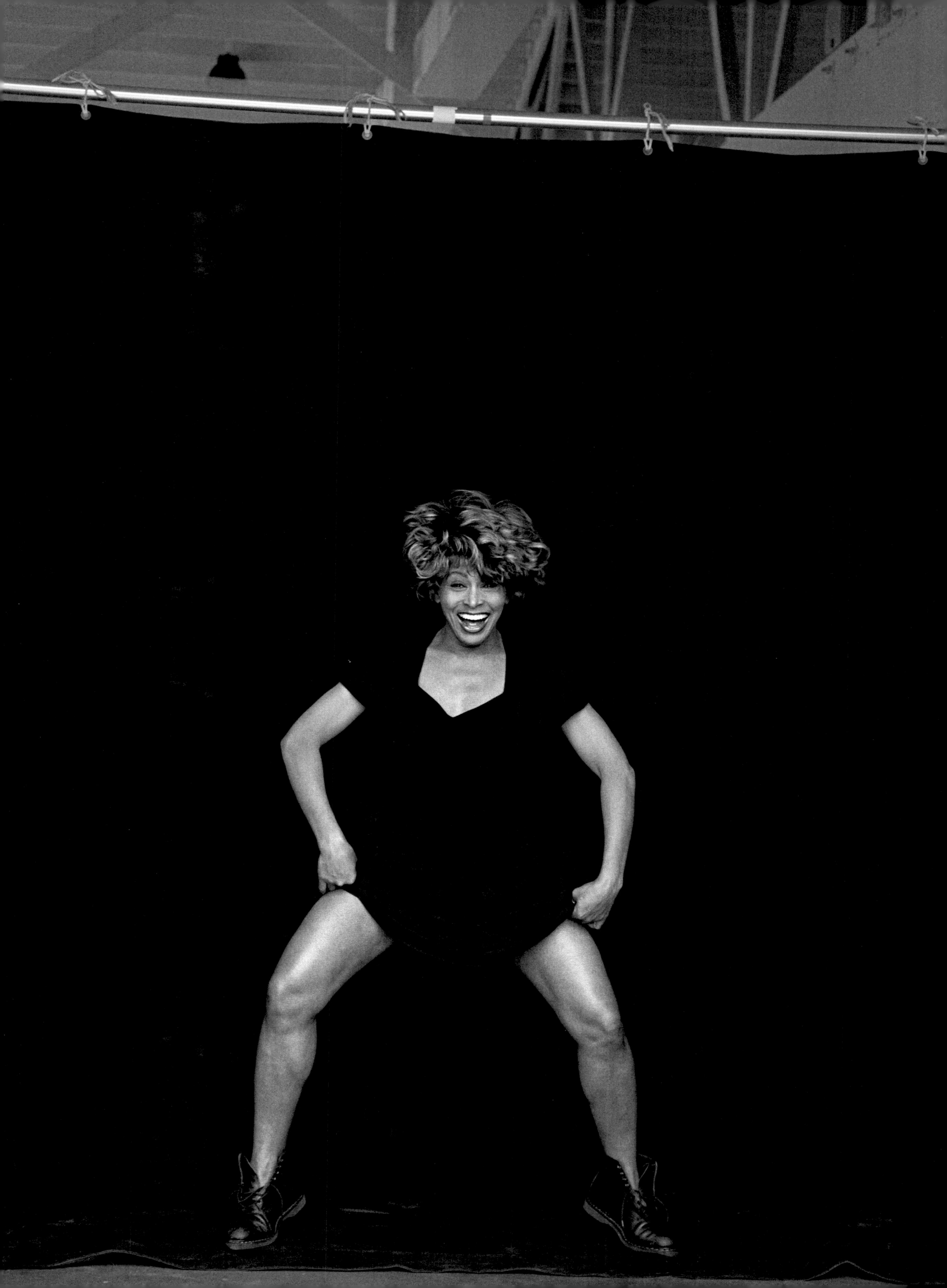

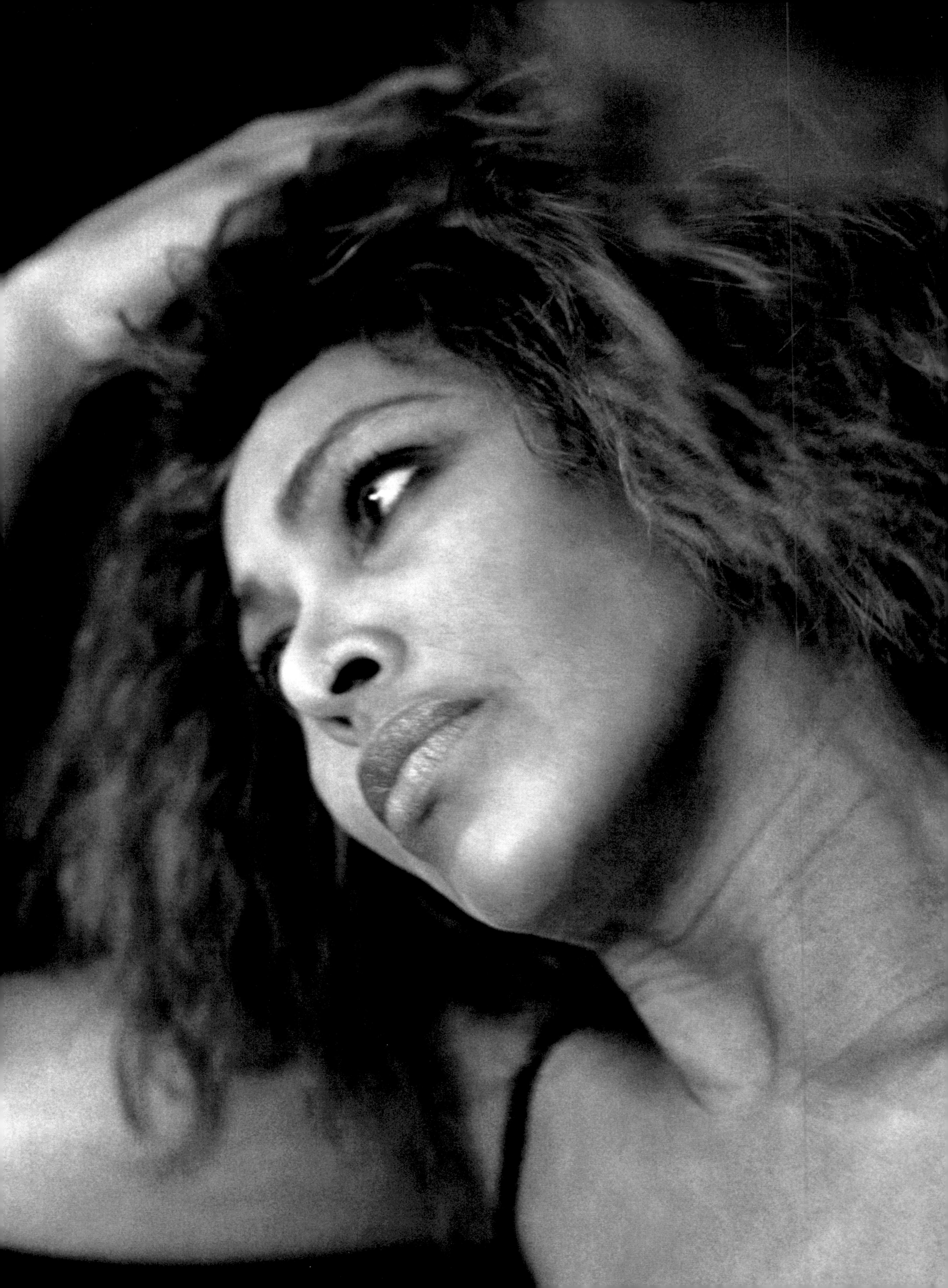

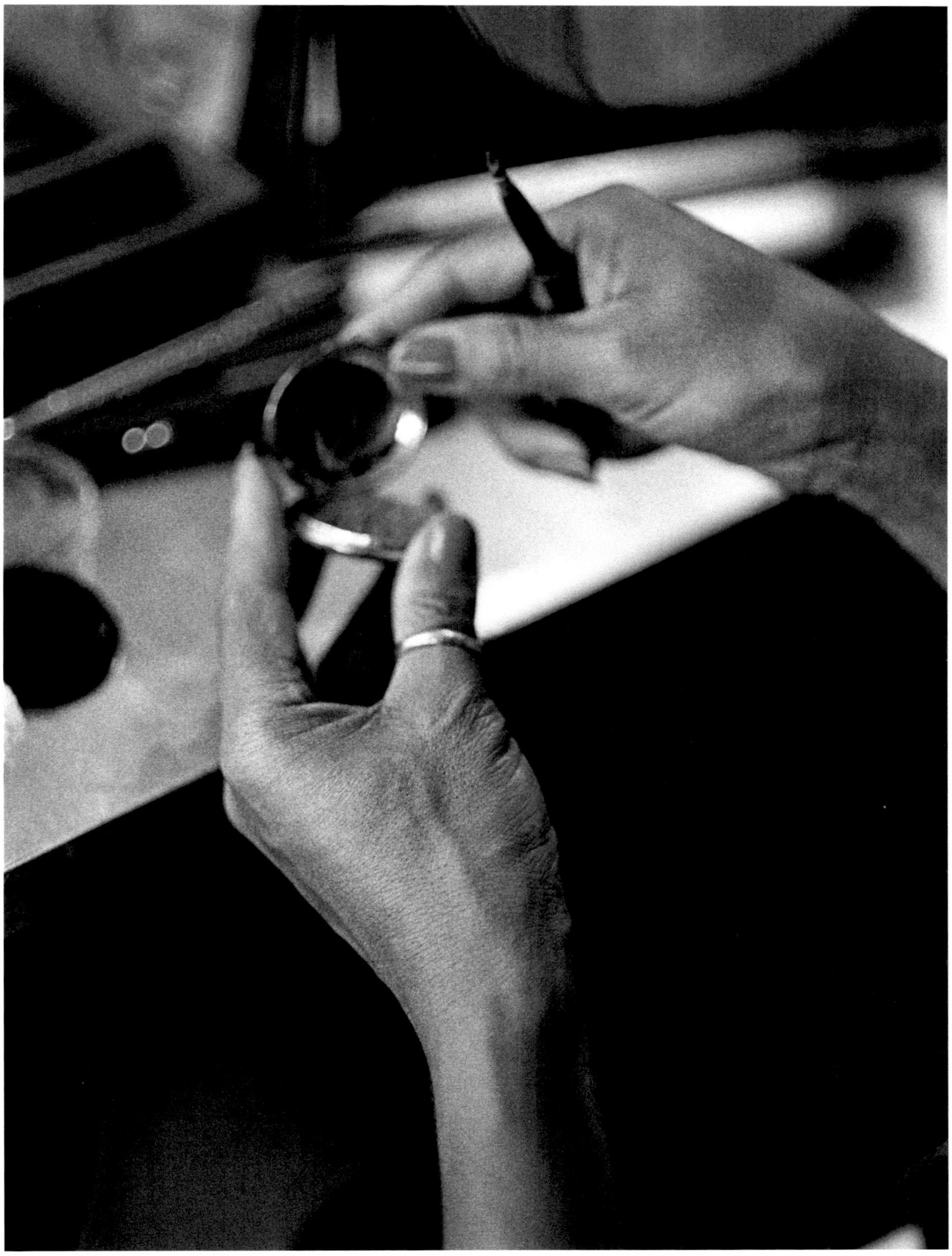

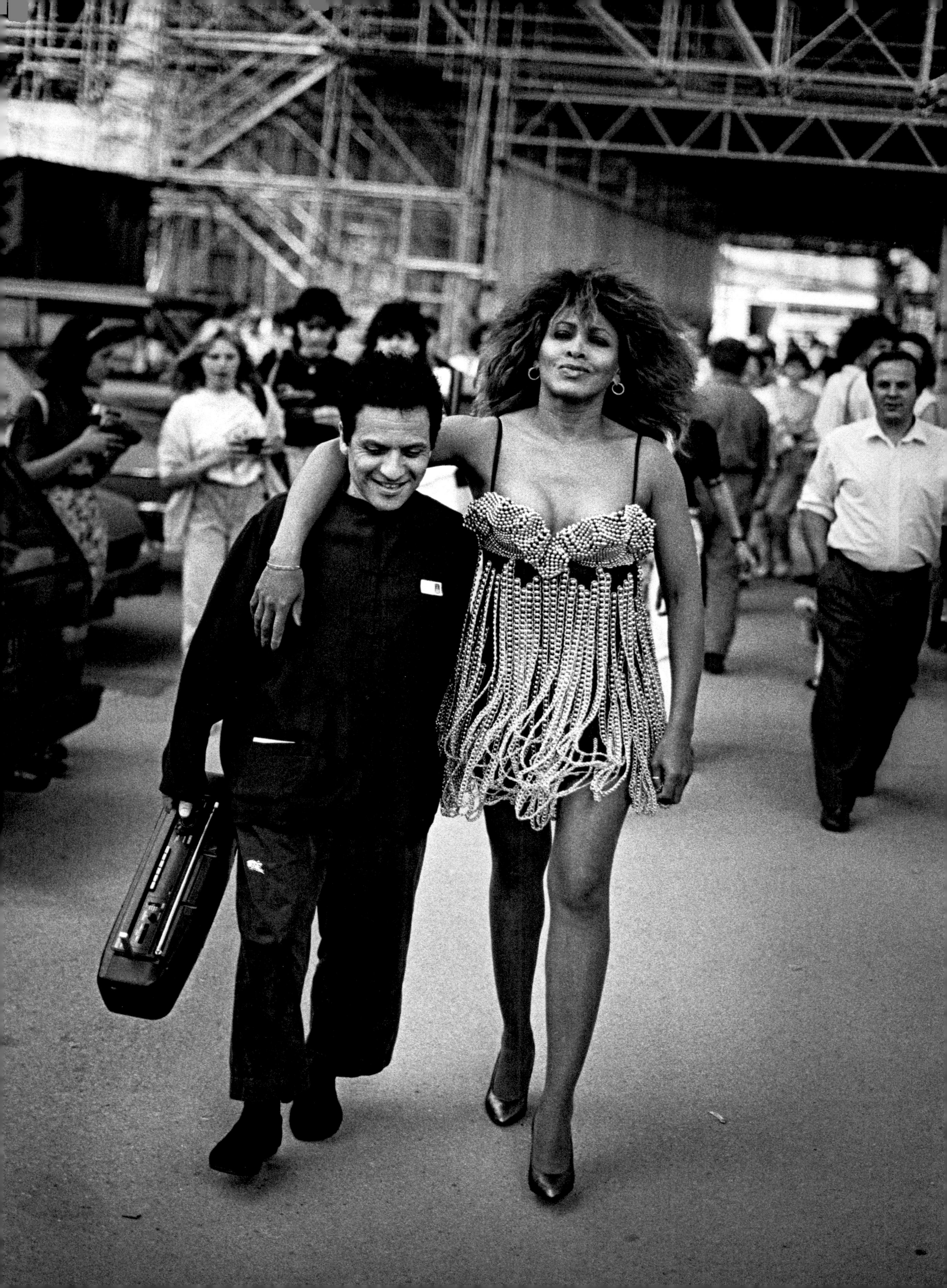

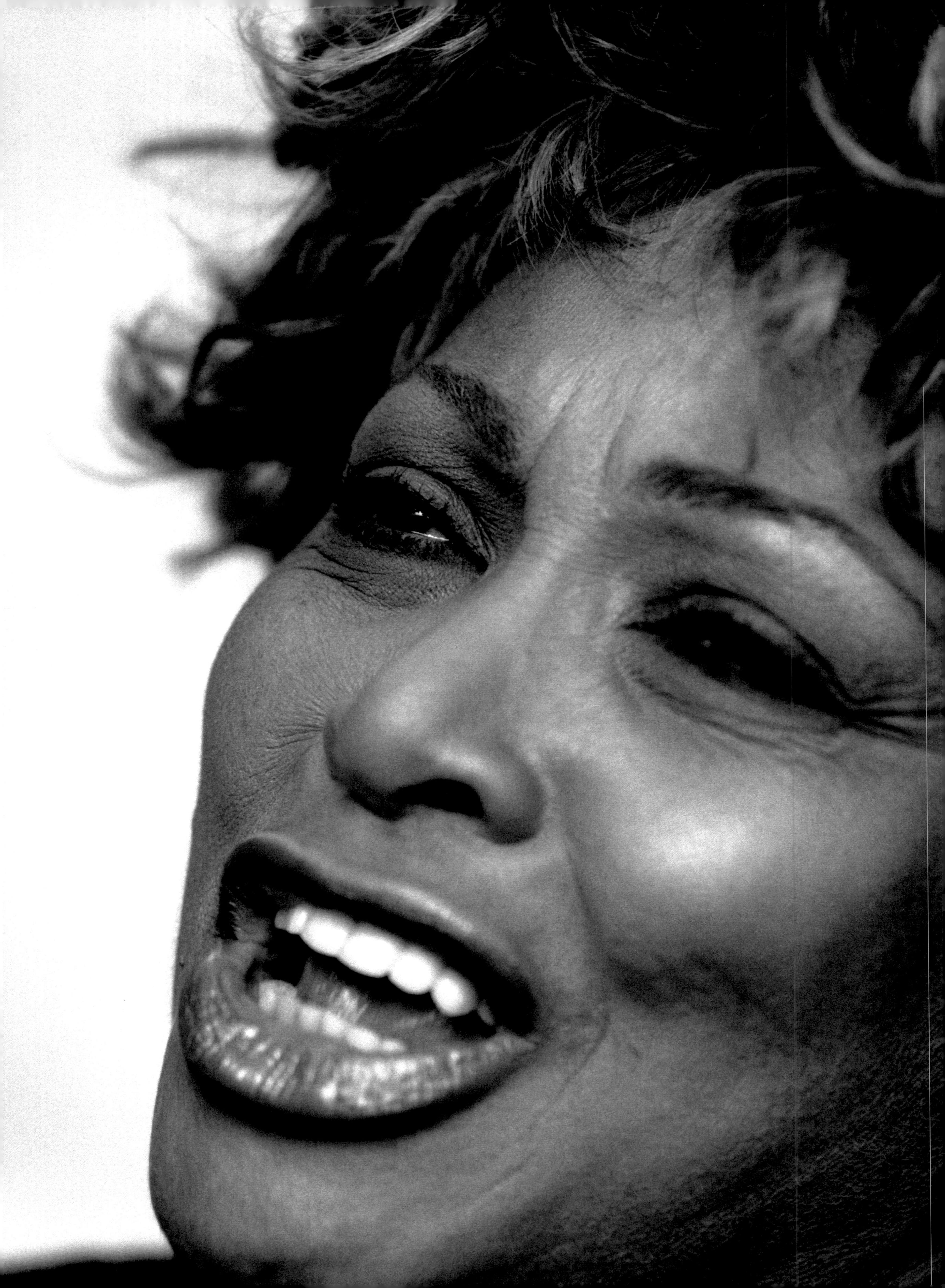

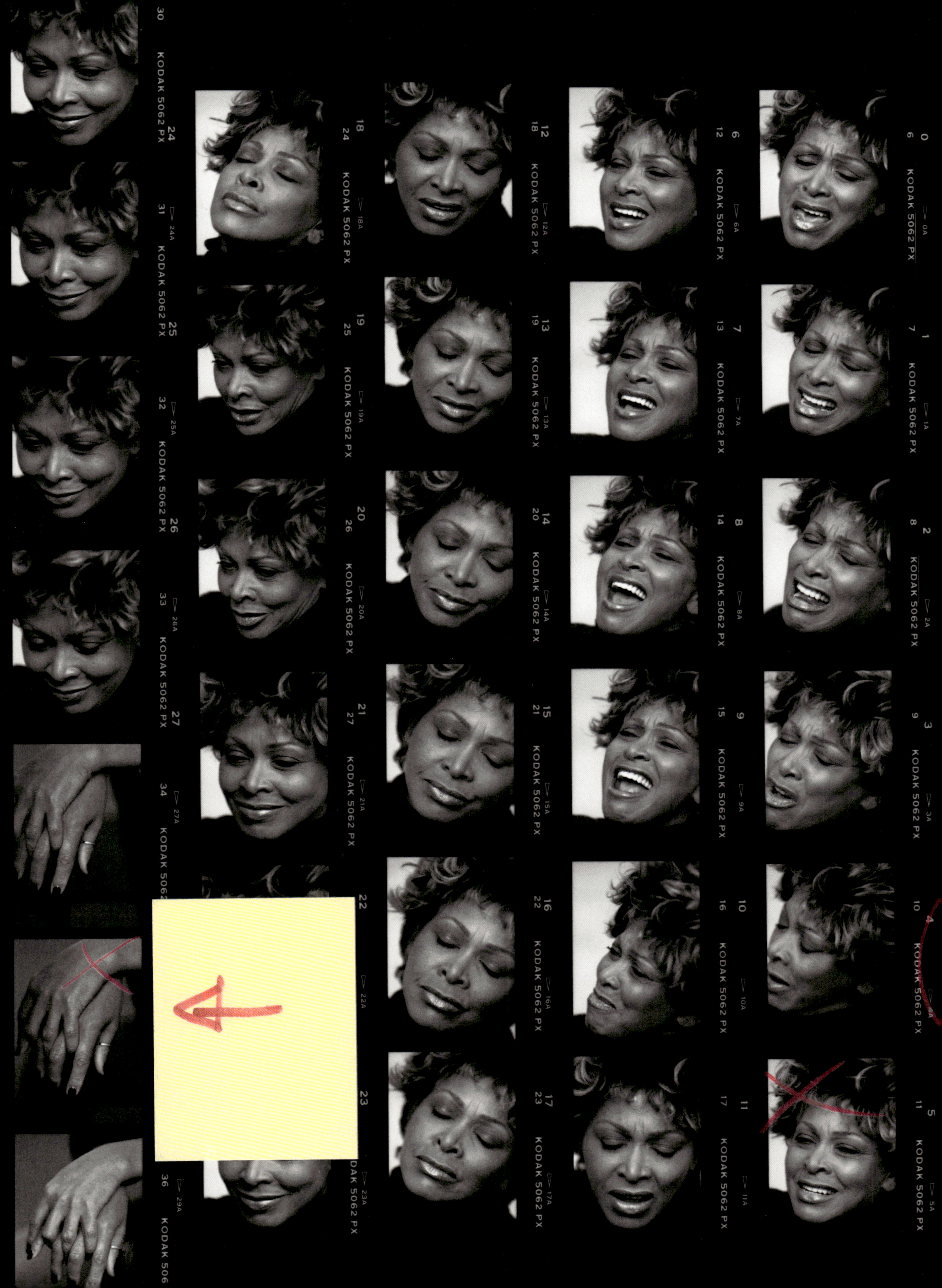
KODAK 5062 PX

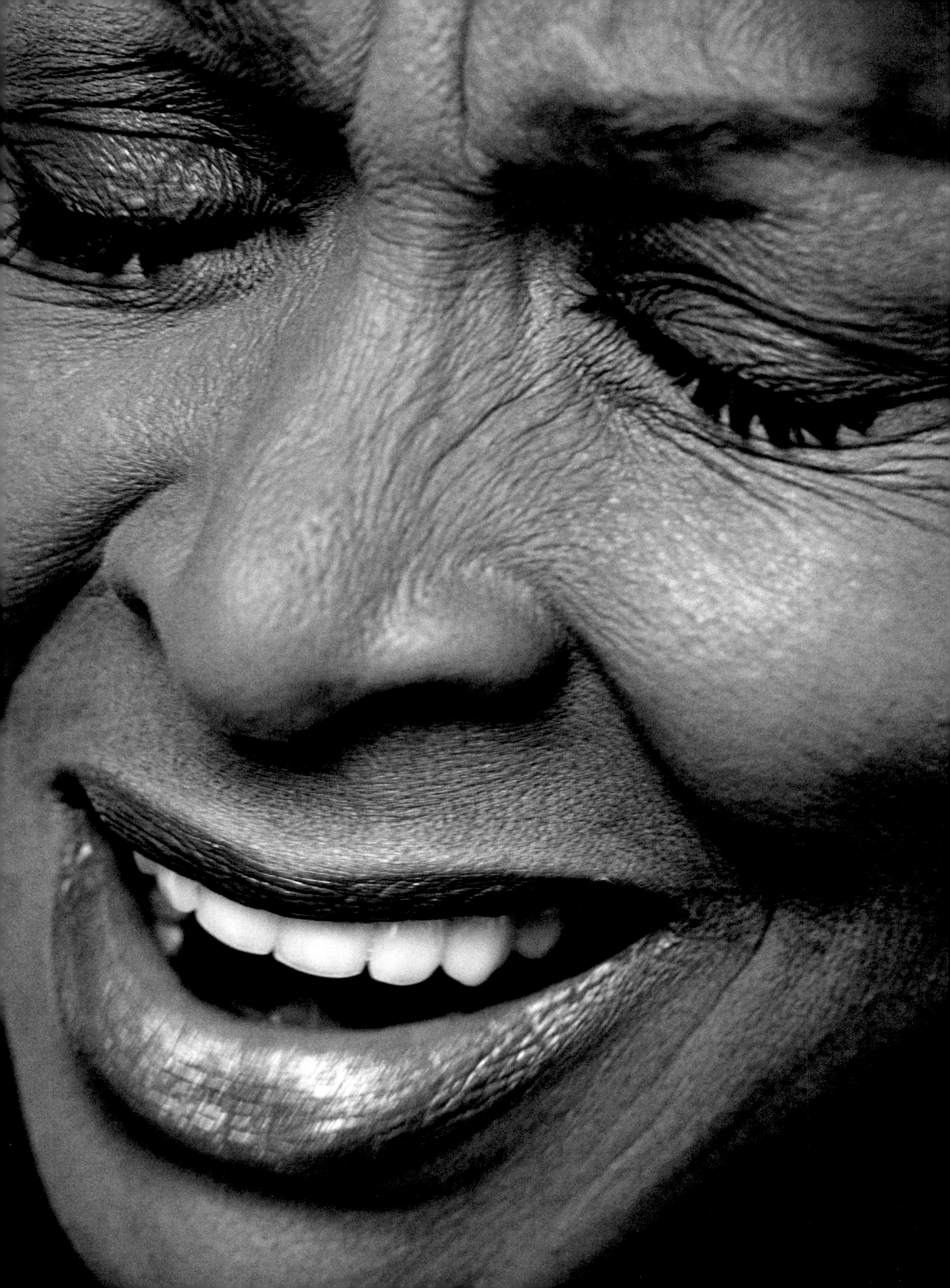

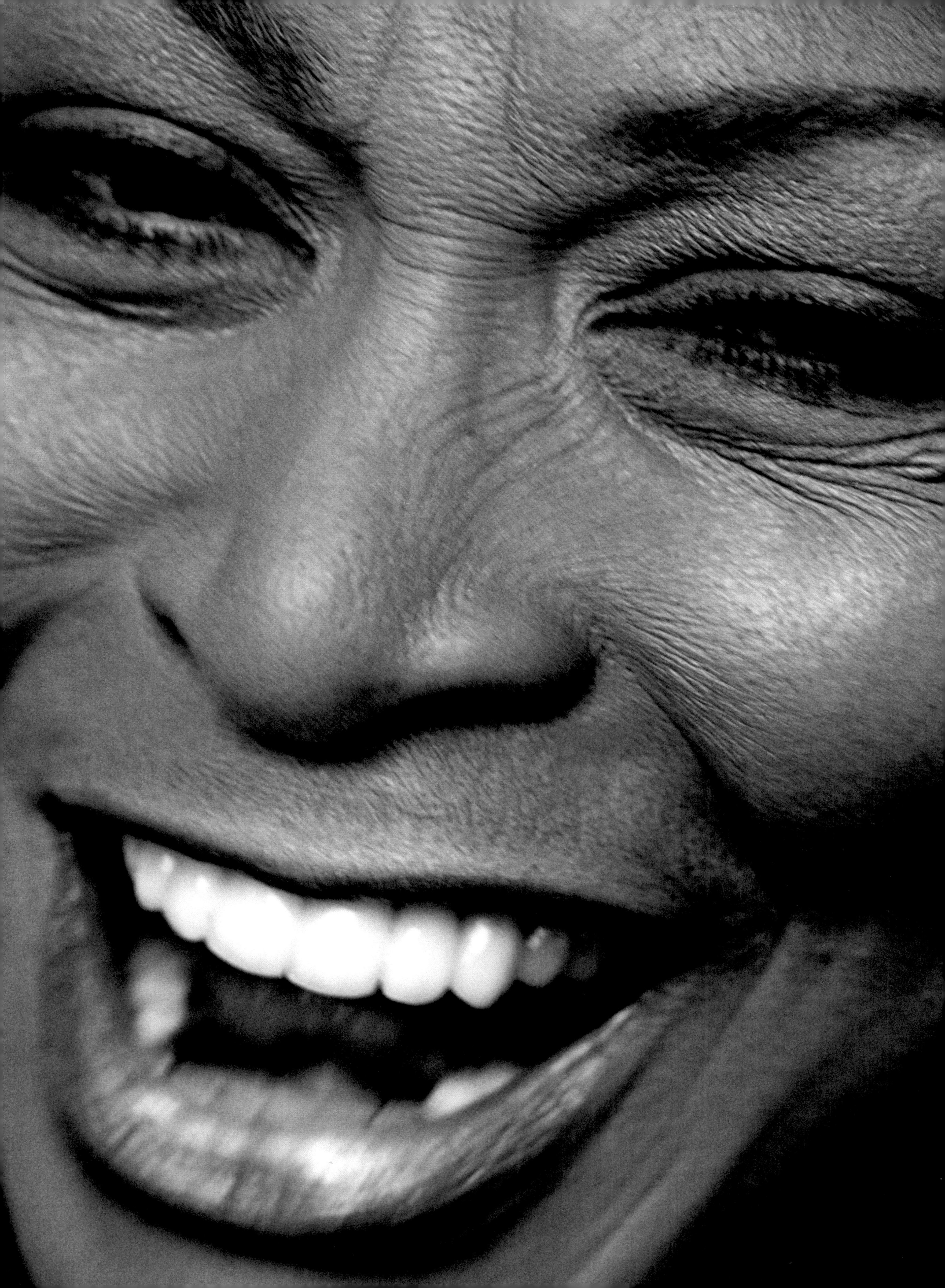

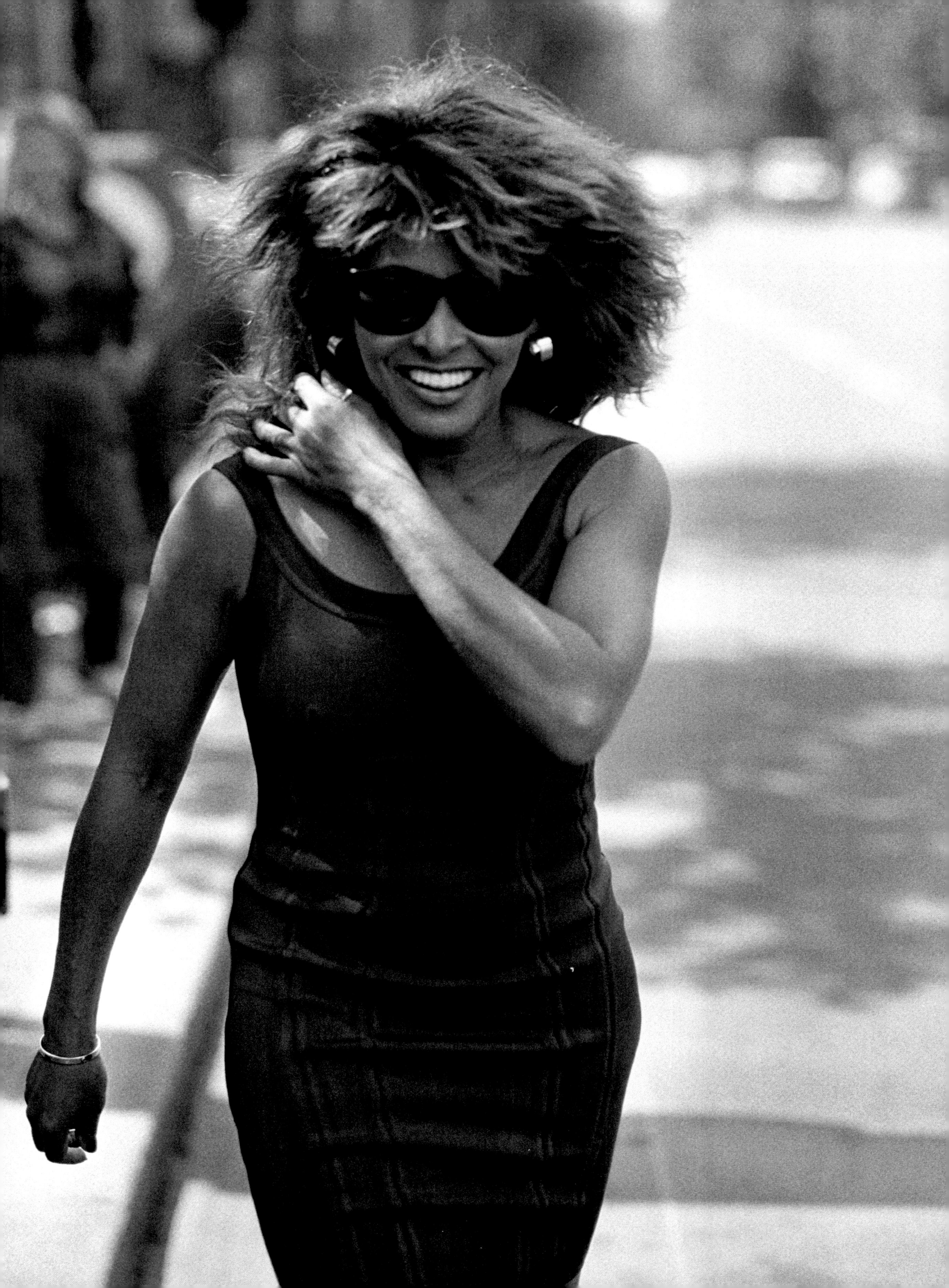

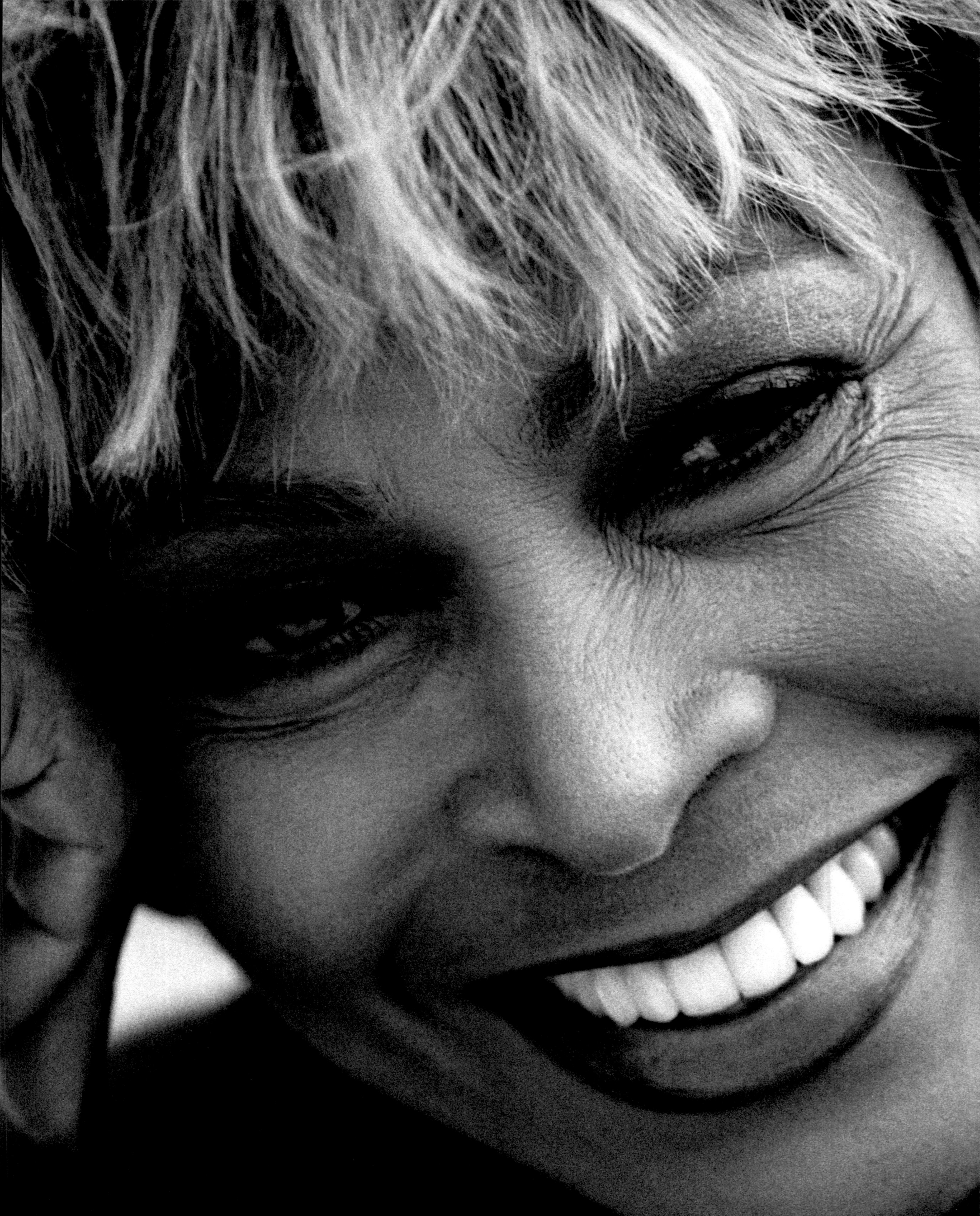

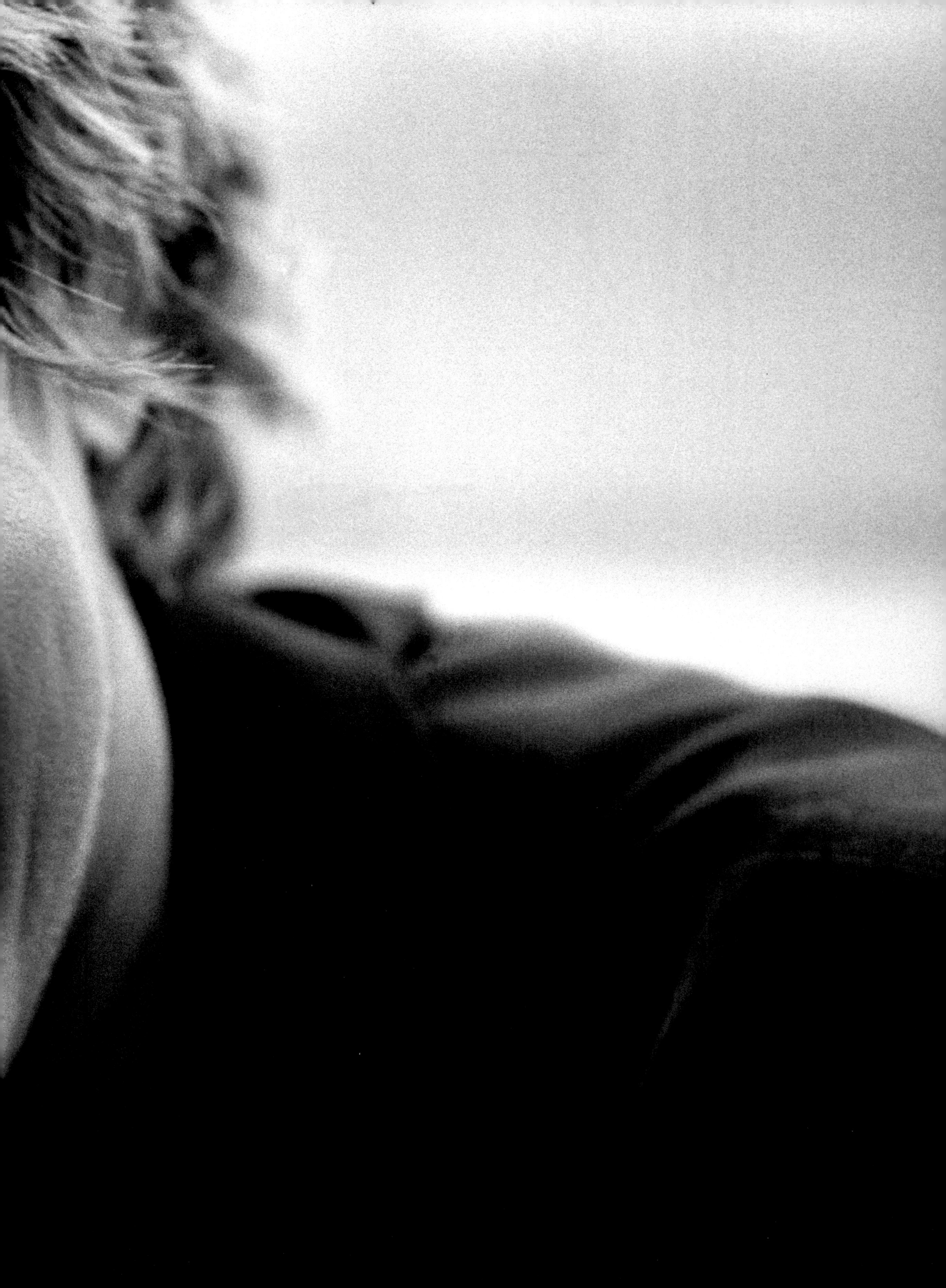

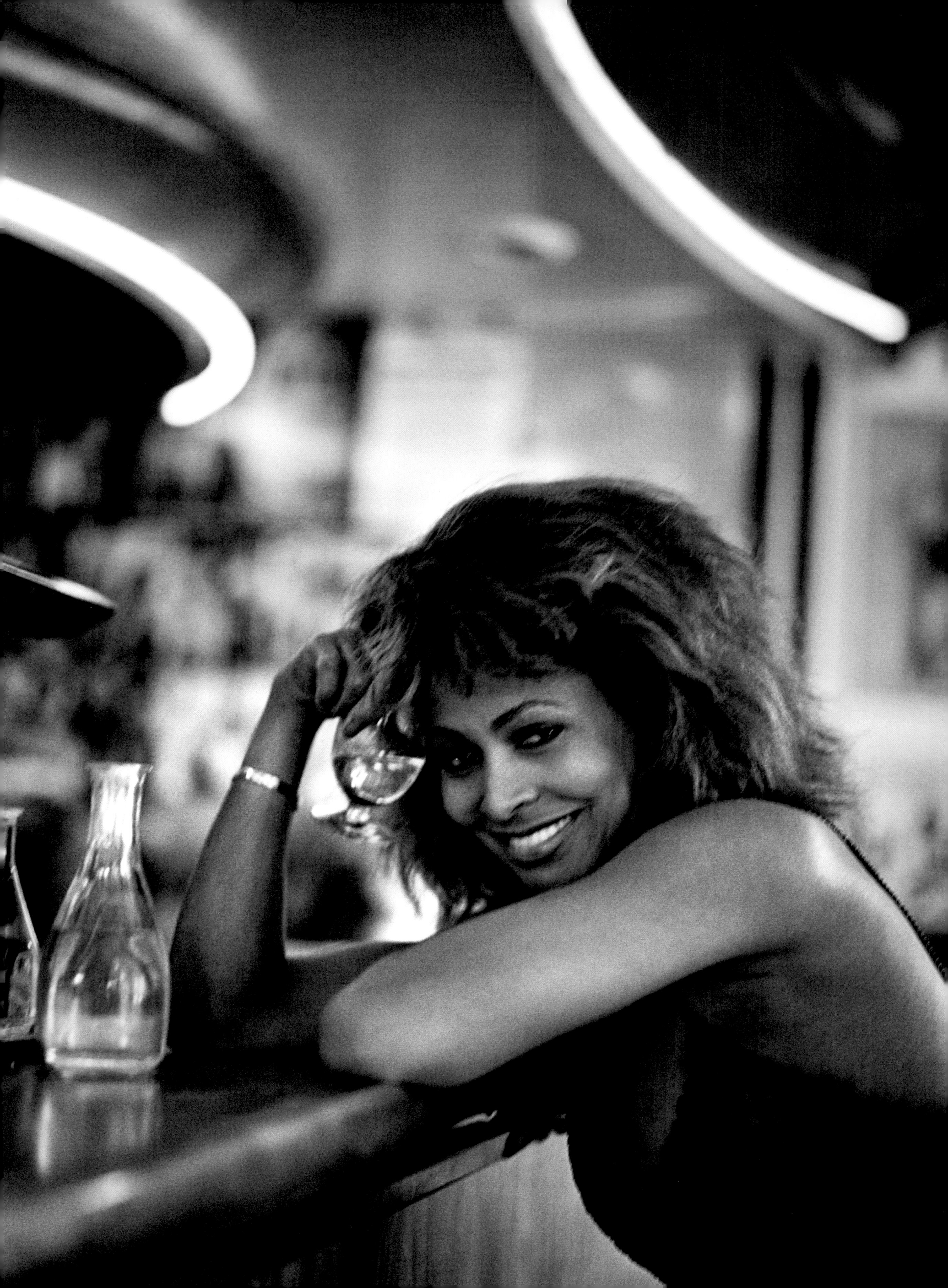

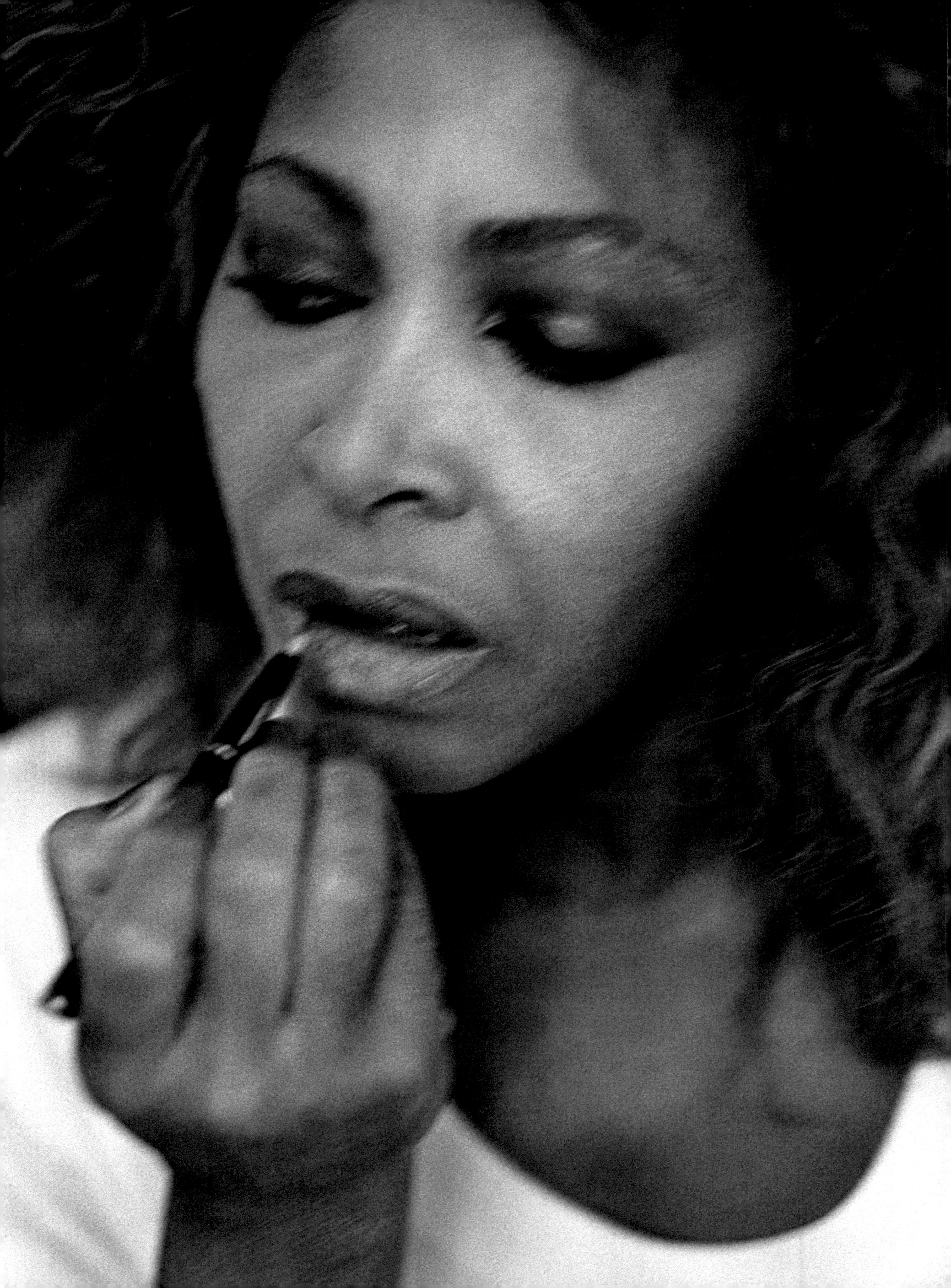

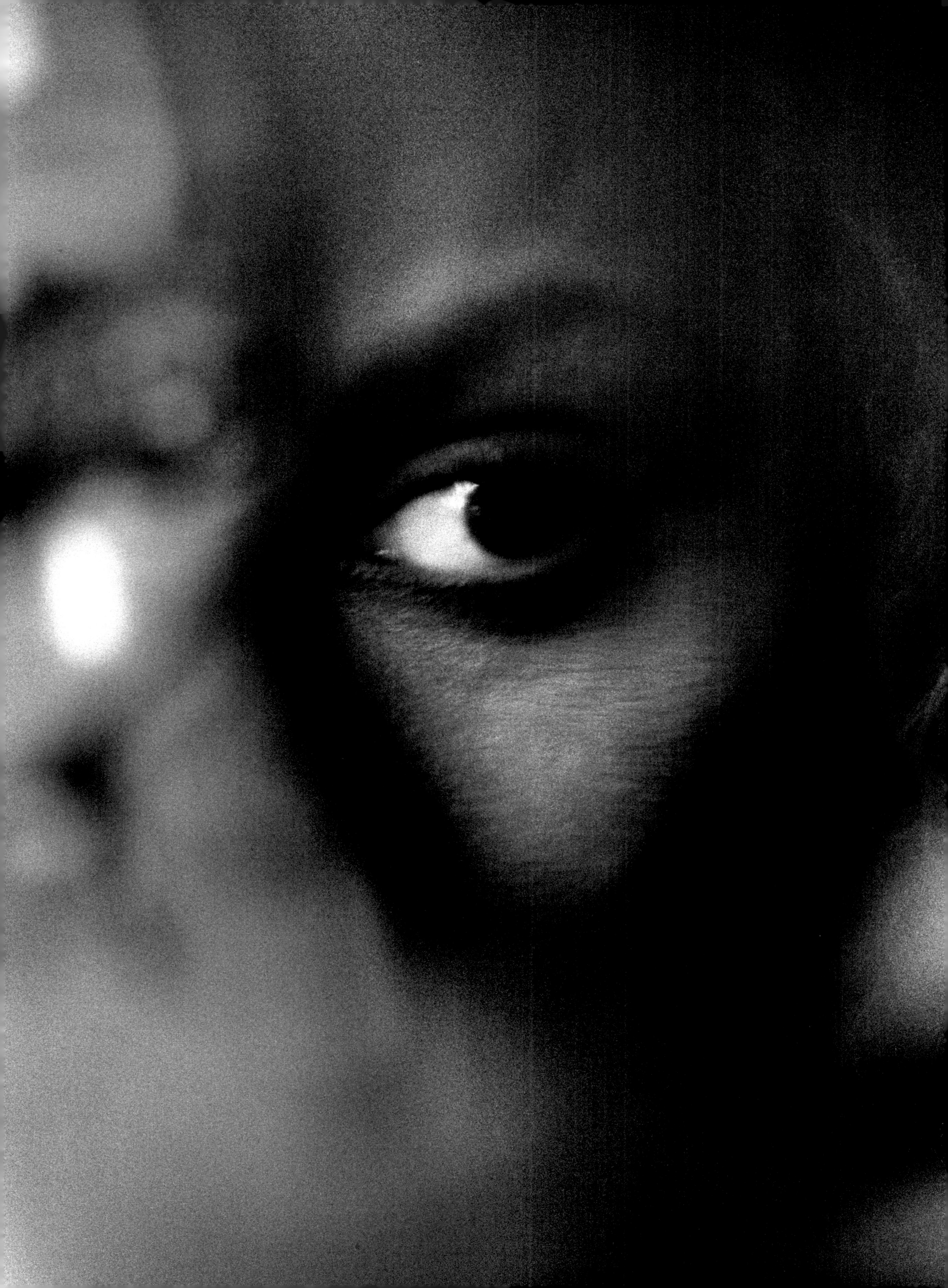

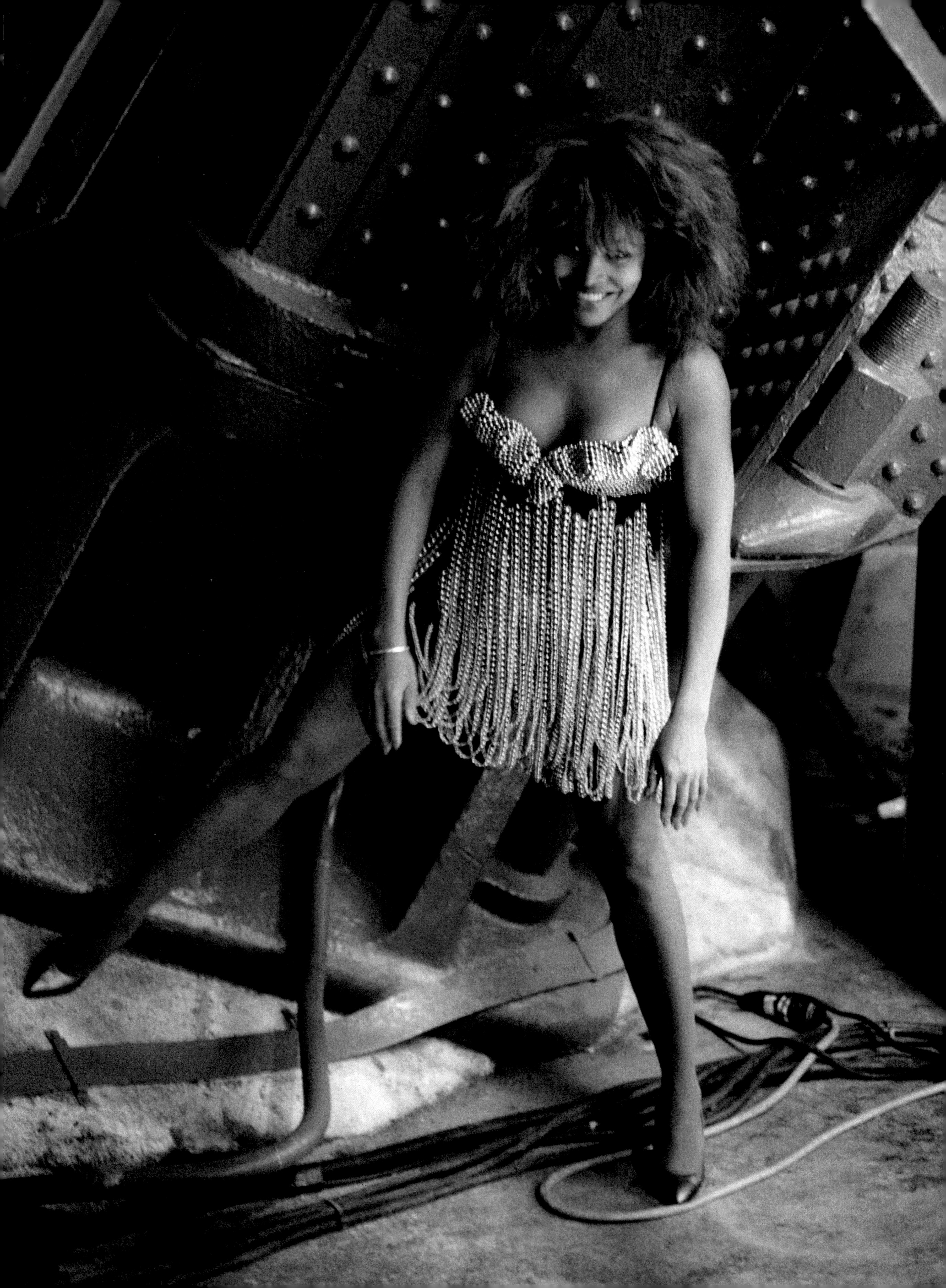

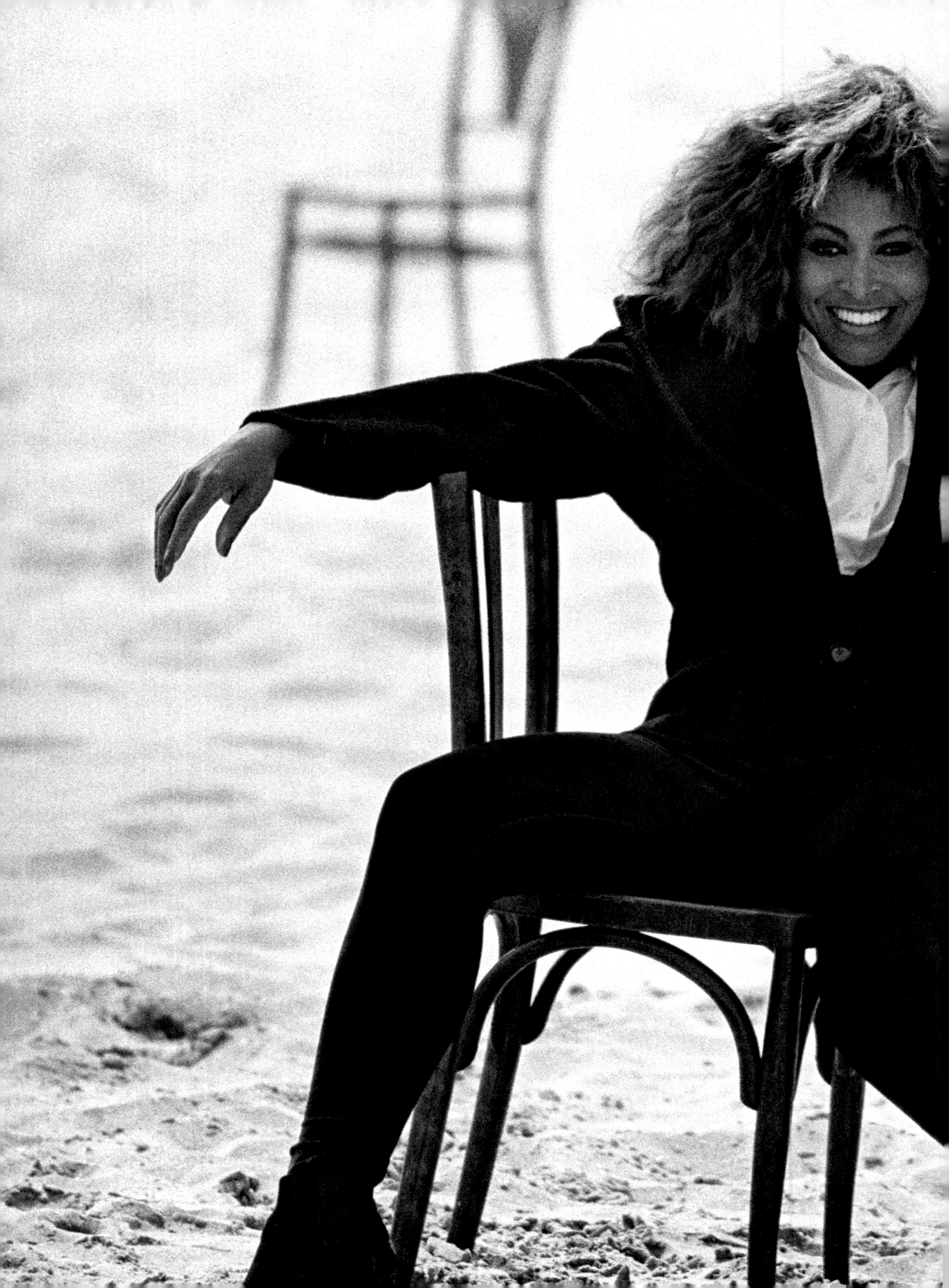

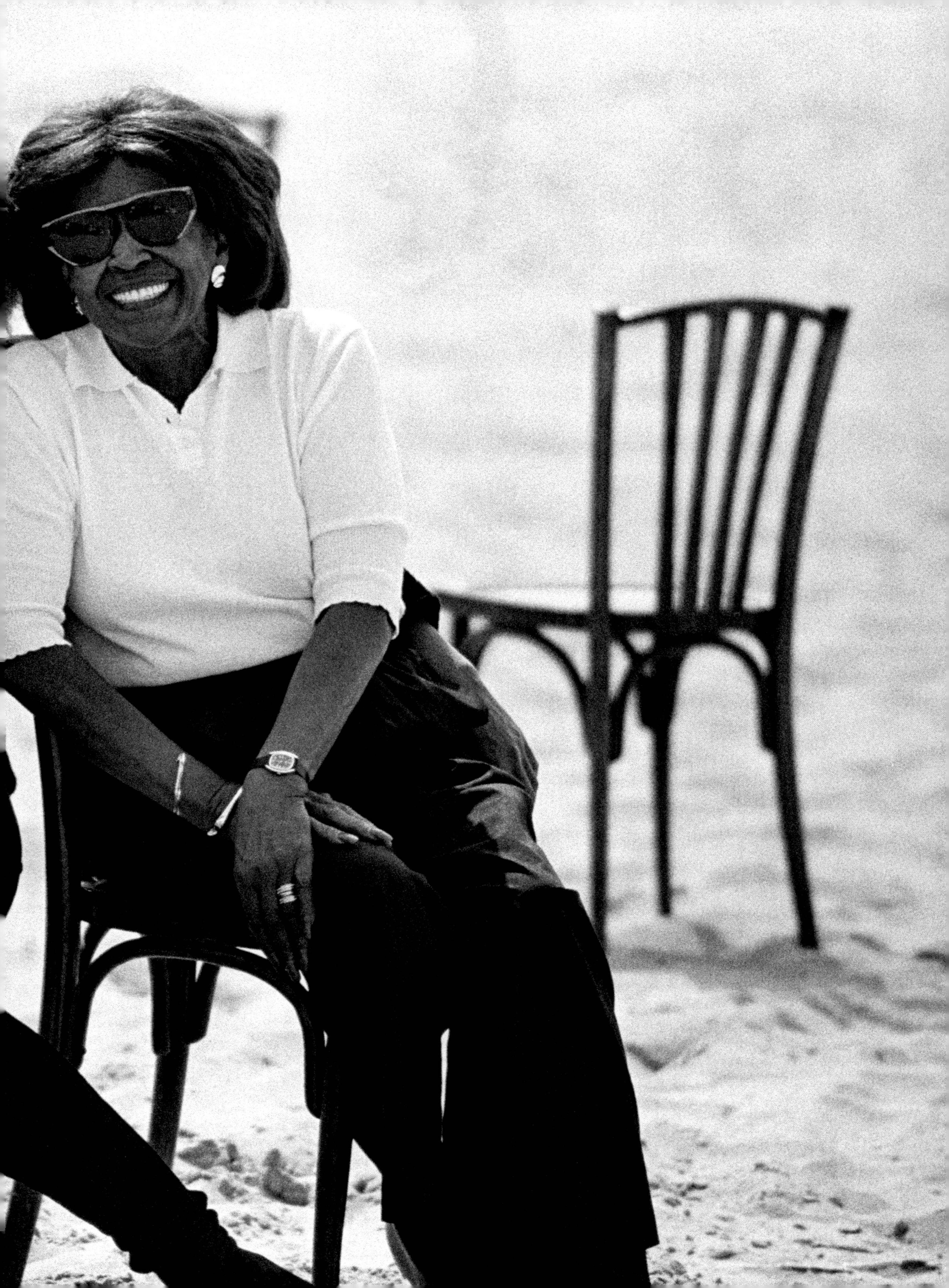

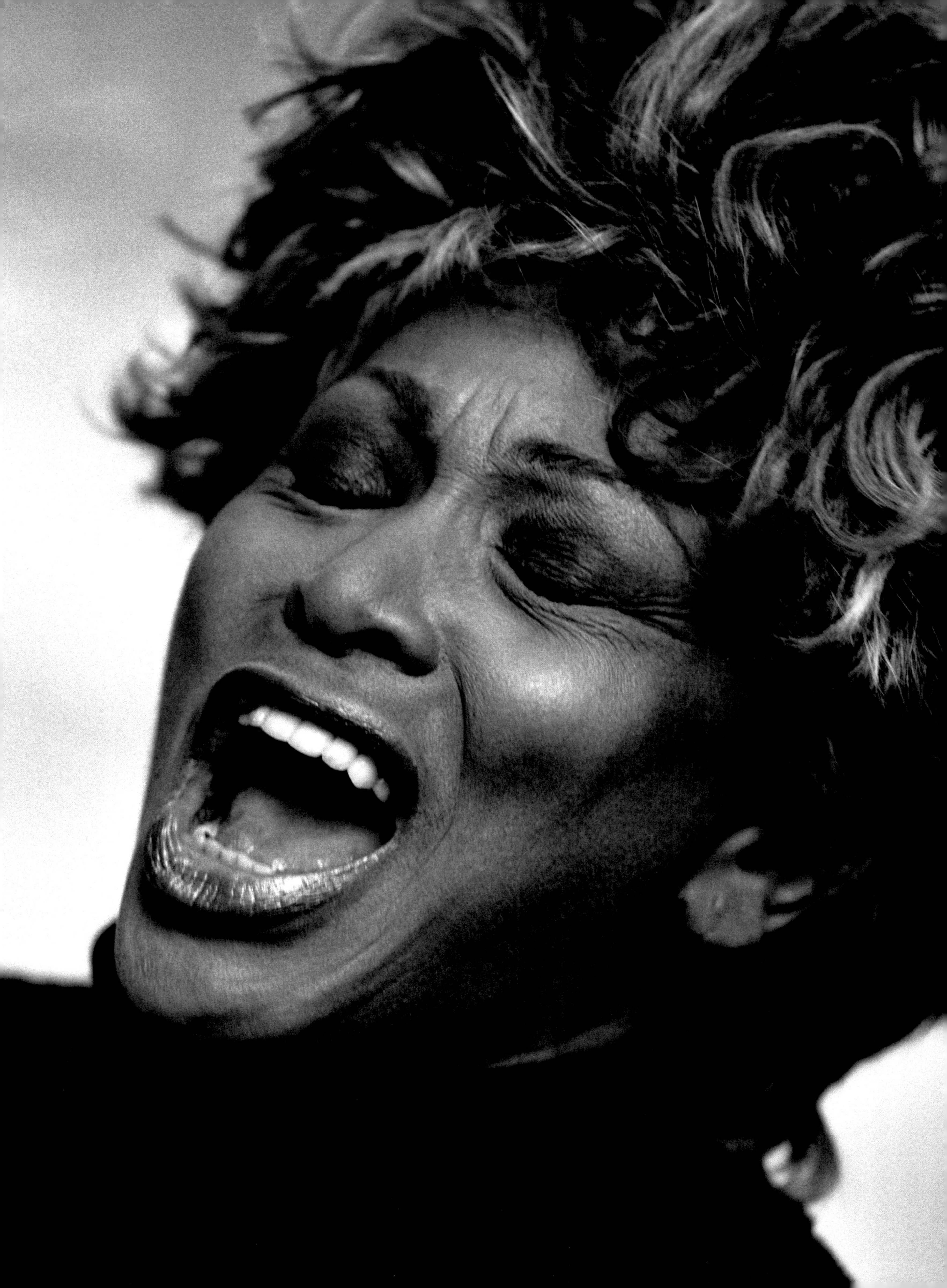

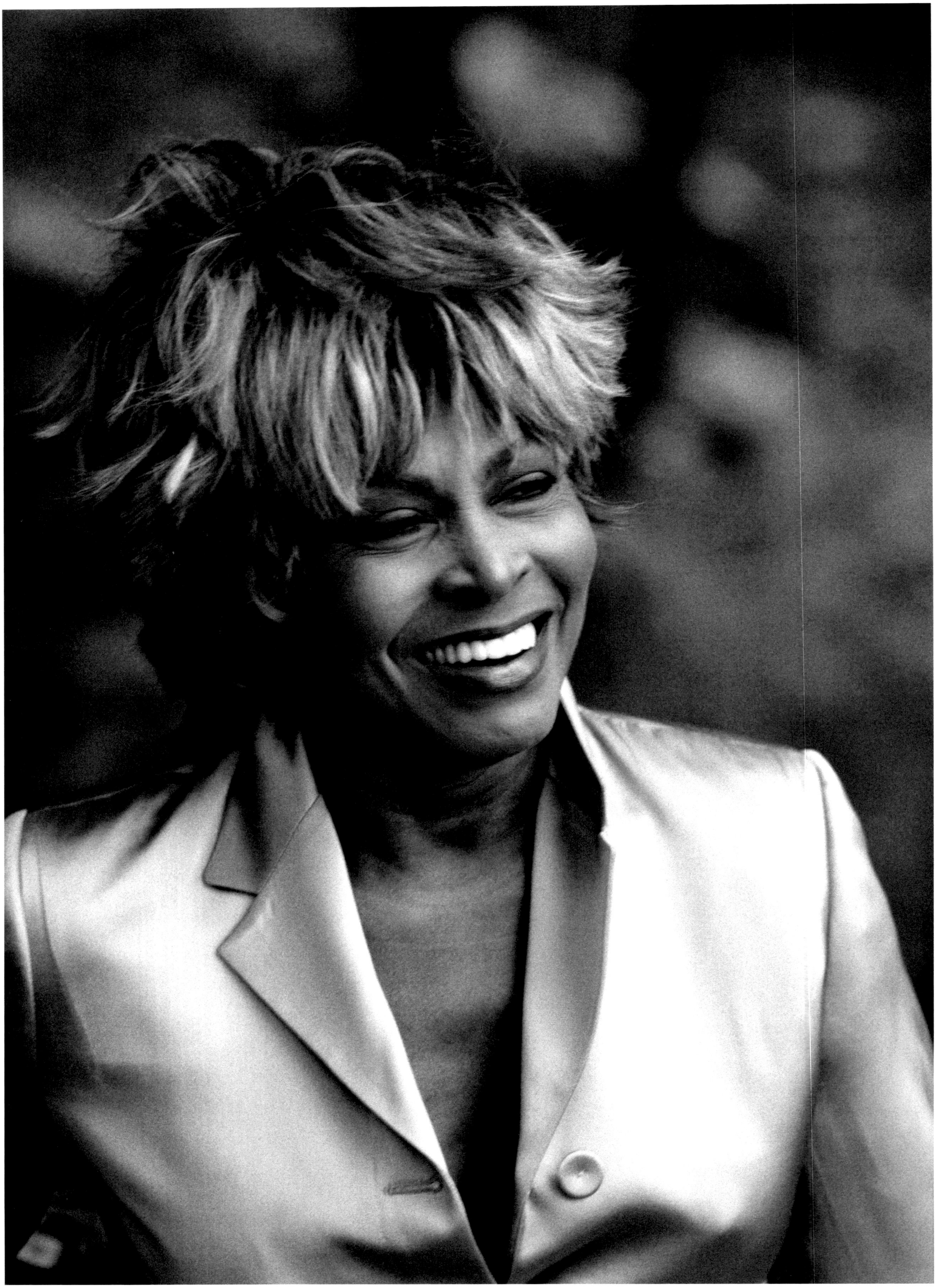

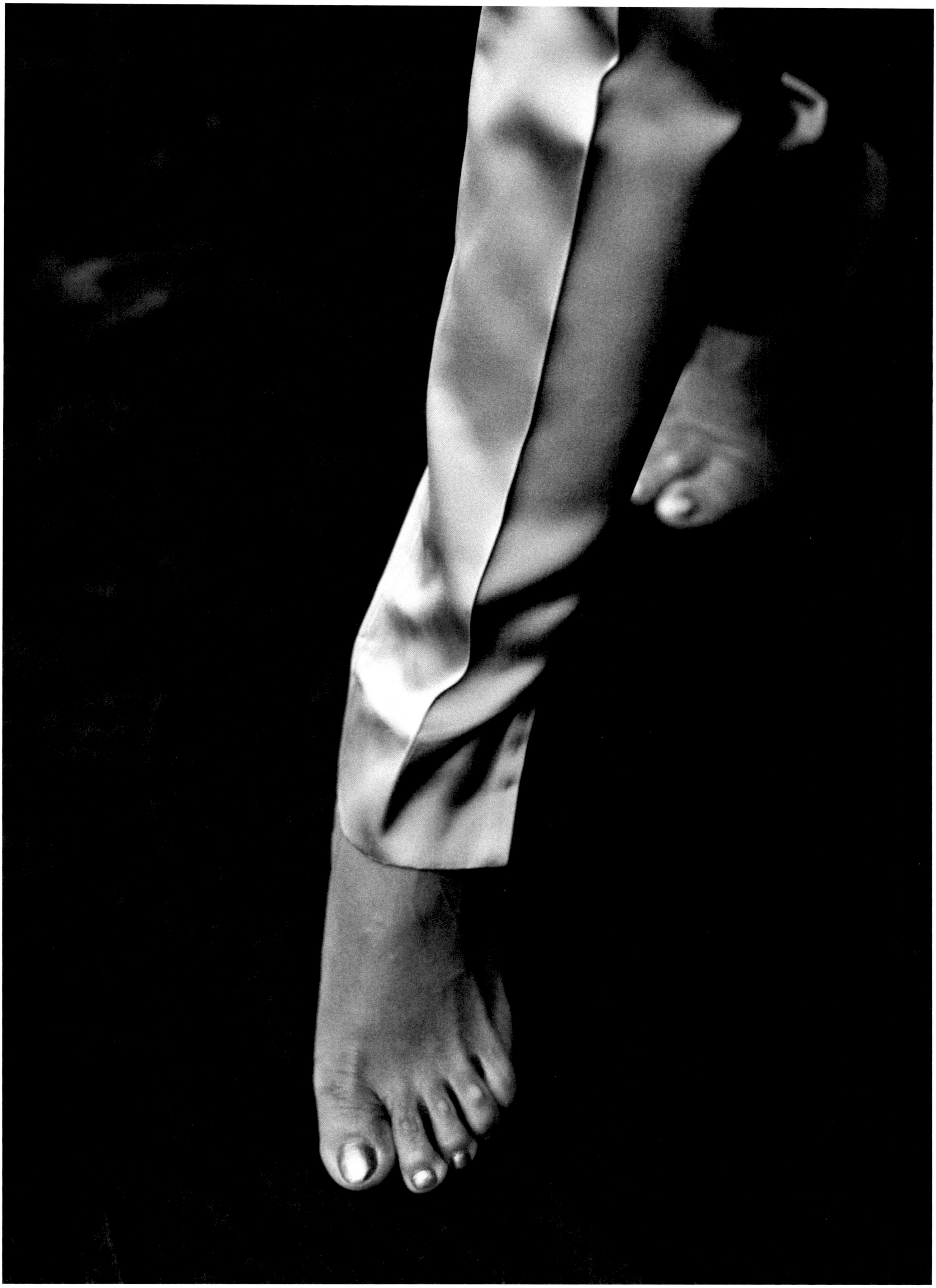

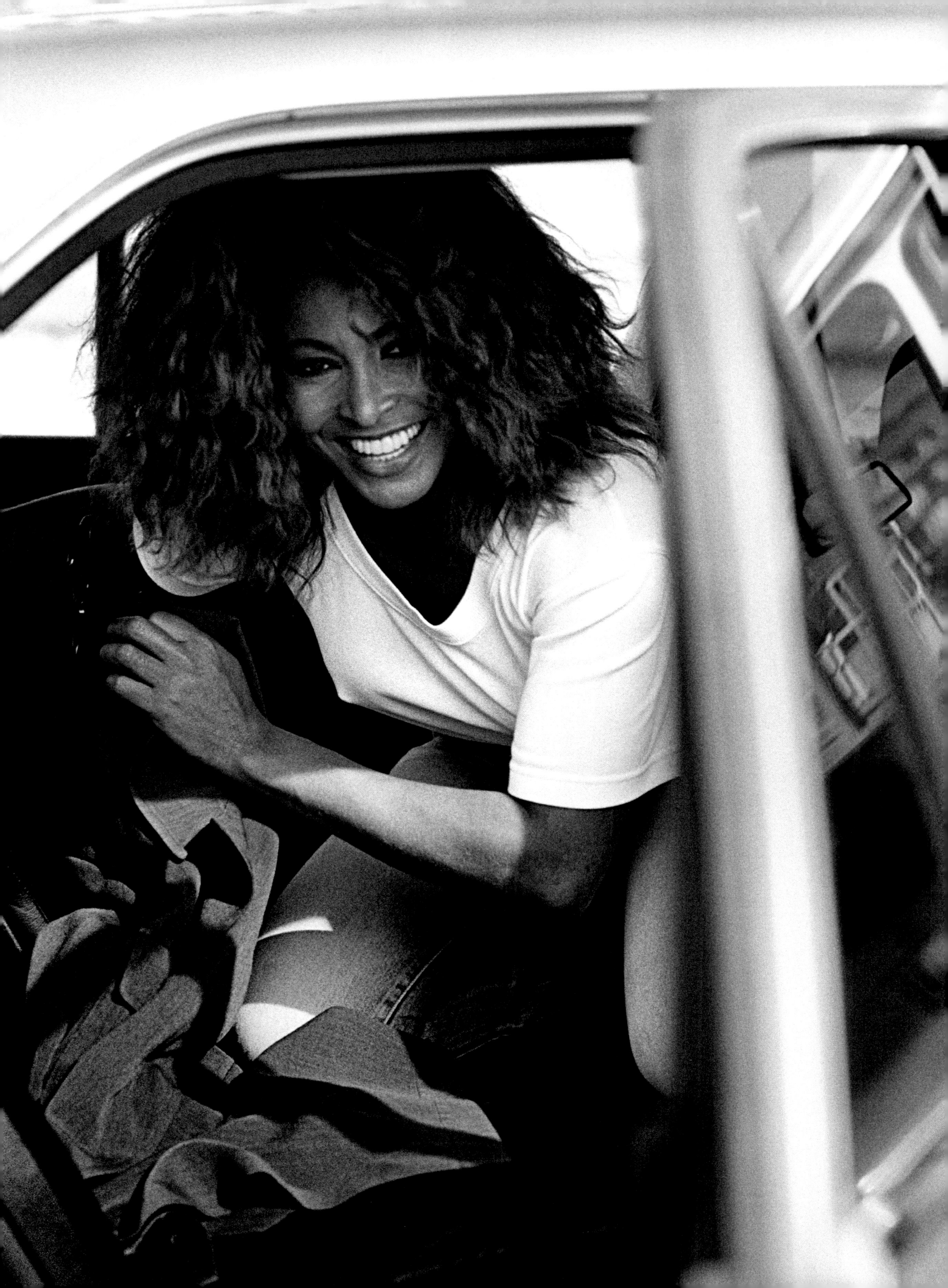

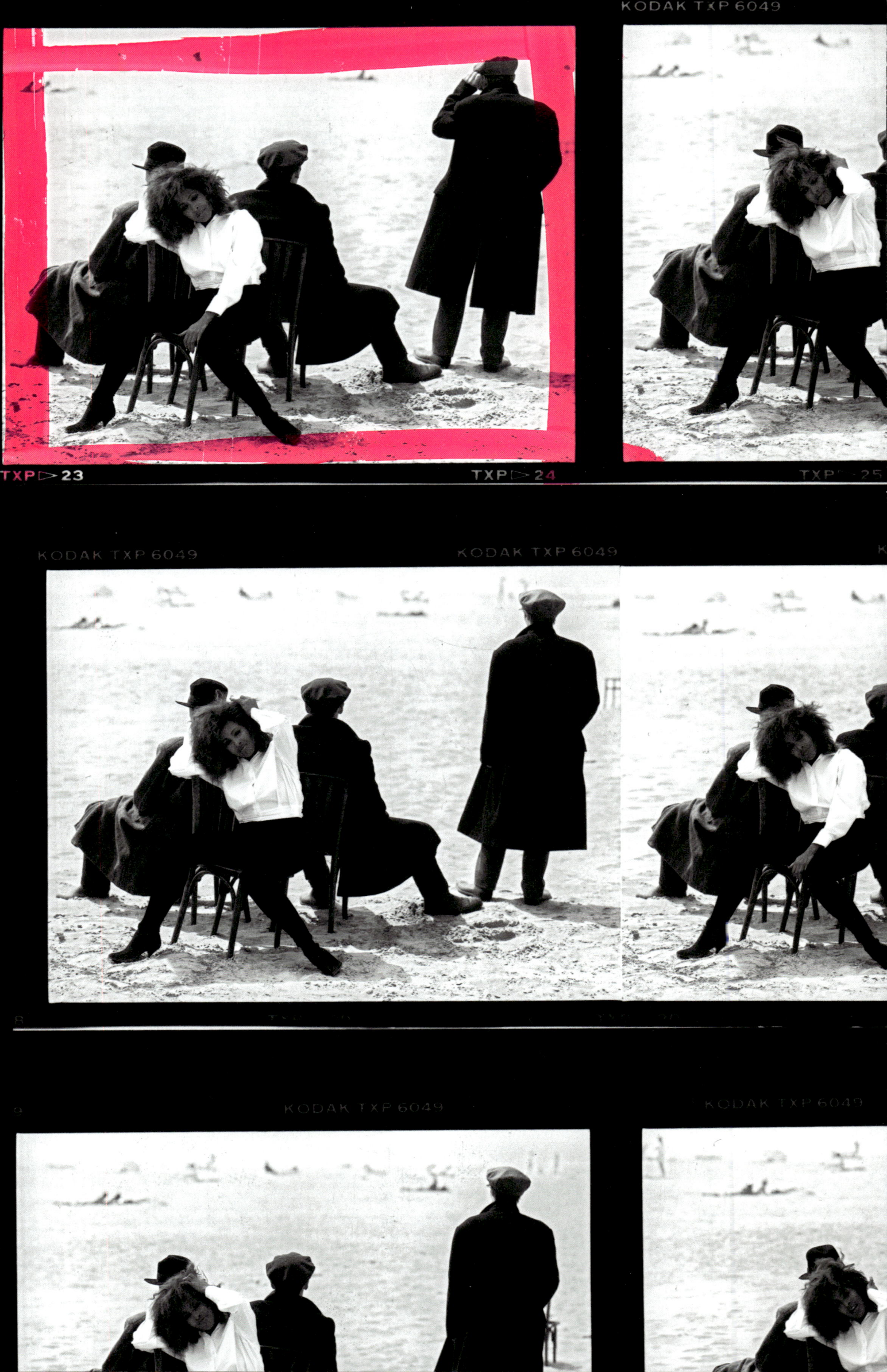
KODAK TXP 6049
TXP▷23
TXP▷24
KODAK TXP 6049
KODAK TXP 6049
KODAK TXP 6049
KODAK TXP 6049

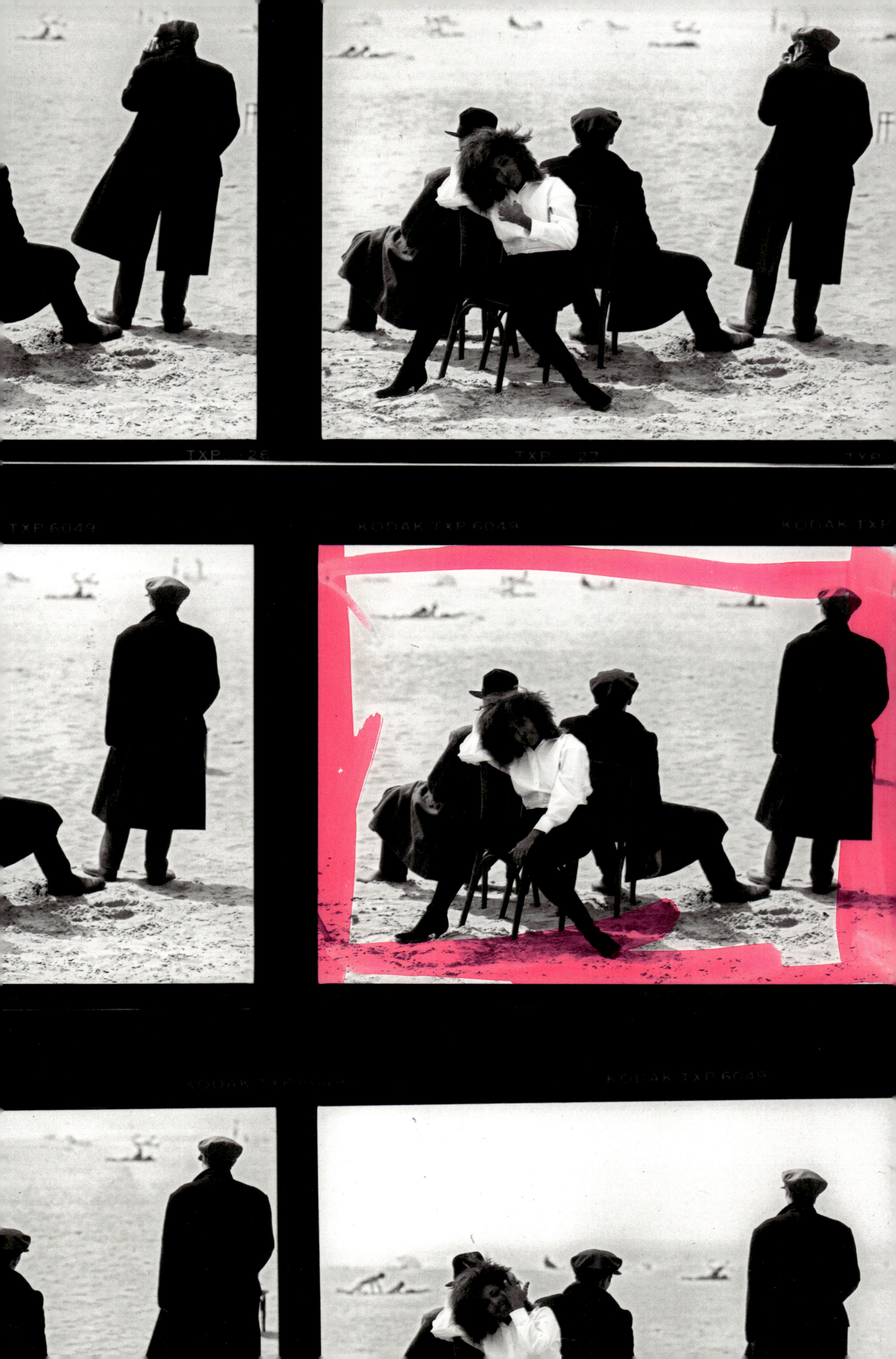
TXP 6049
KODAK TXP 6049
KODAK TXP
KODAK TXP 6049

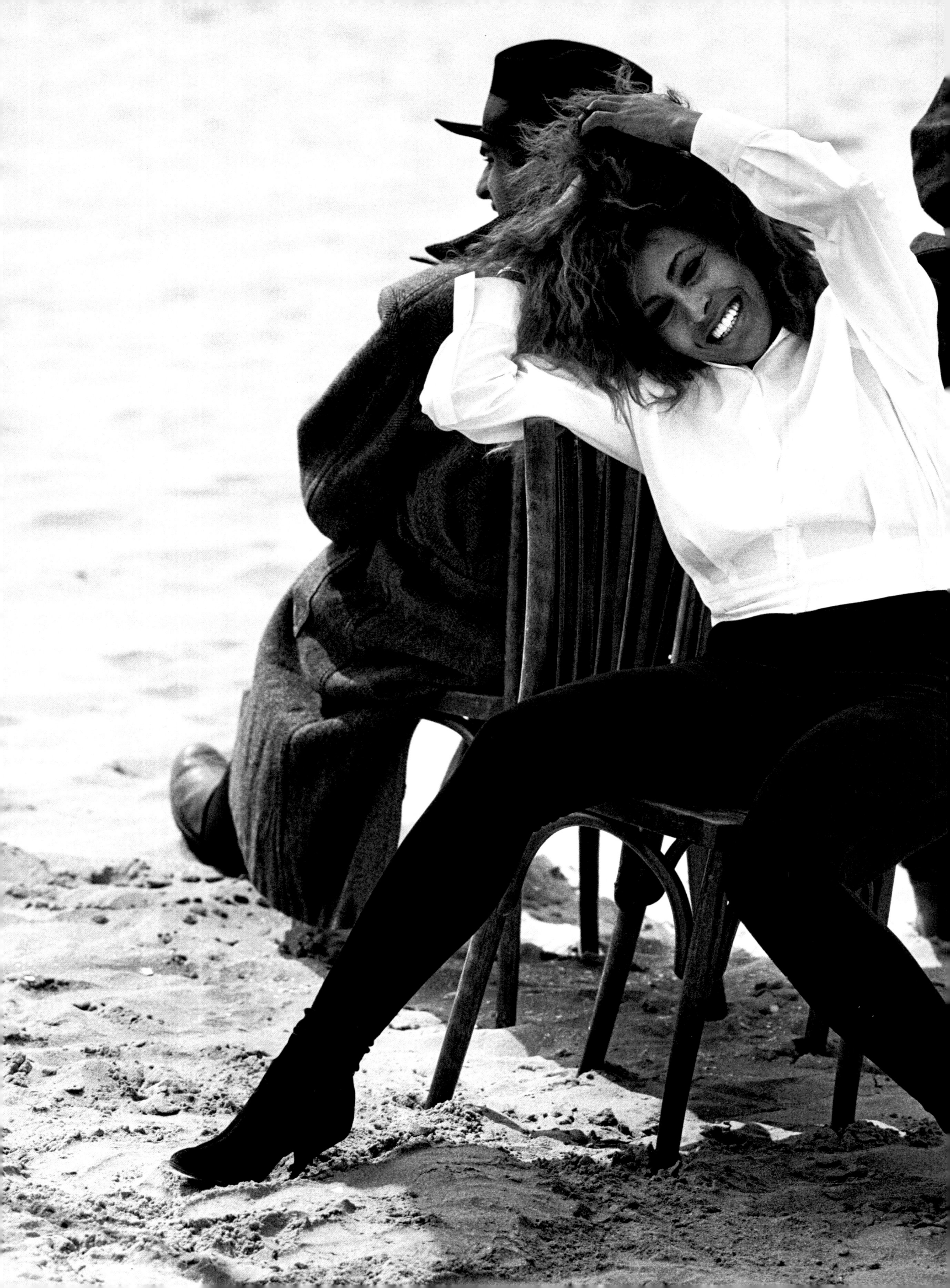

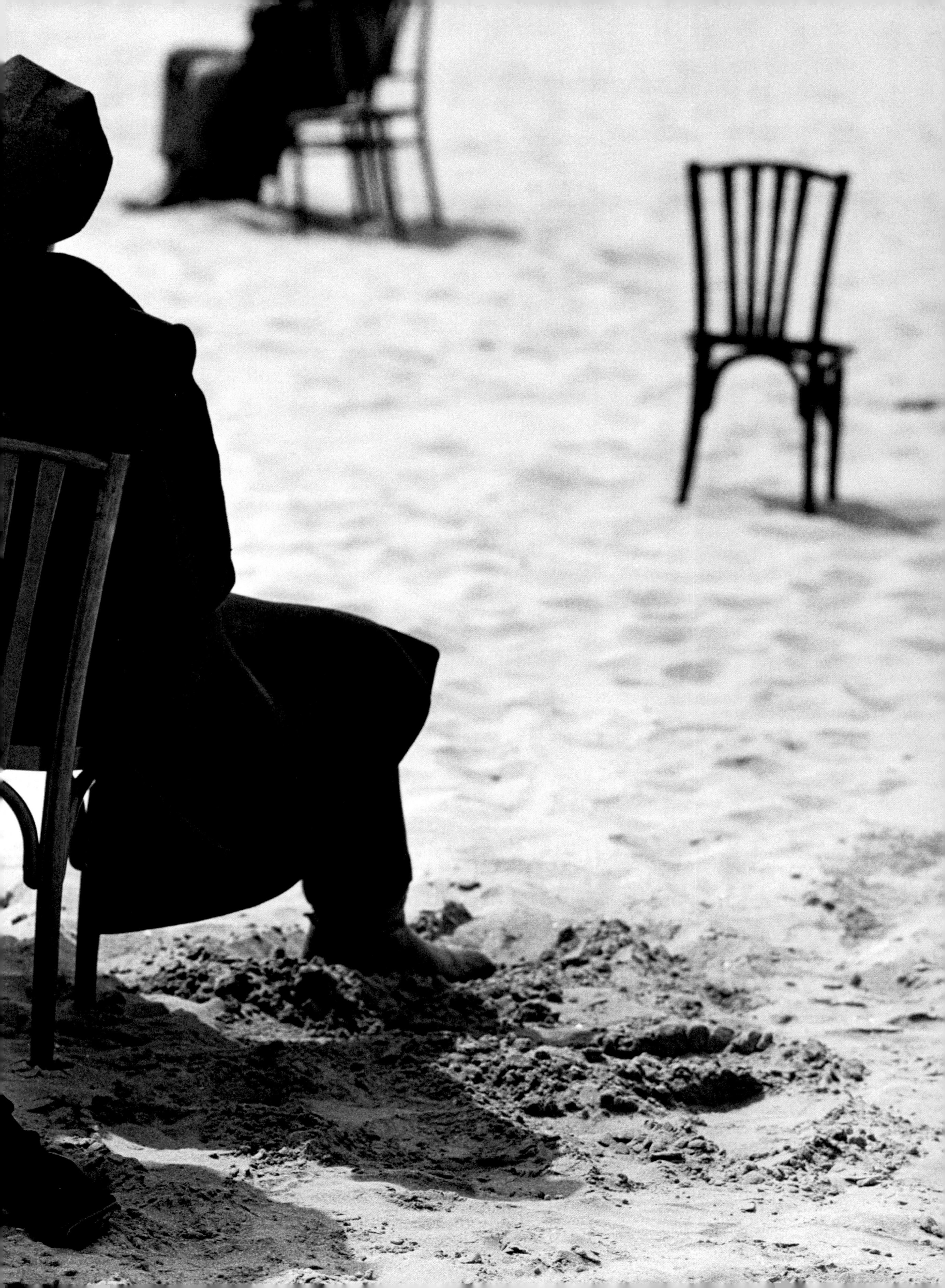

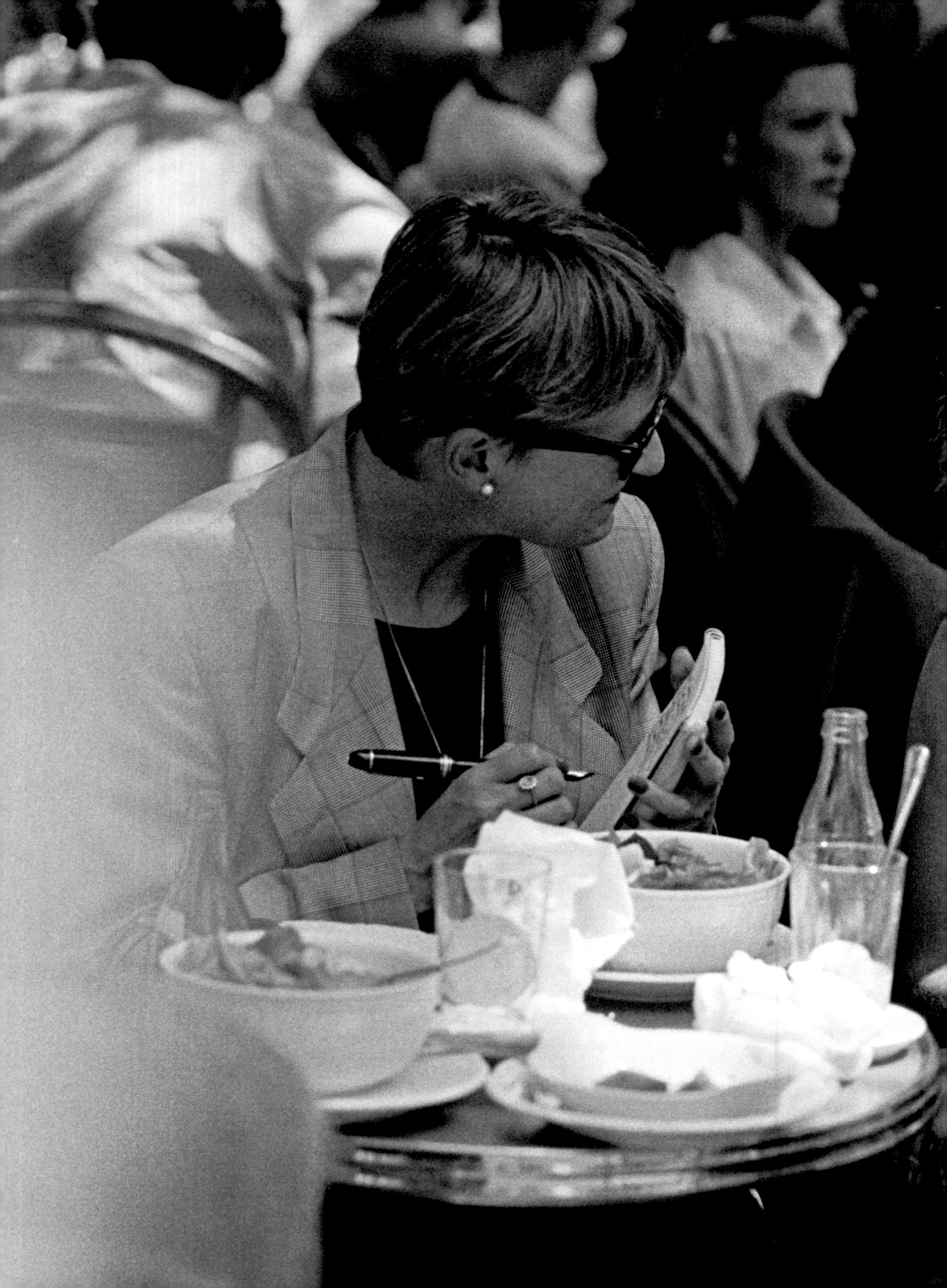

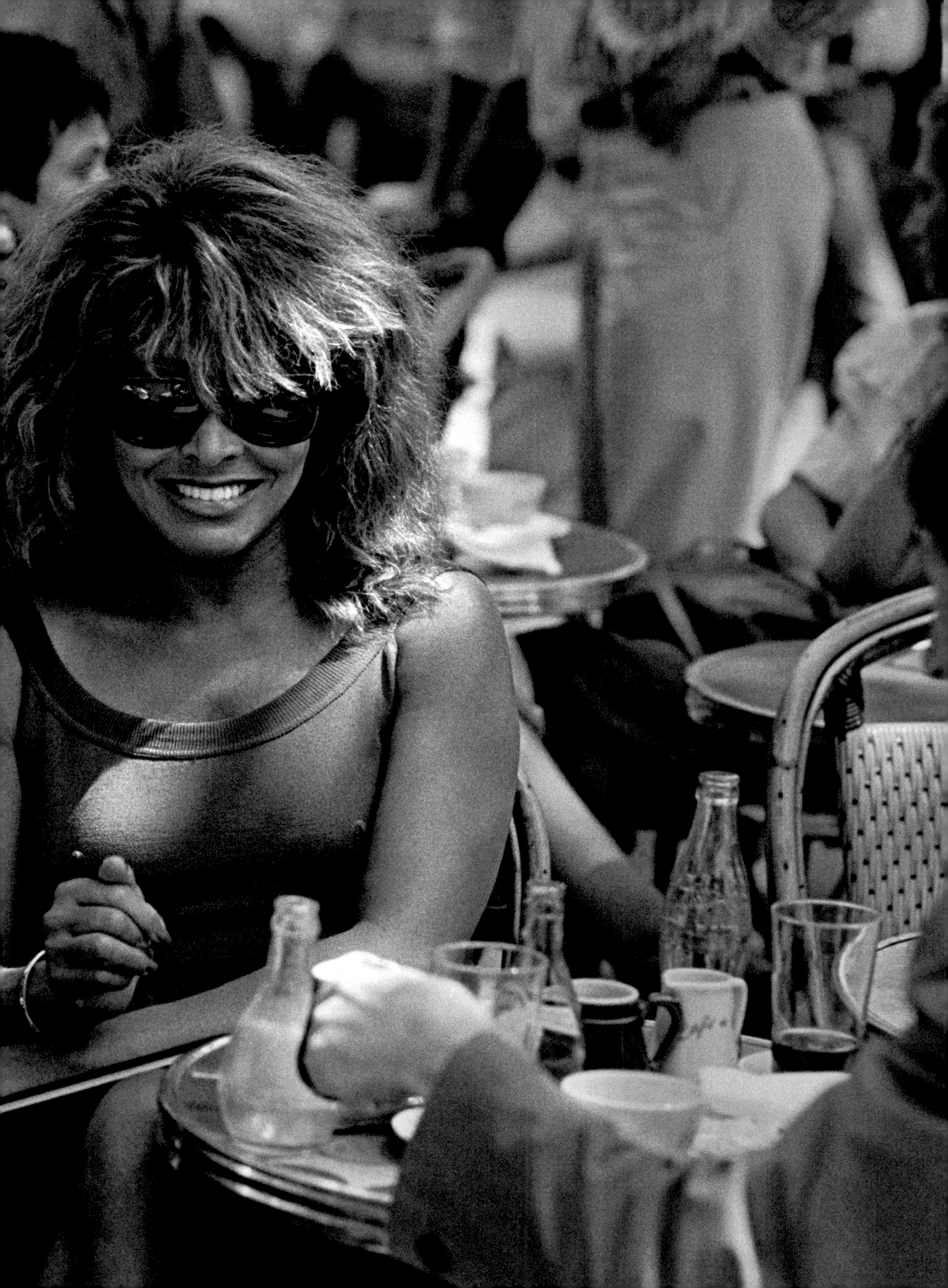

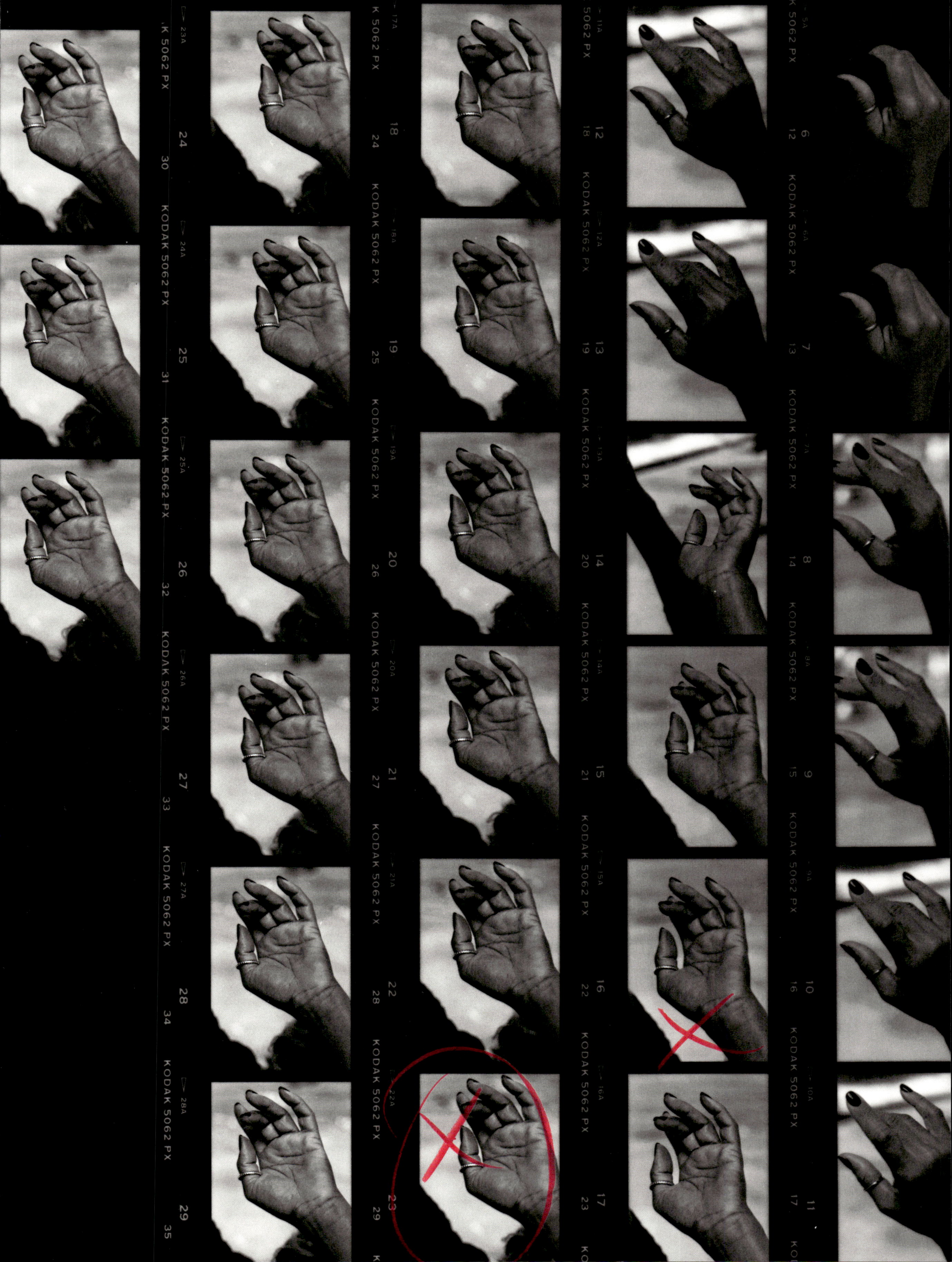
KODAK 5062 PX

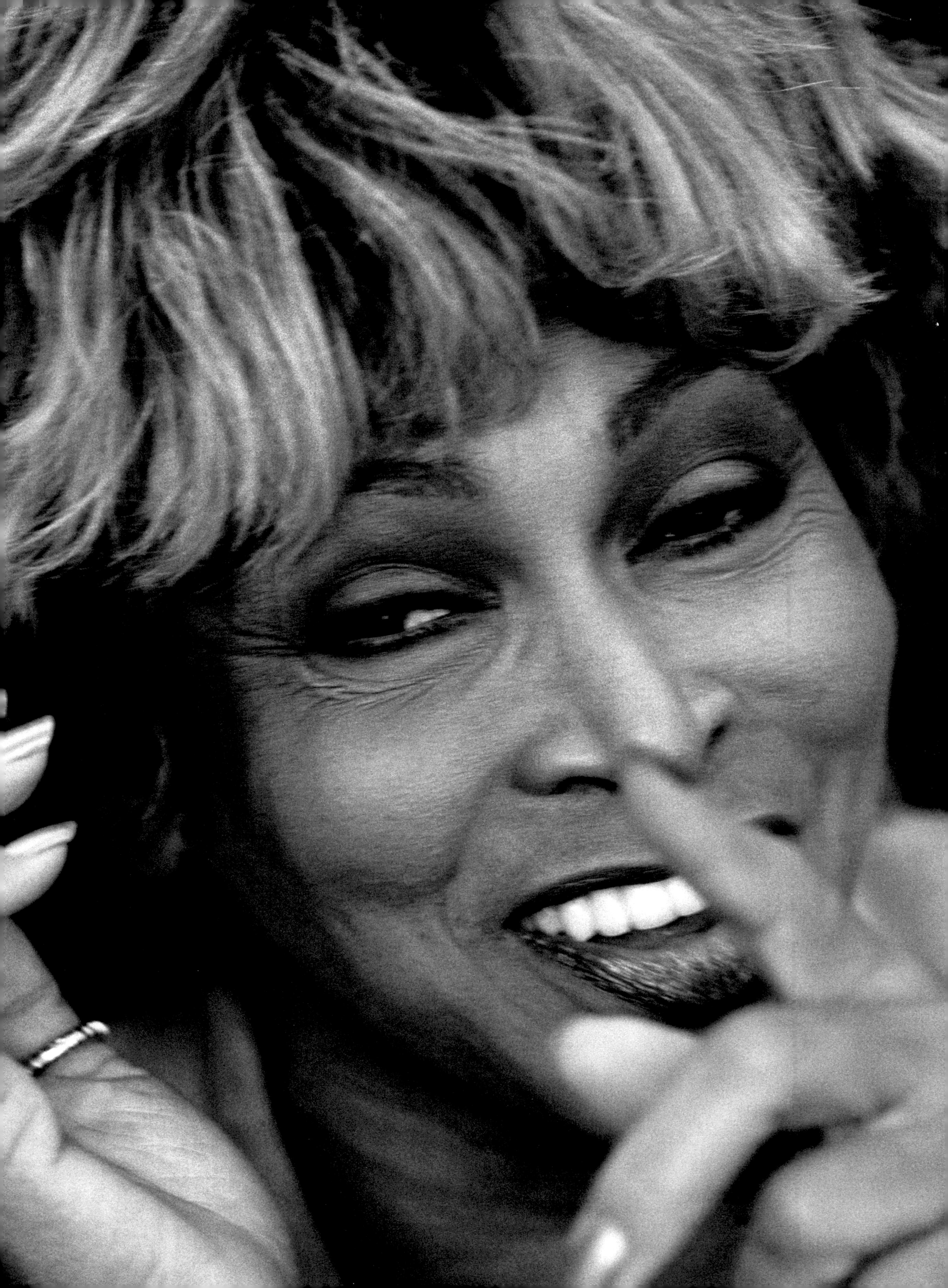

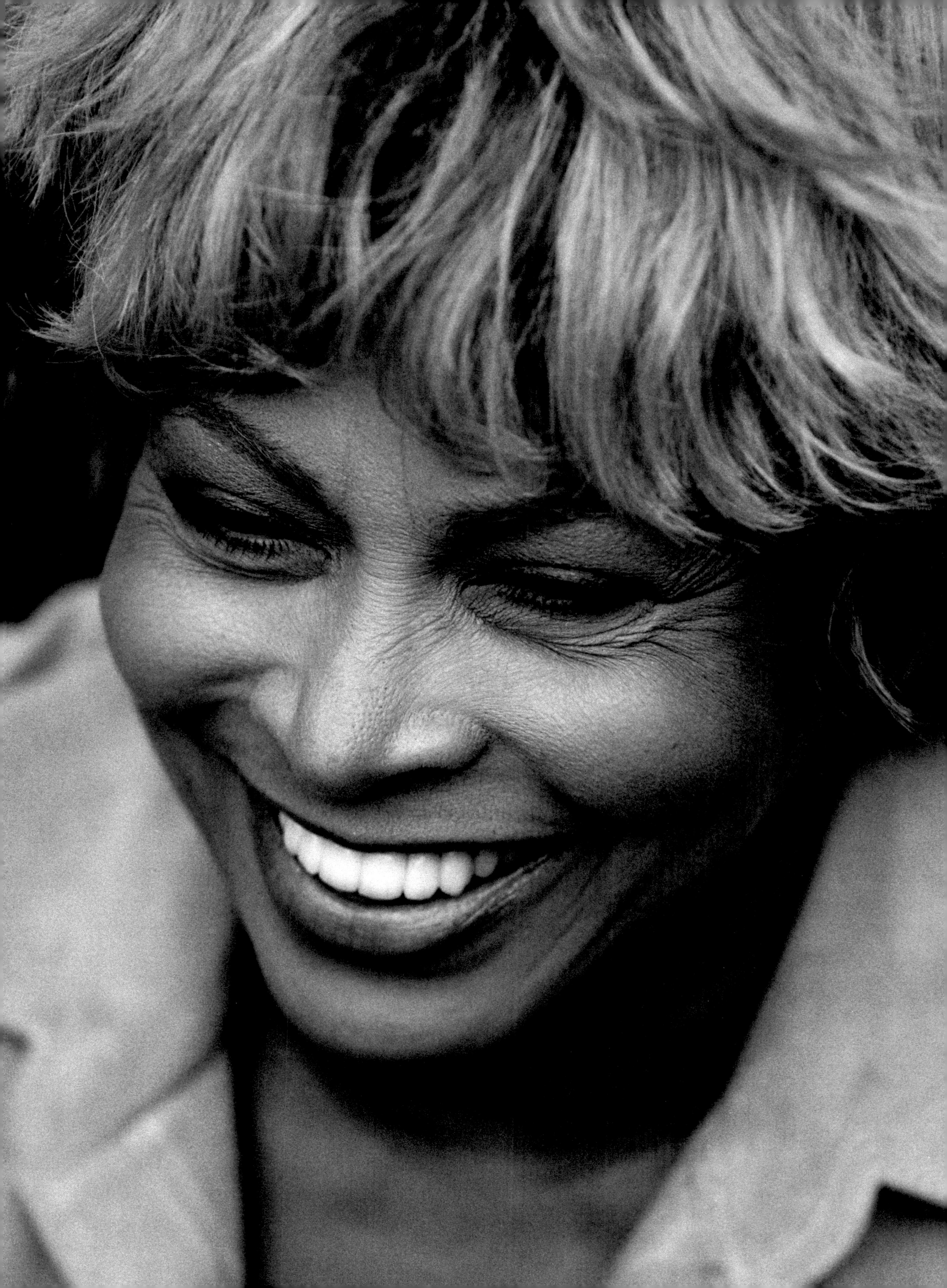

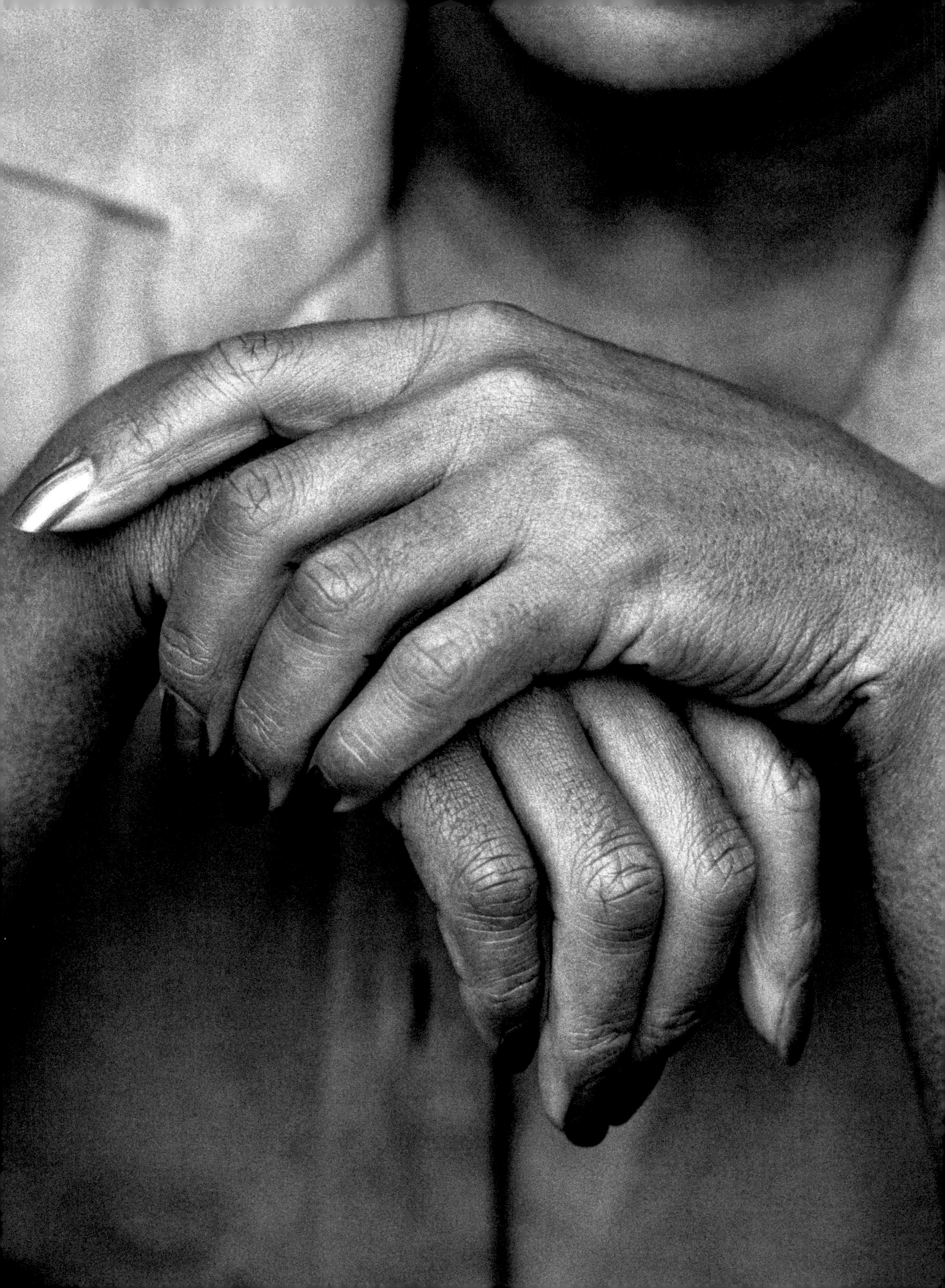

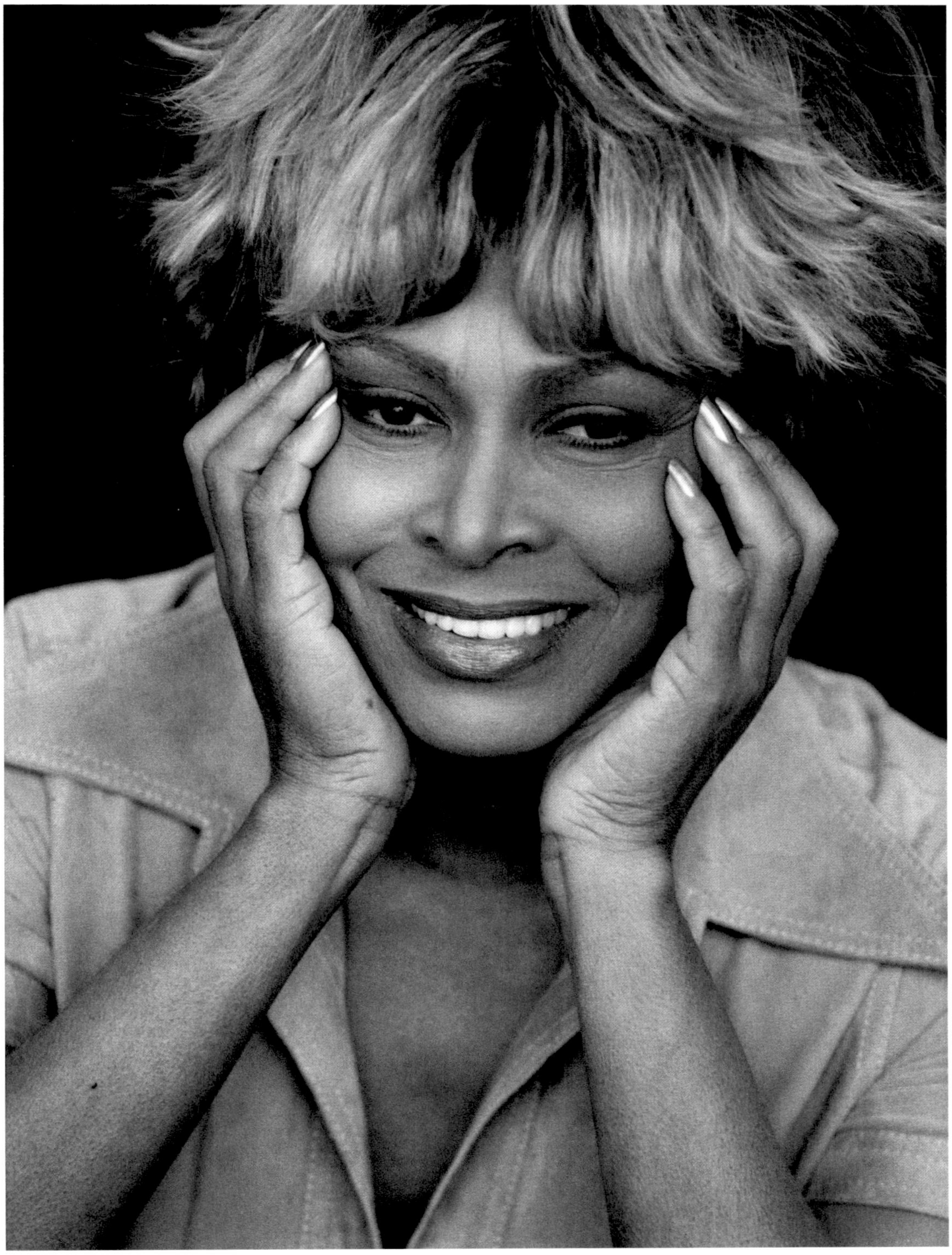

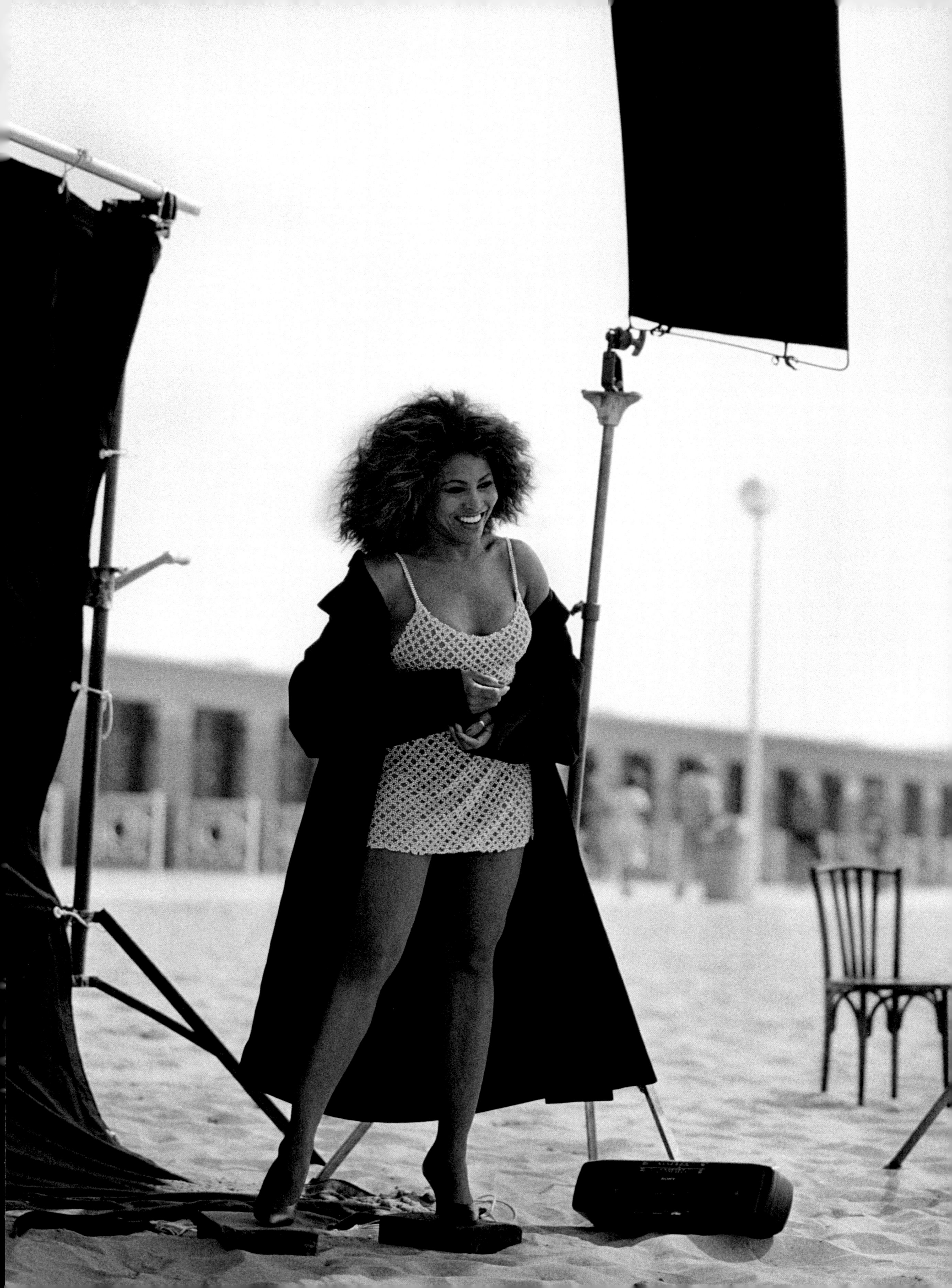

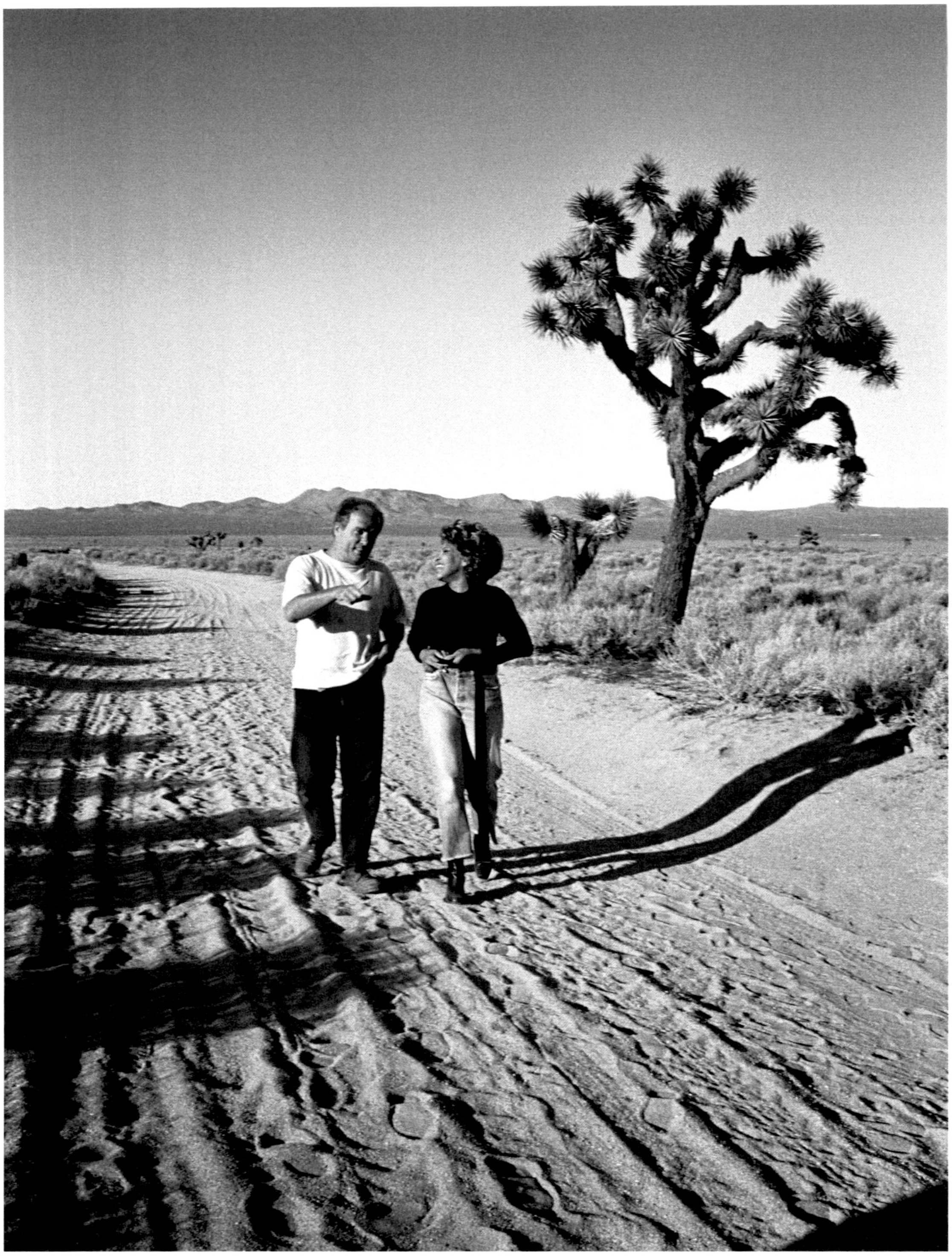

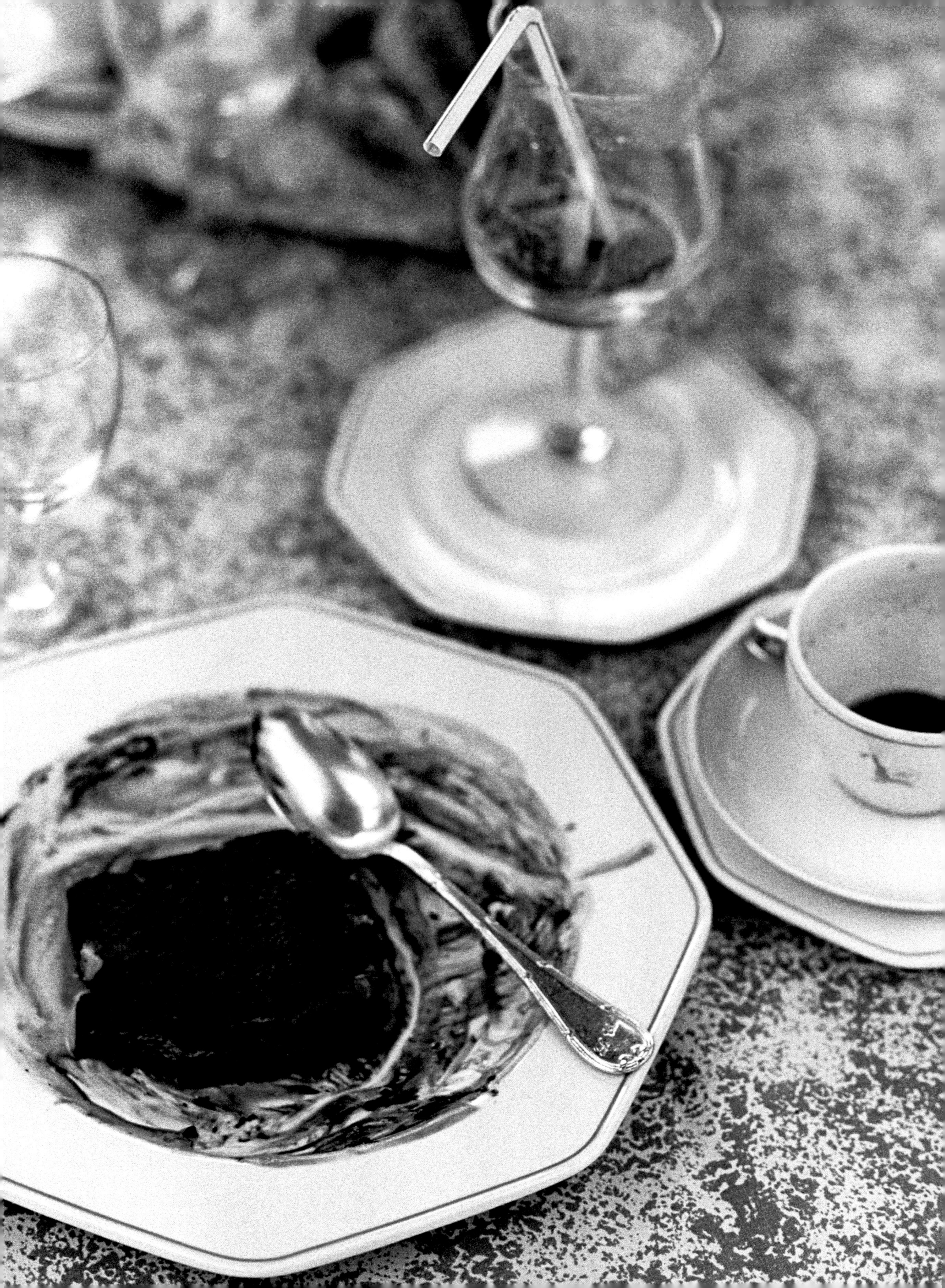

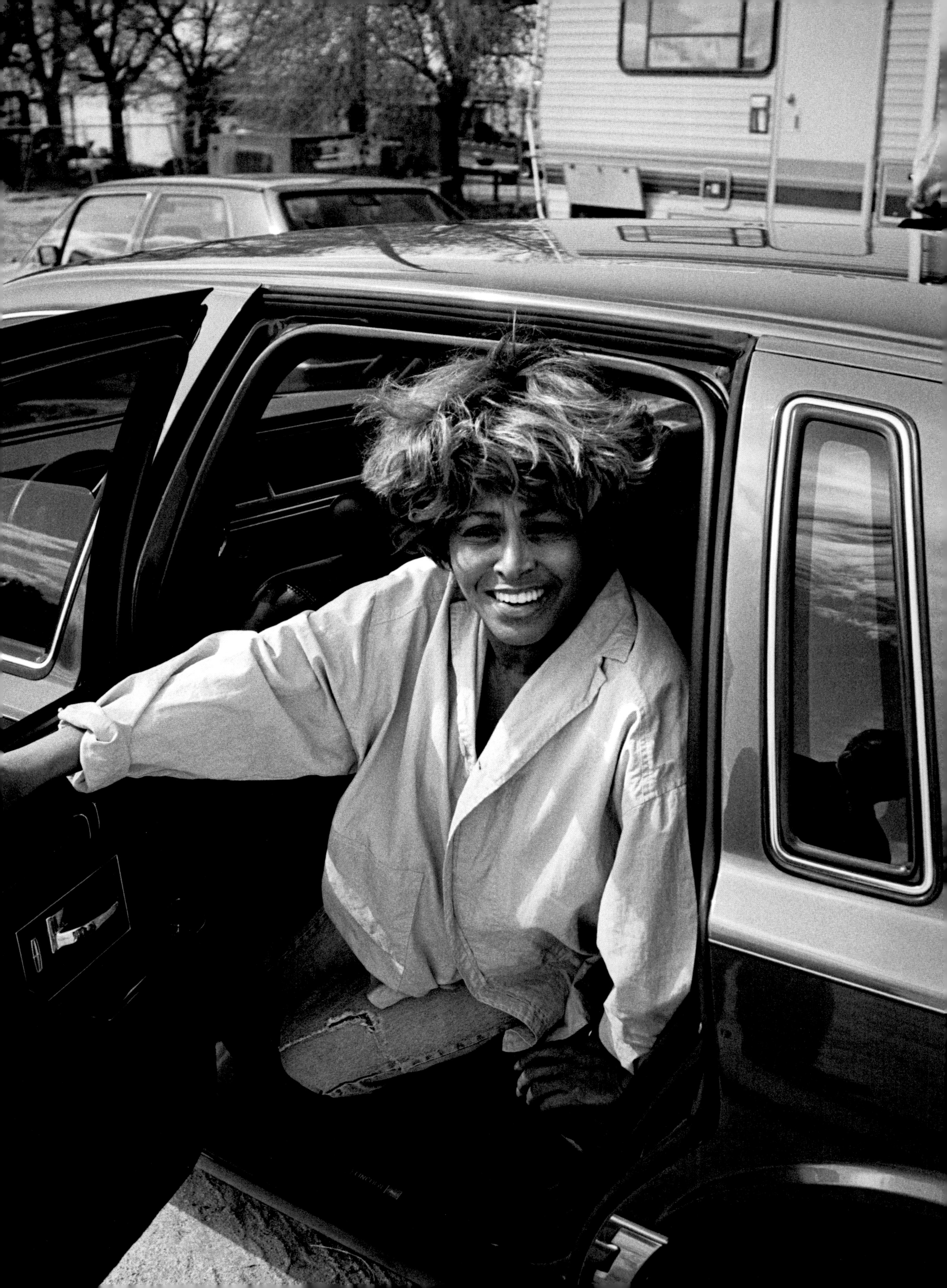

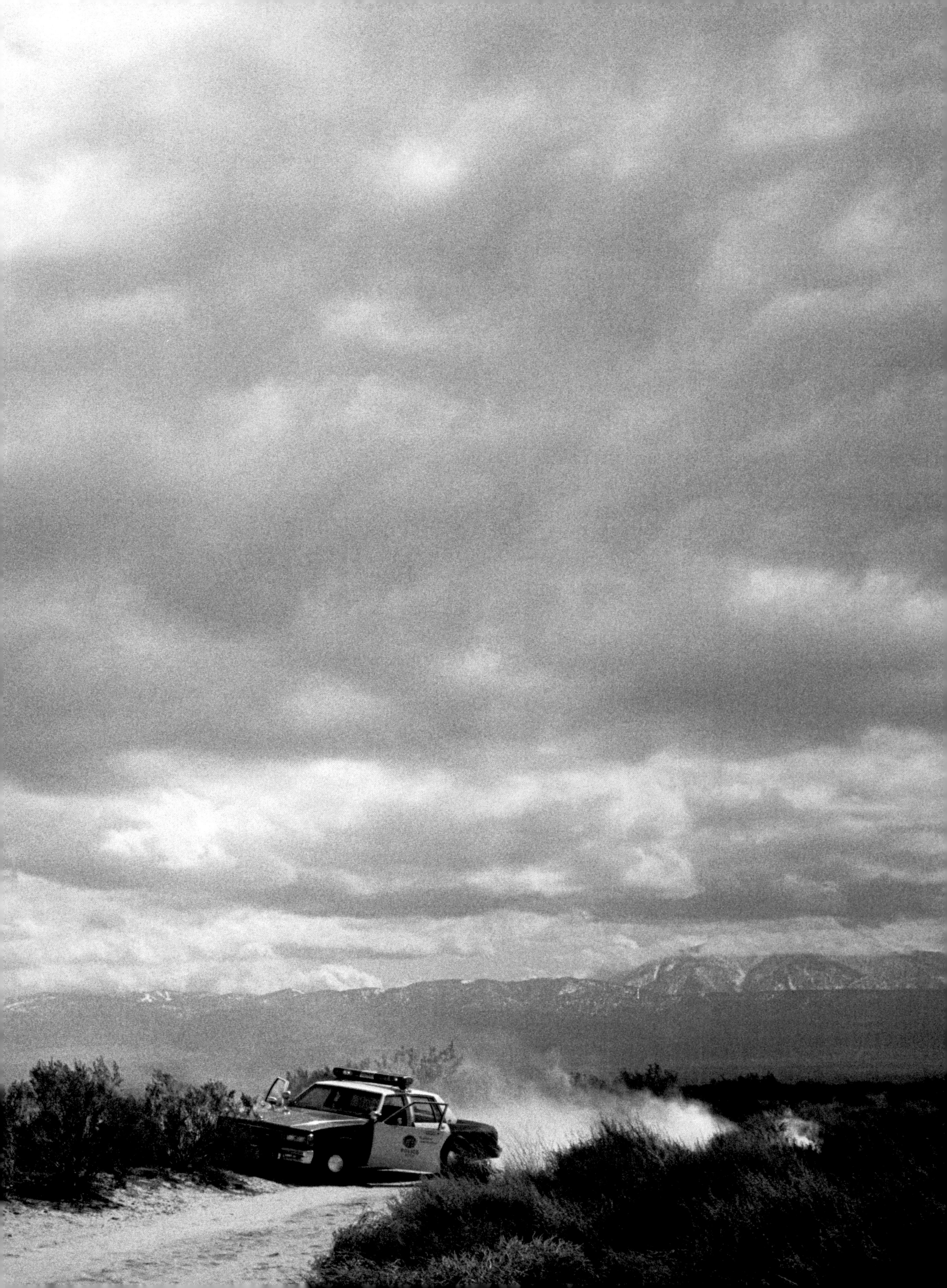

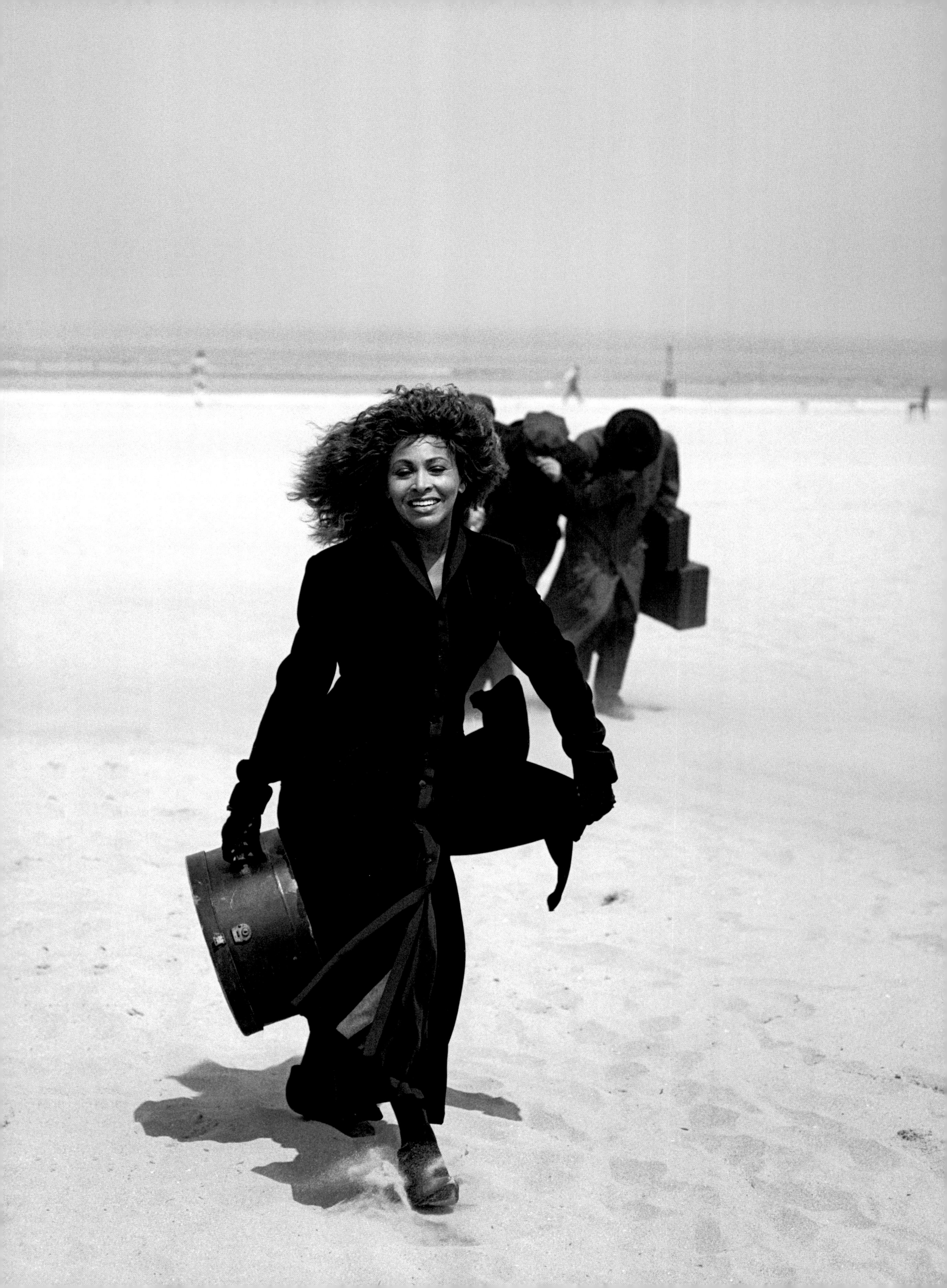

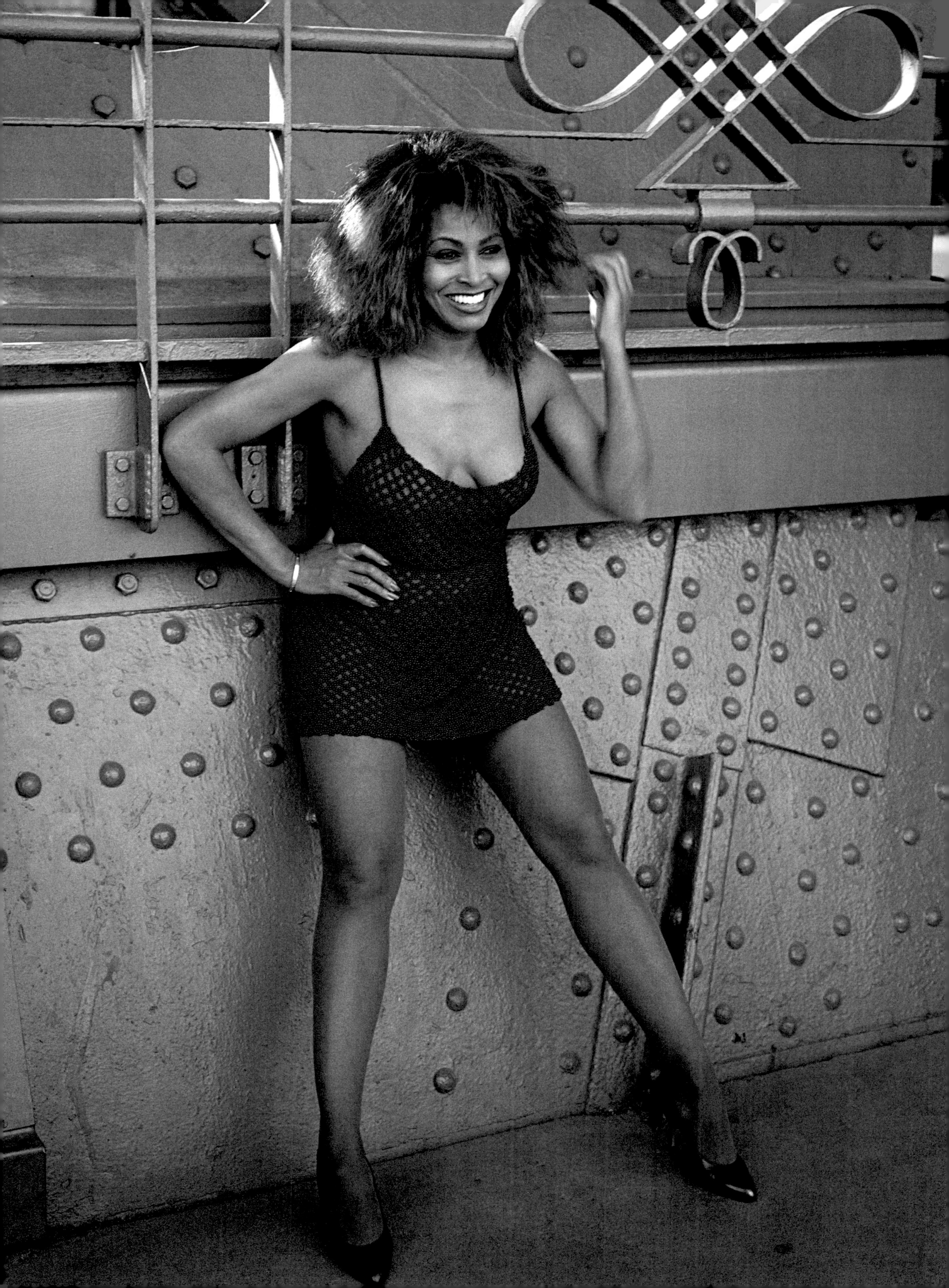

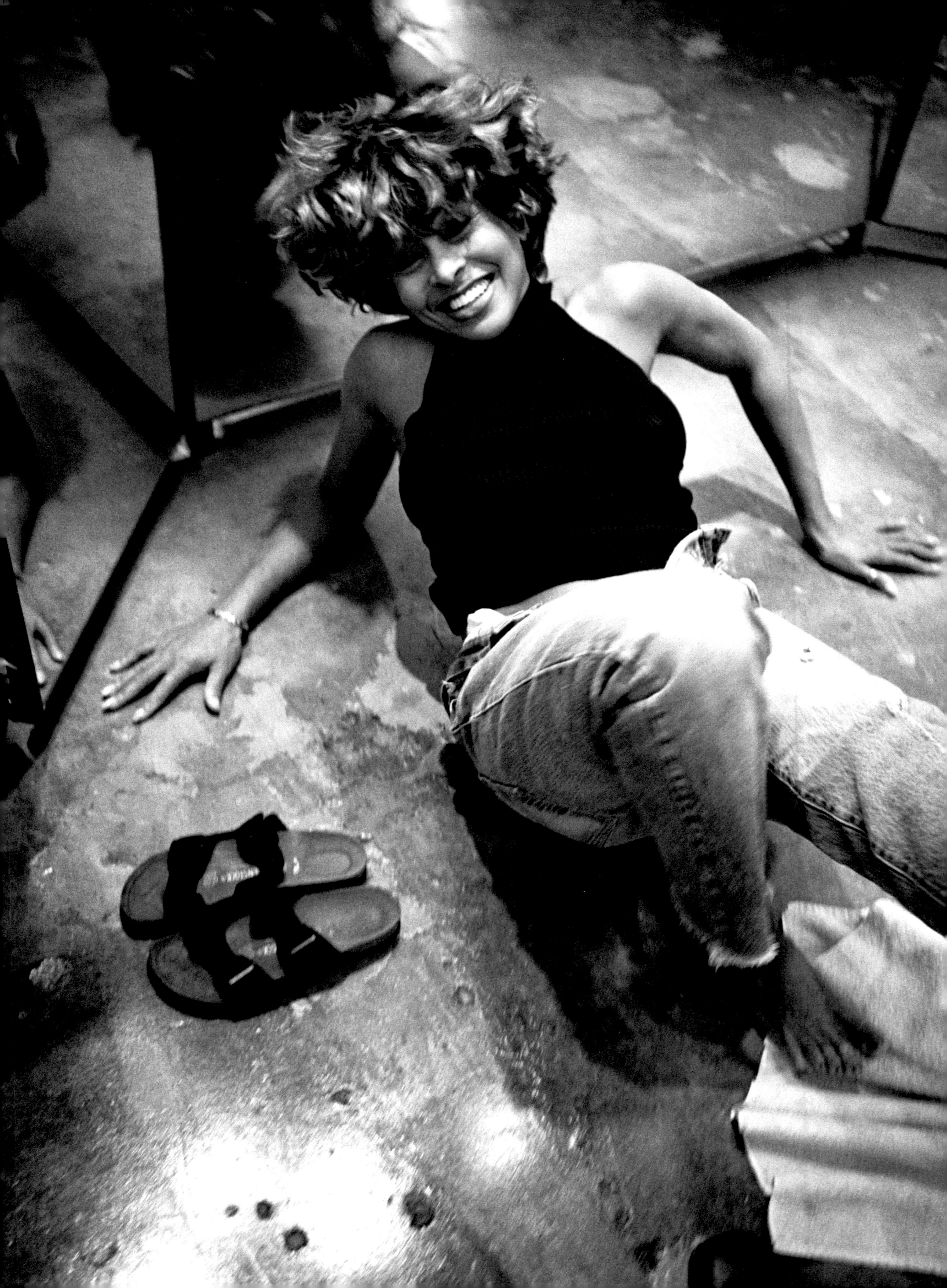

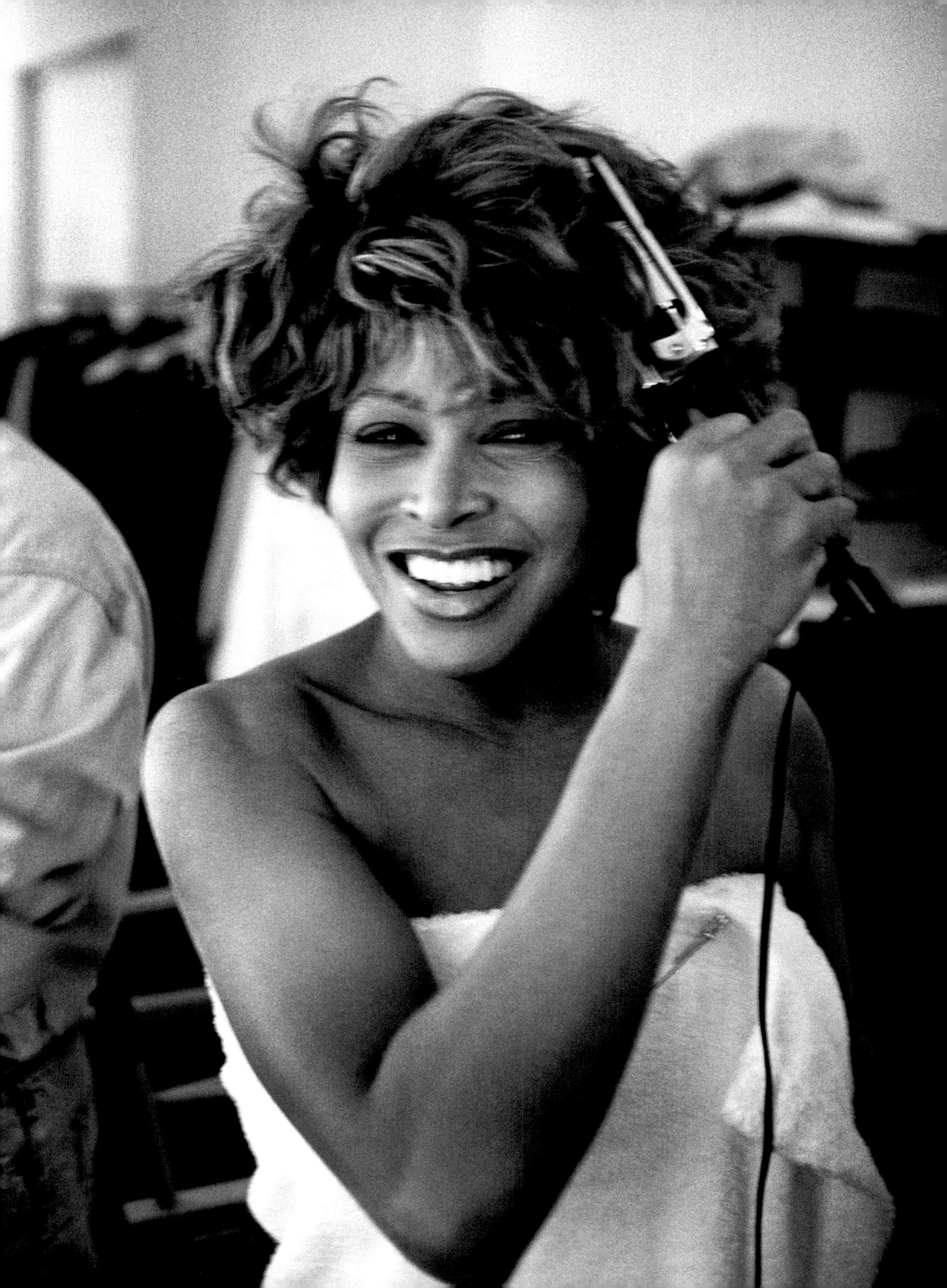

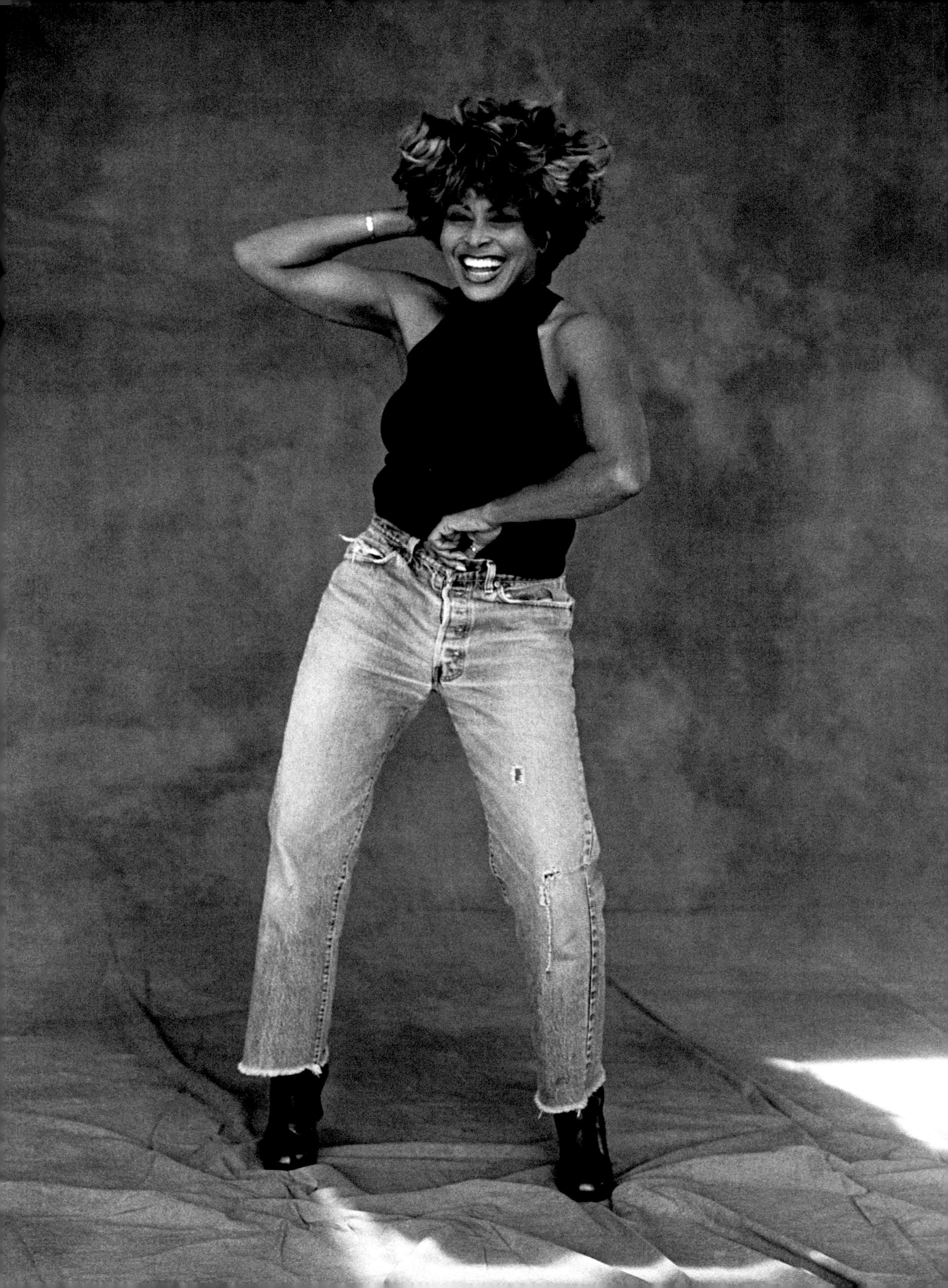

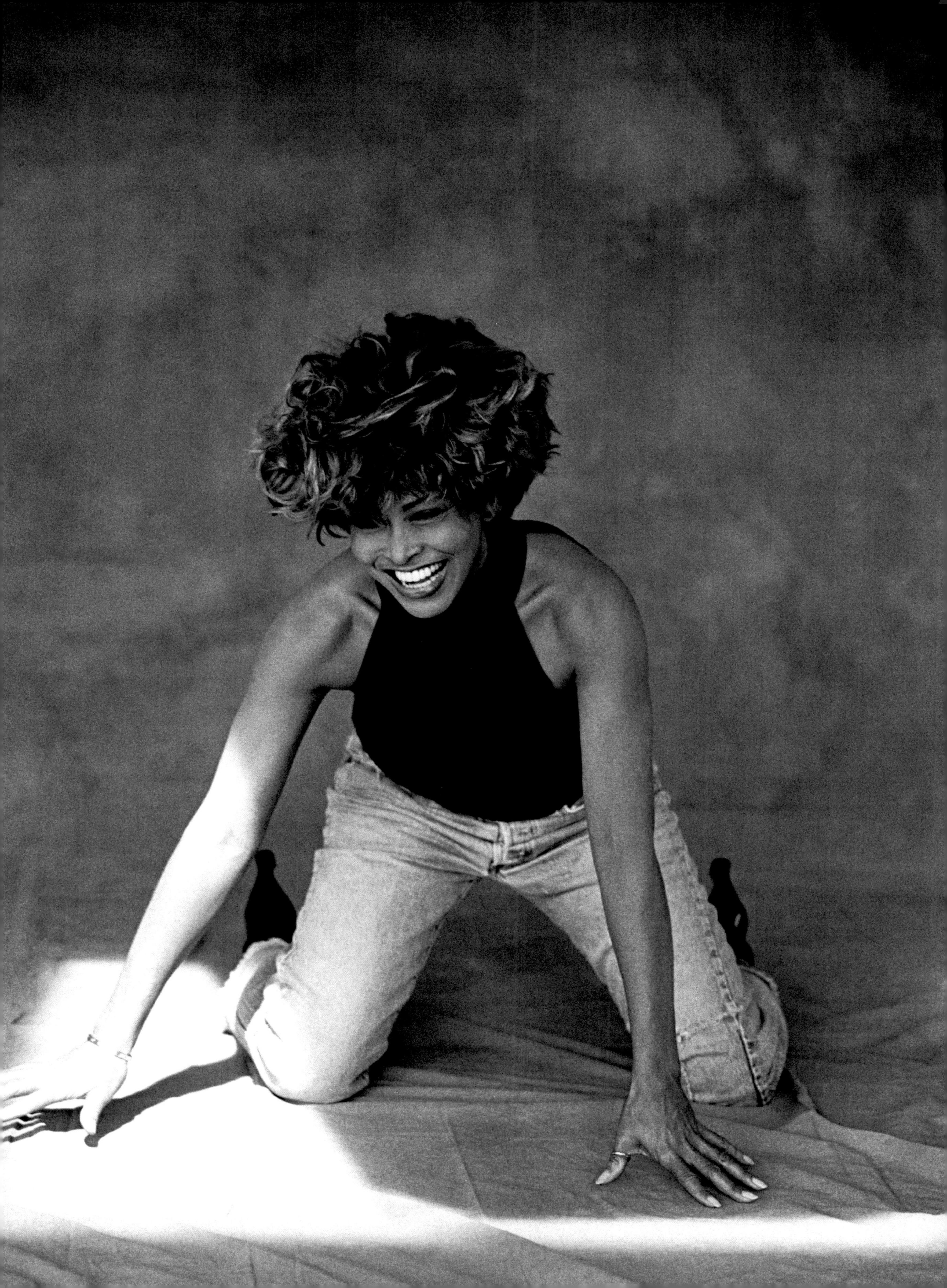

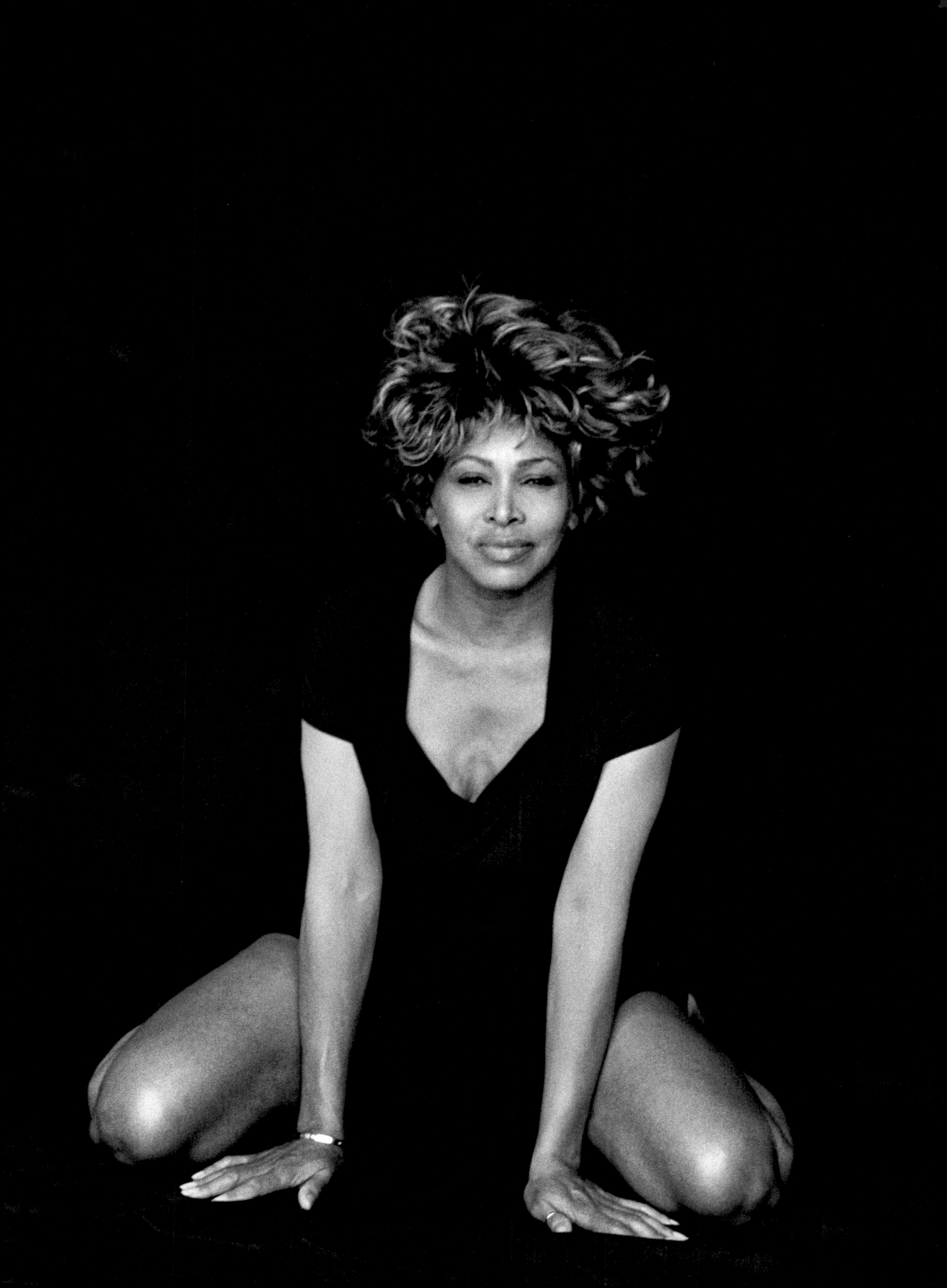

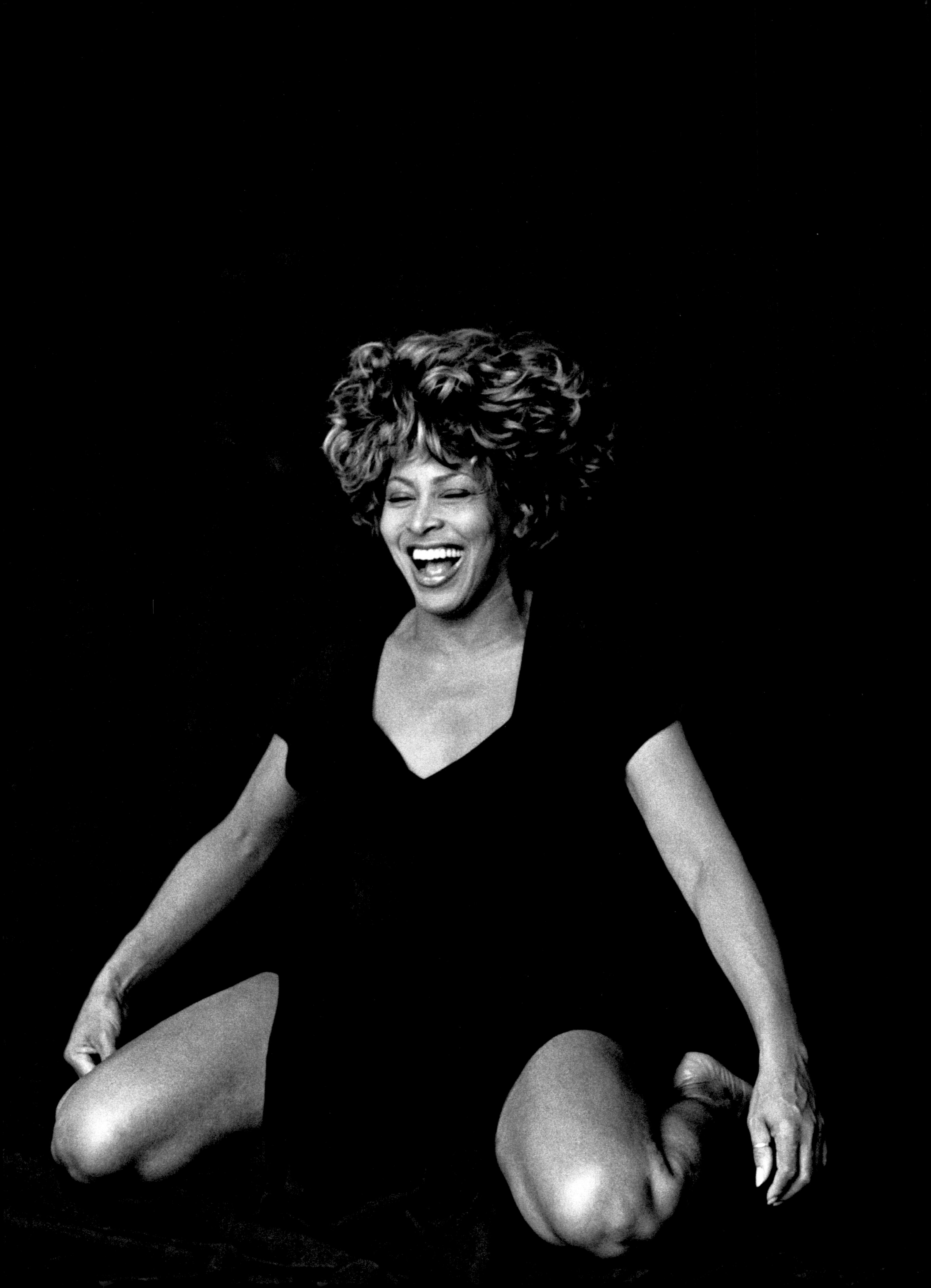

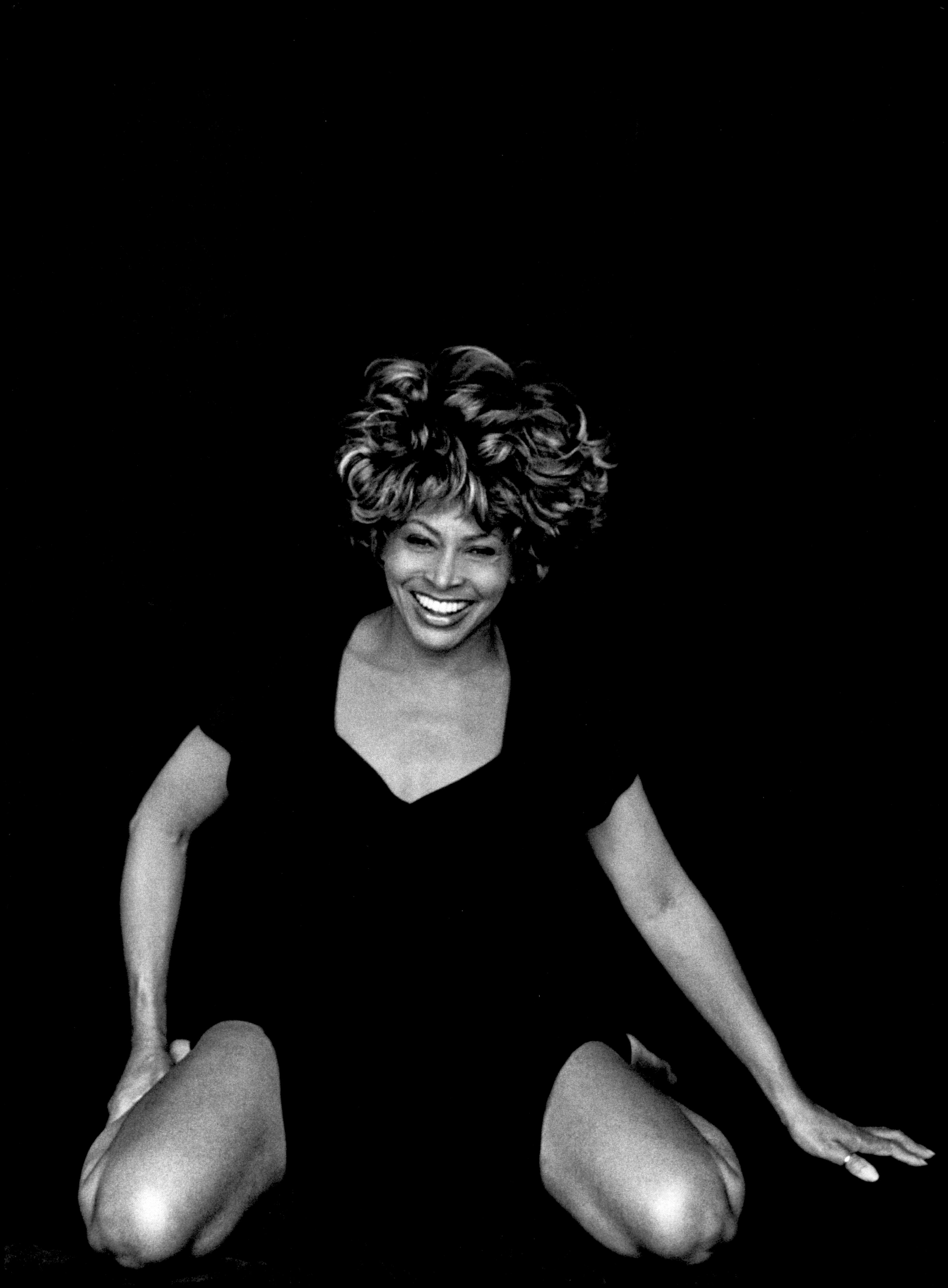

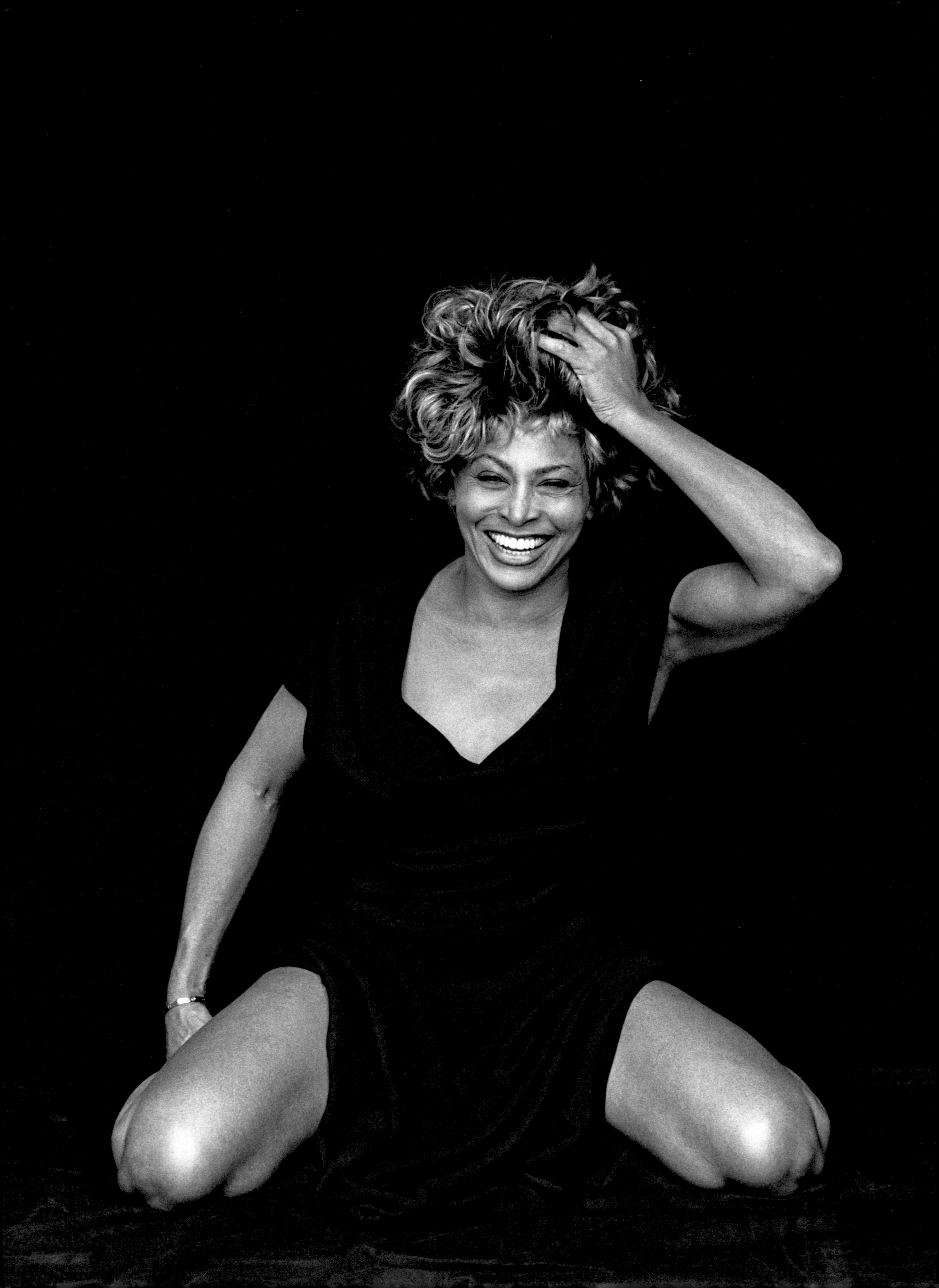

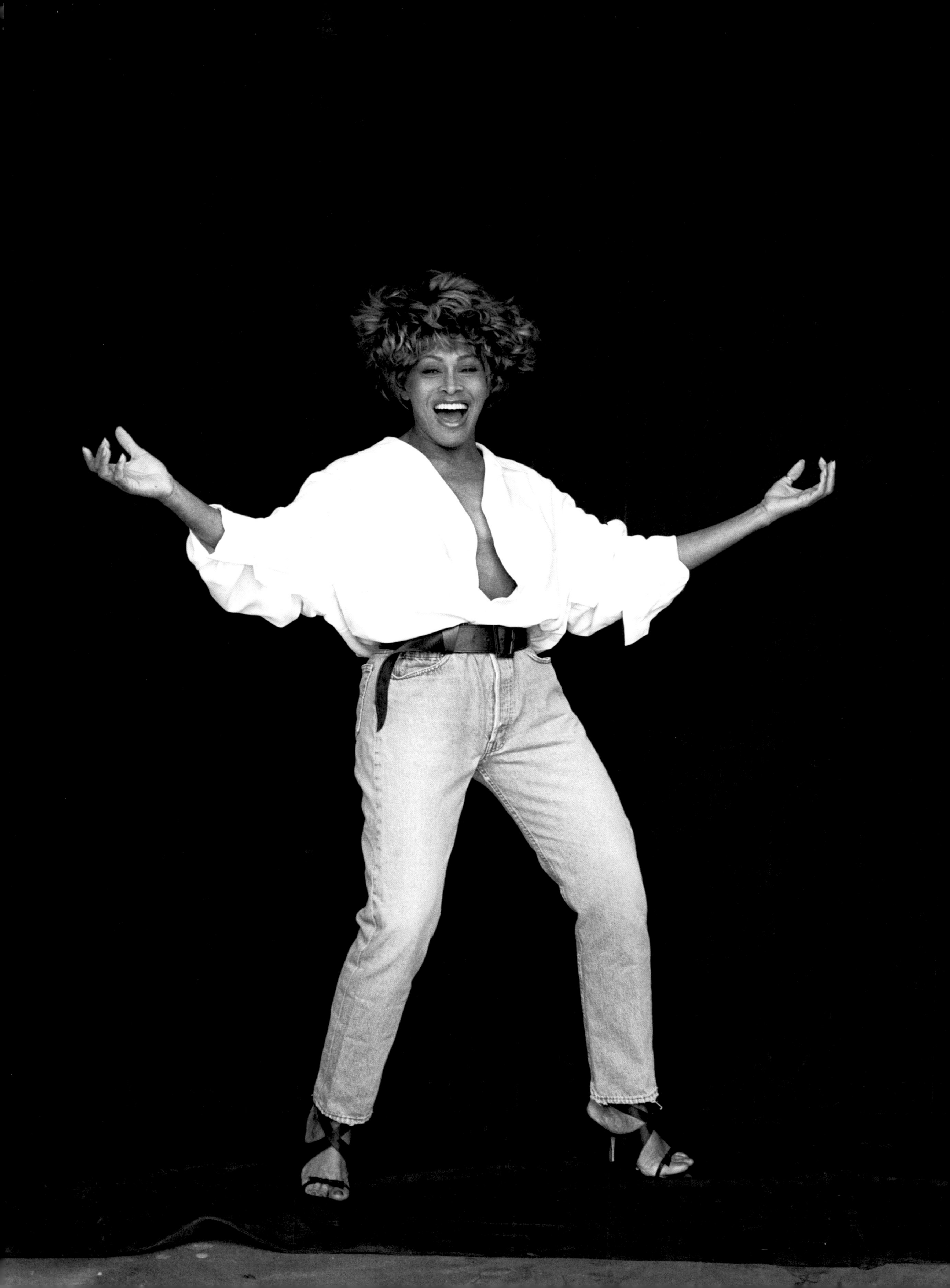

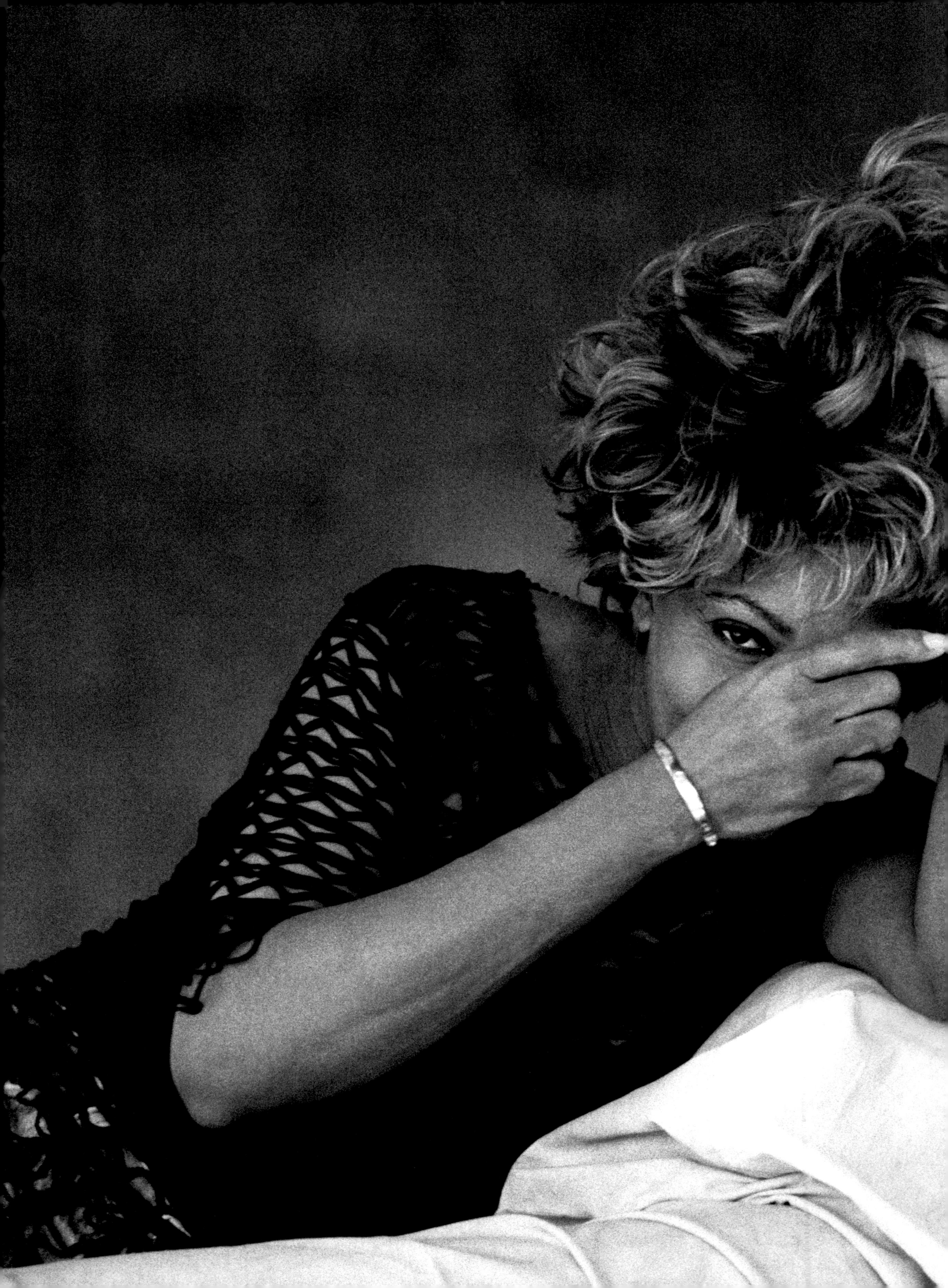

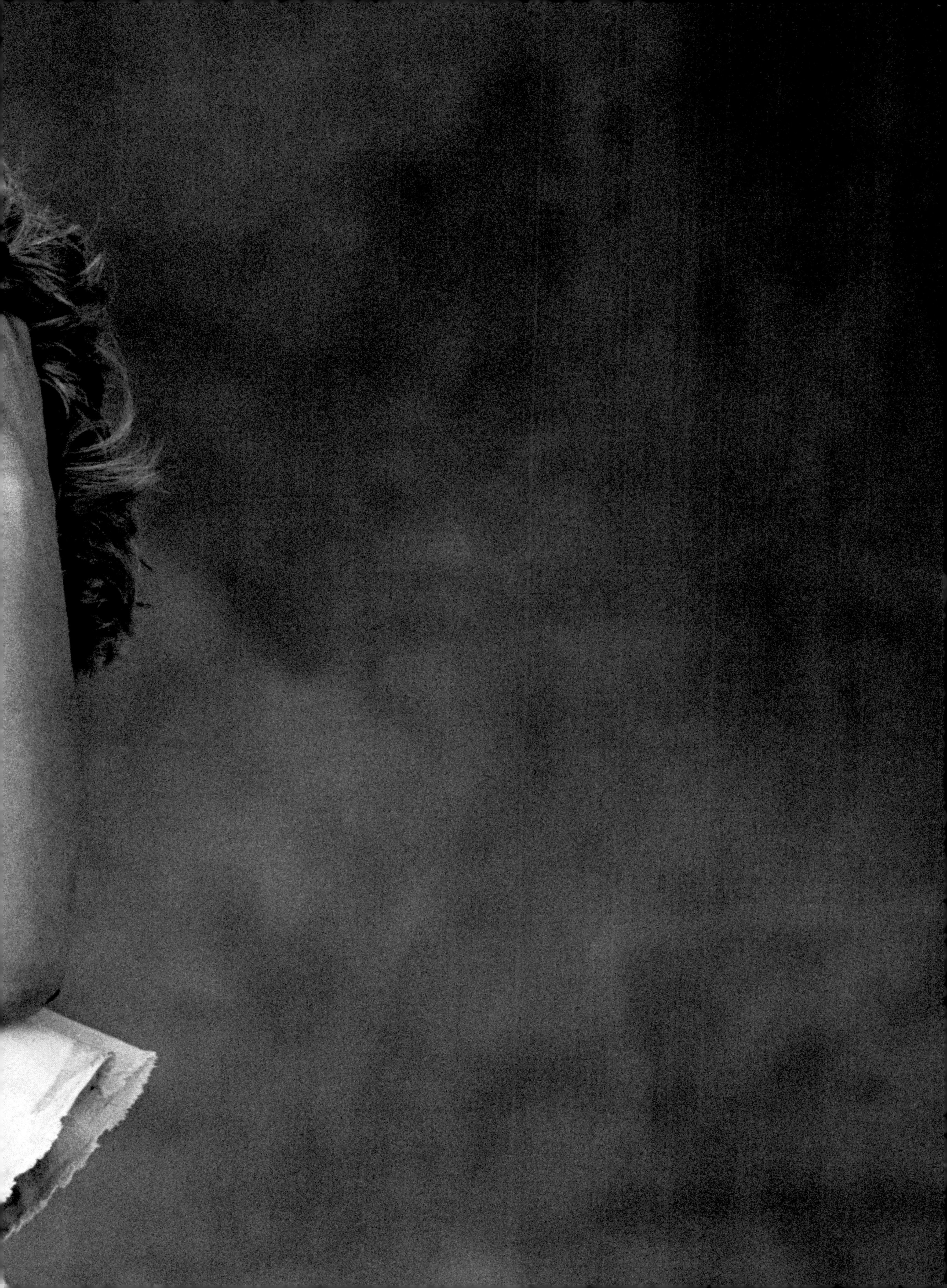

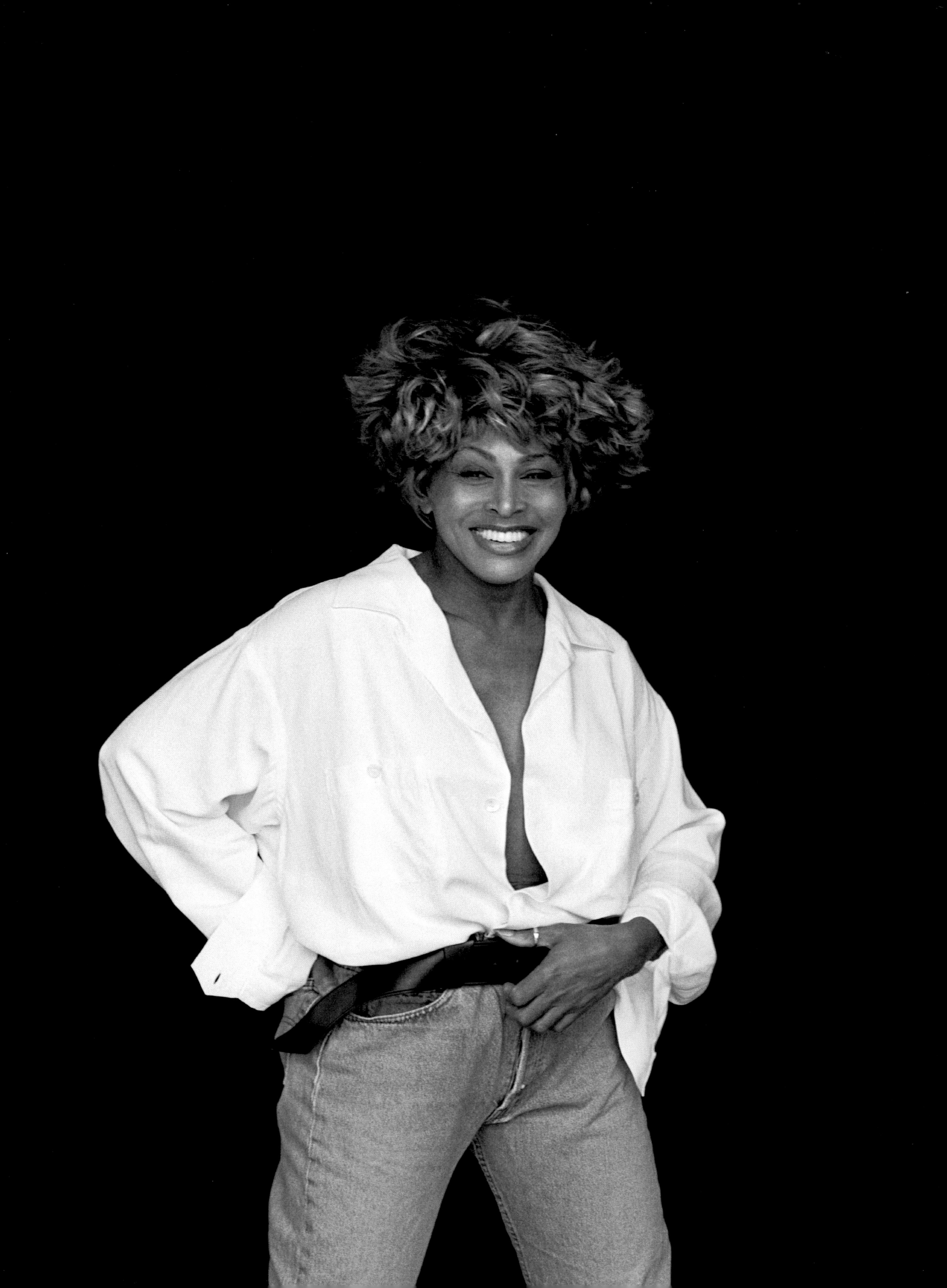

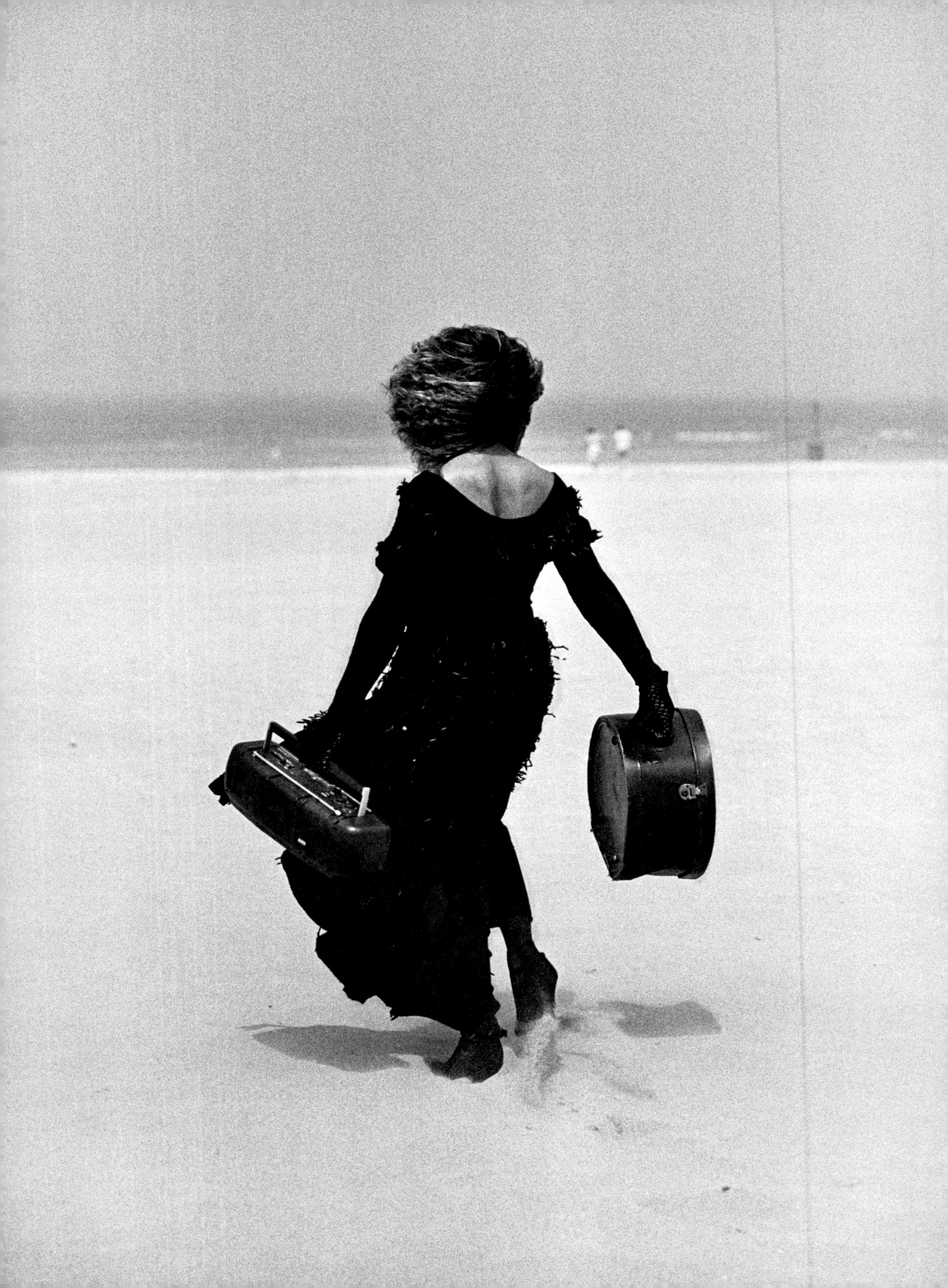

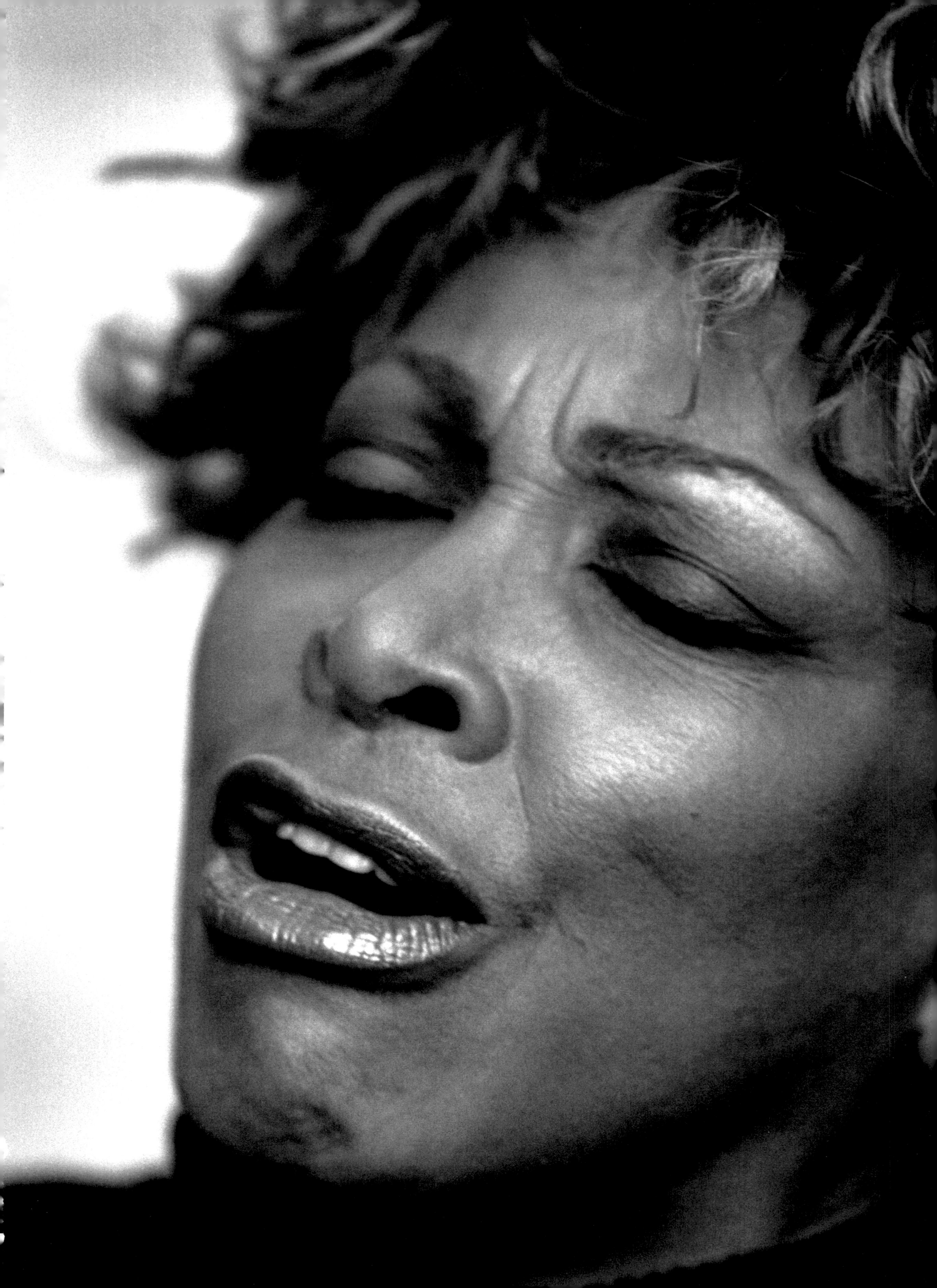

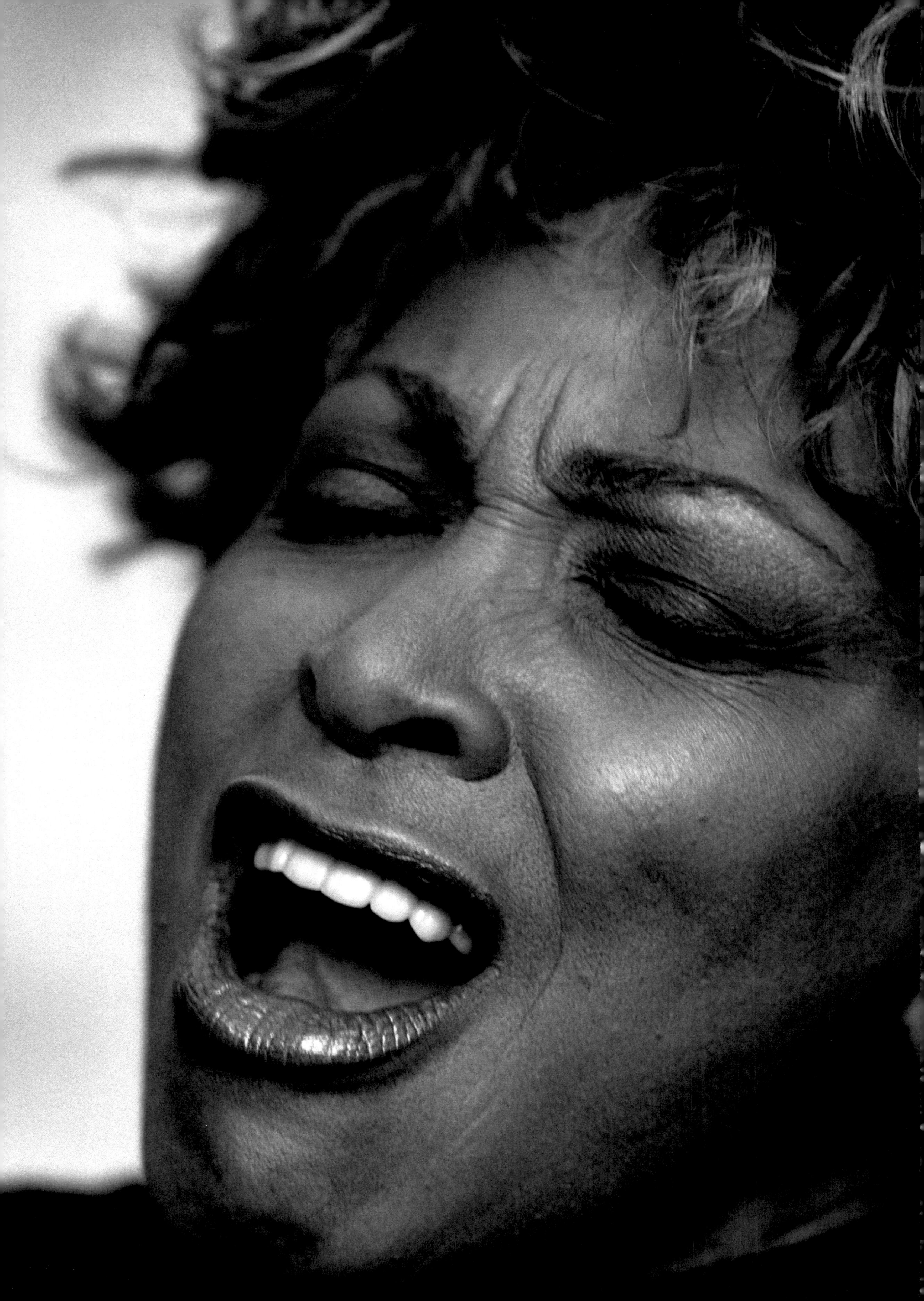

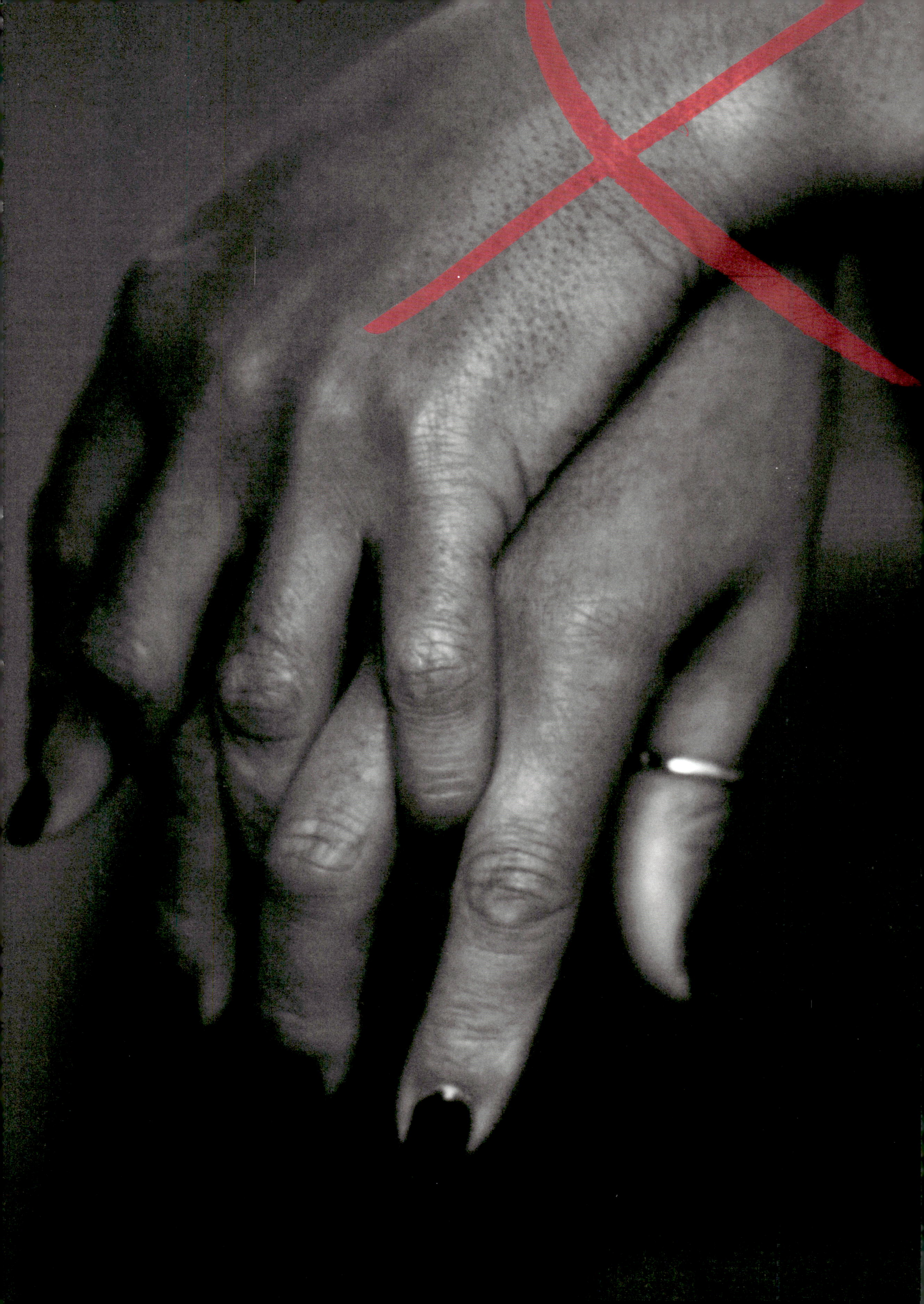

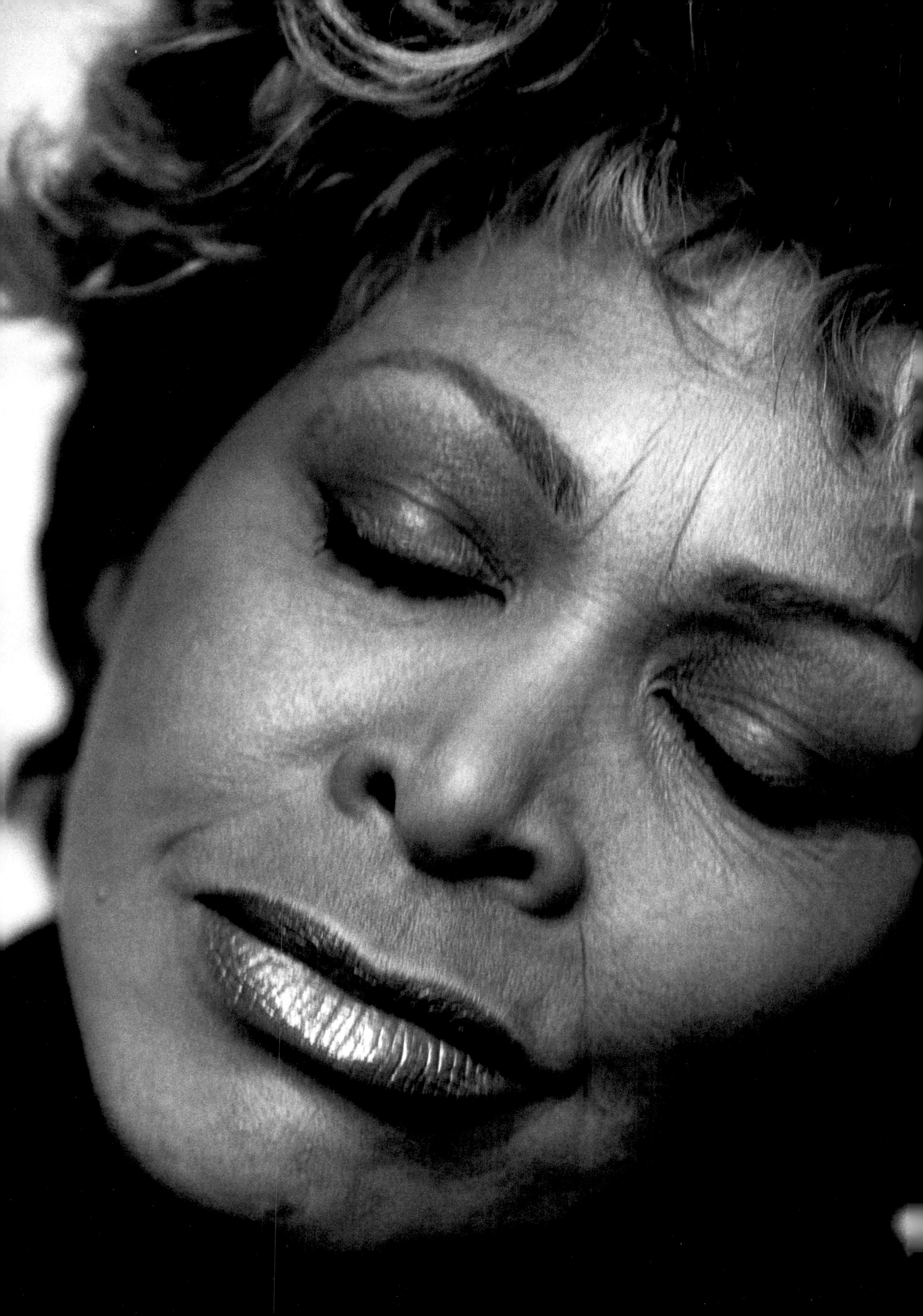

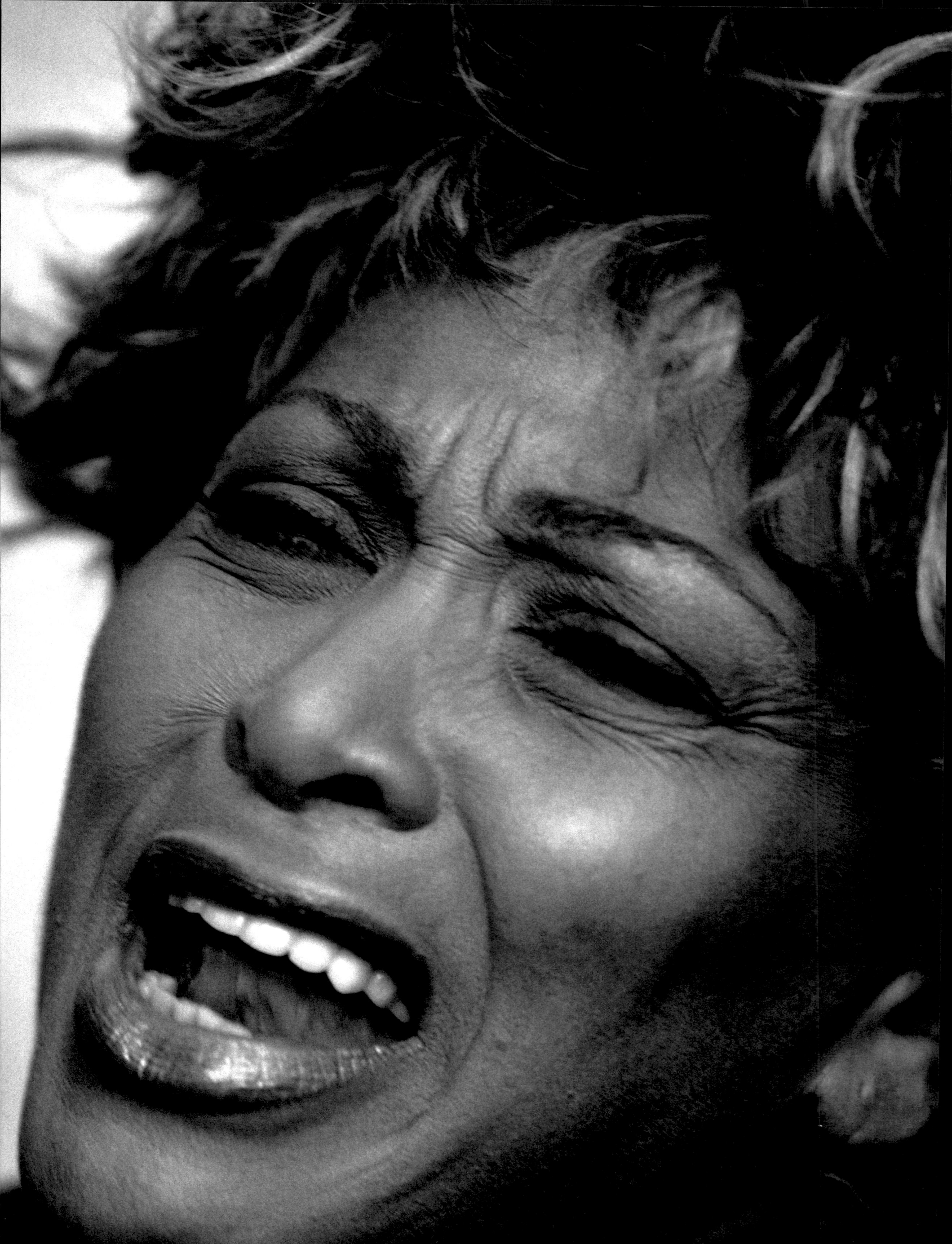

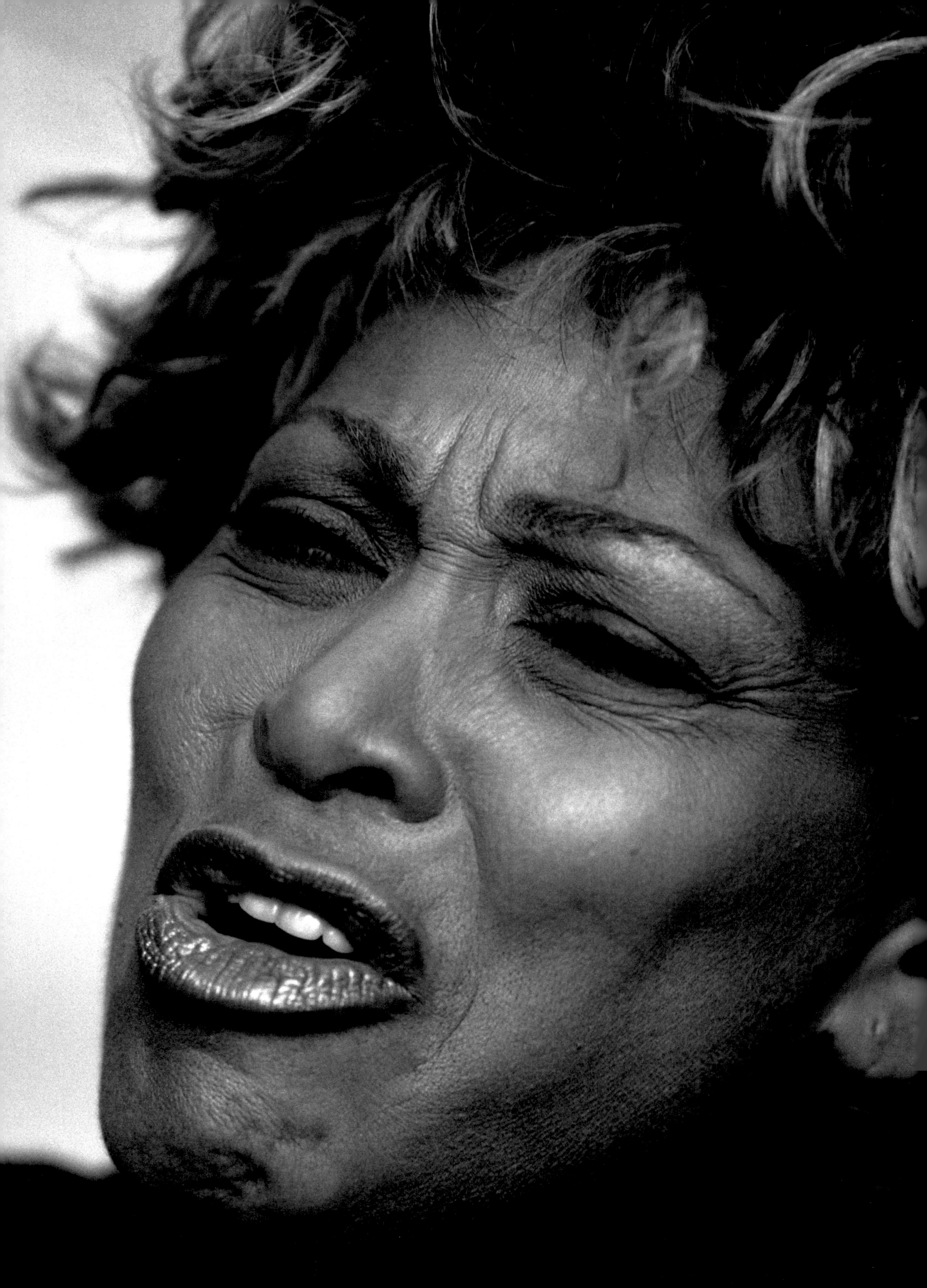

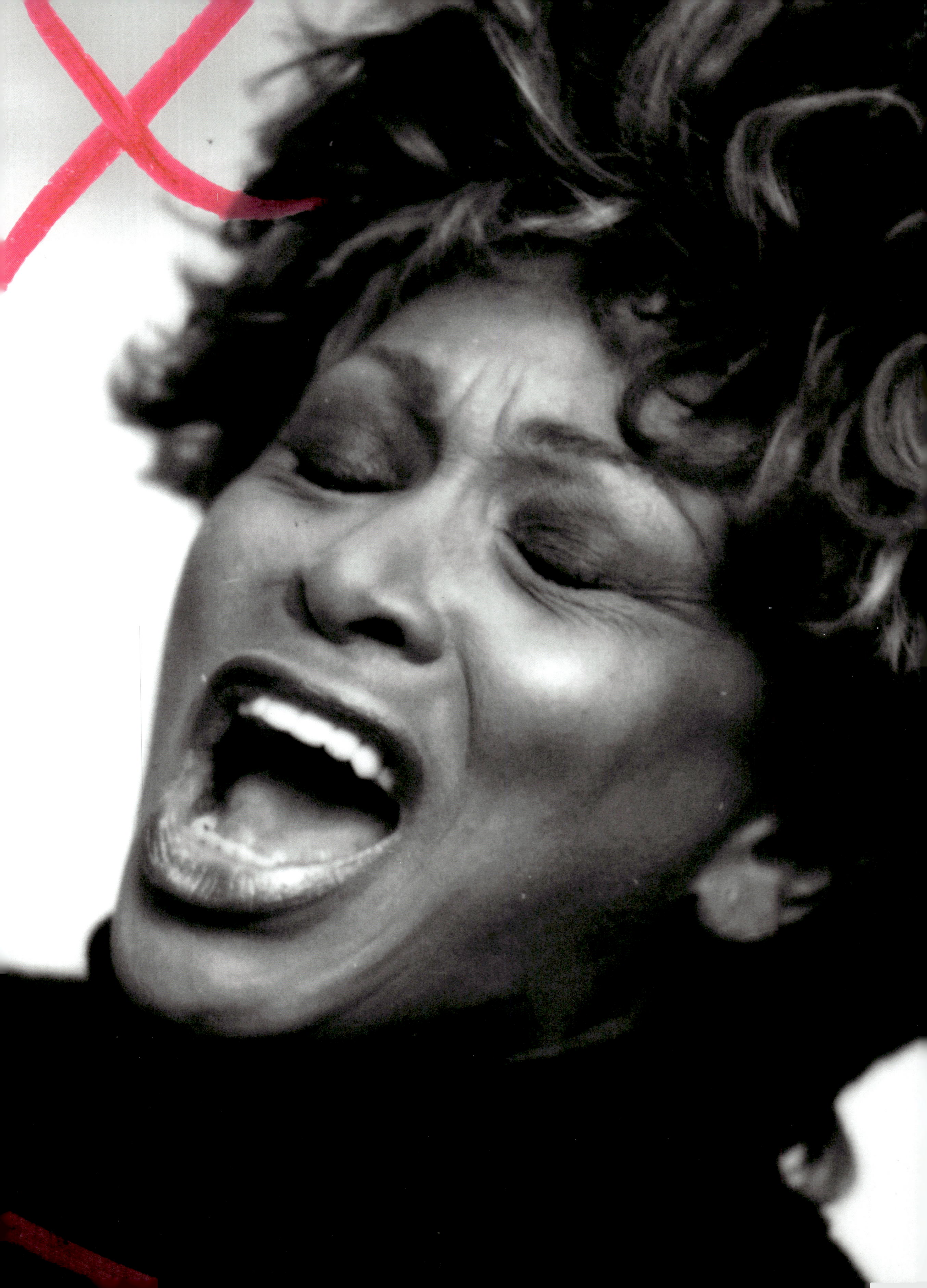

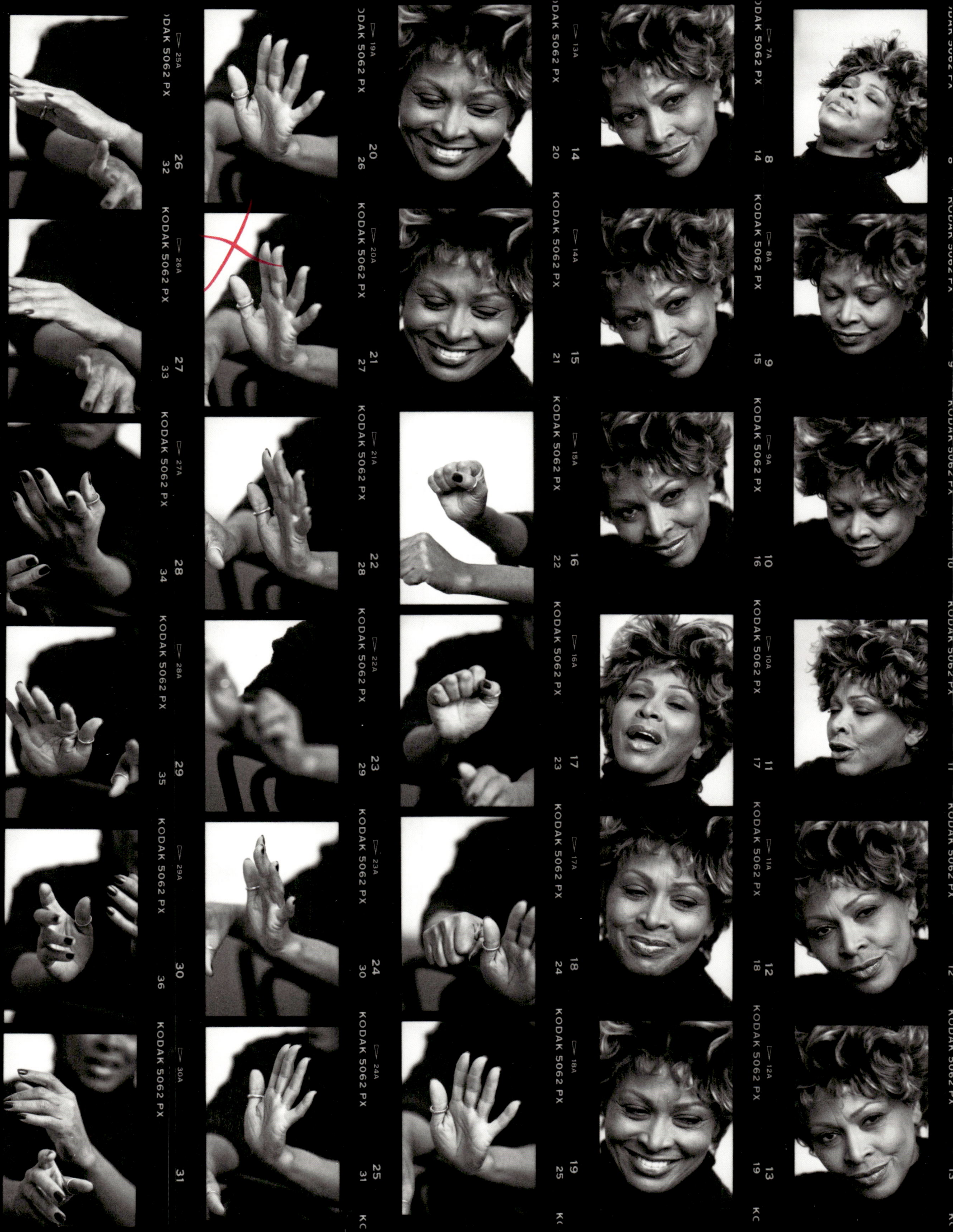
KODAK 5062 PX

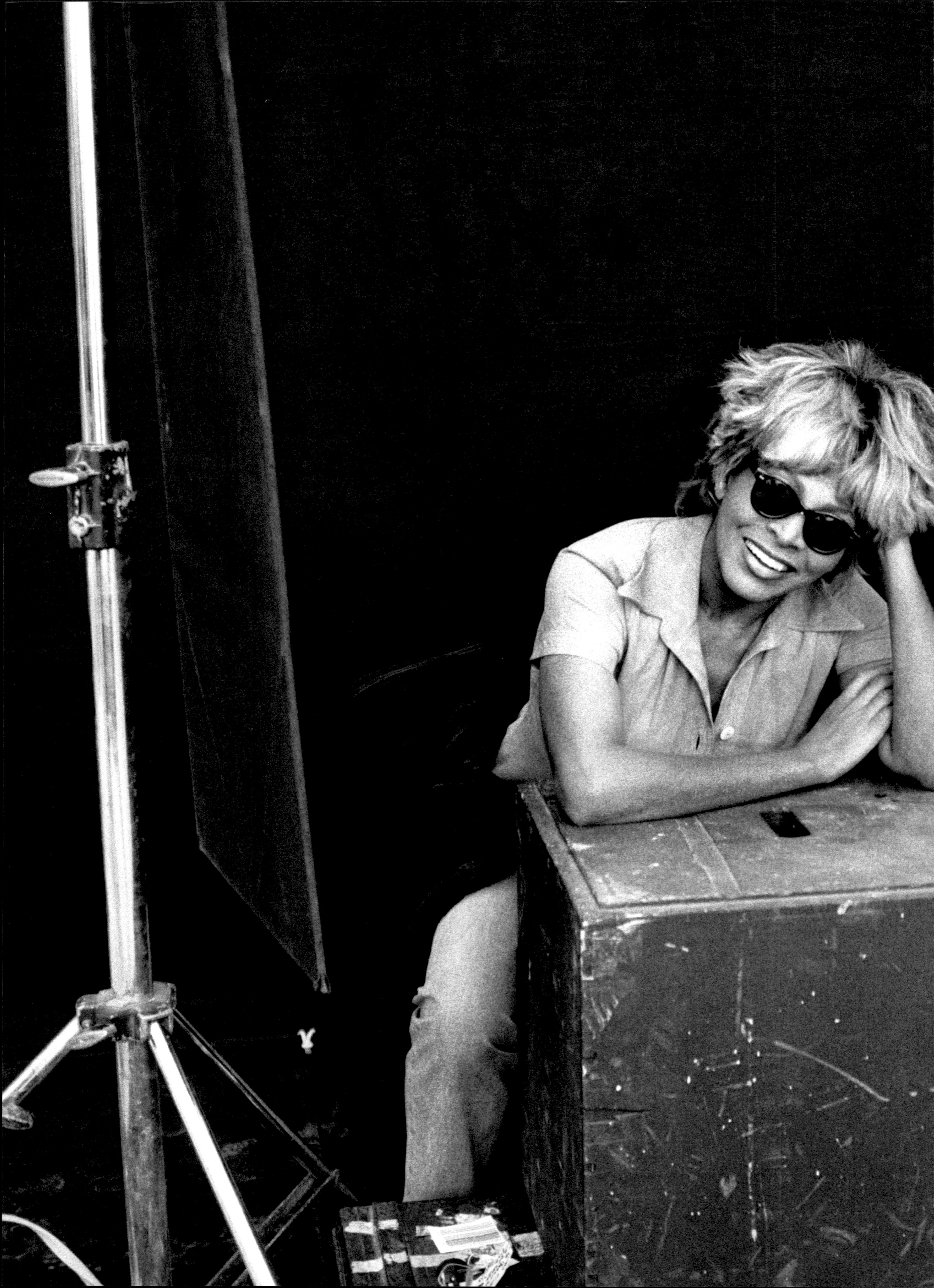

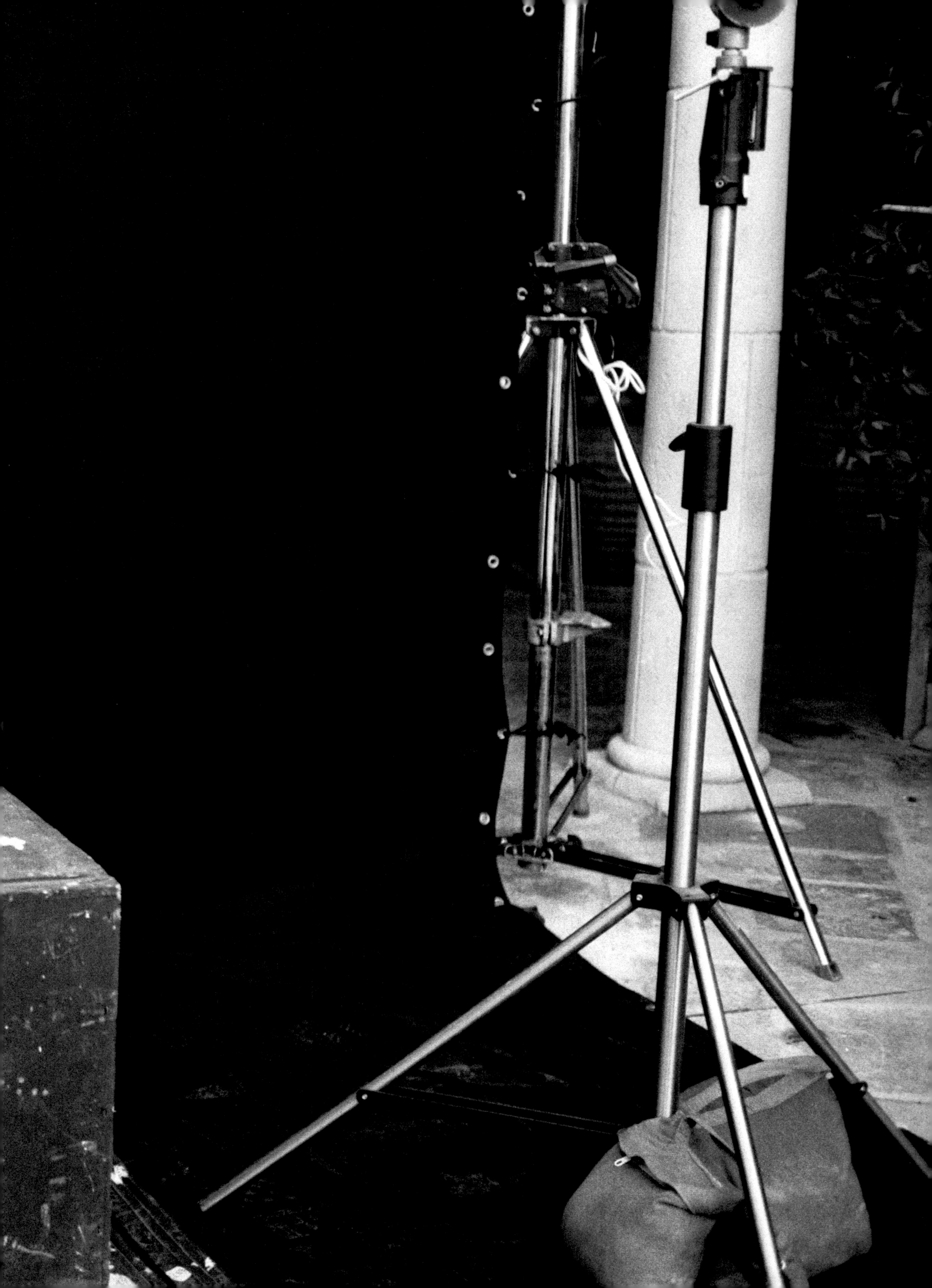

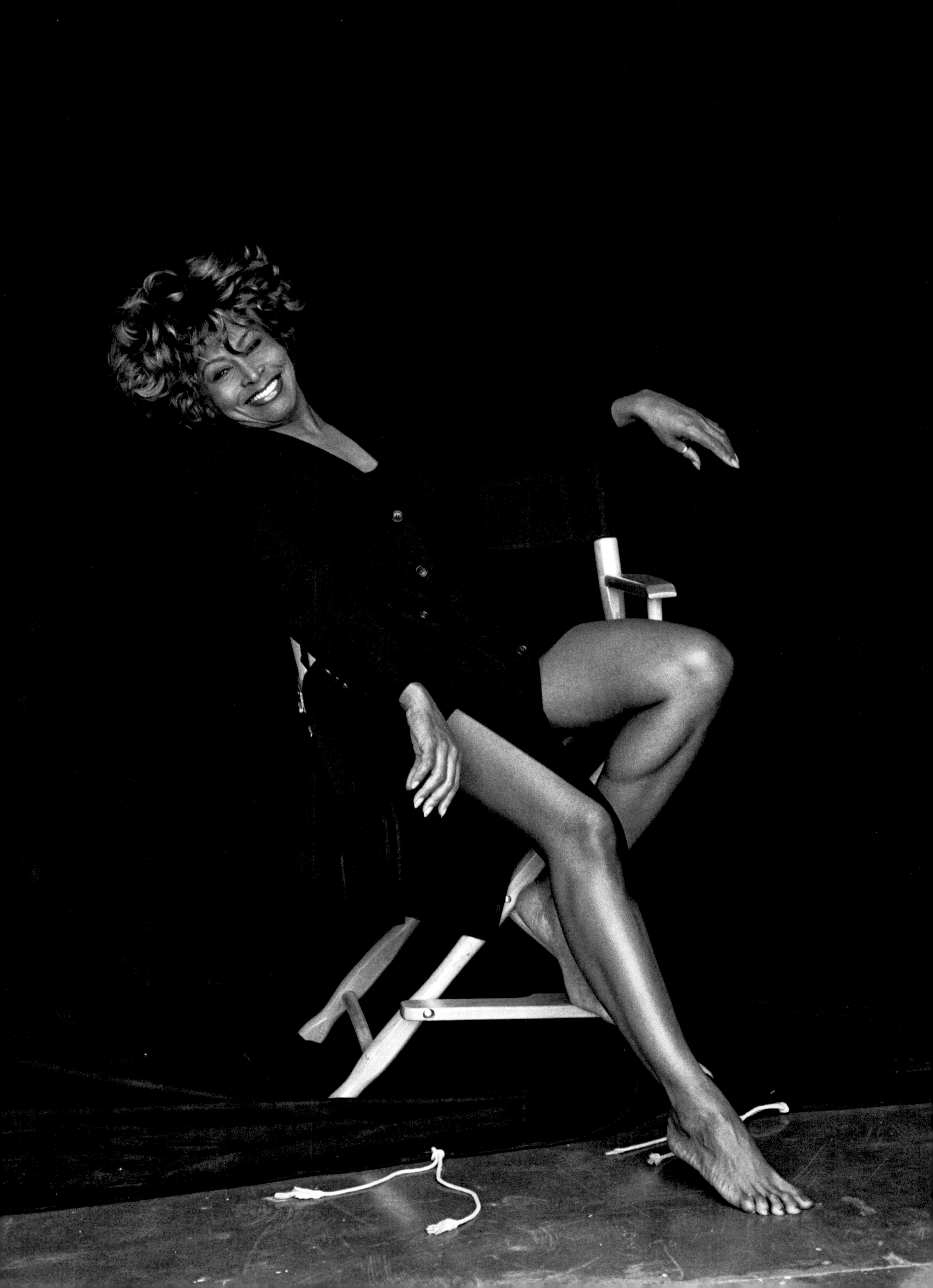

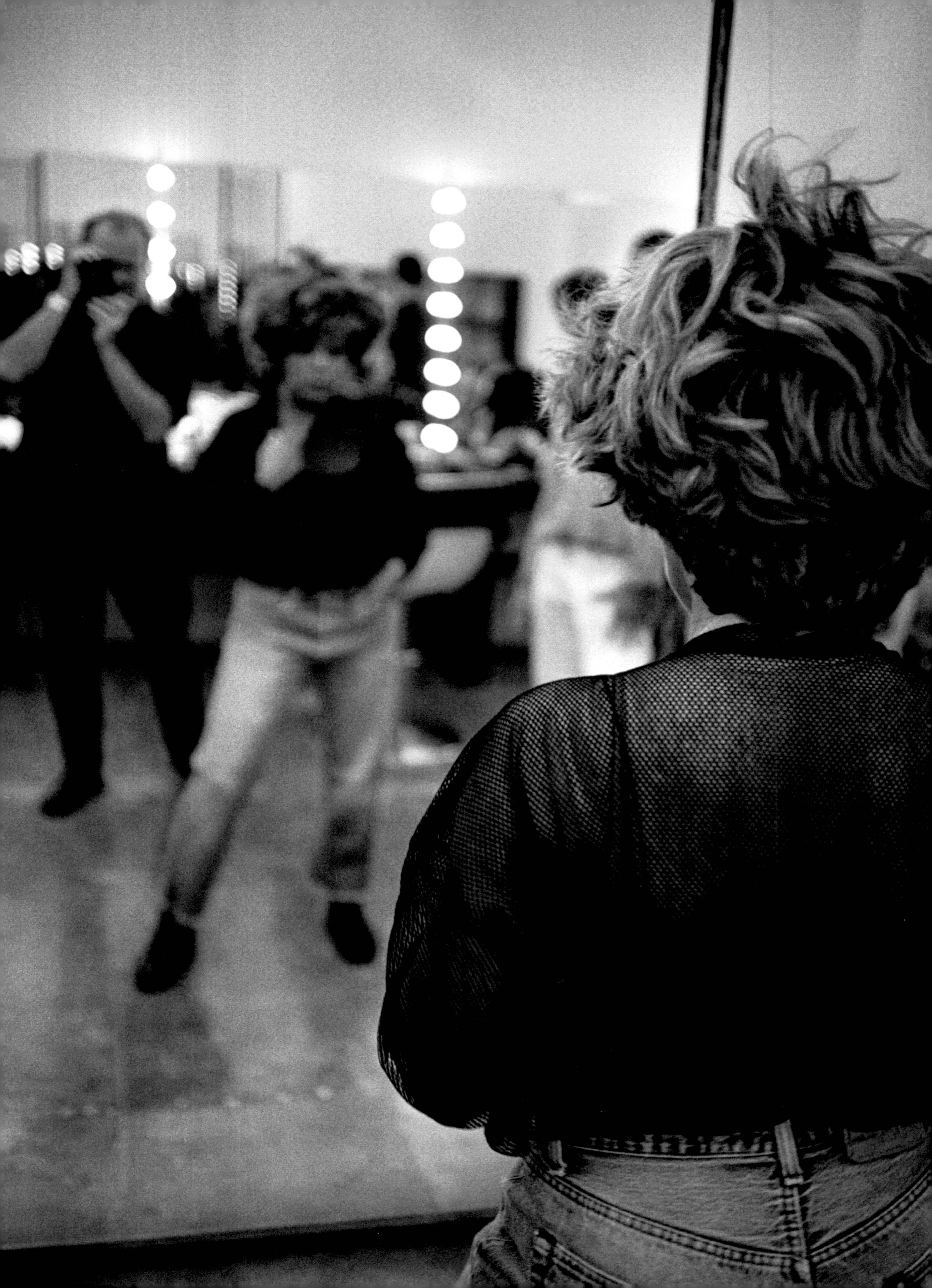

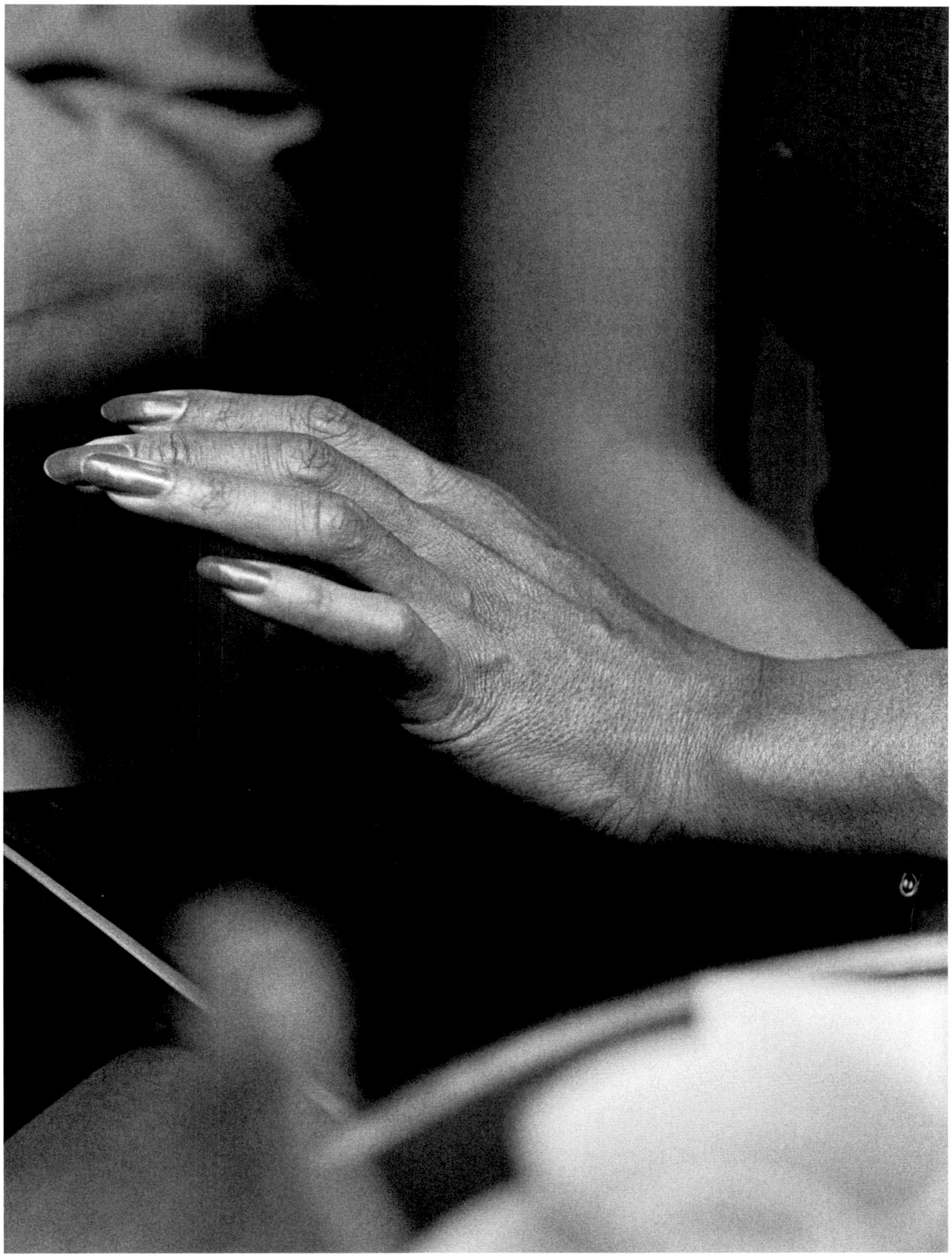

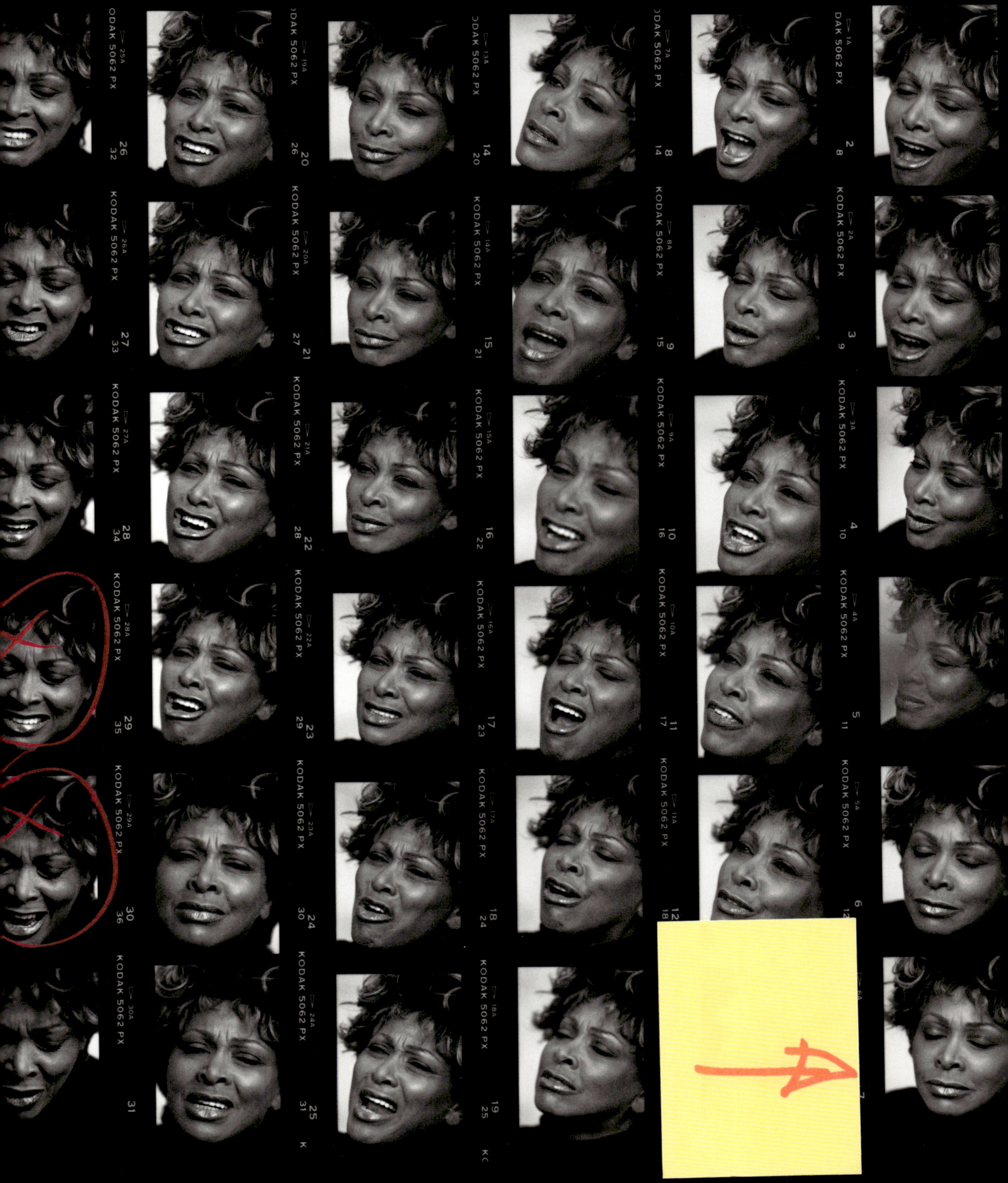
KODAK 5062 PX

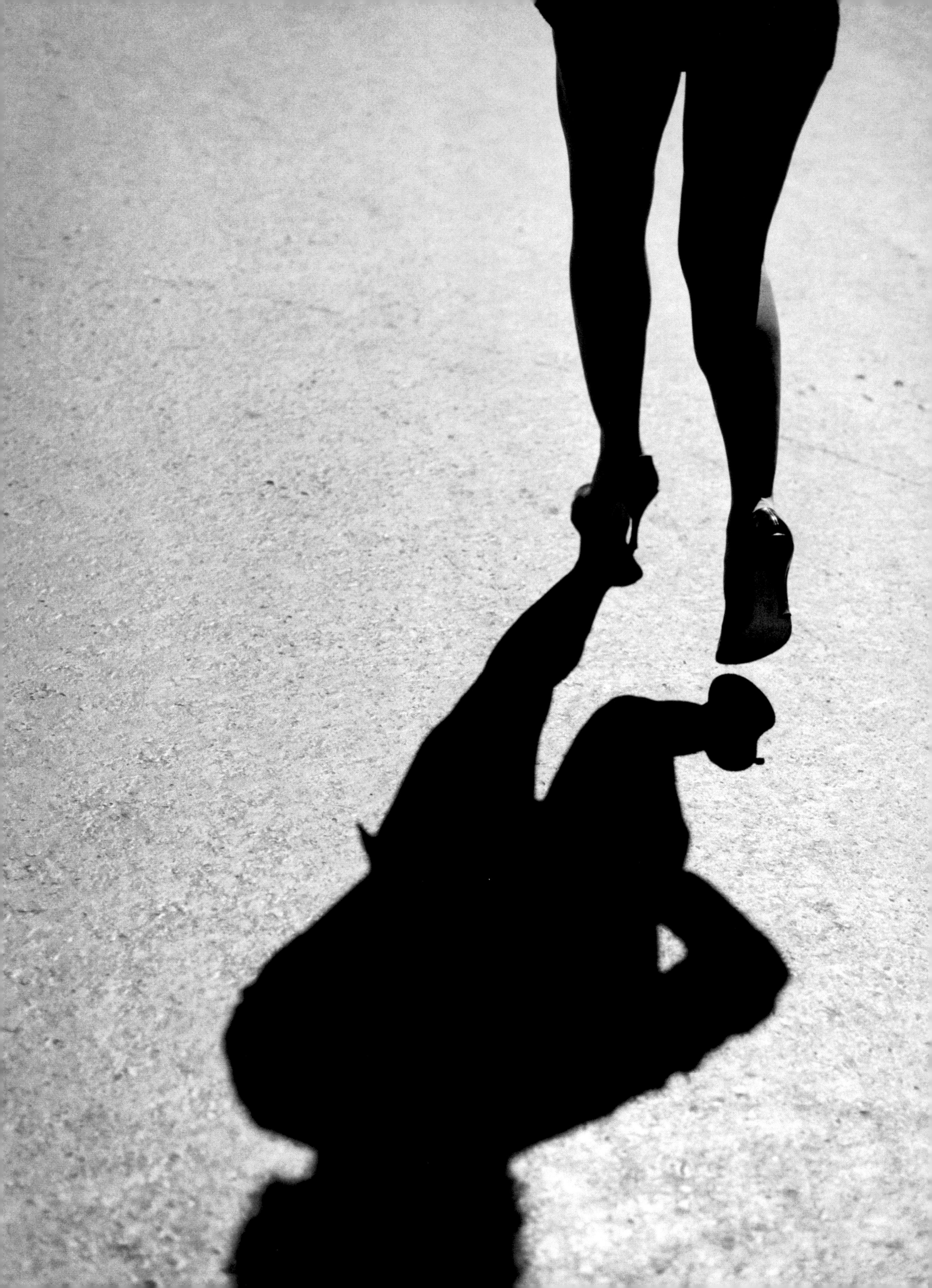

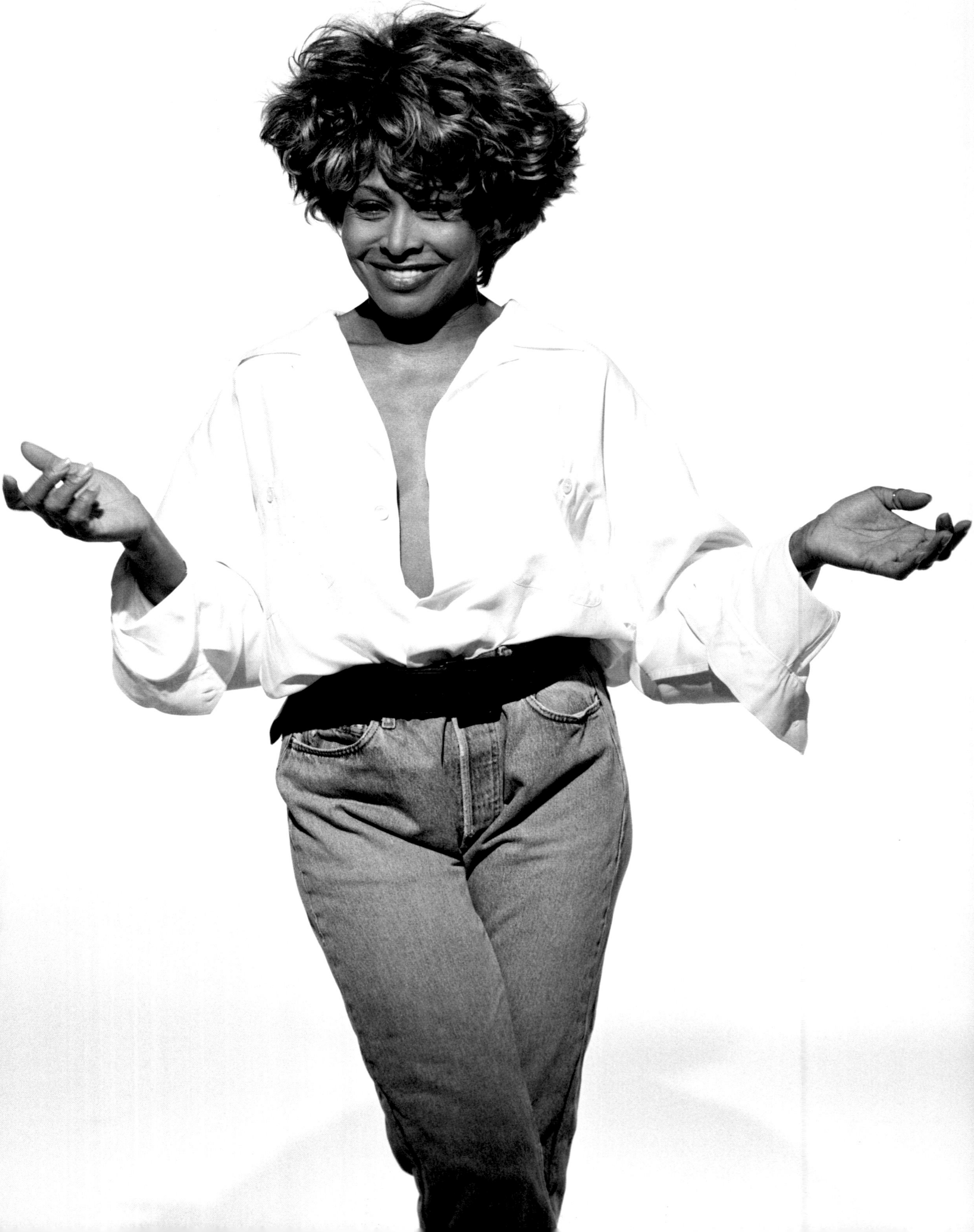

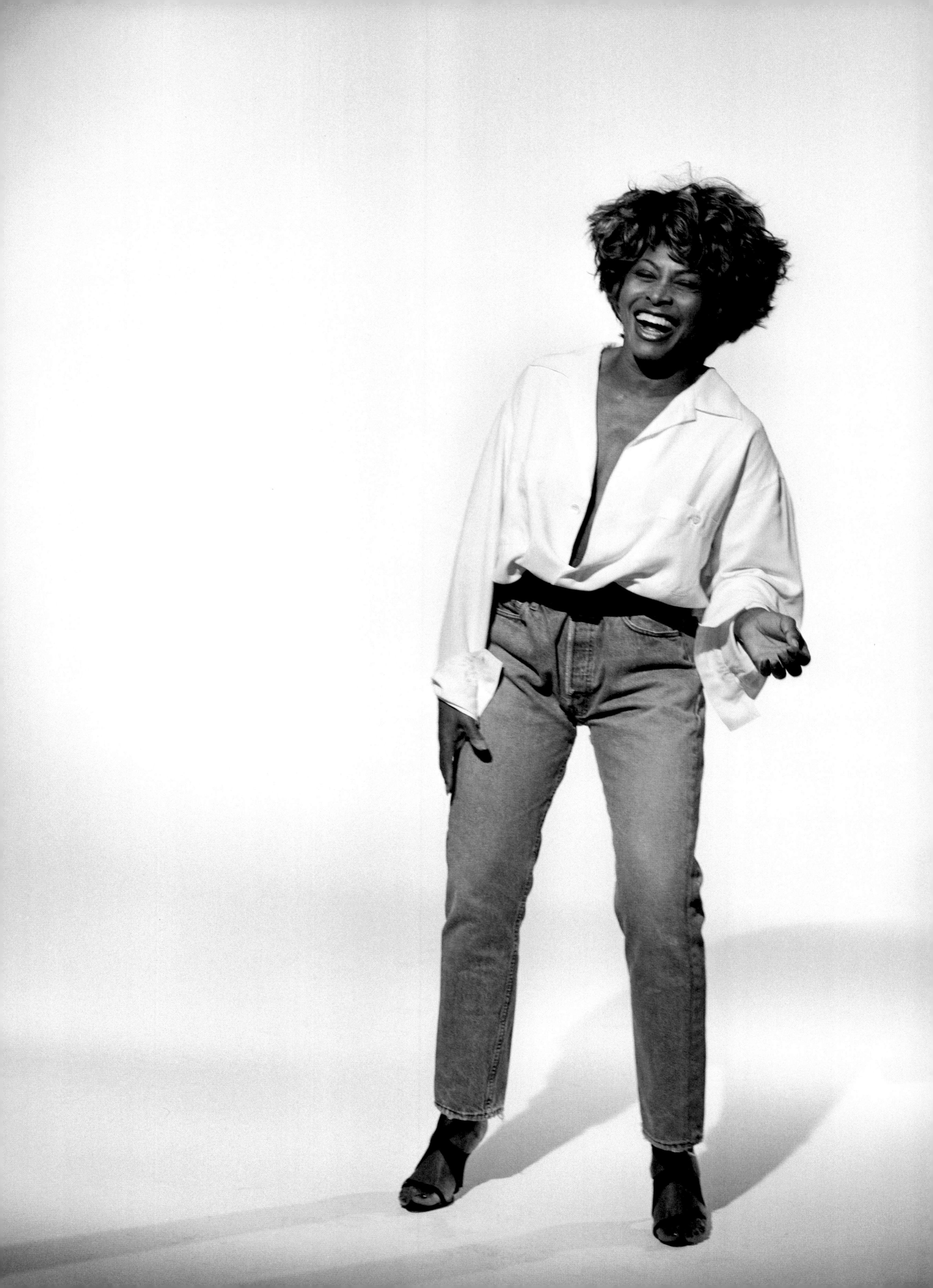

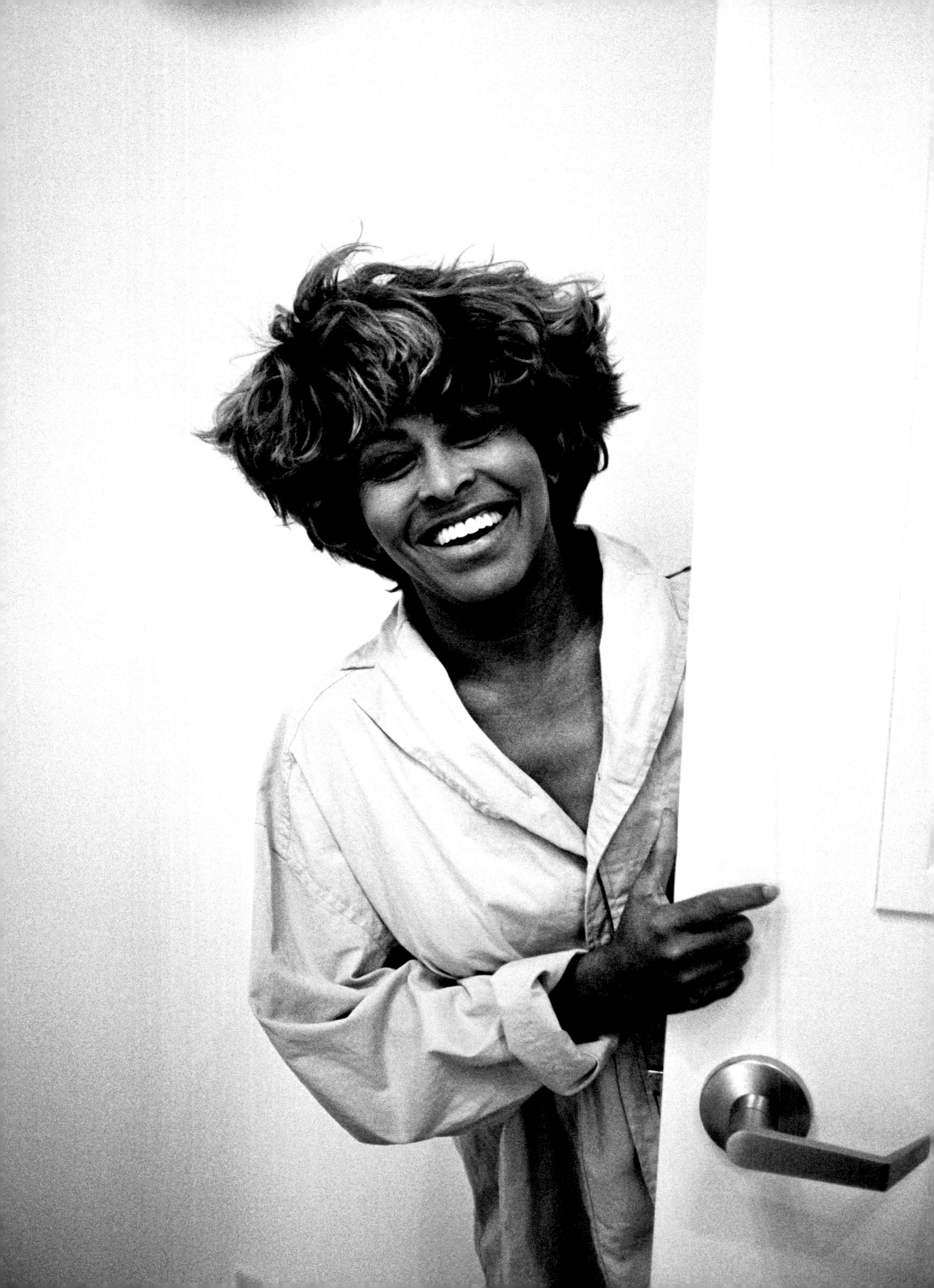

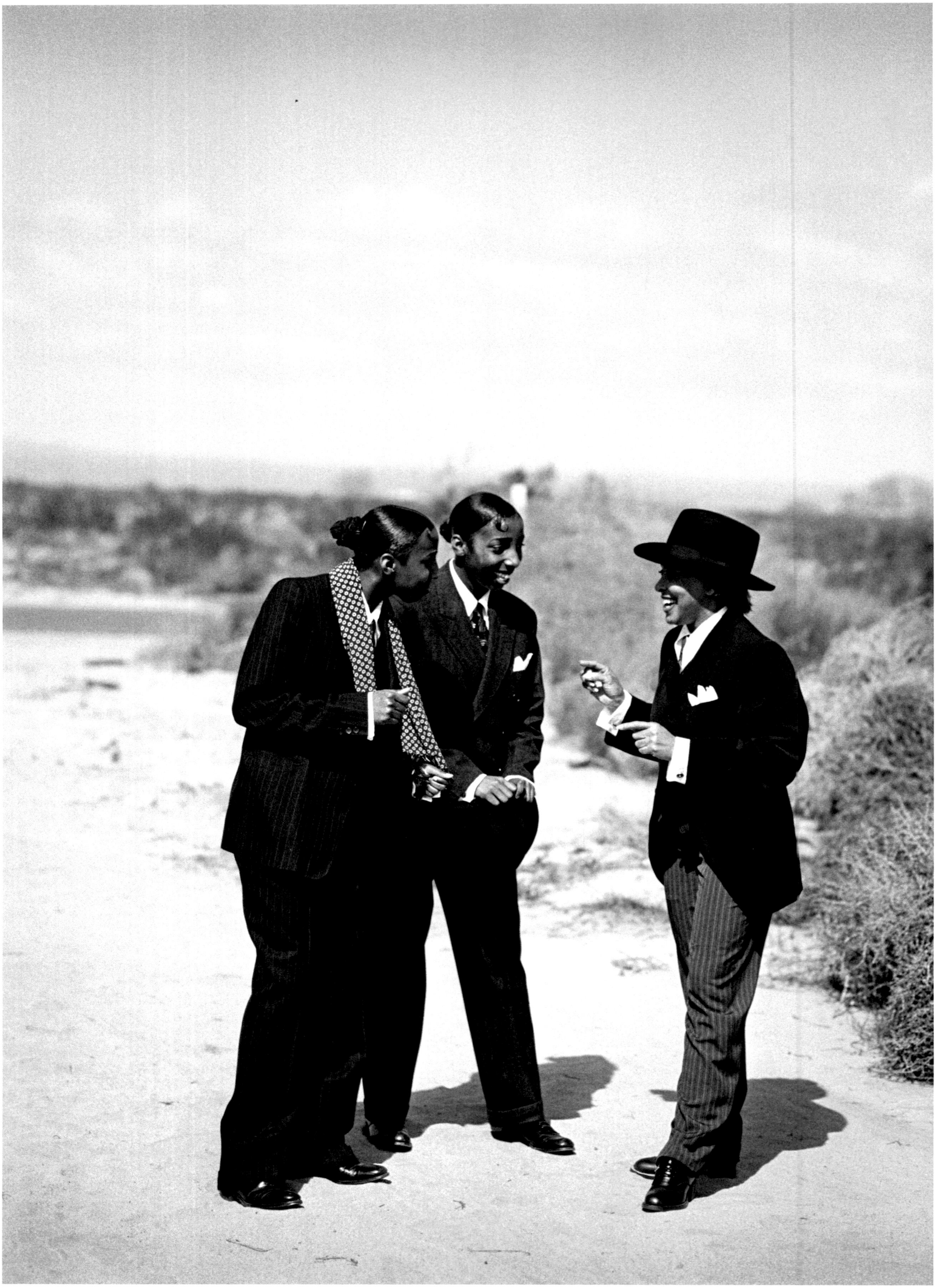

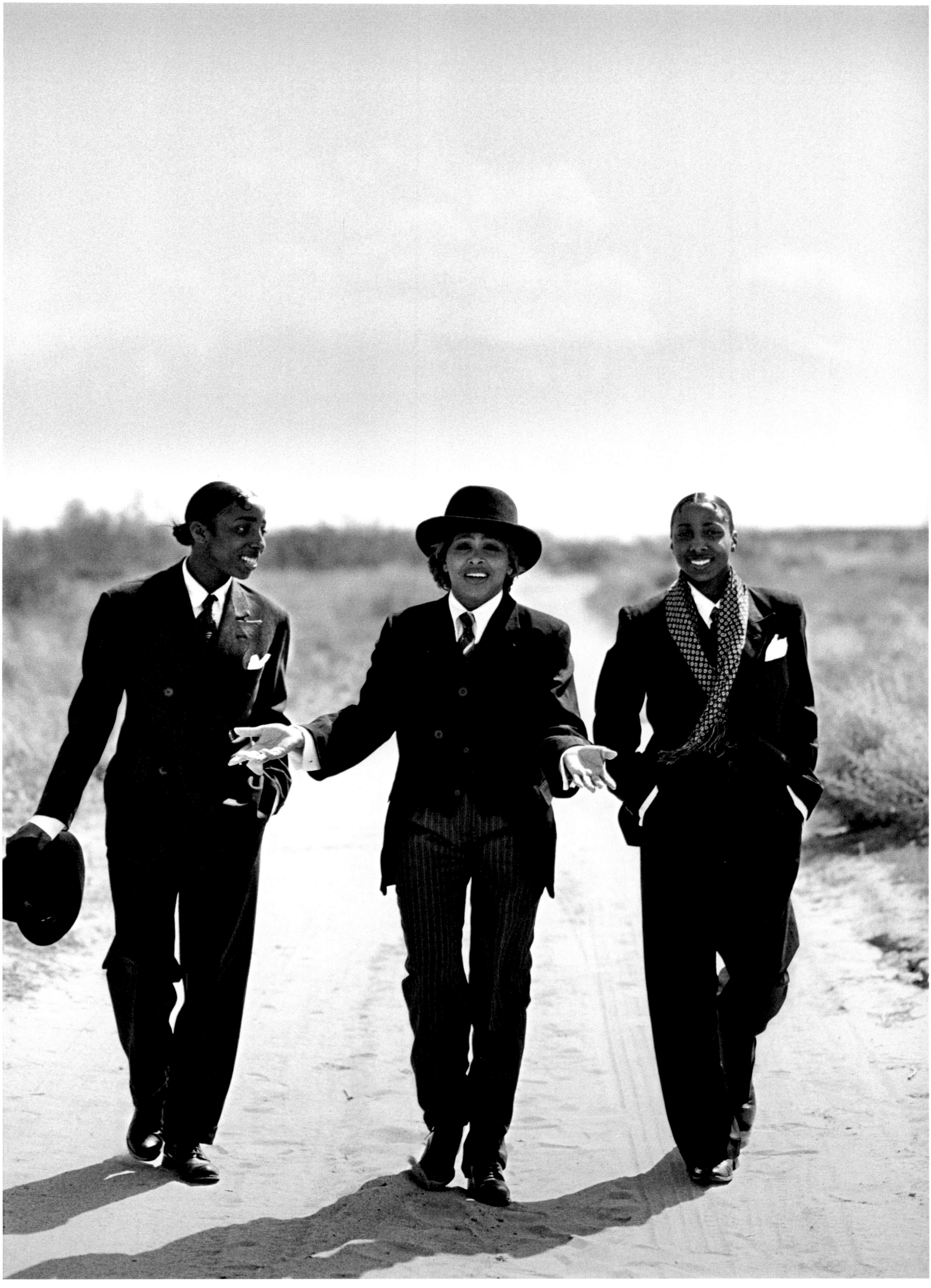

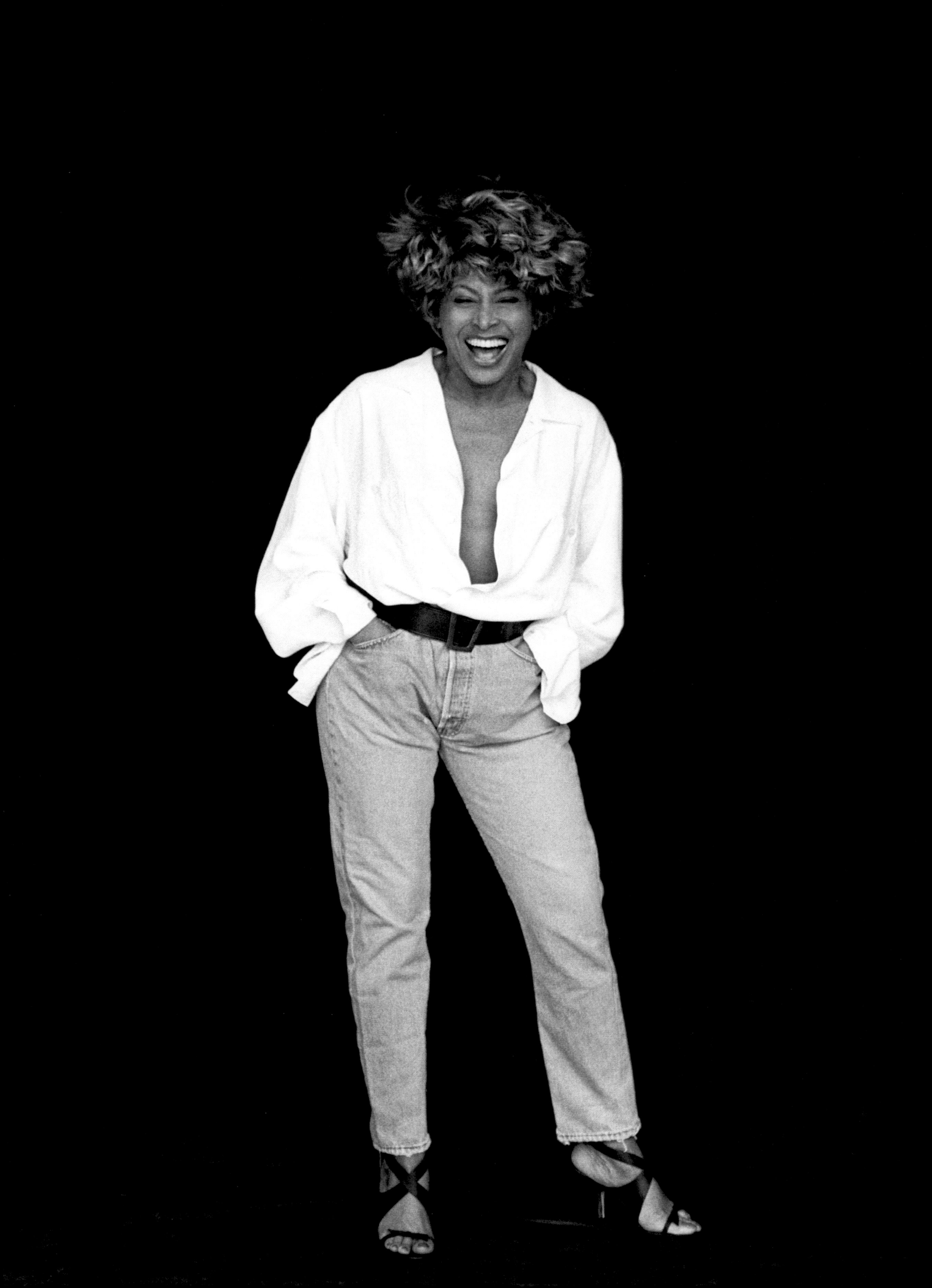

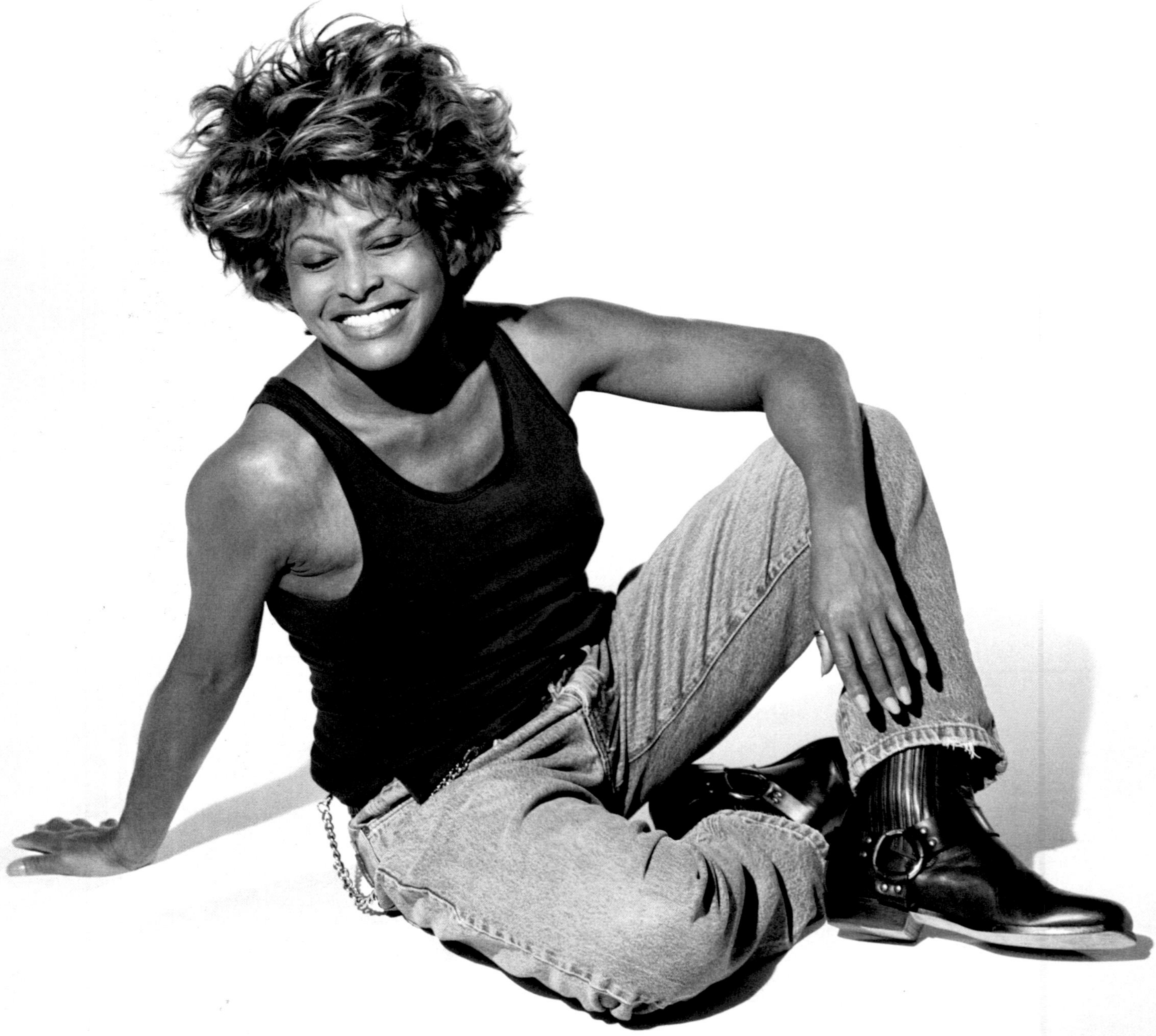

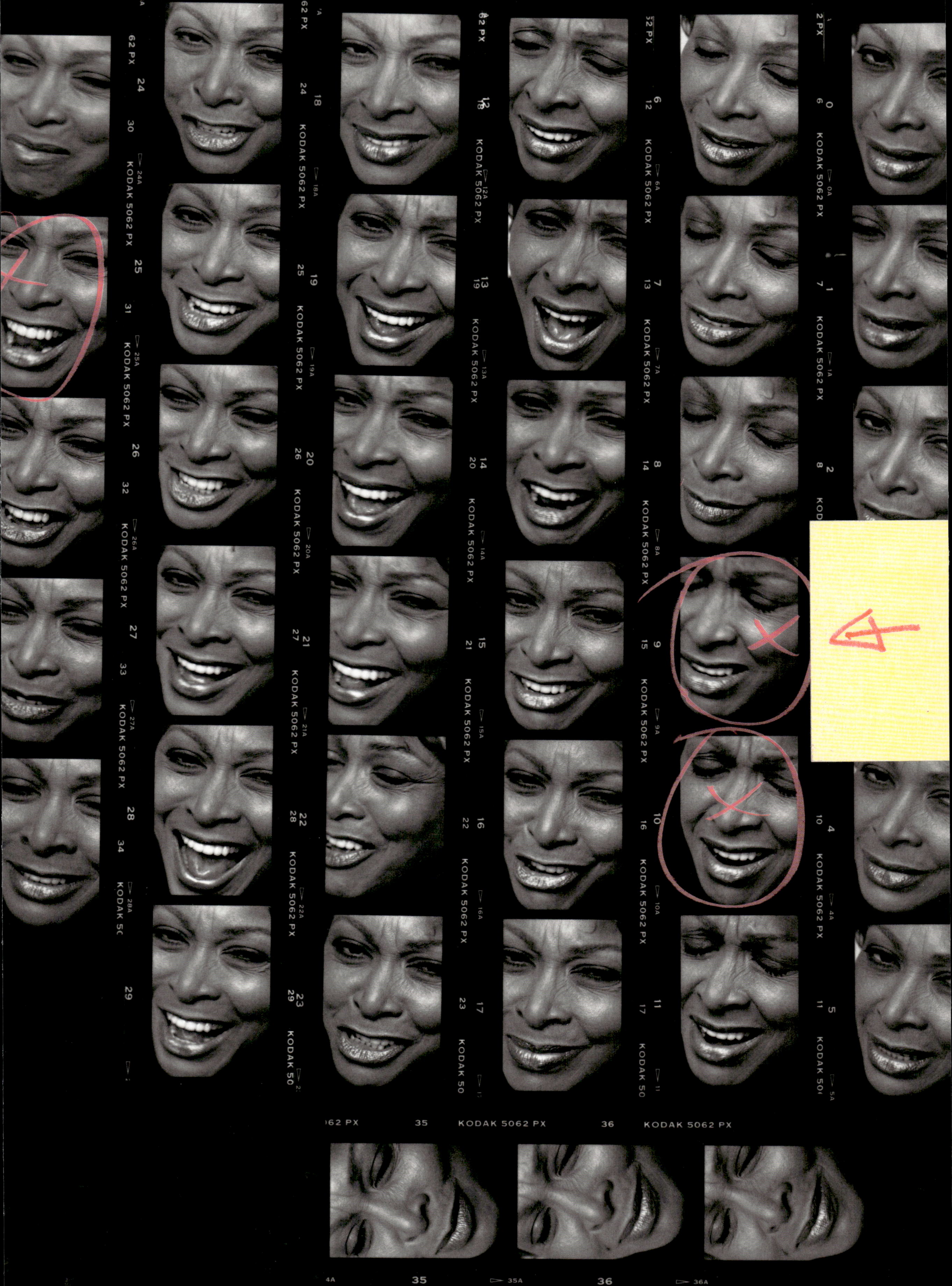
KODAK 5062 PX
35
KODAK 5062 PX
36
KODAK 5062 PX

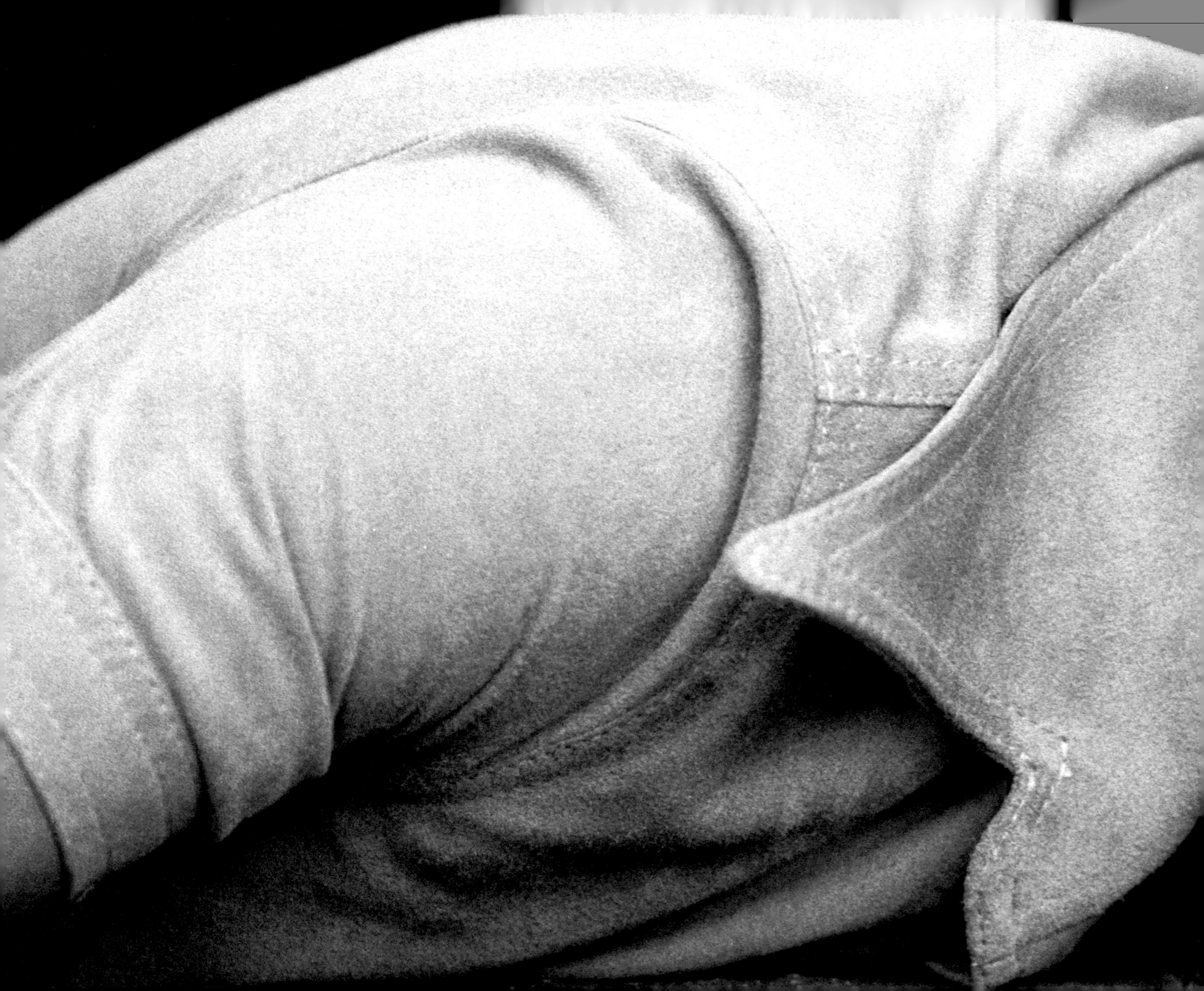

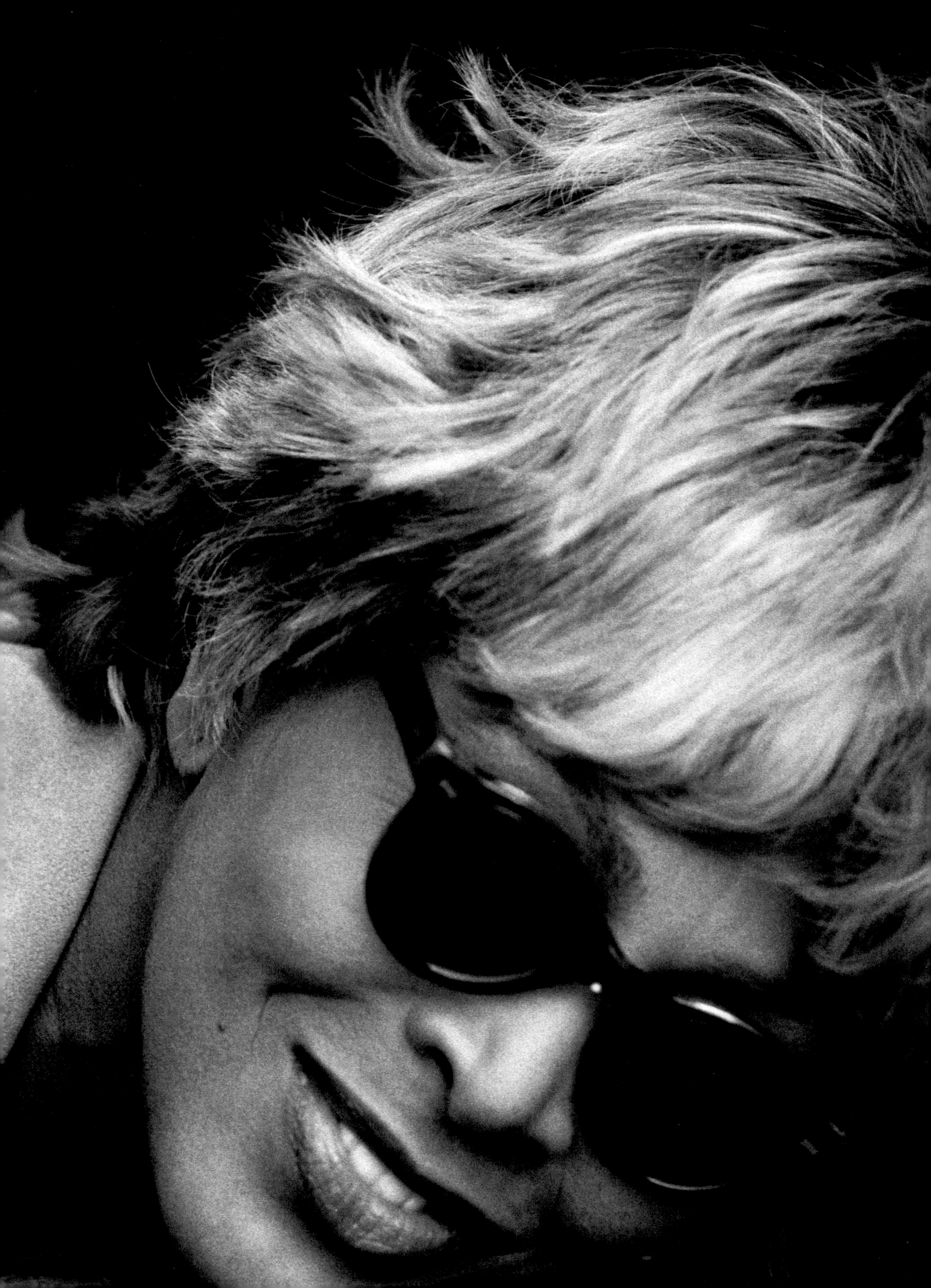

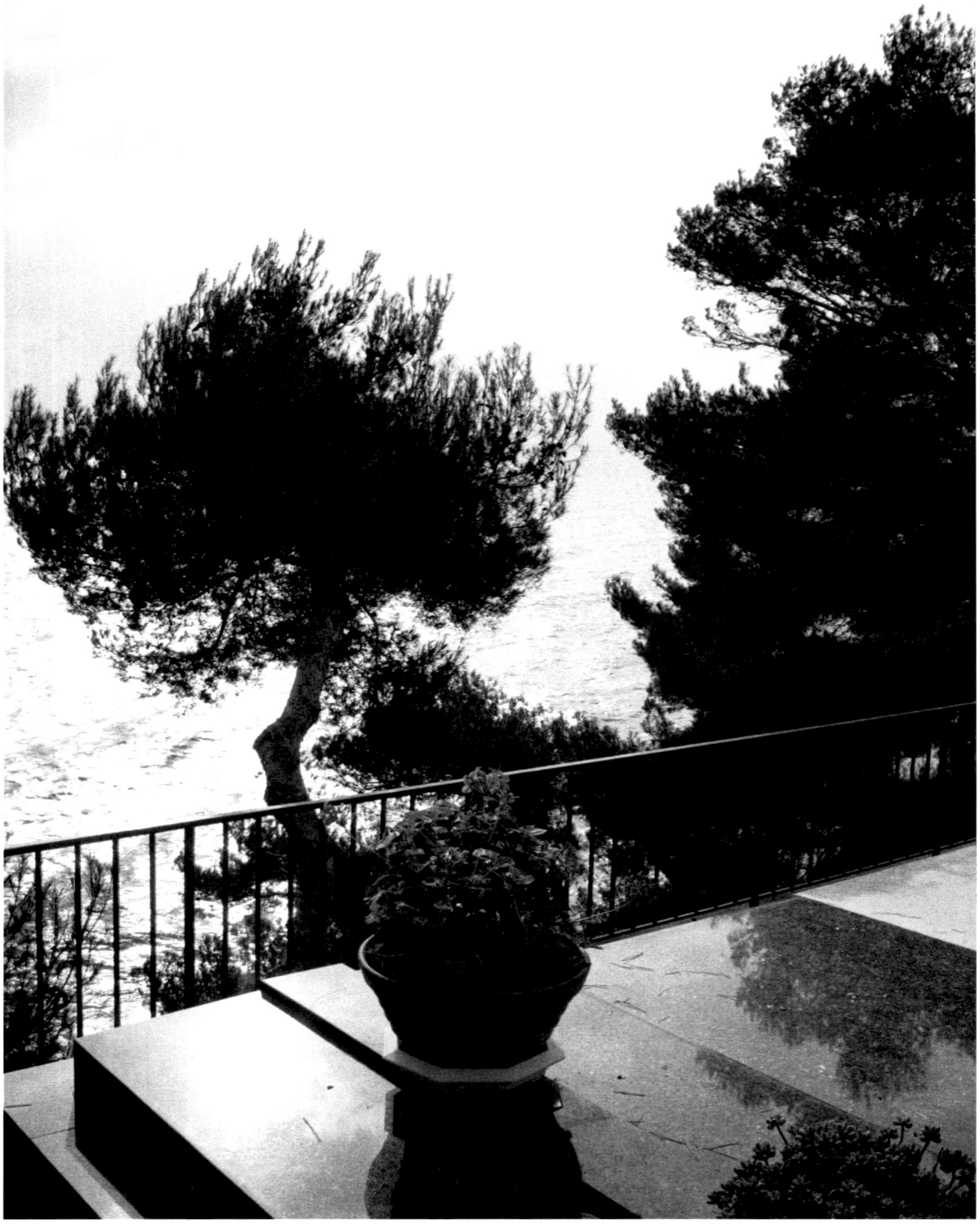

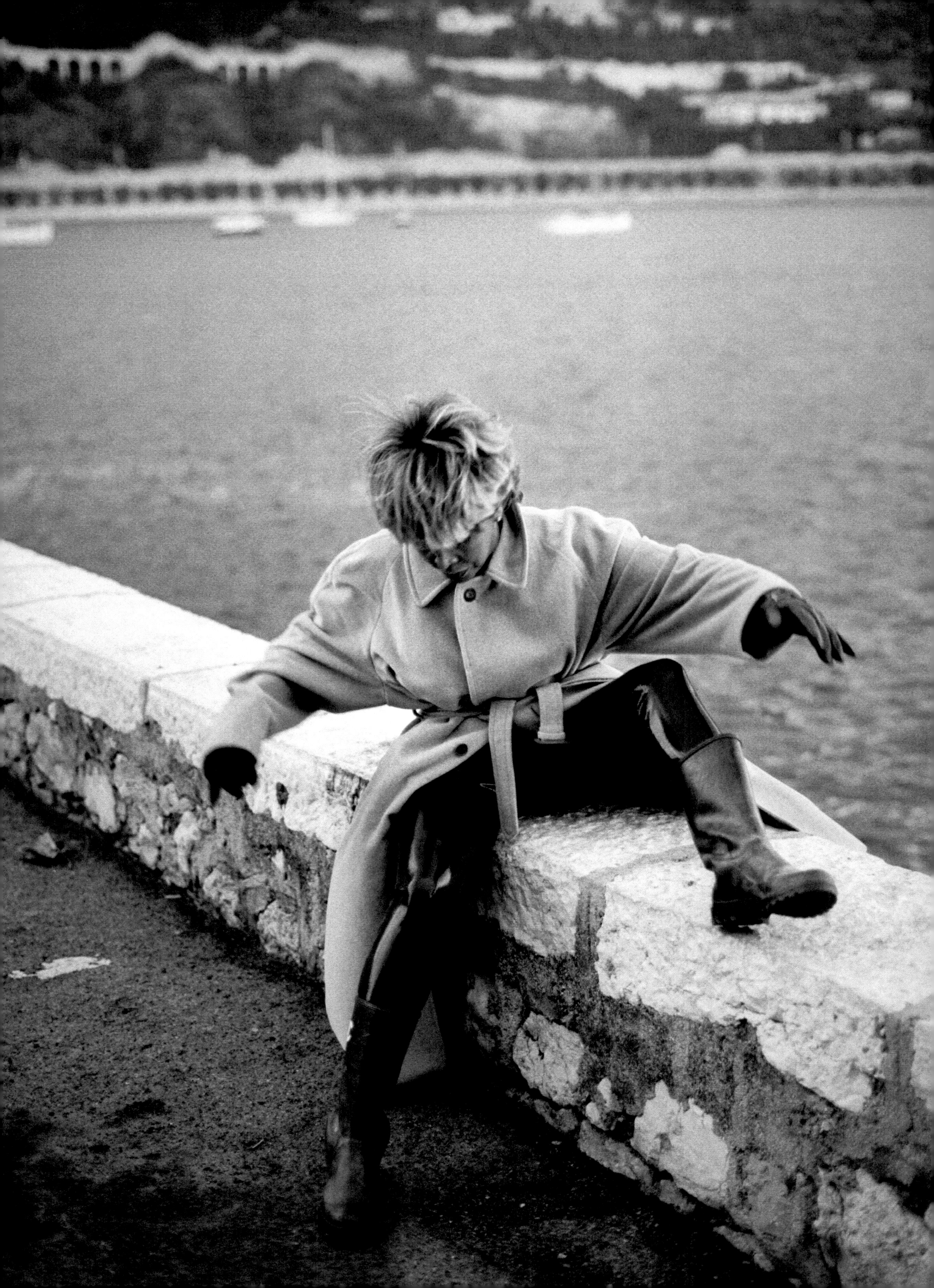

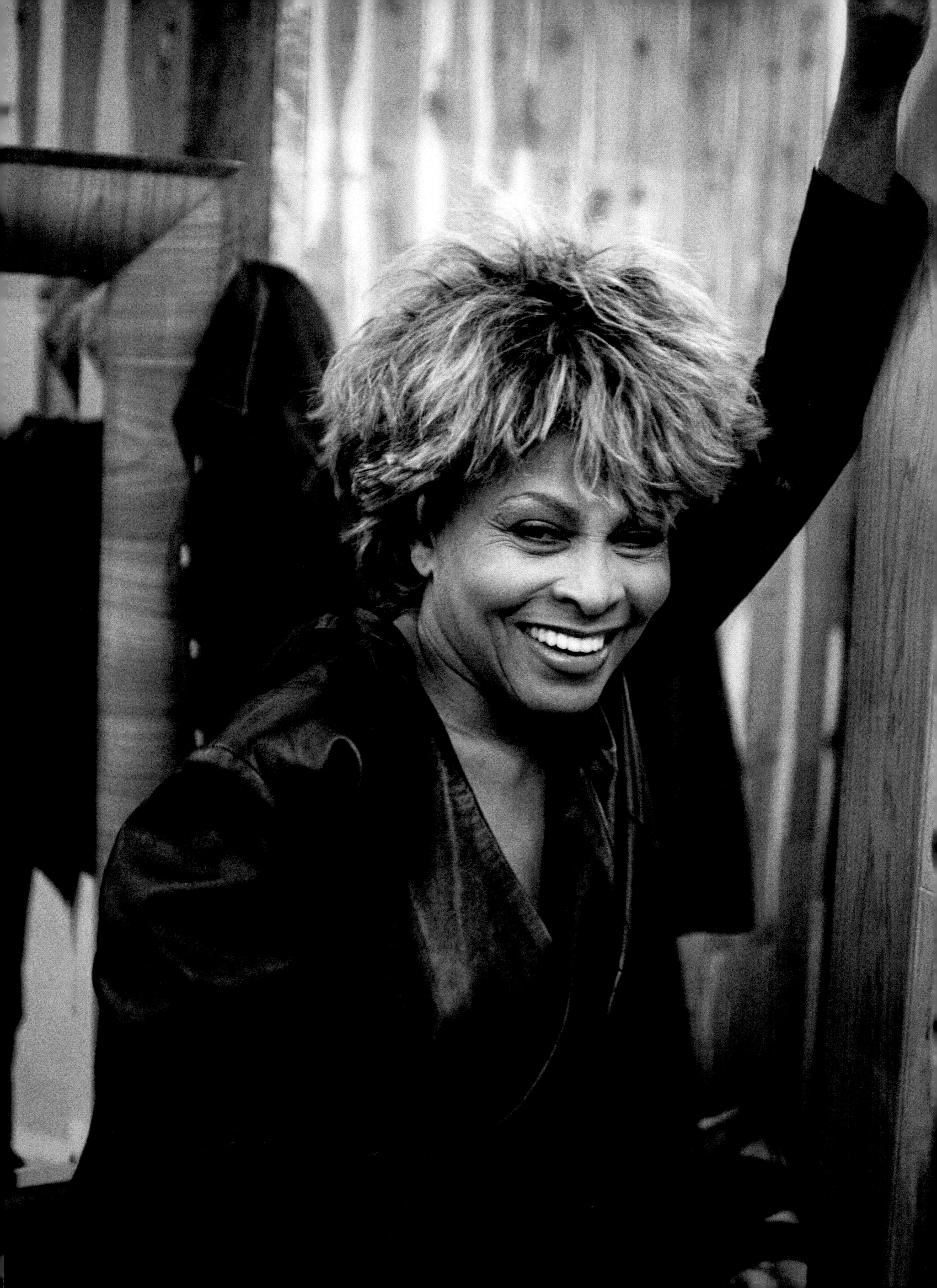

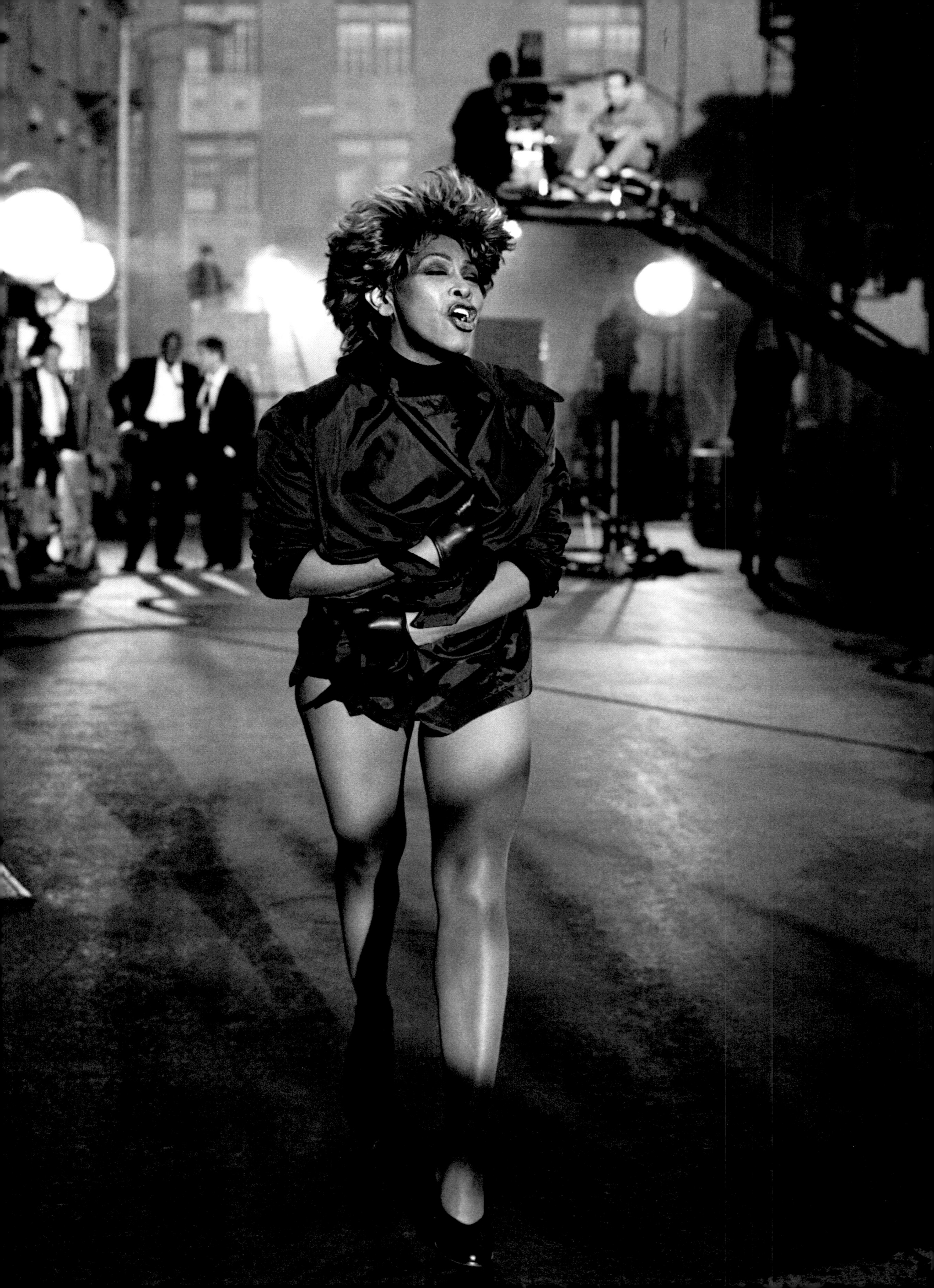

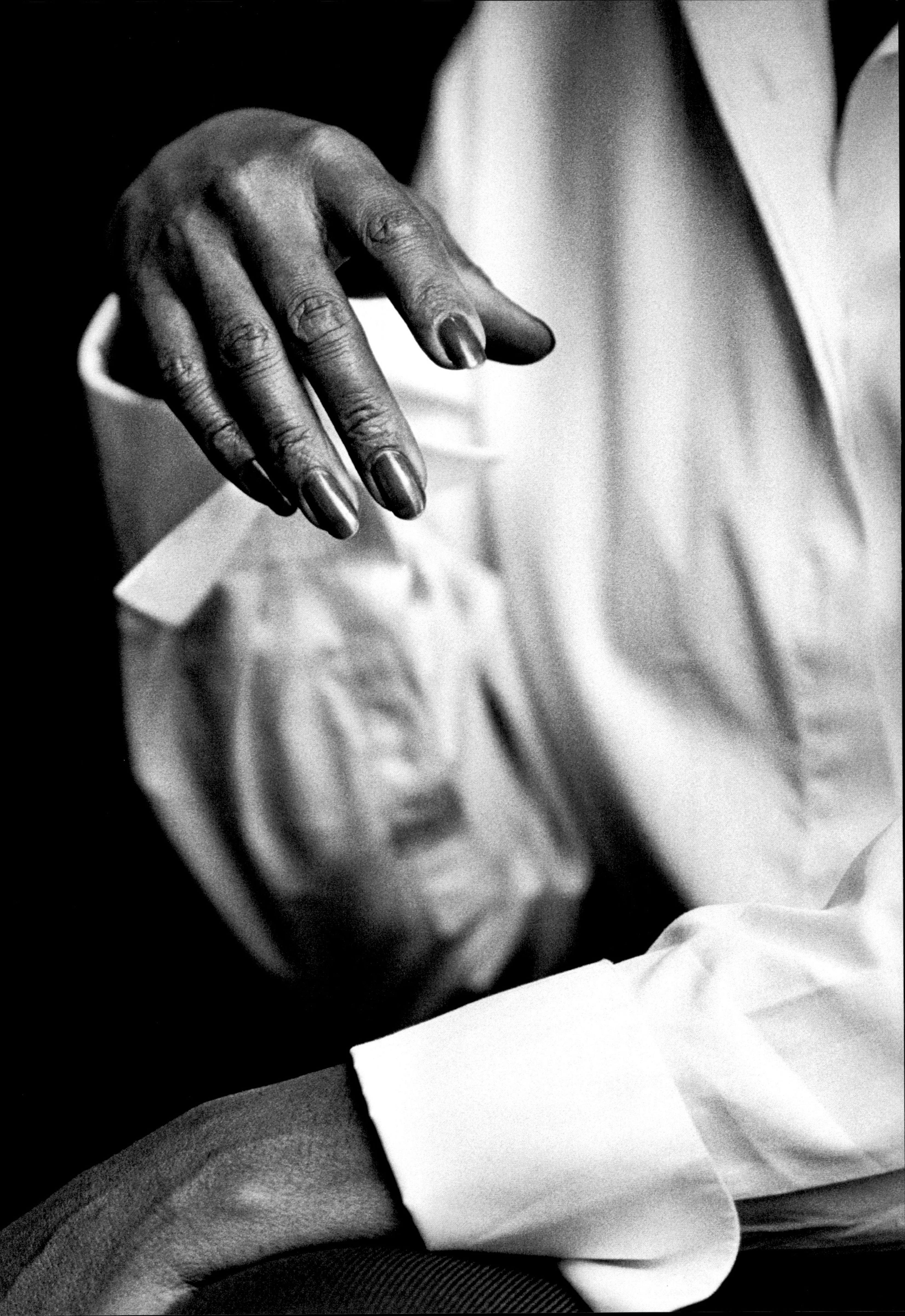

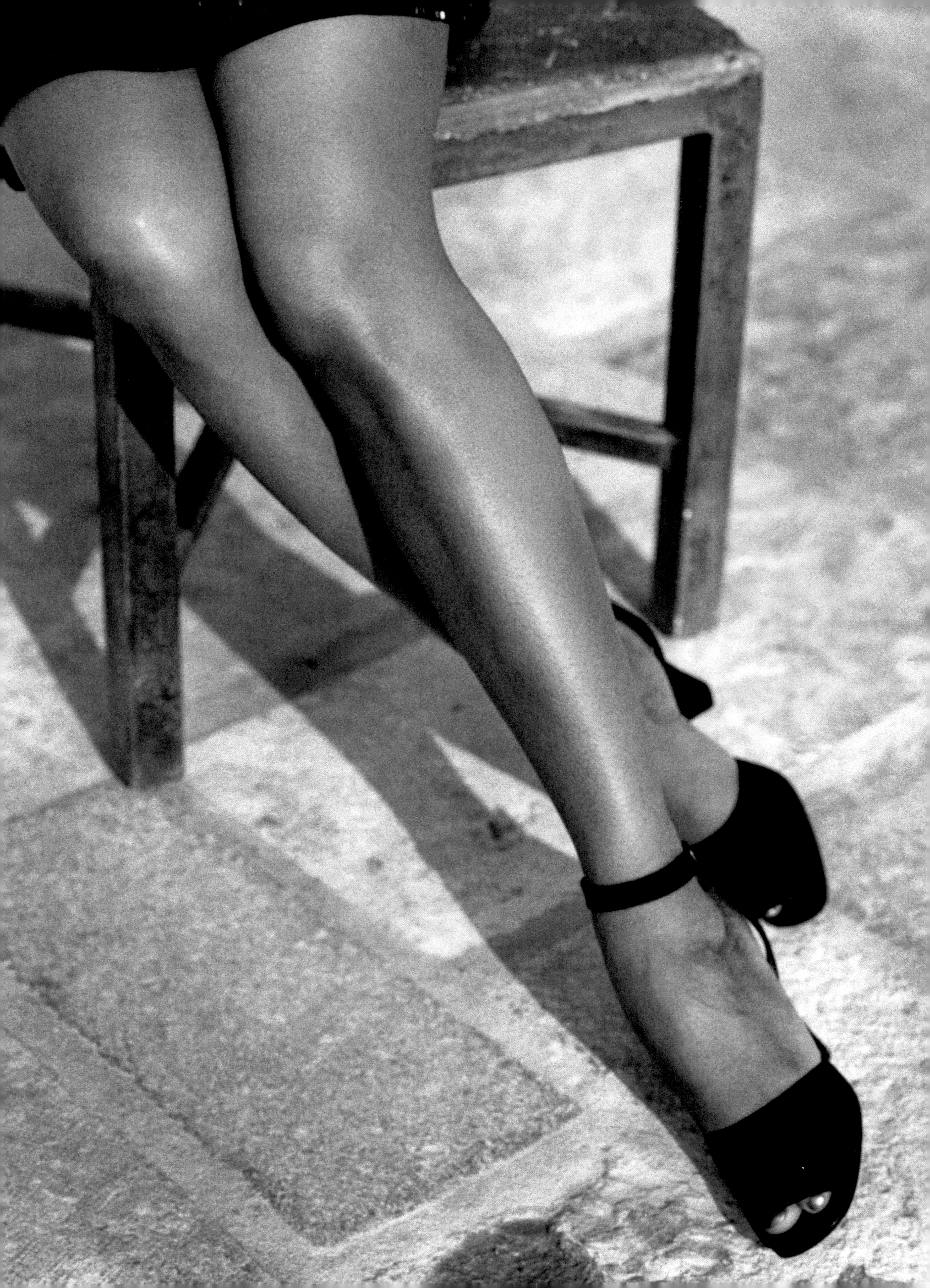

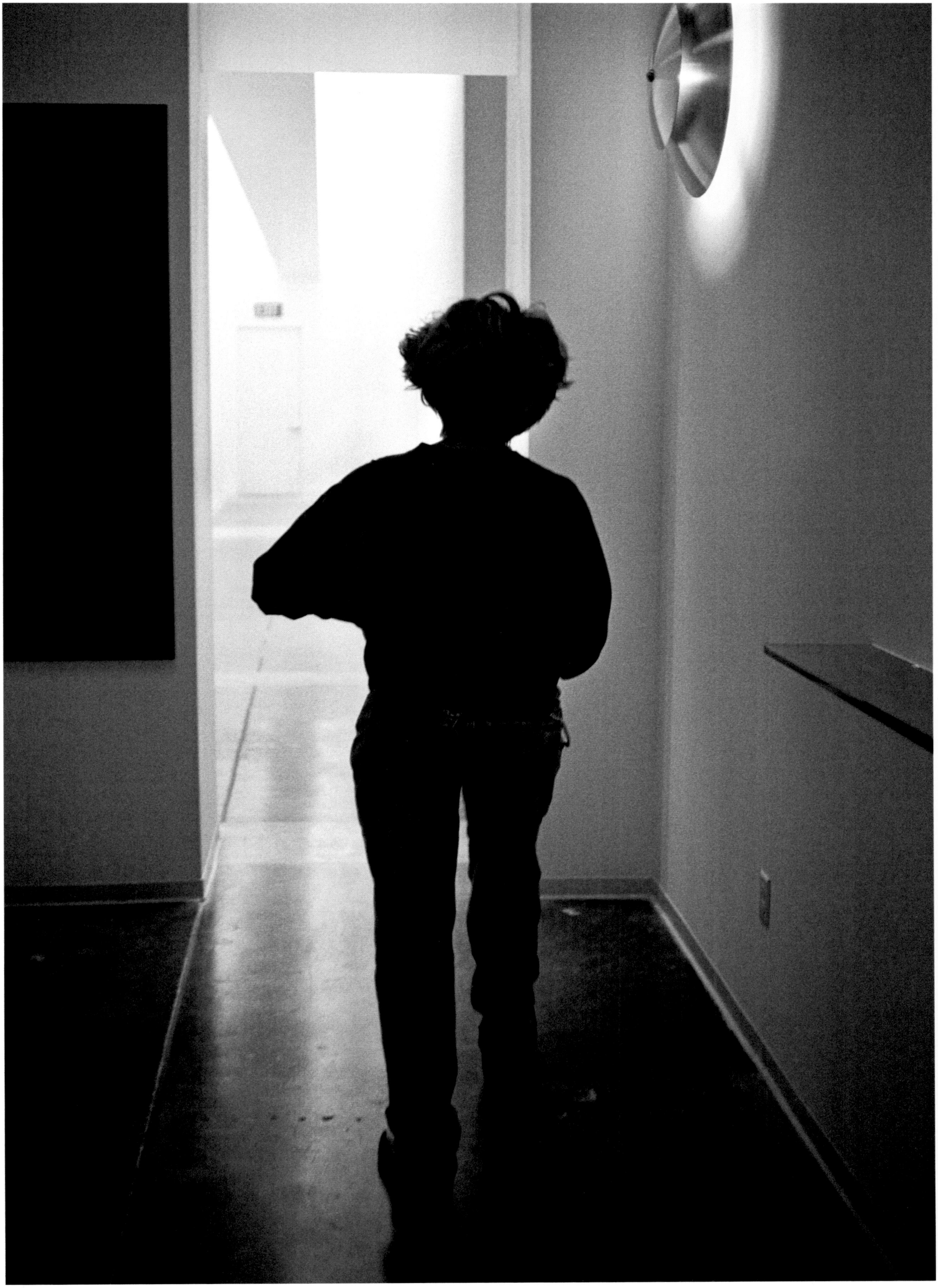

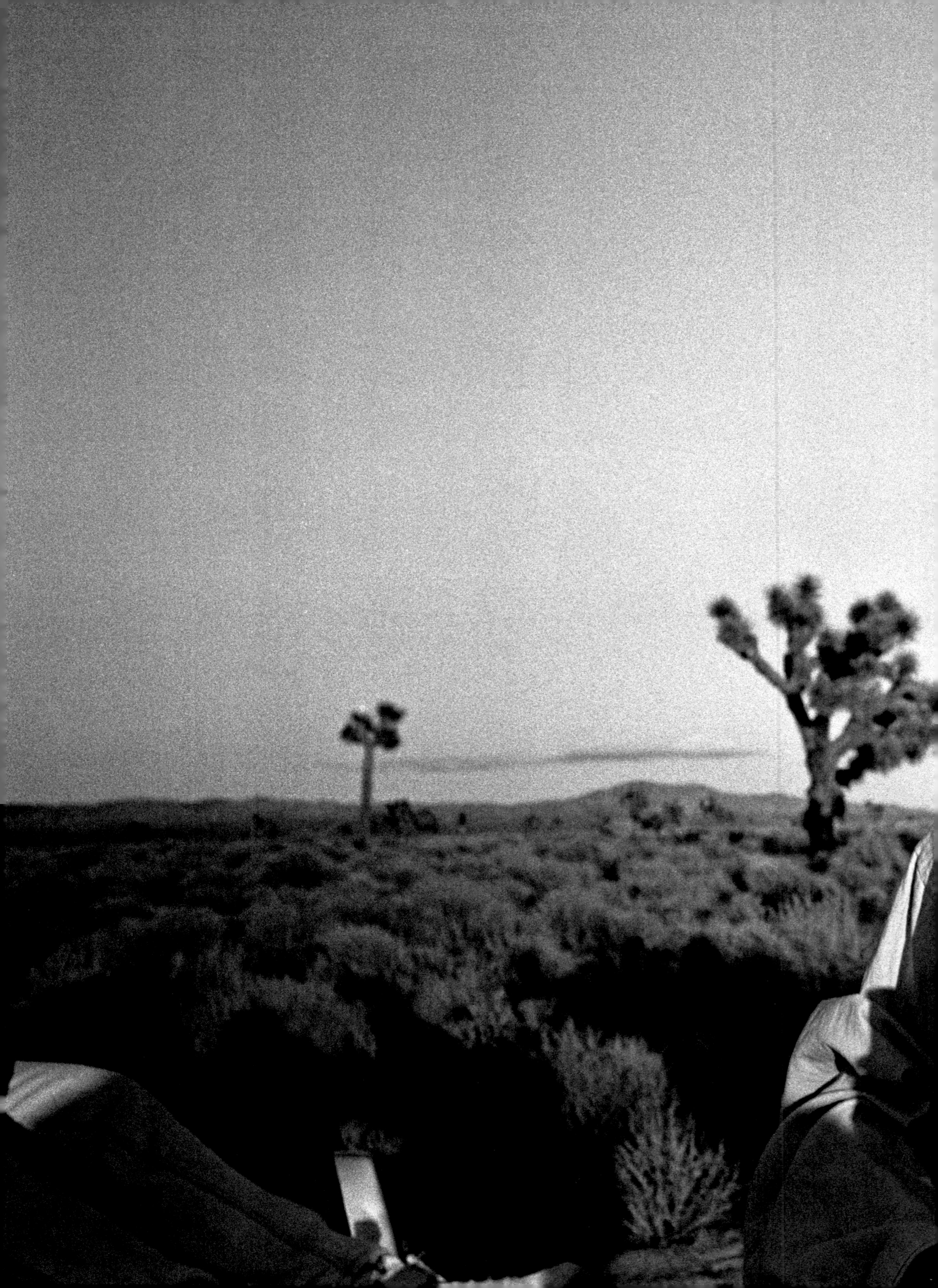

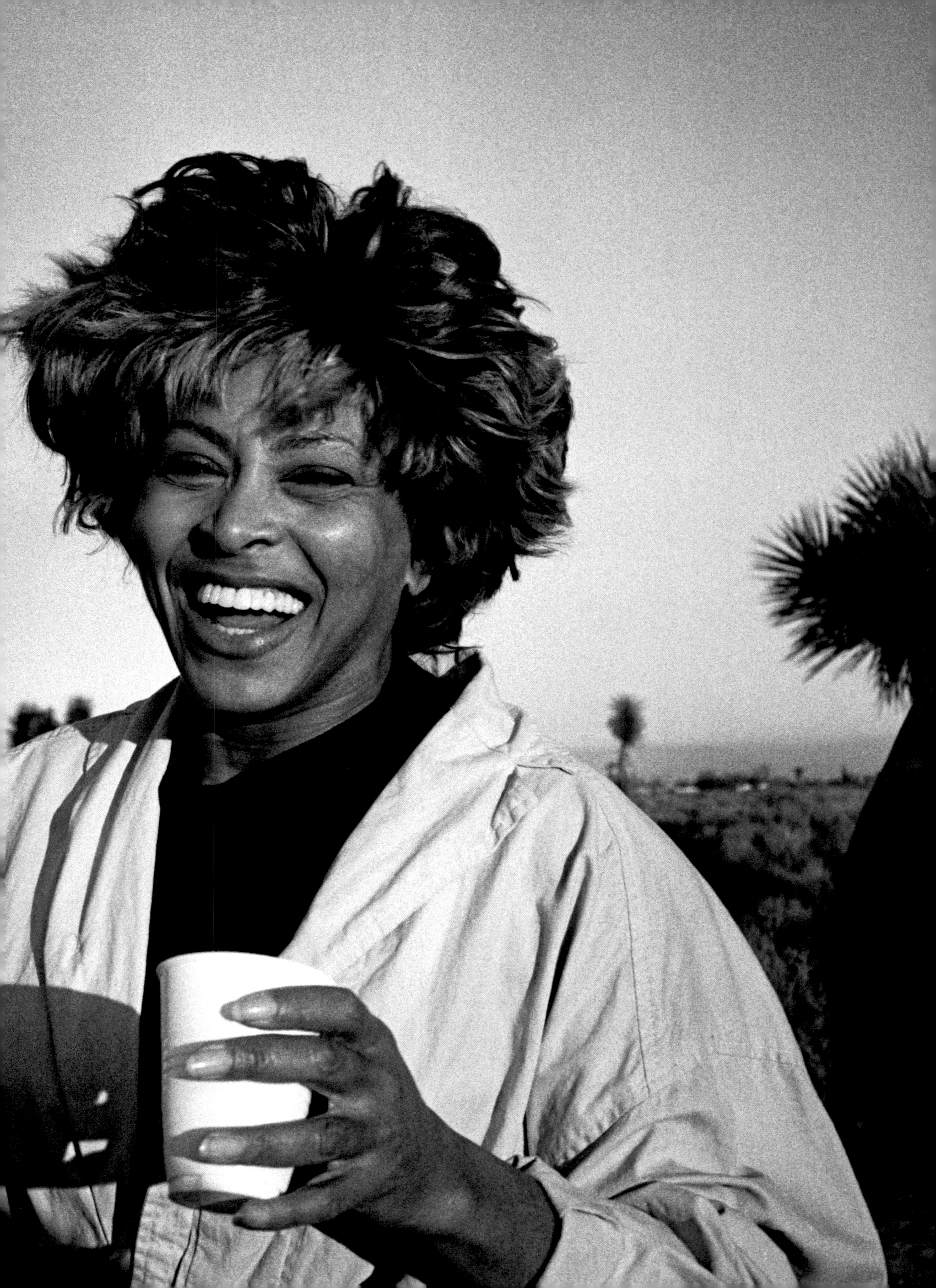

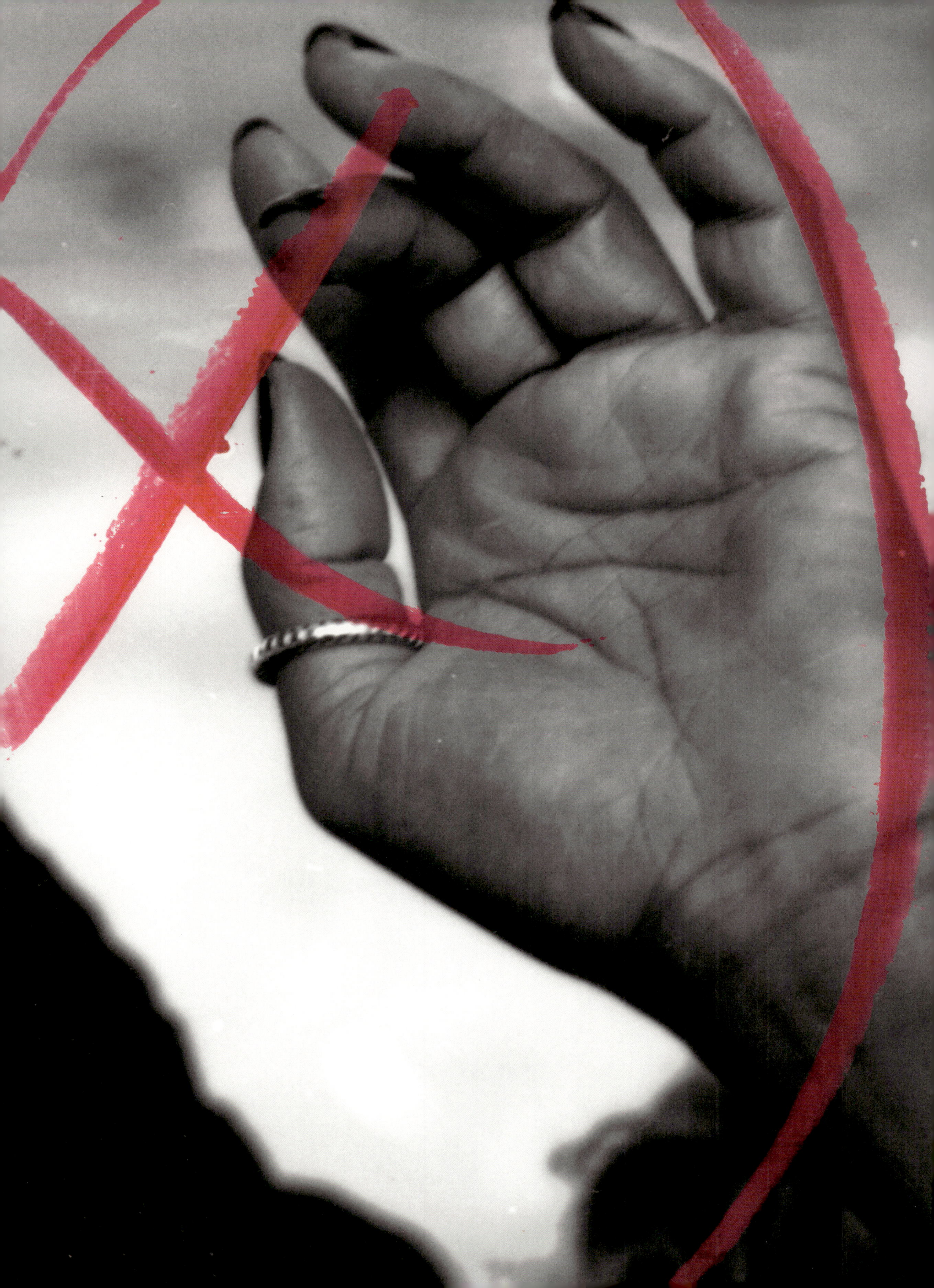

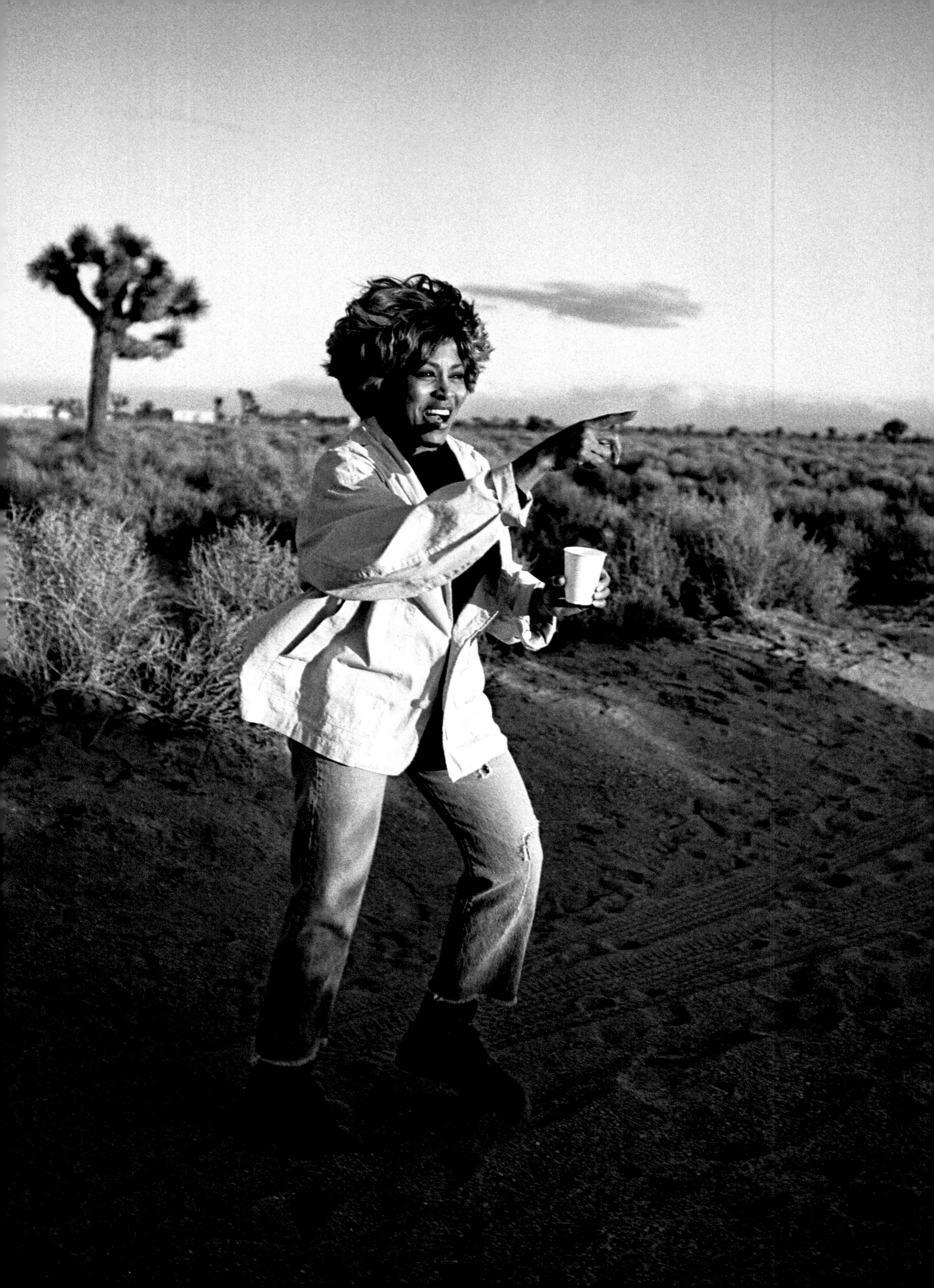

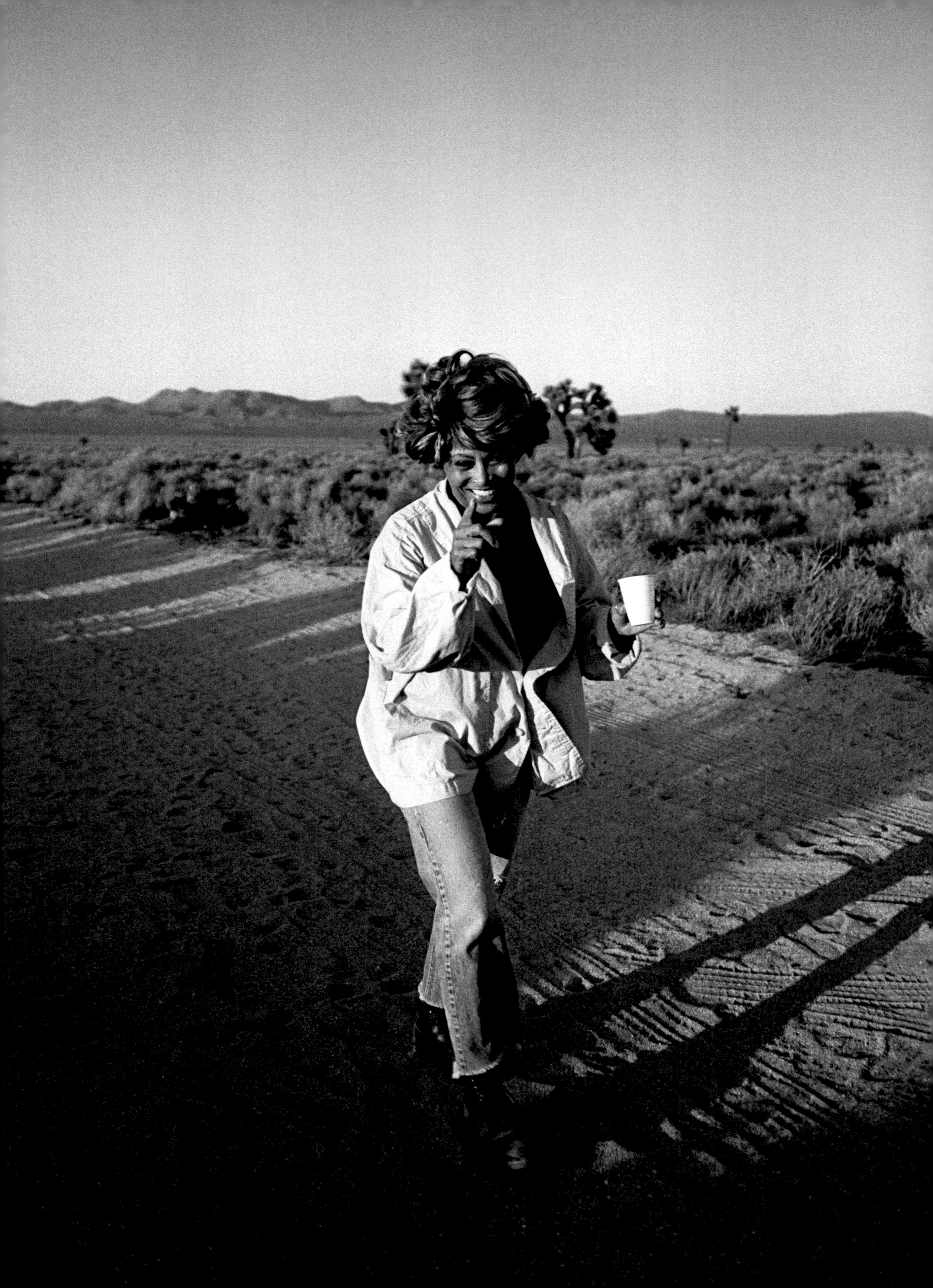

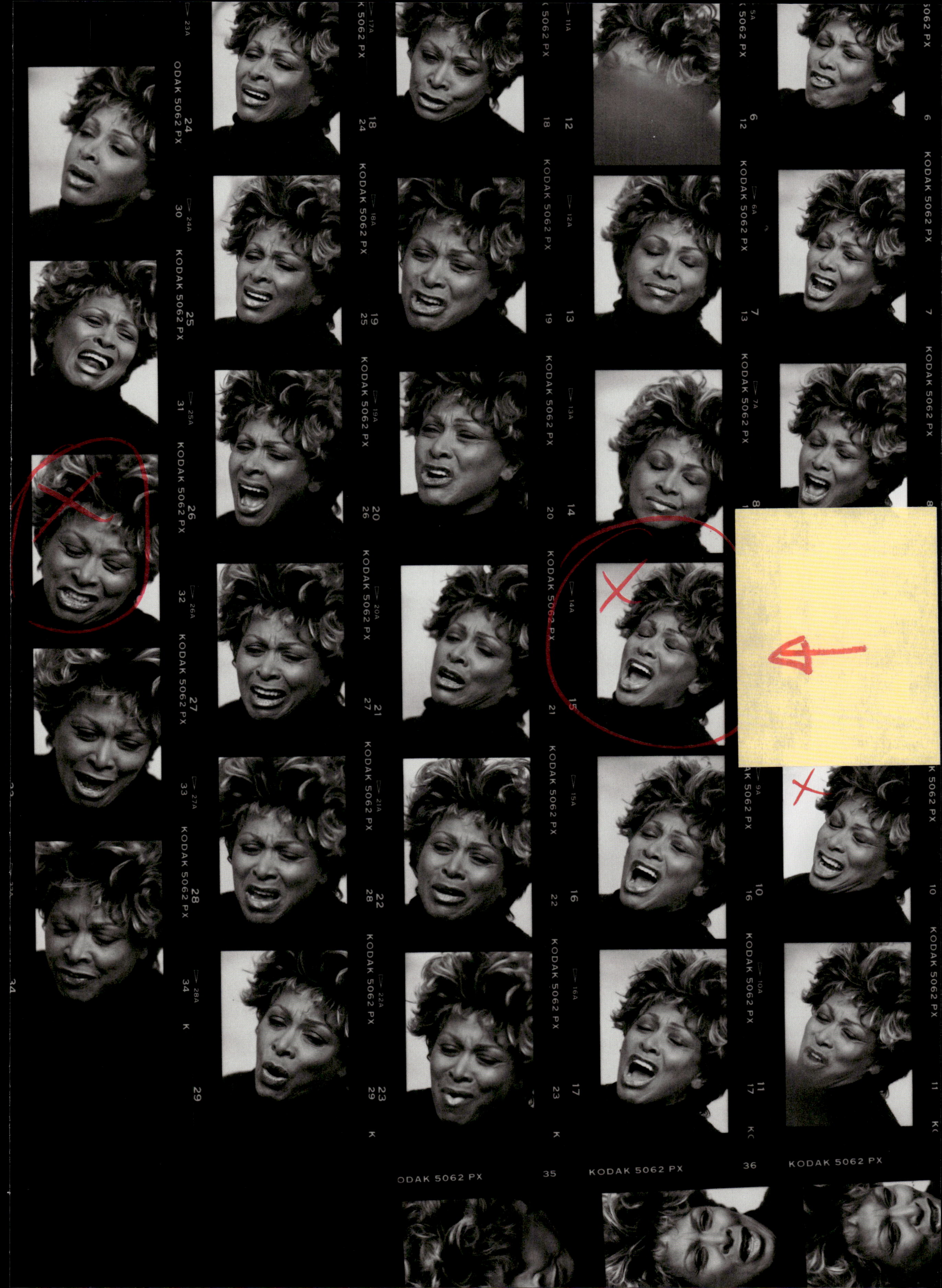
KODAK 5062 PX
KODAK 5062 PX
KODAK 5062 PX

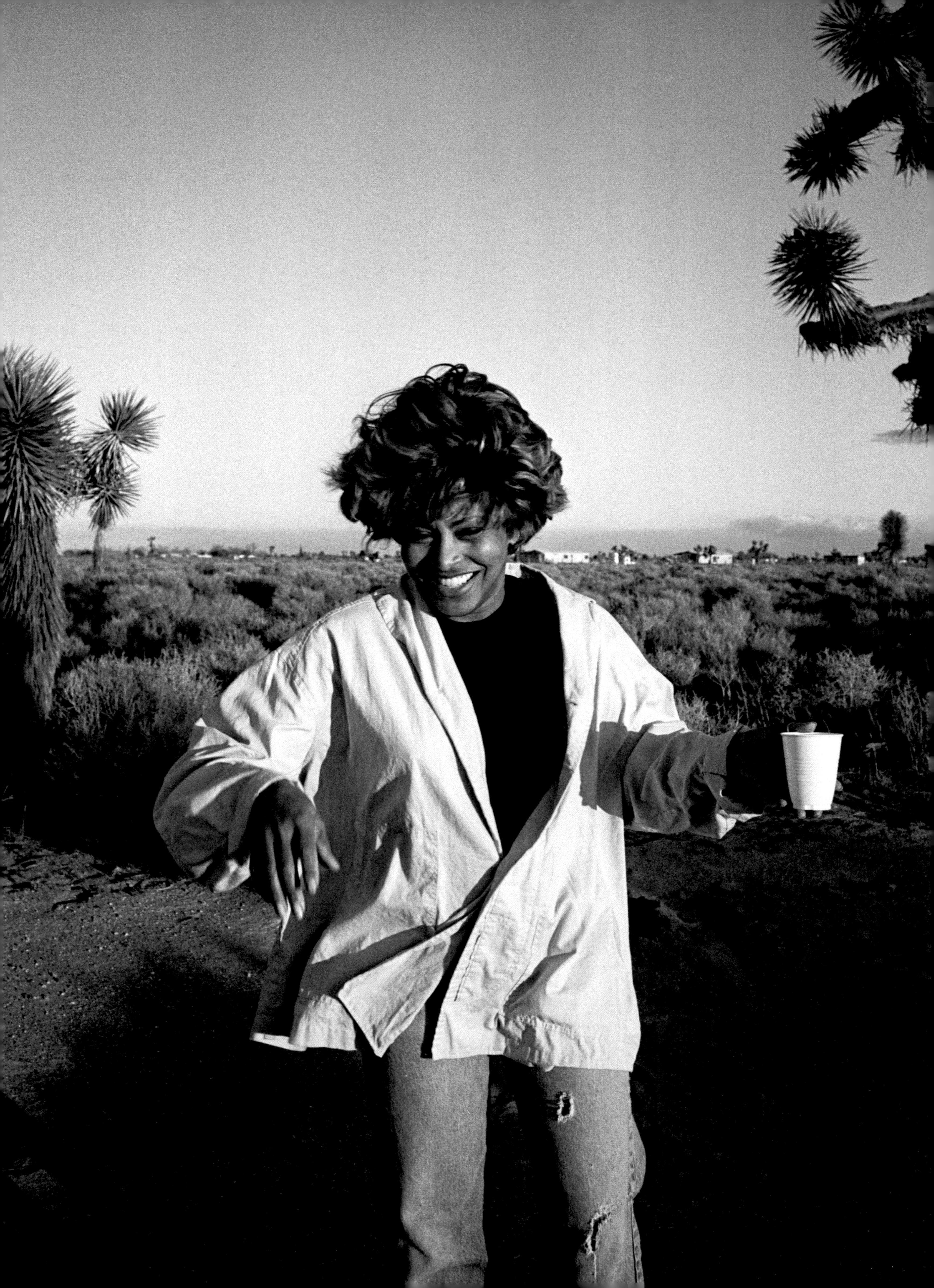

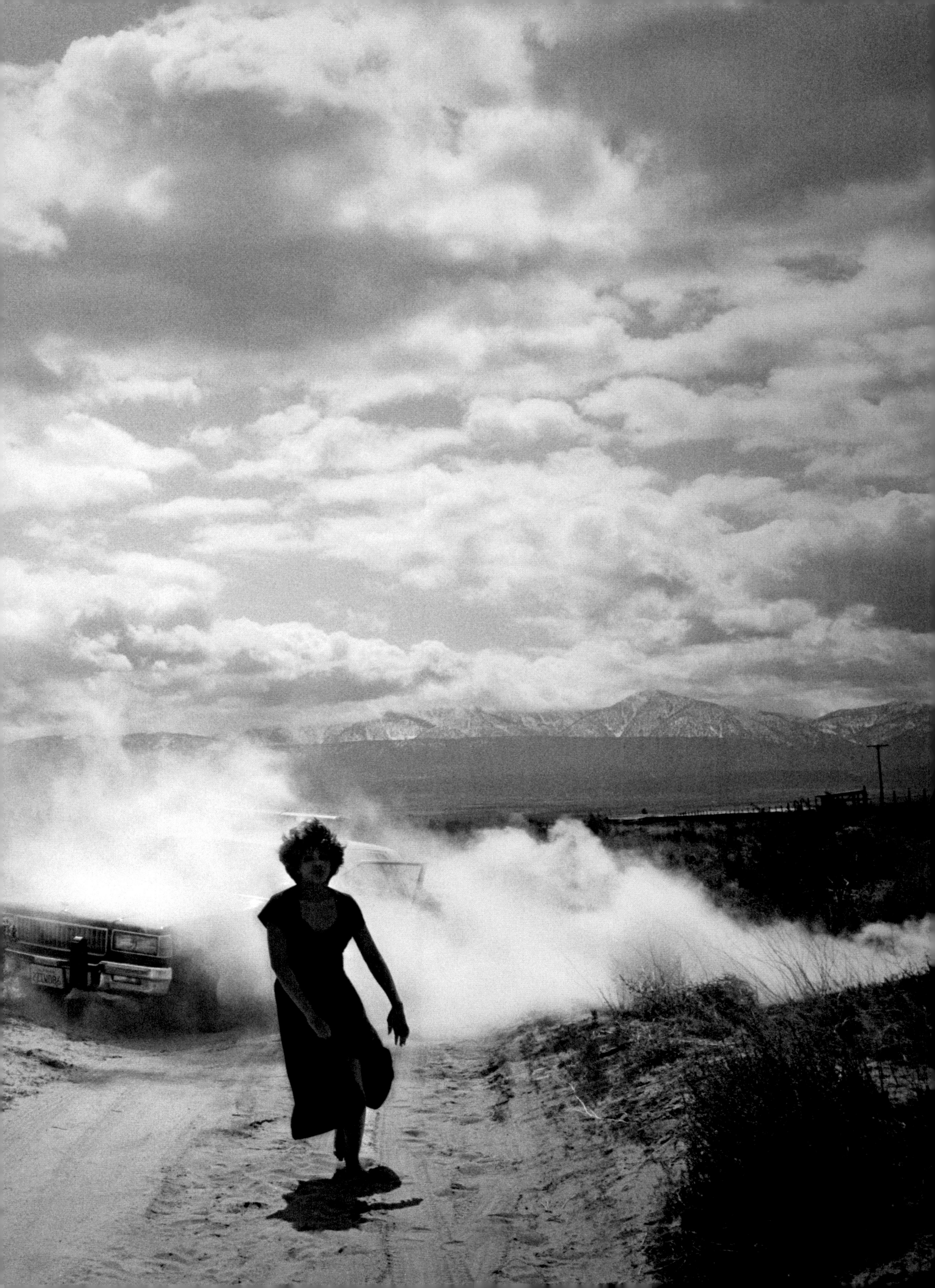

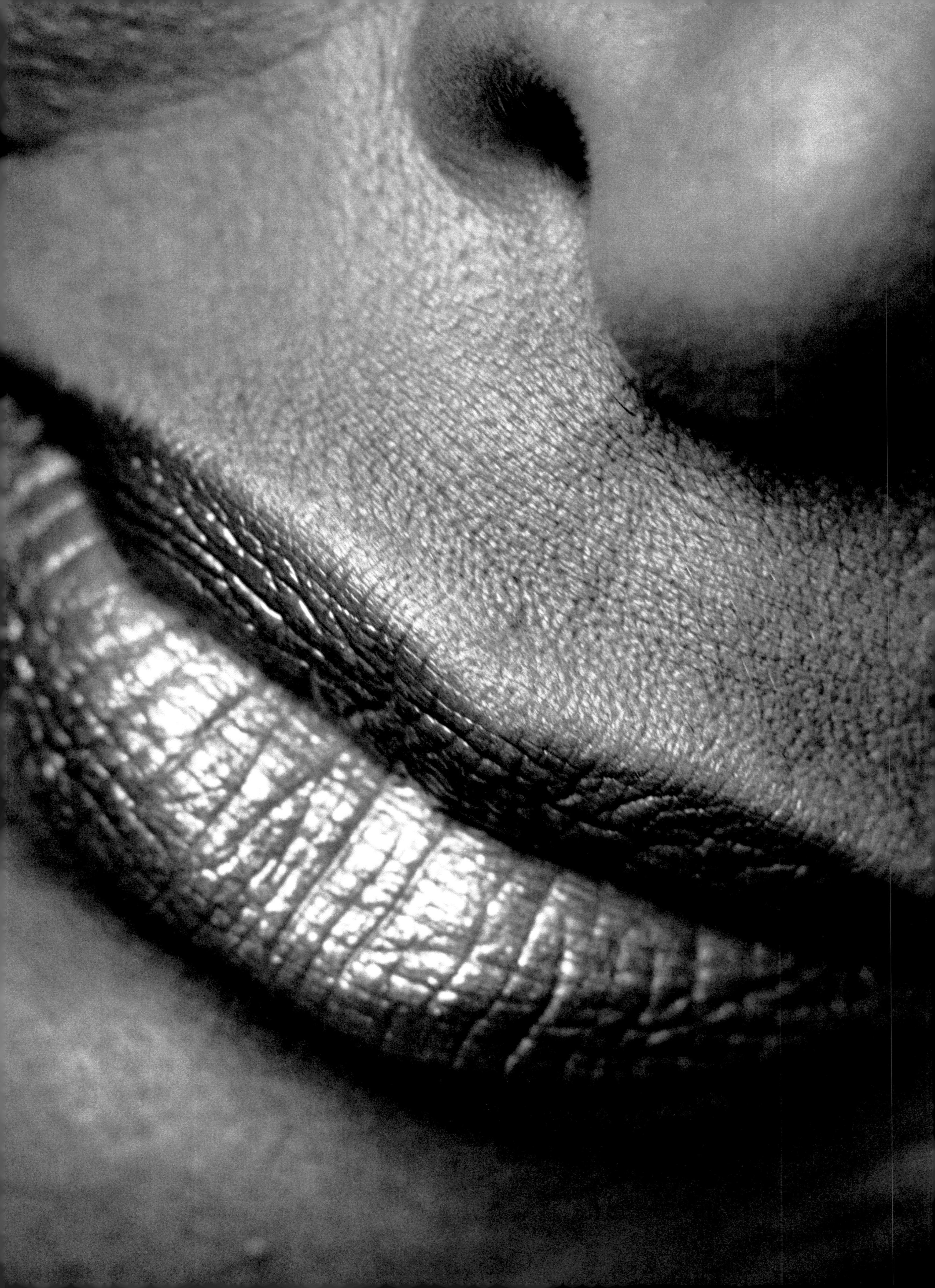

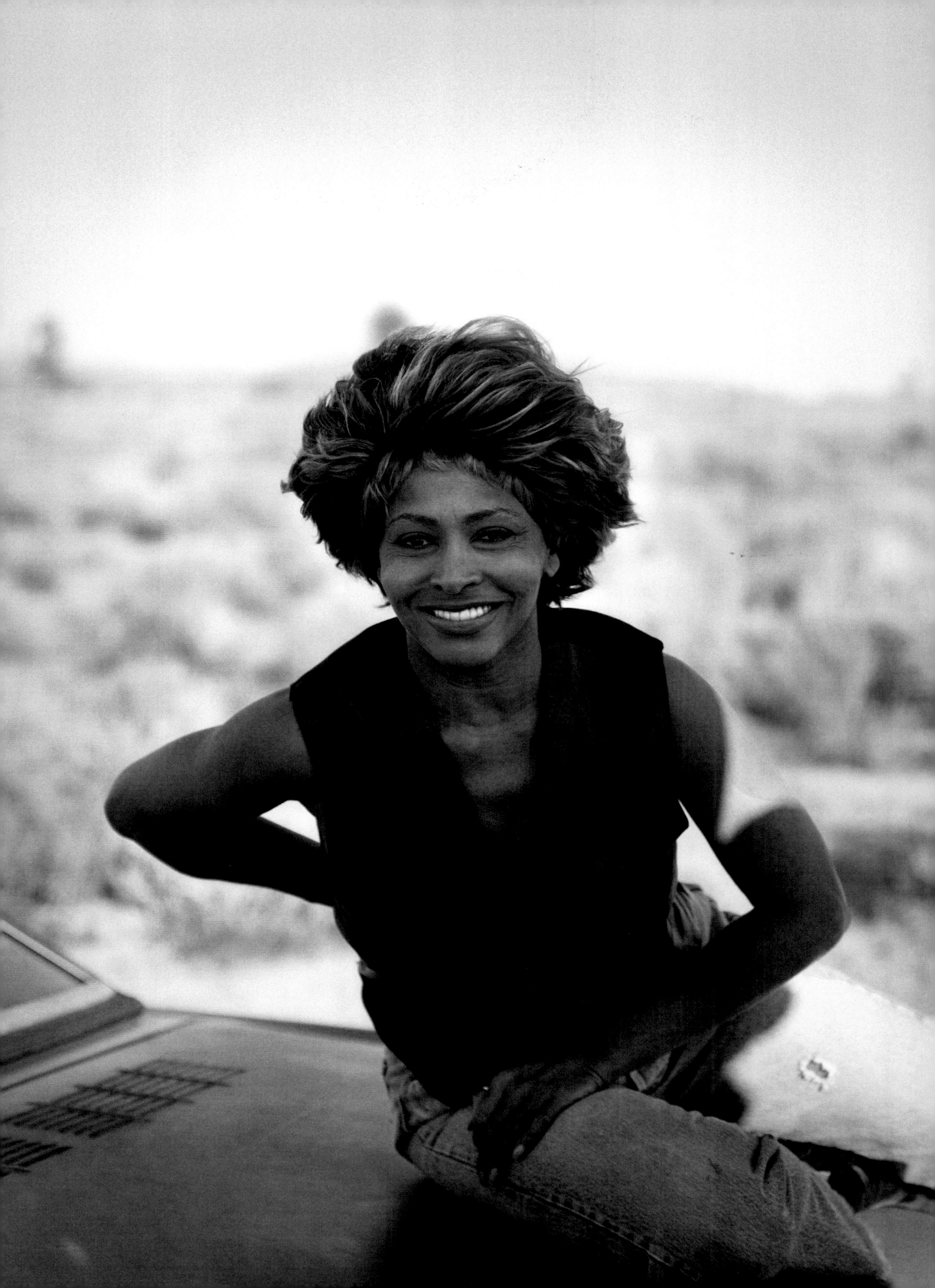

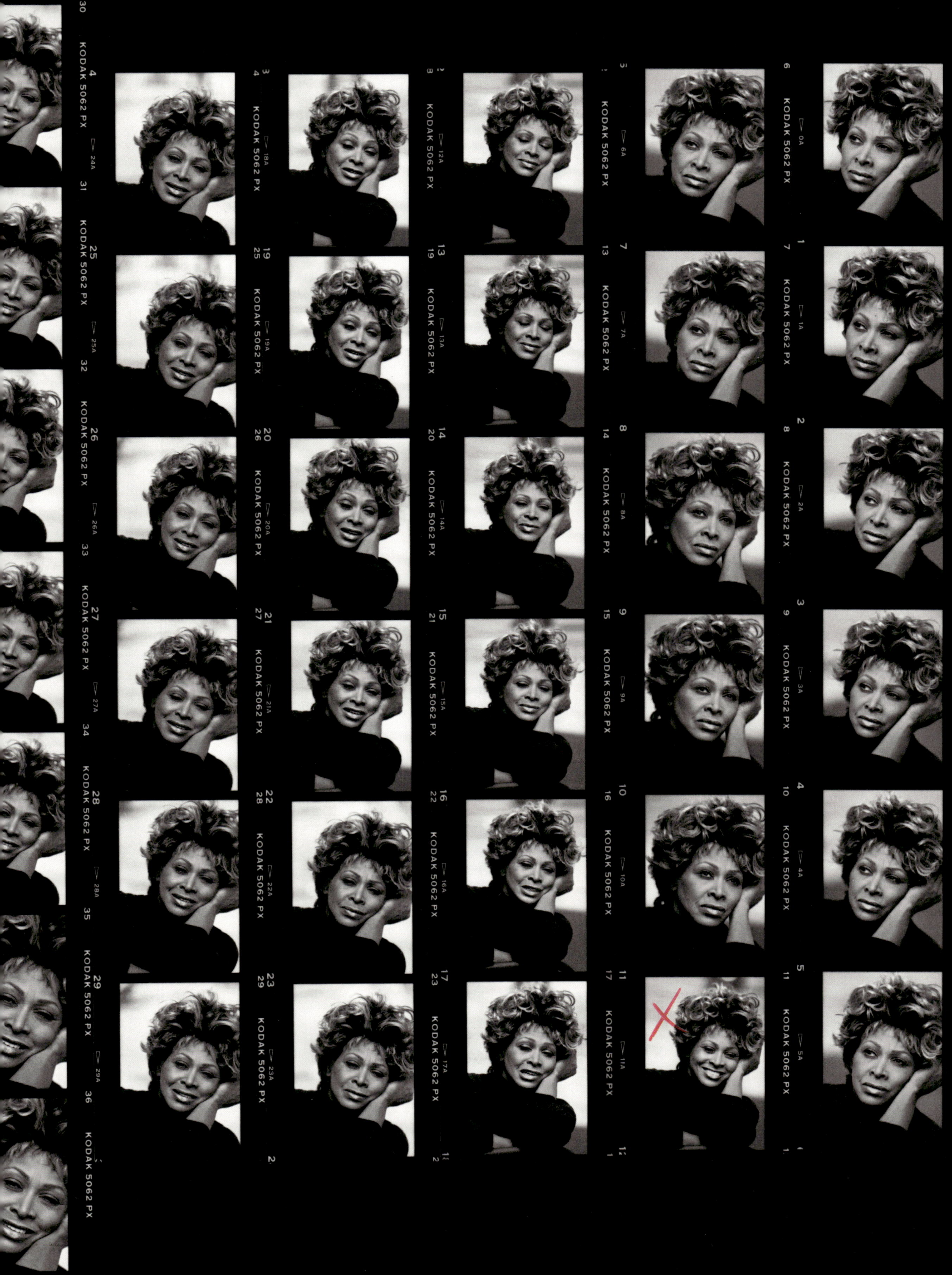
KODAK 5062 PX

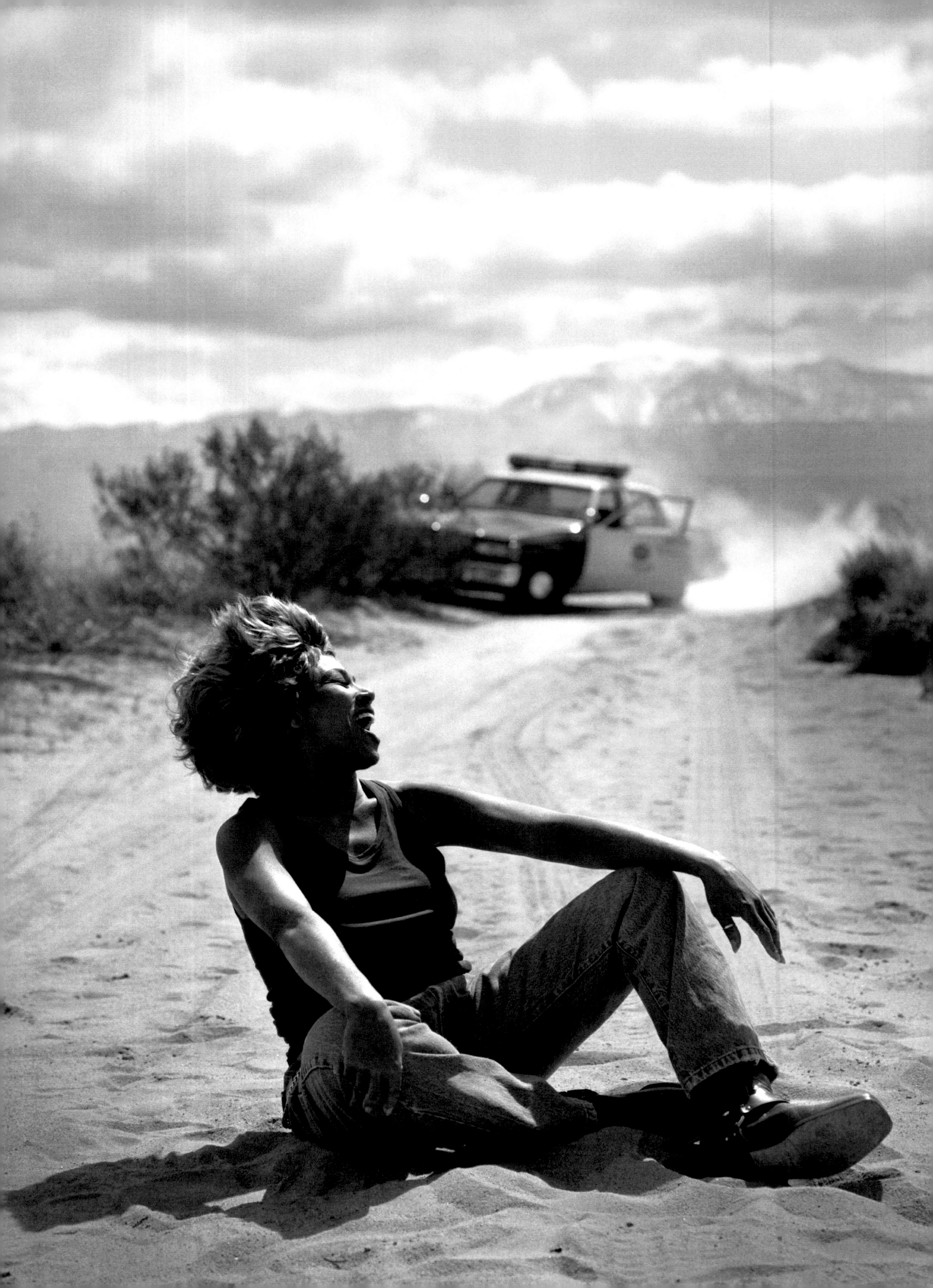

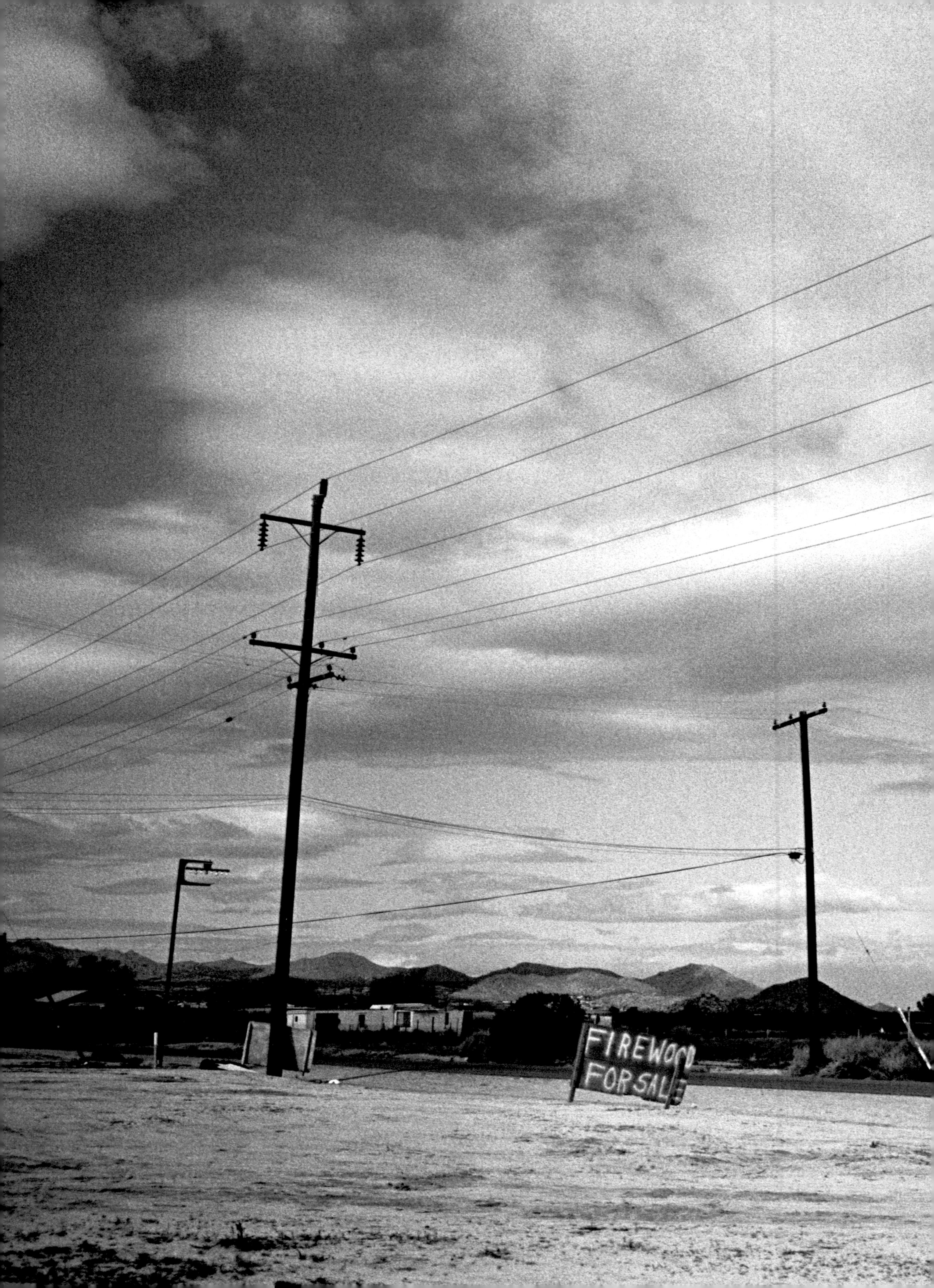
FIREWOOD
FOR SALE

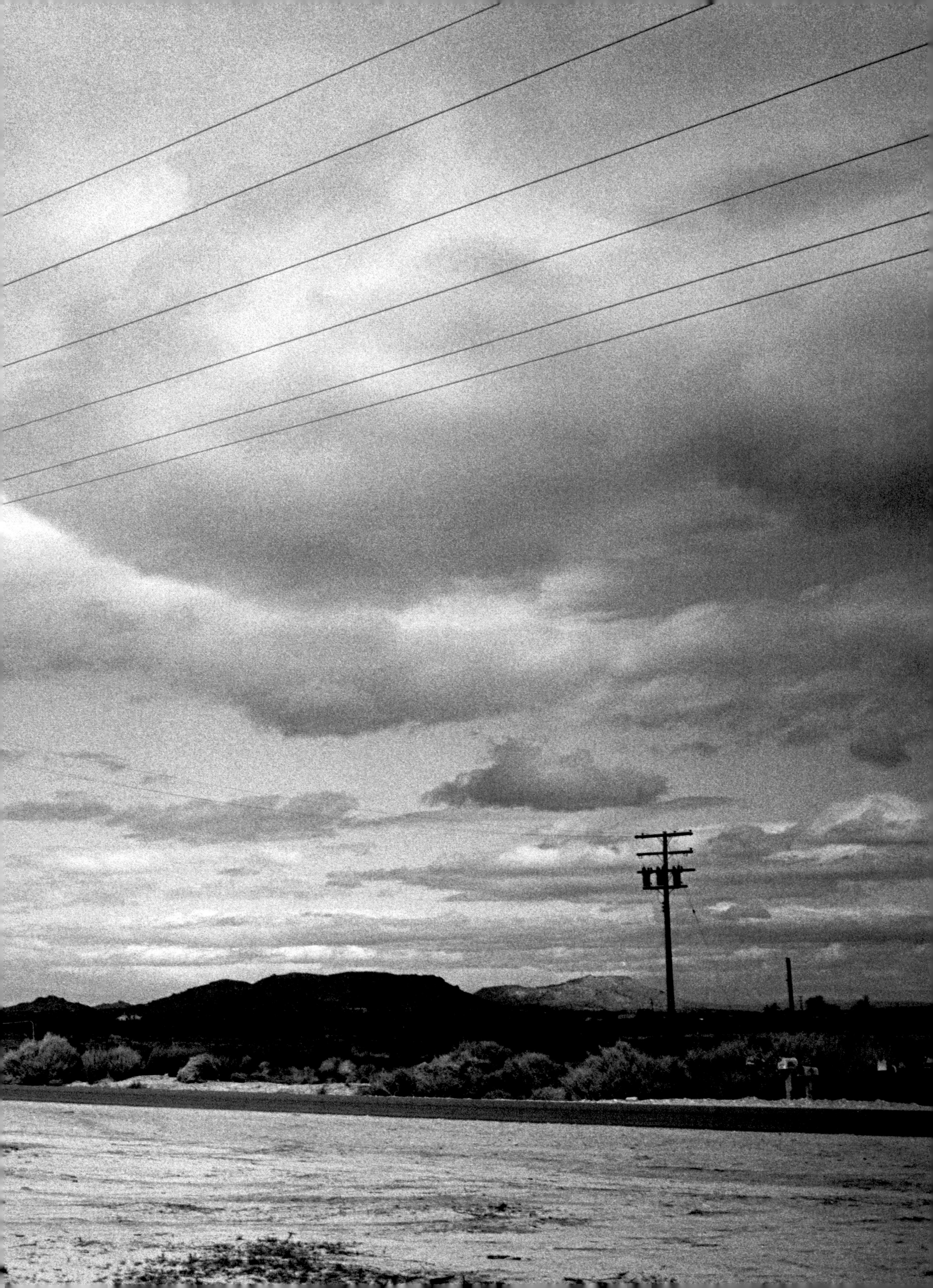

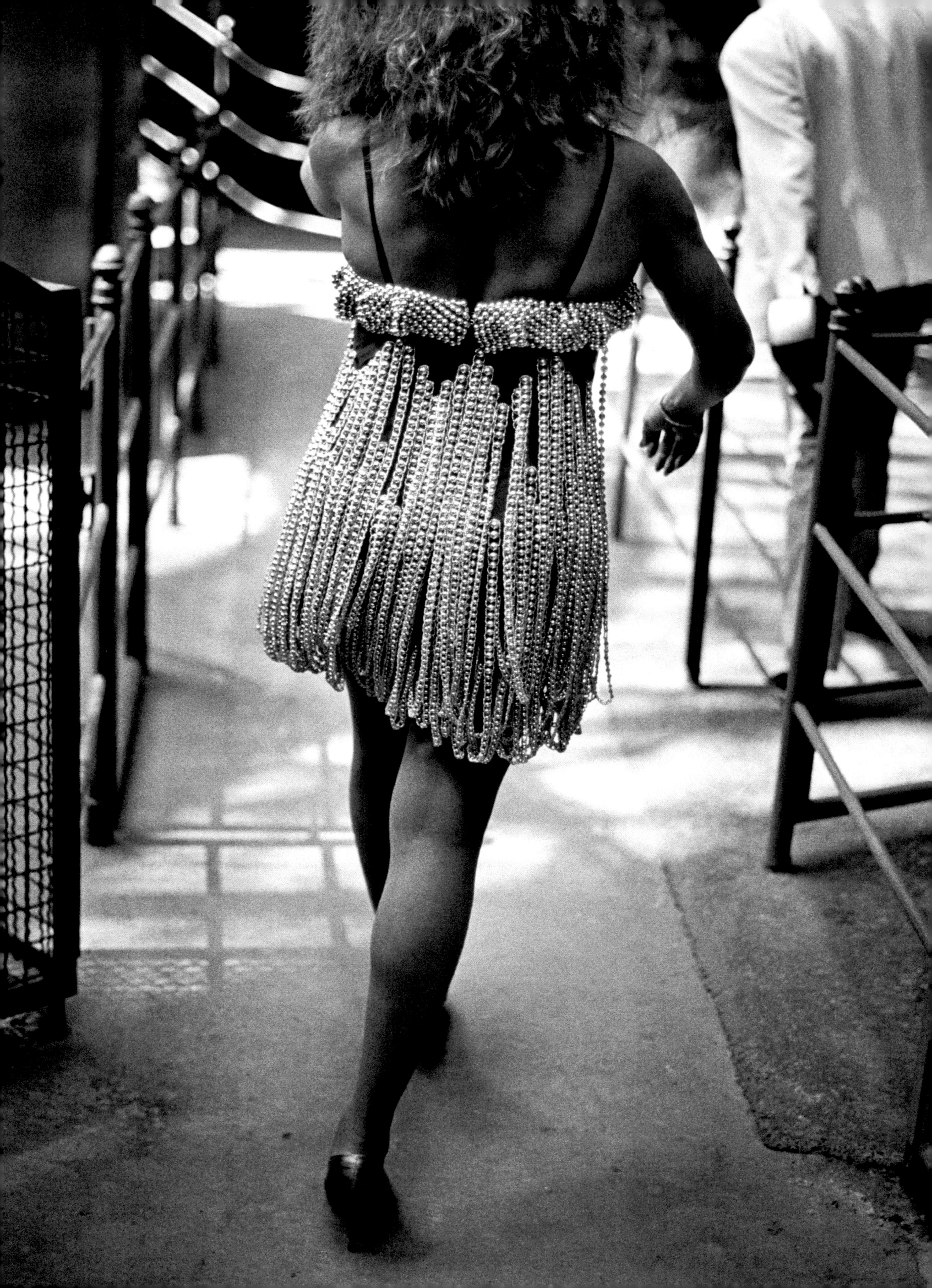

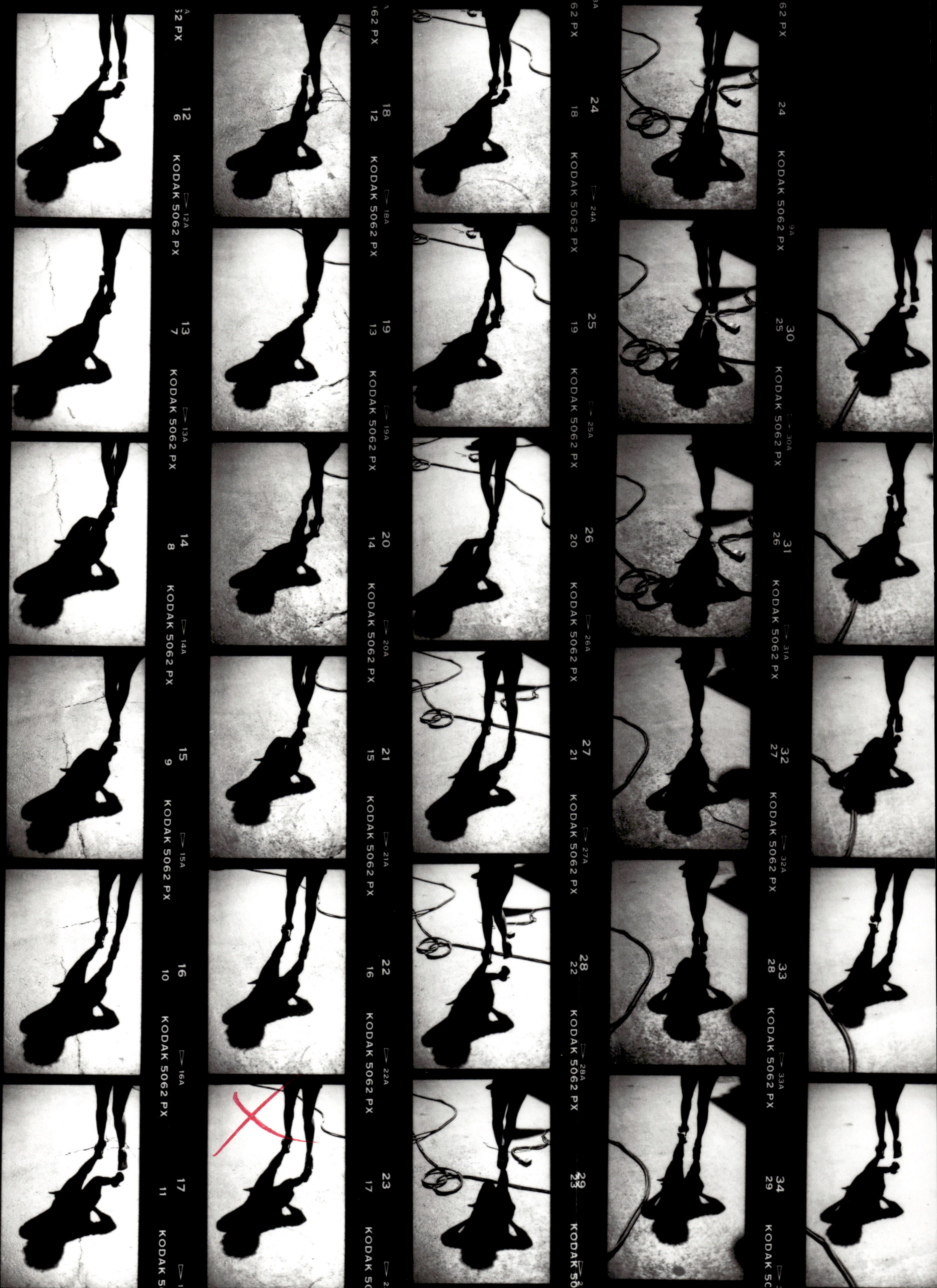
KODAK 5062 PX

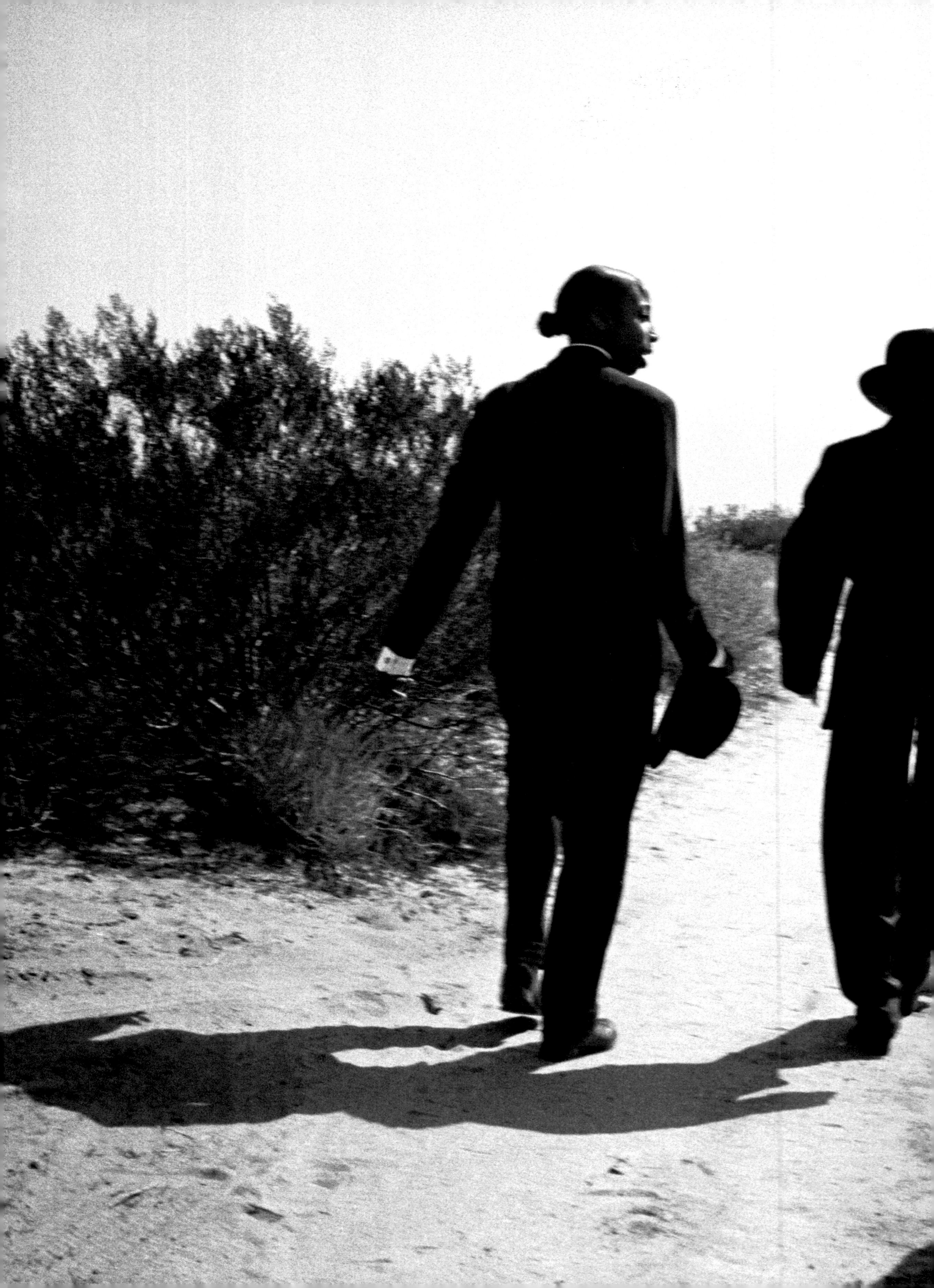

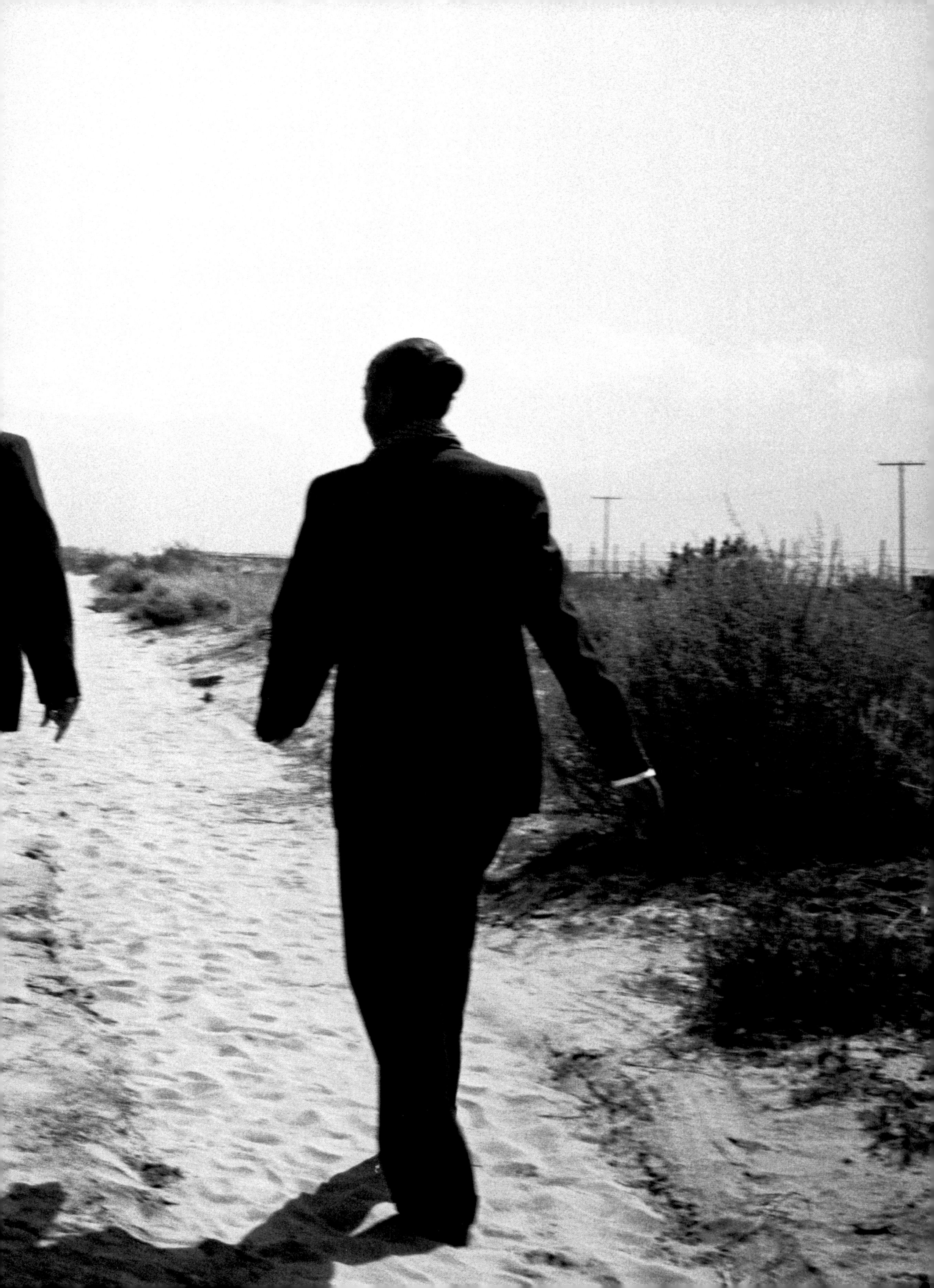

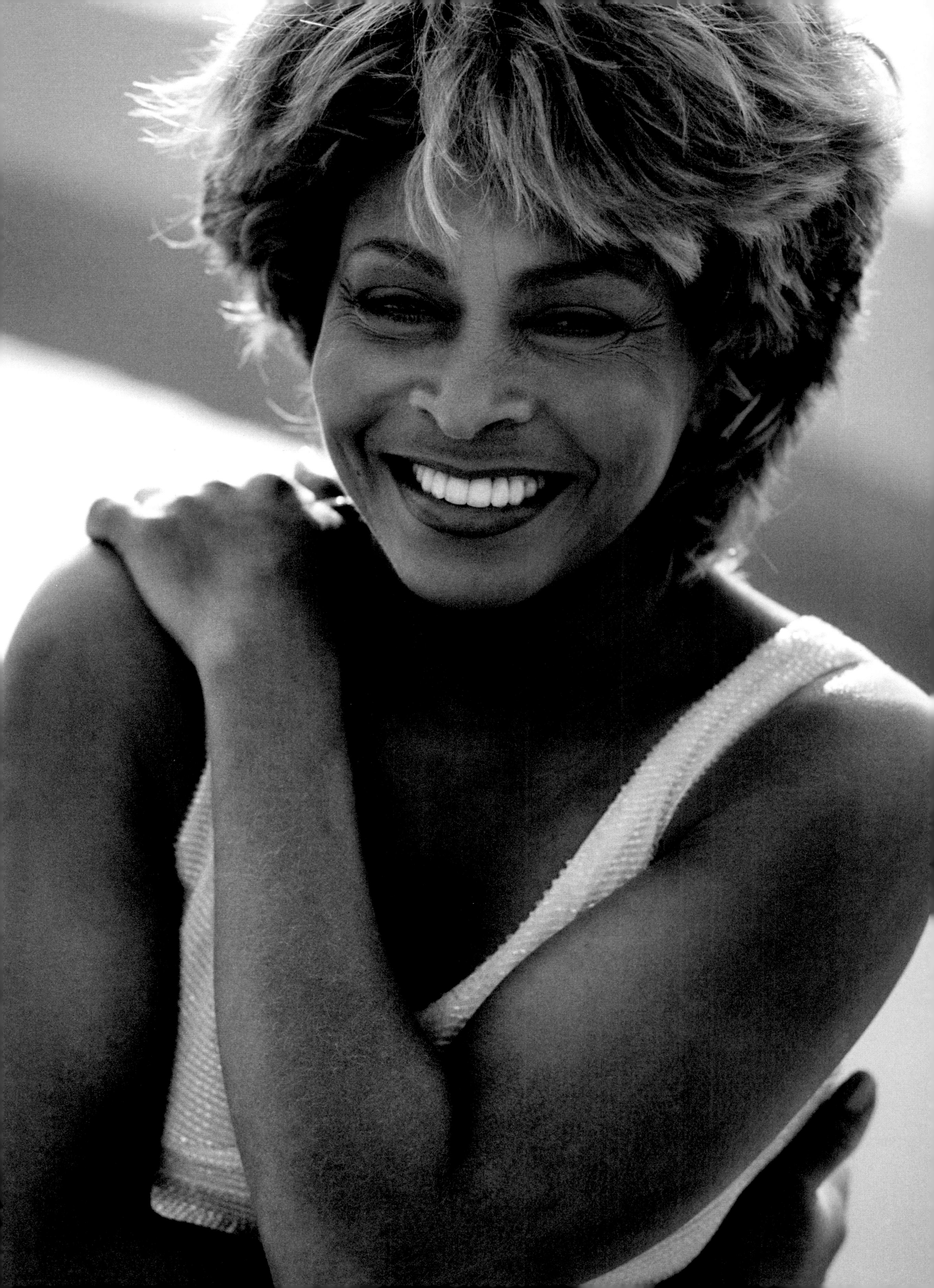

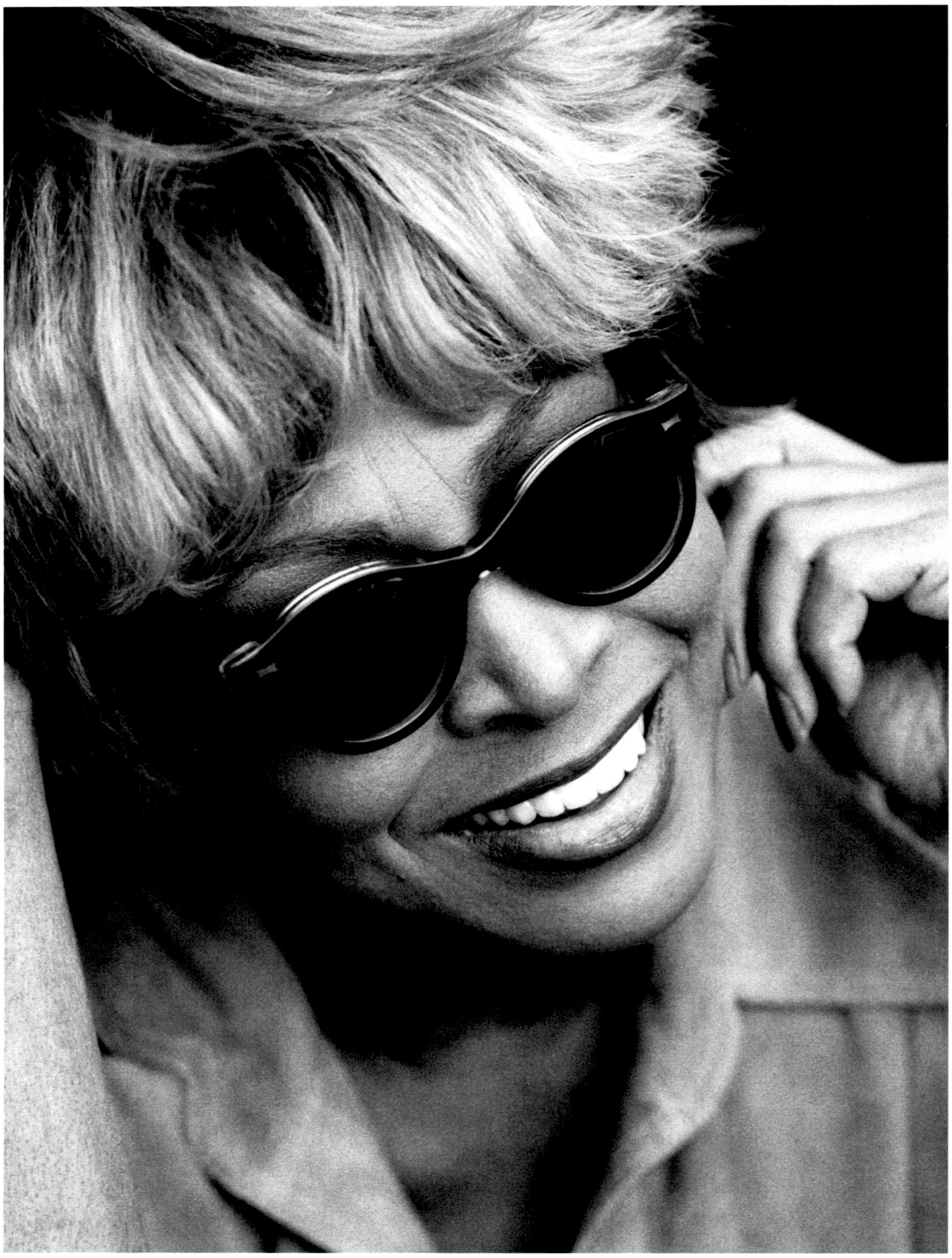

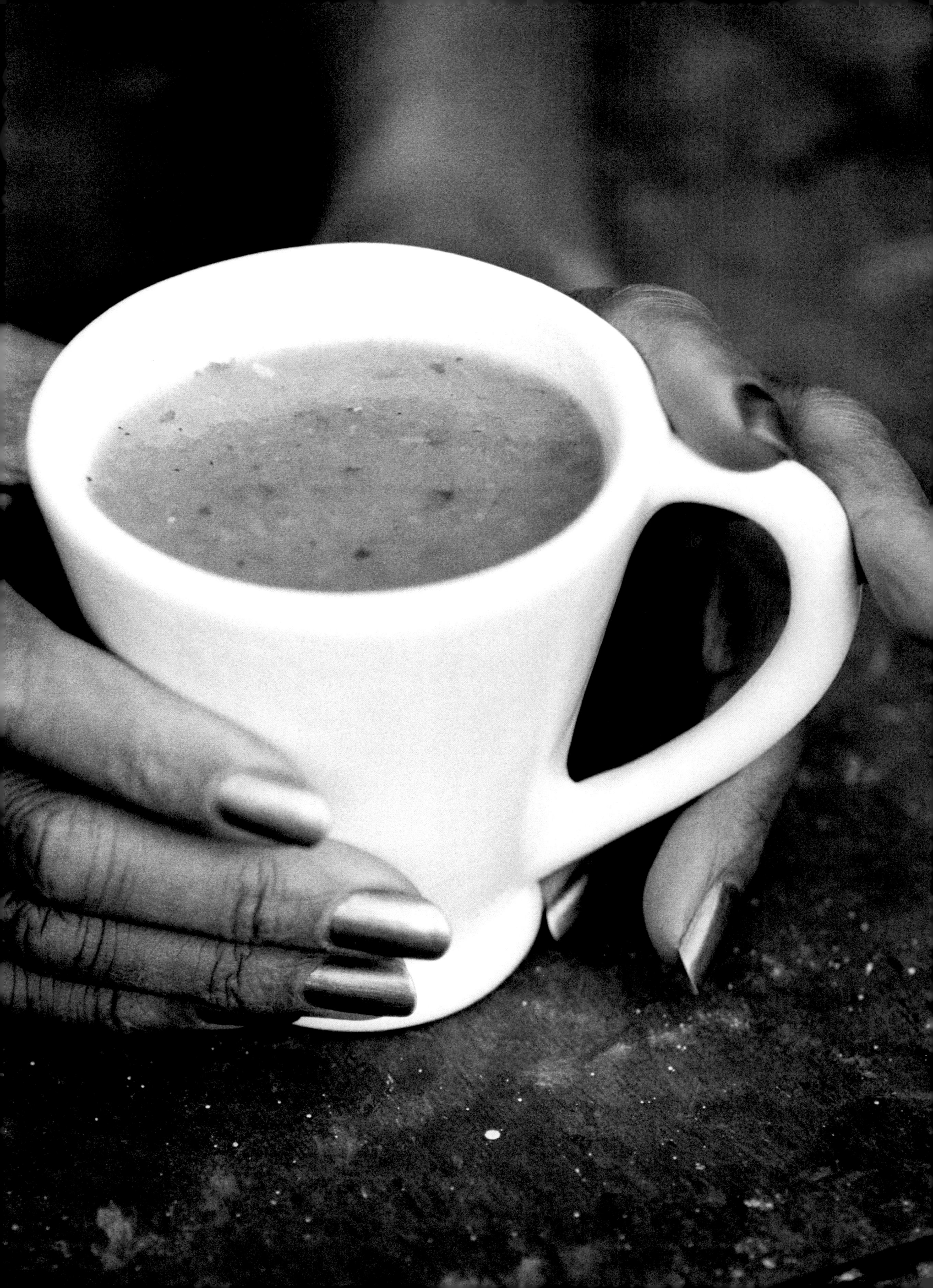

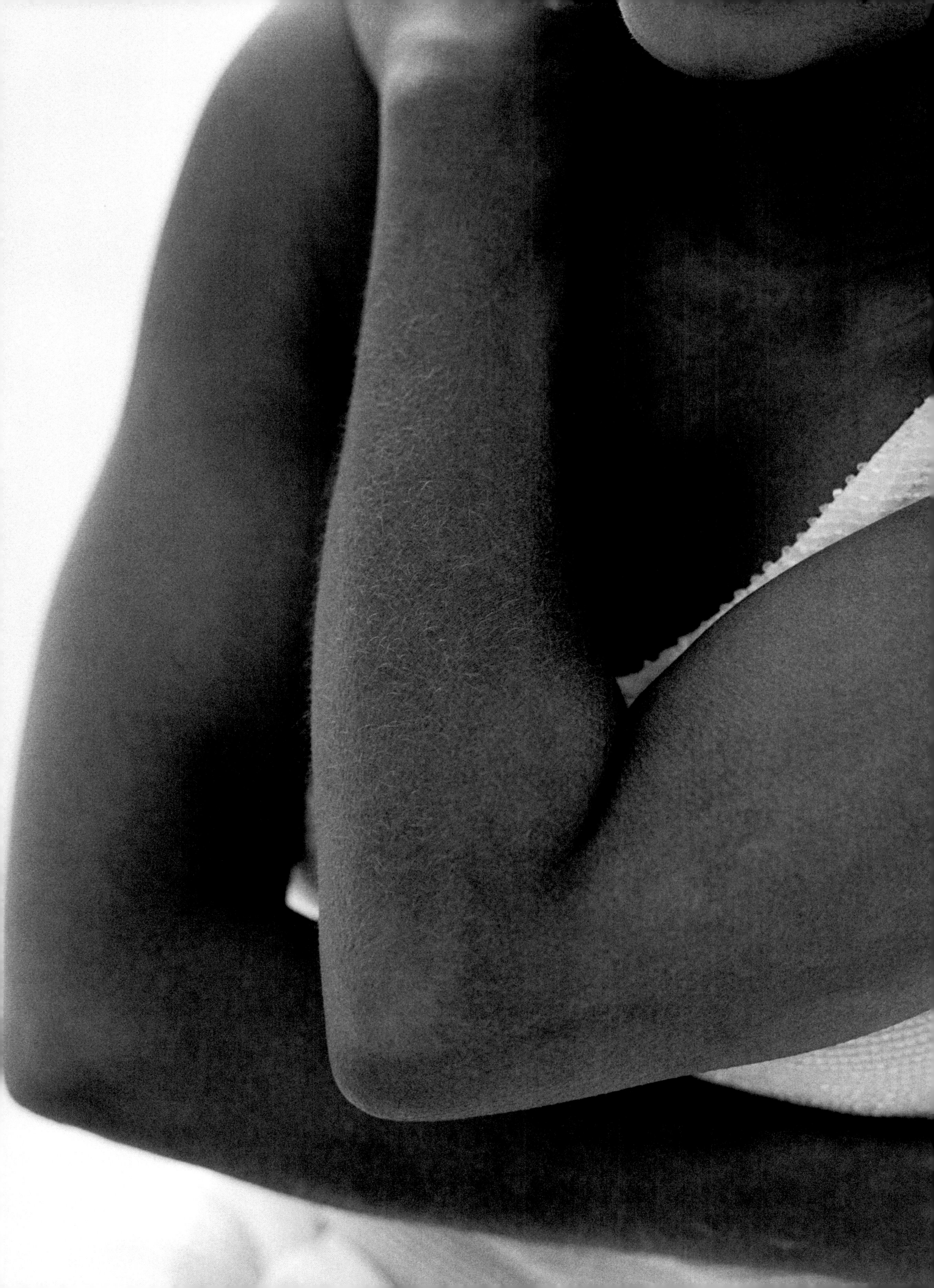

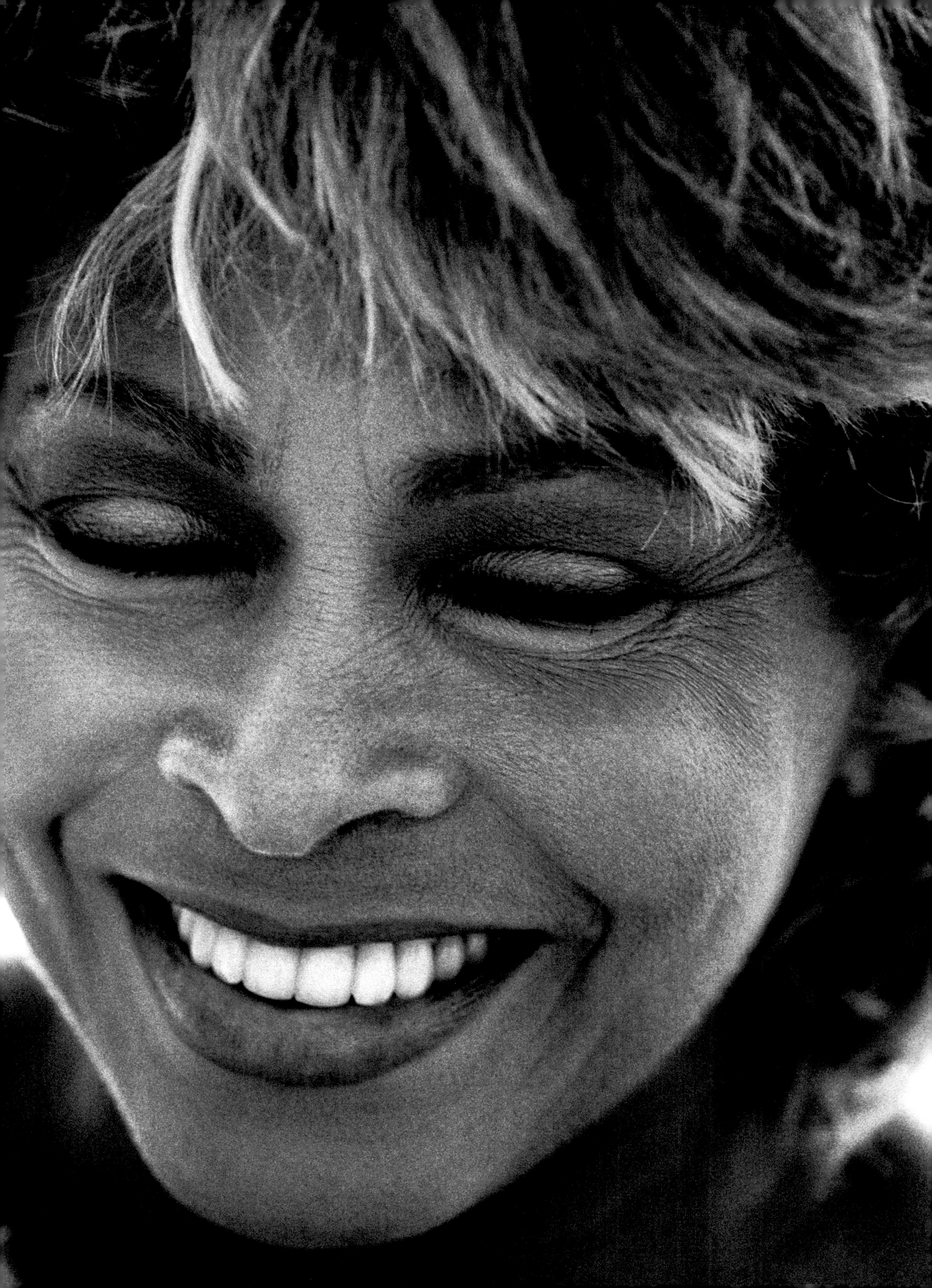

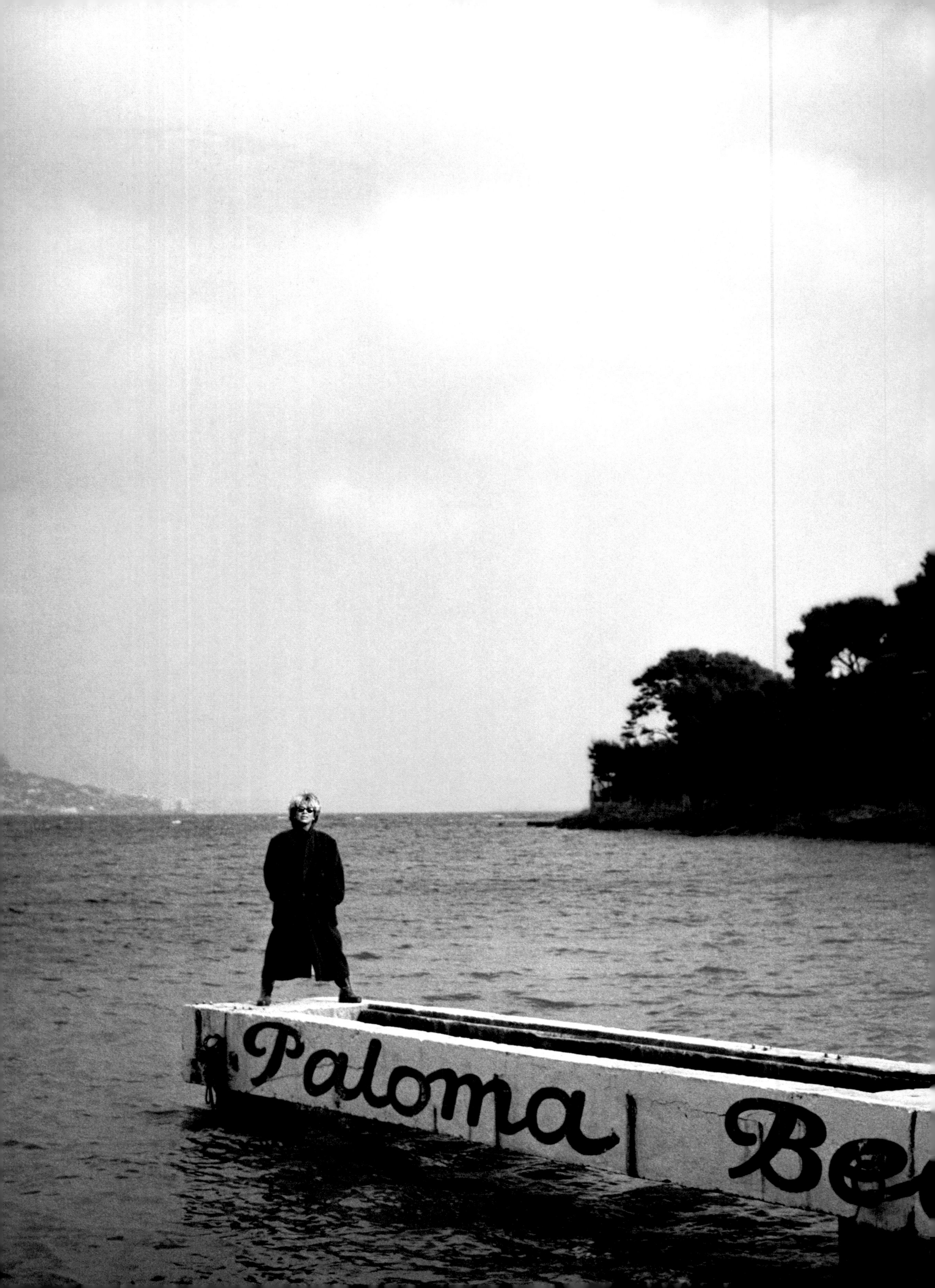
Paloma

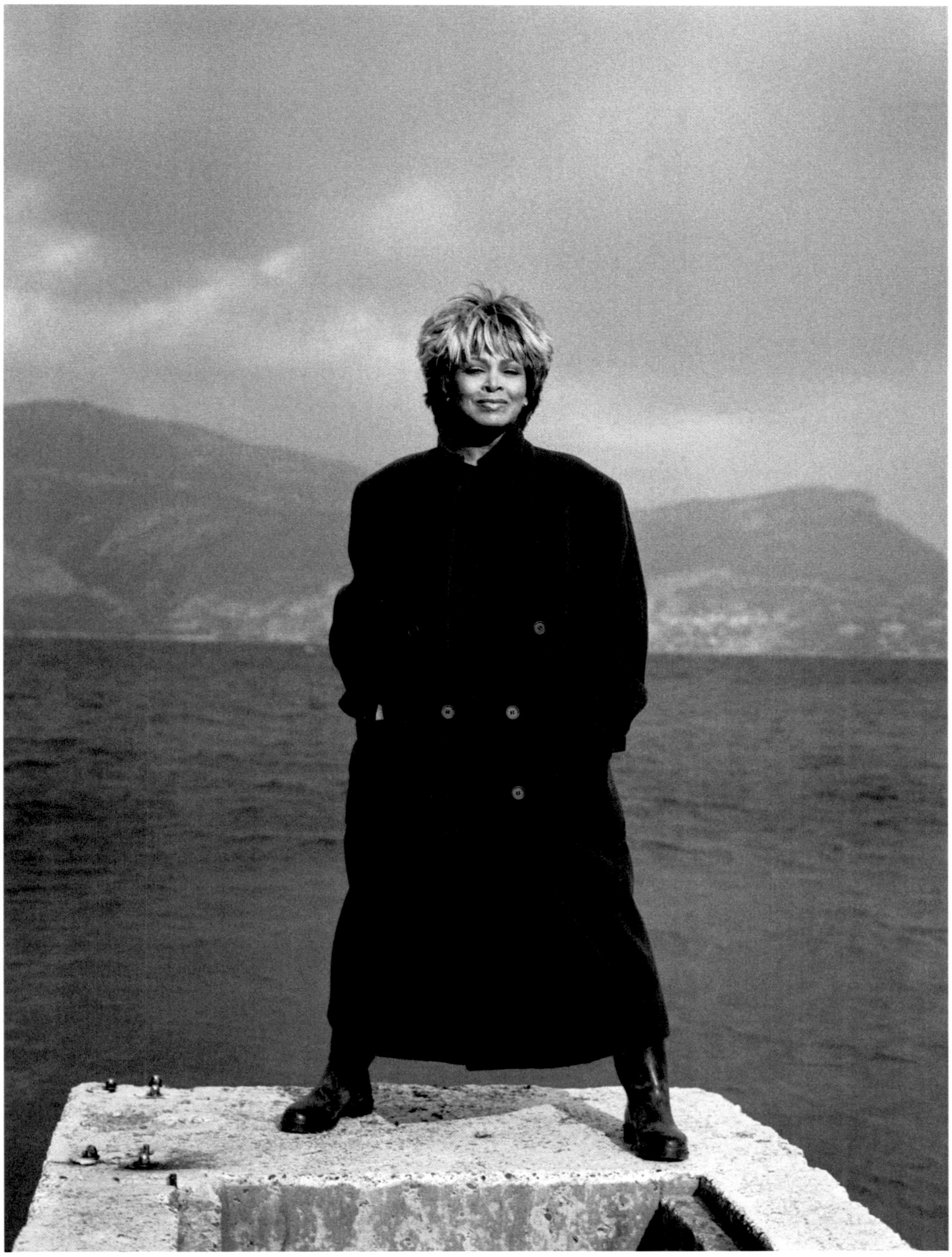

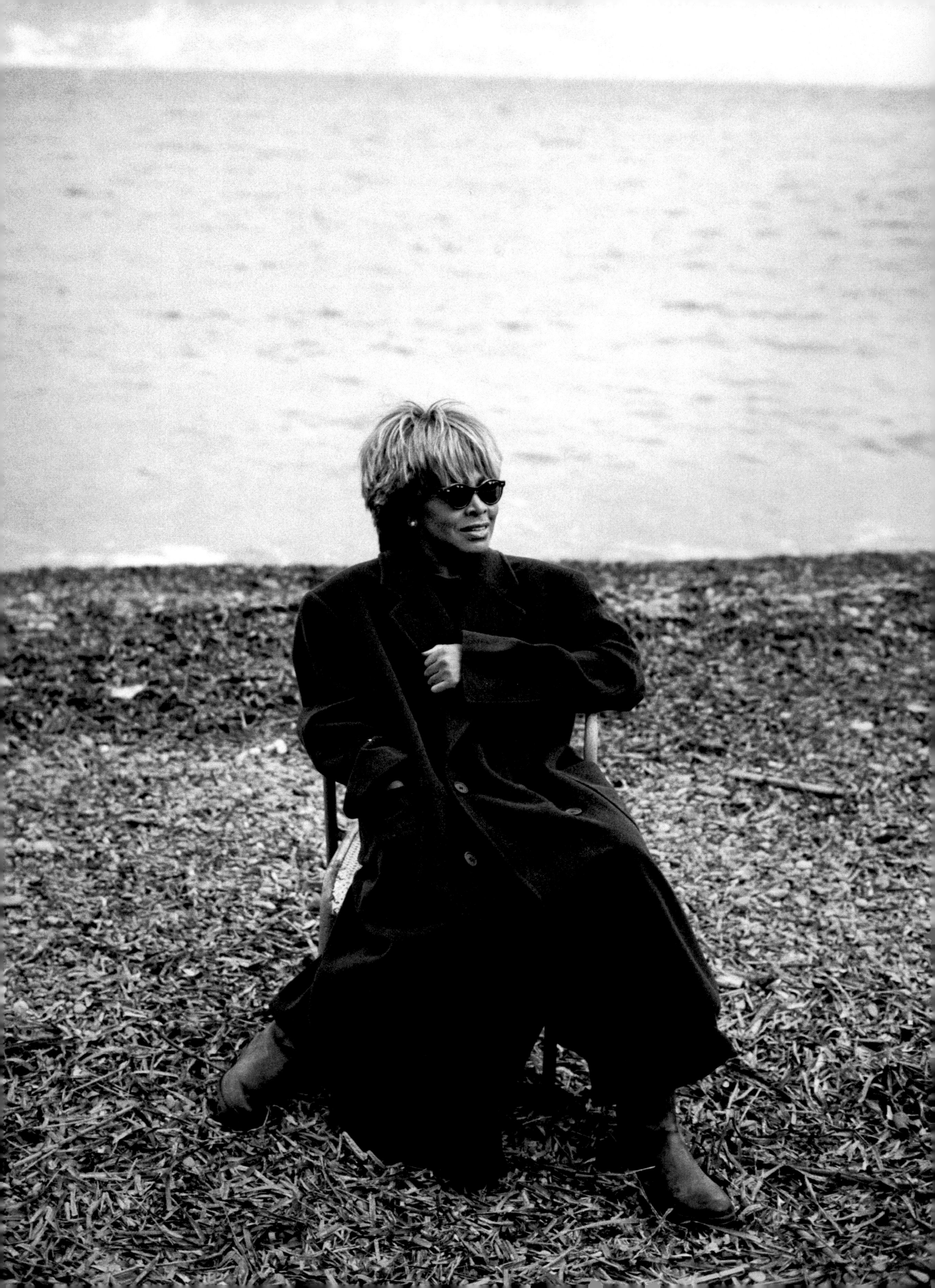

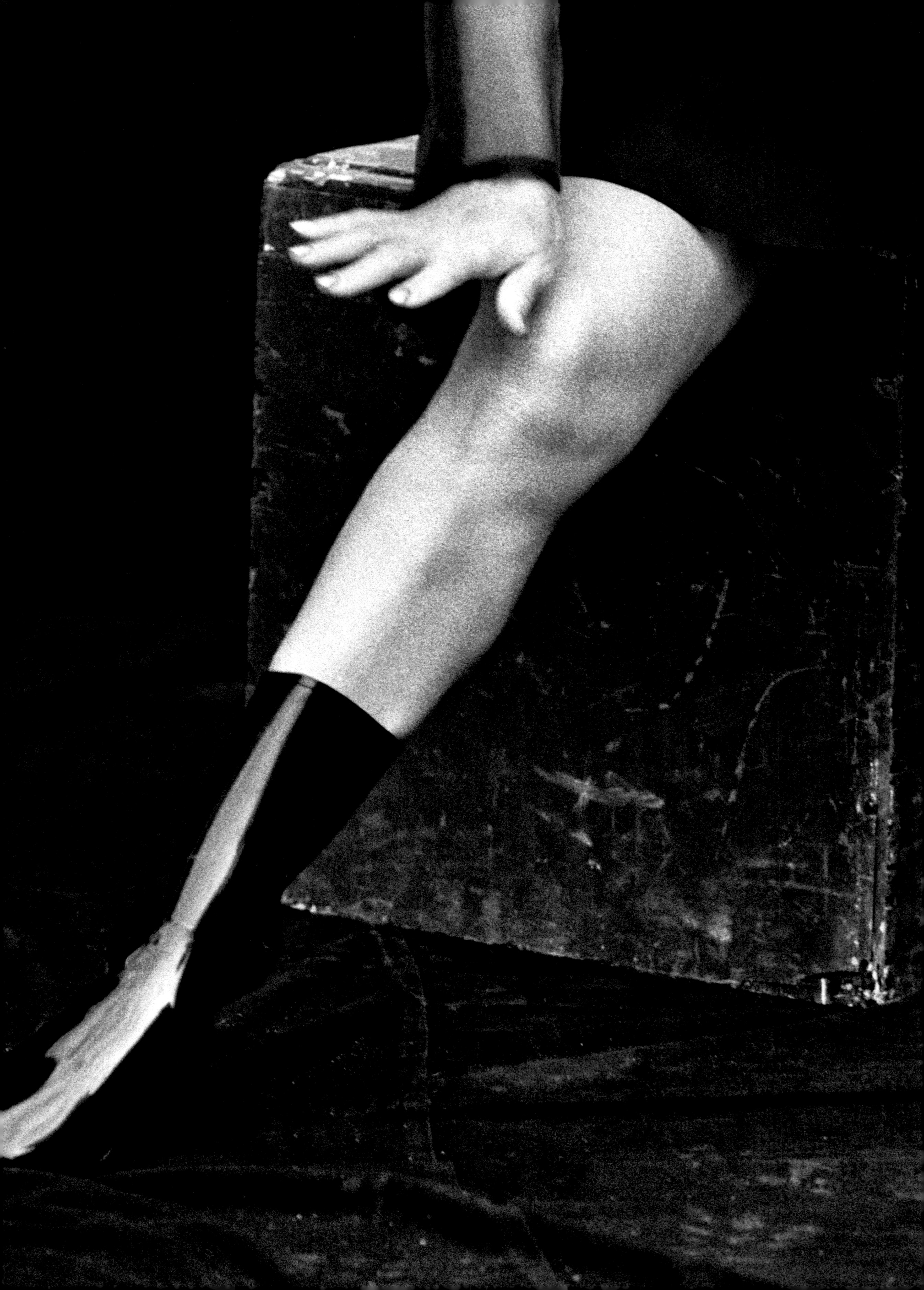

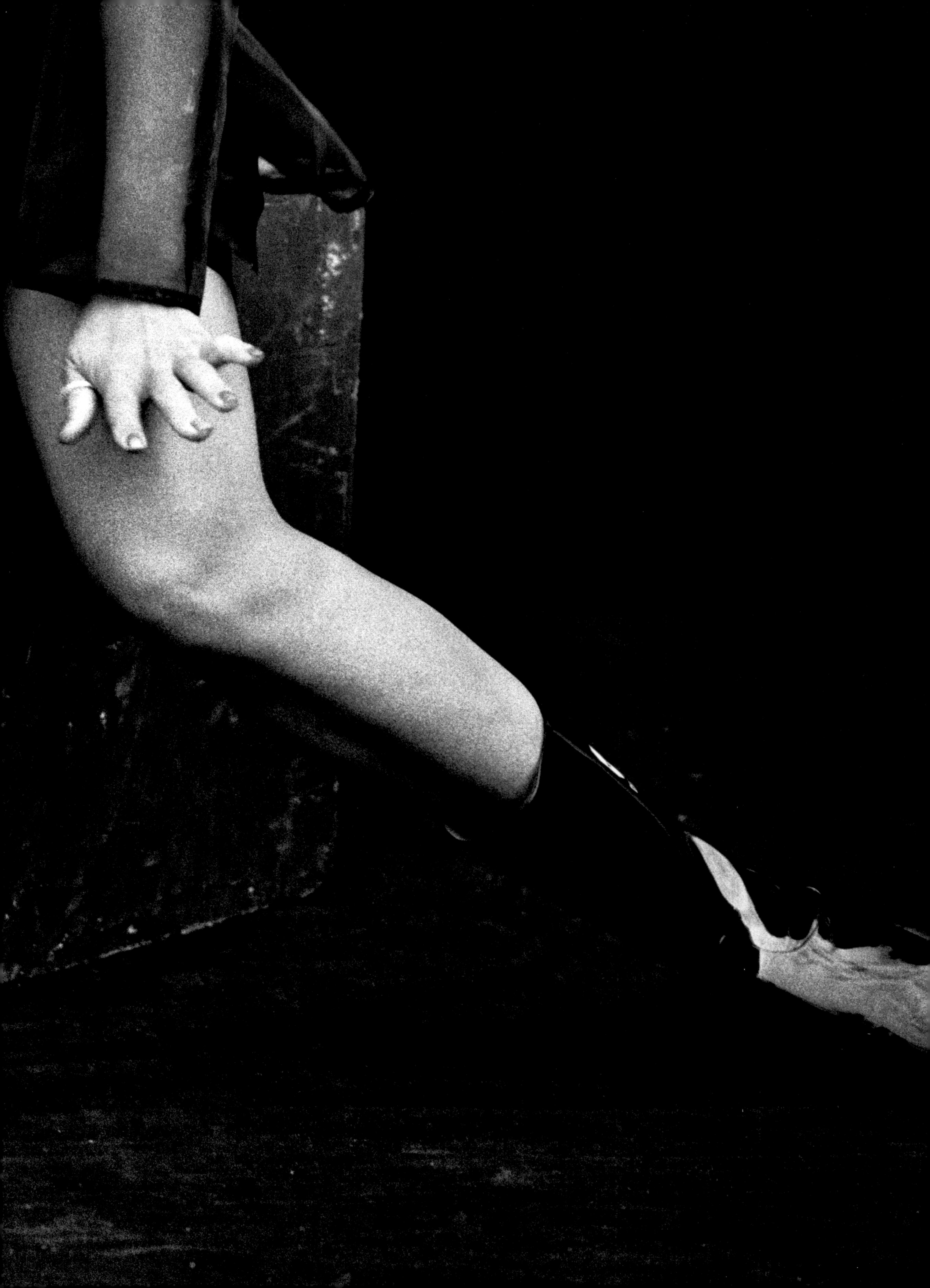

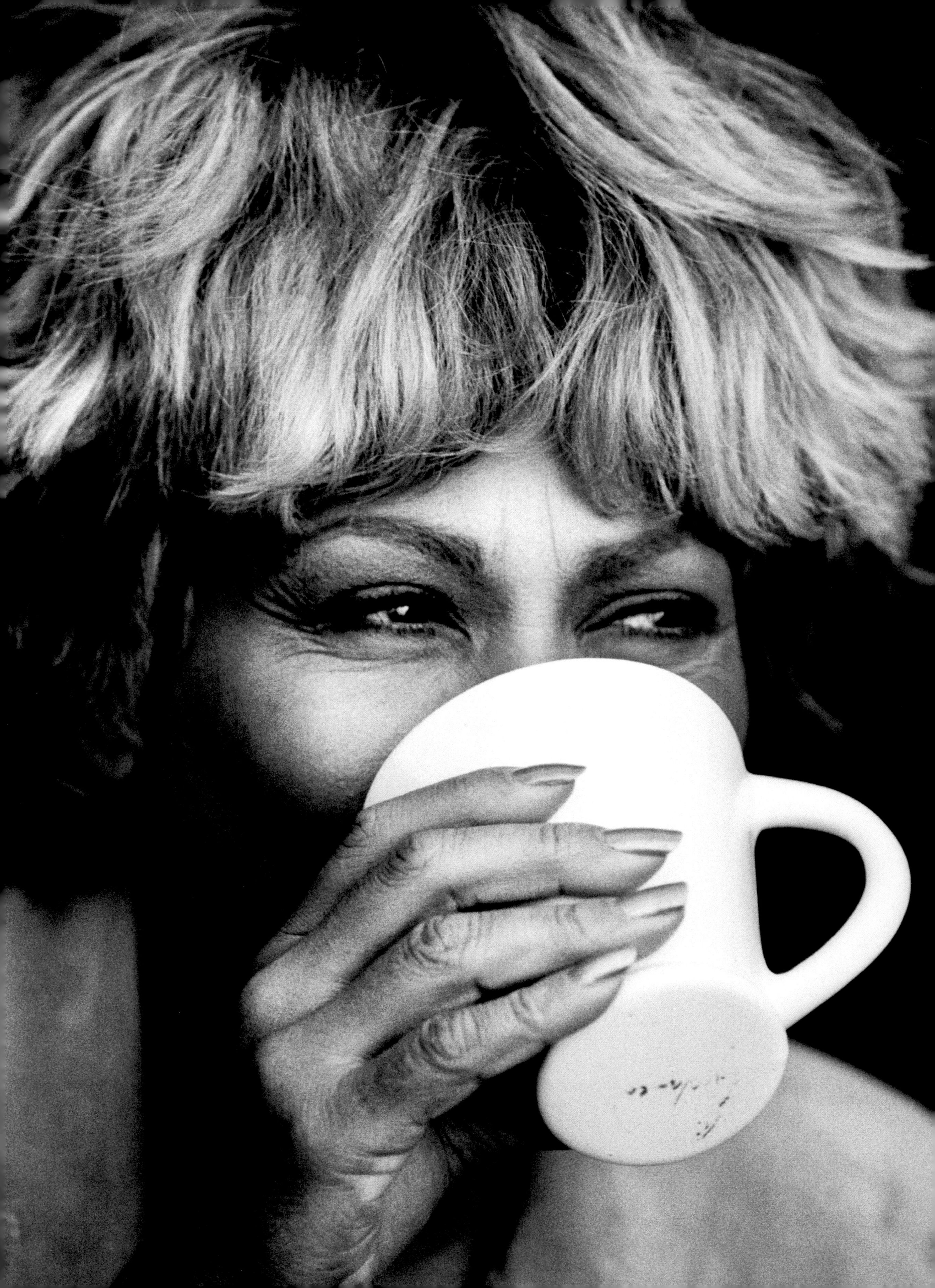

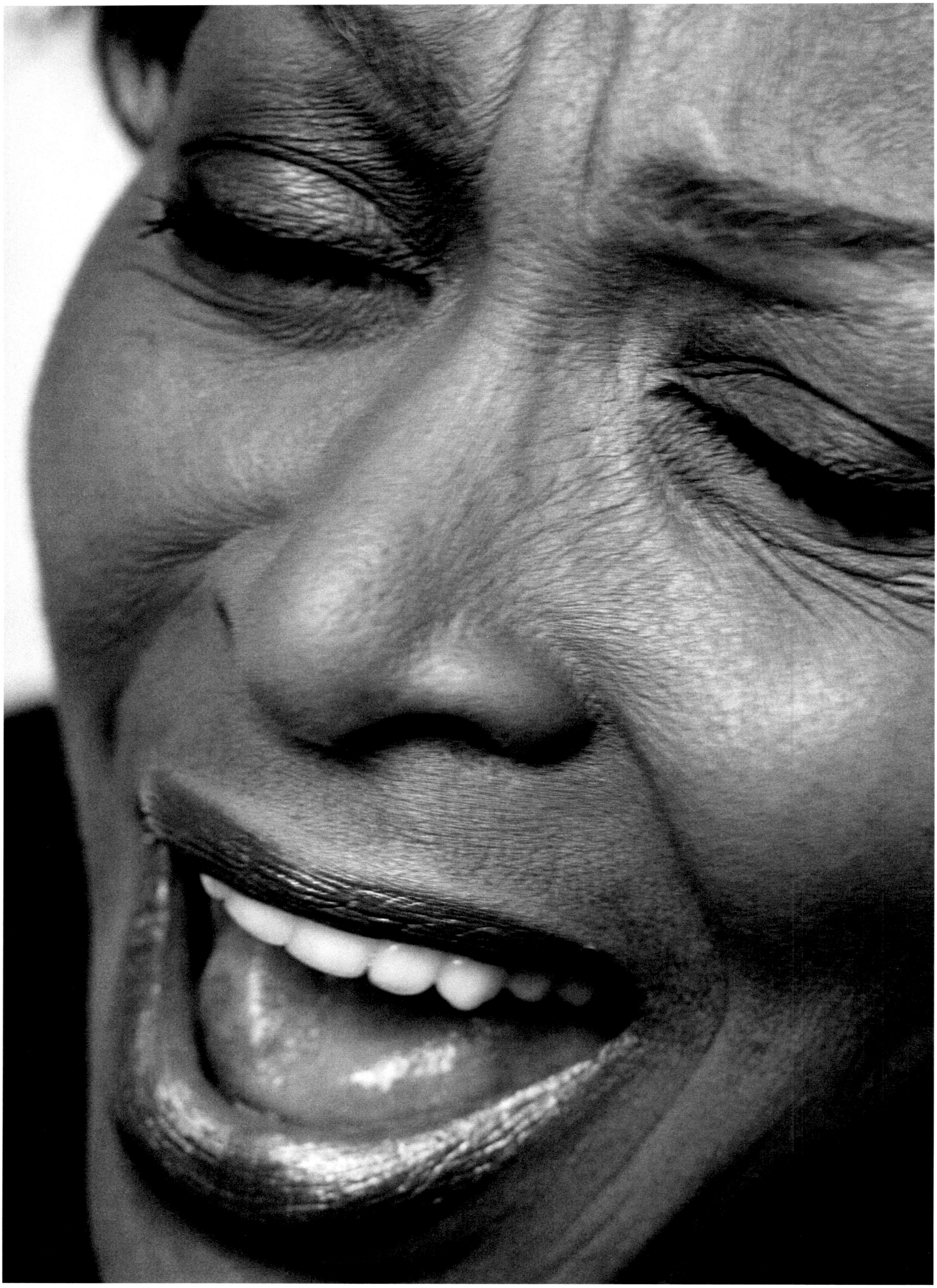

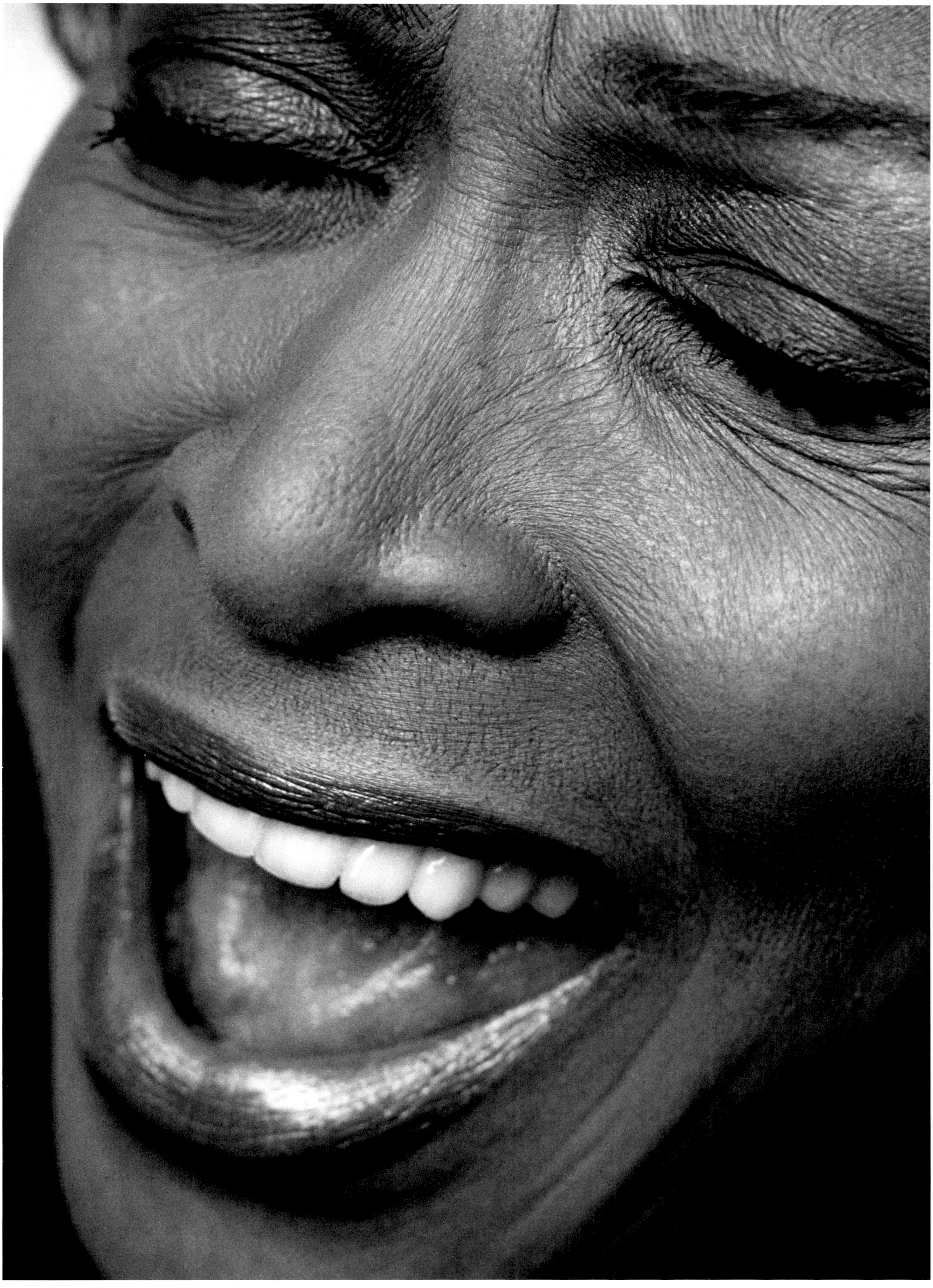

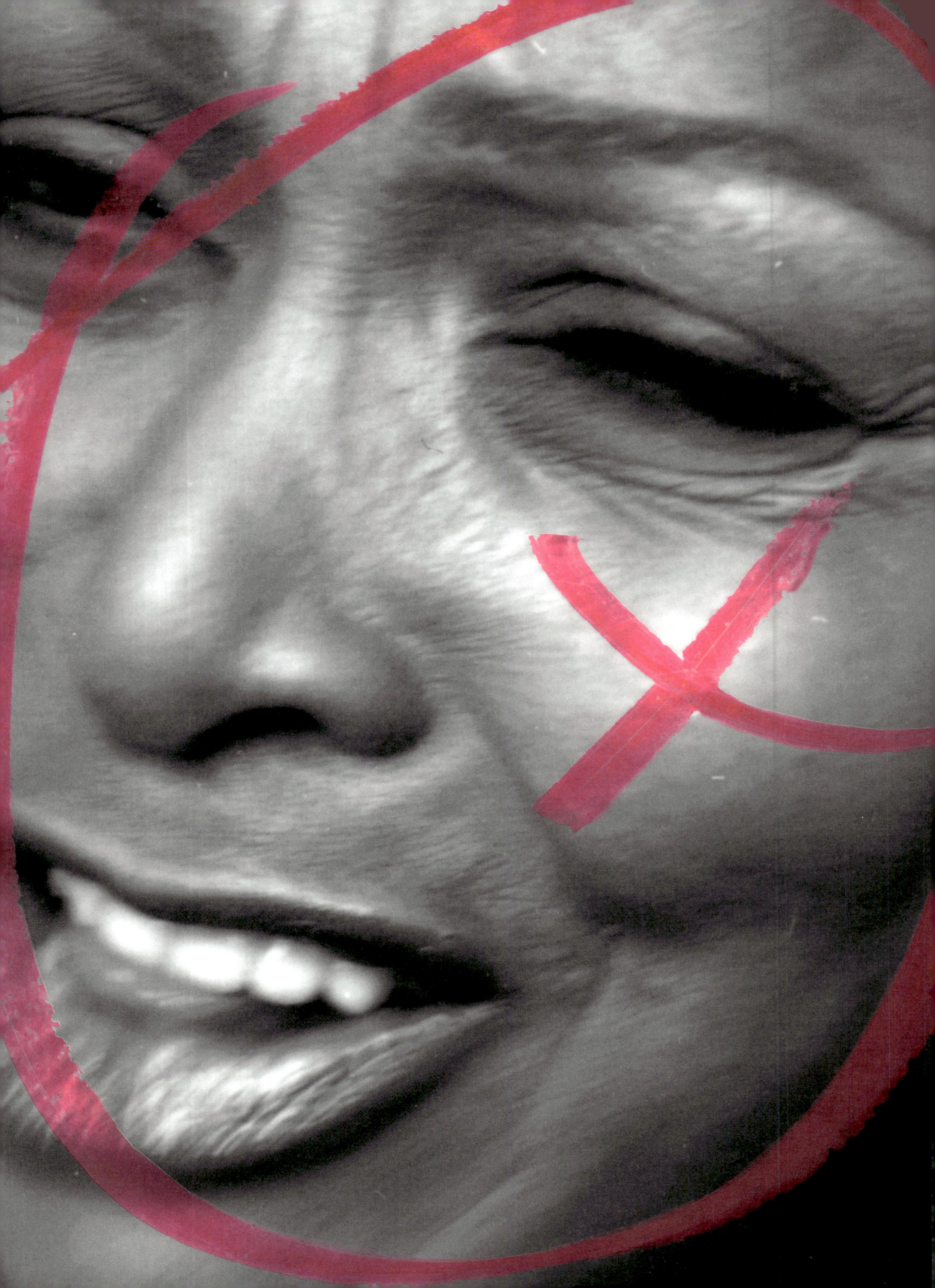

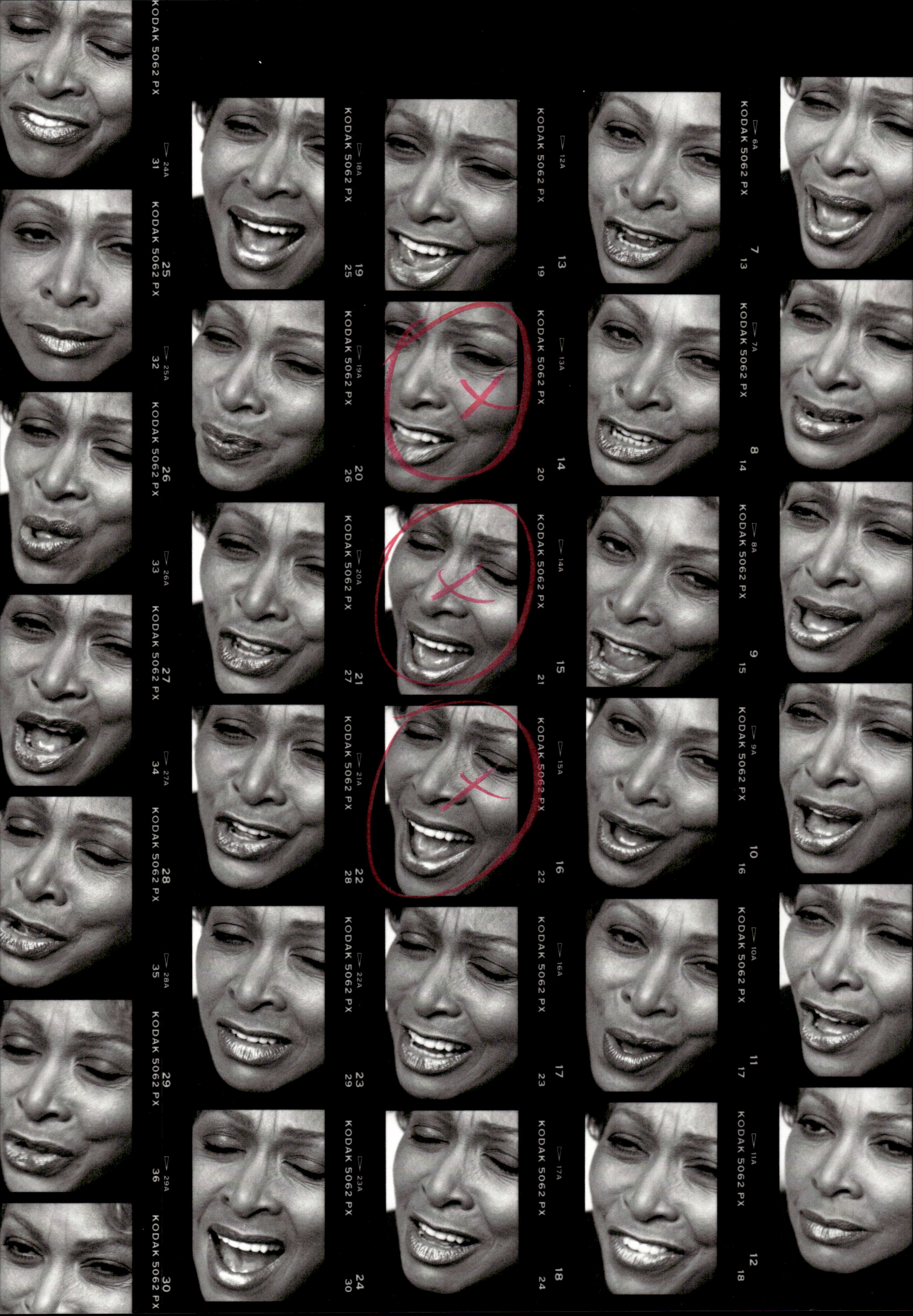

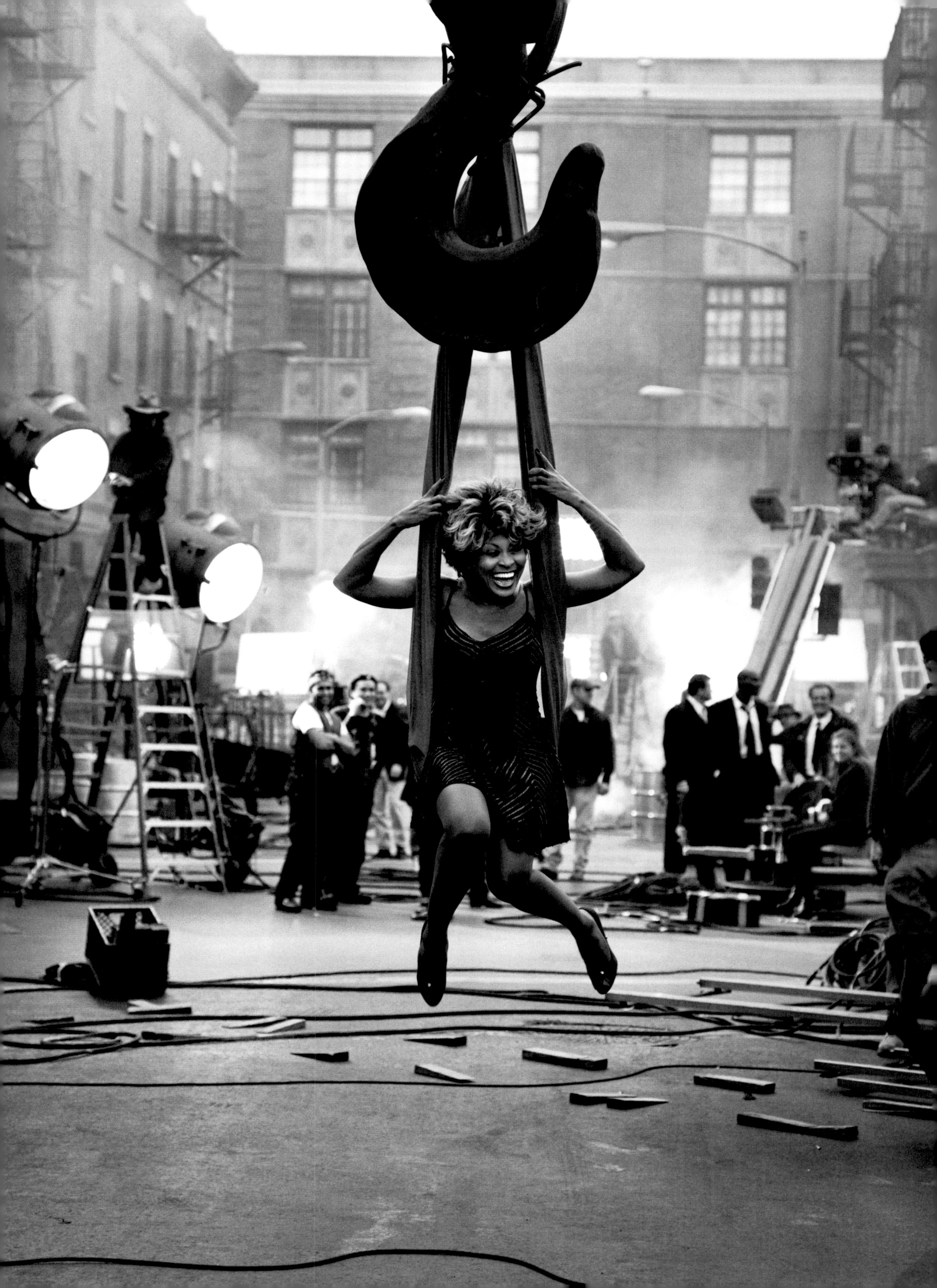

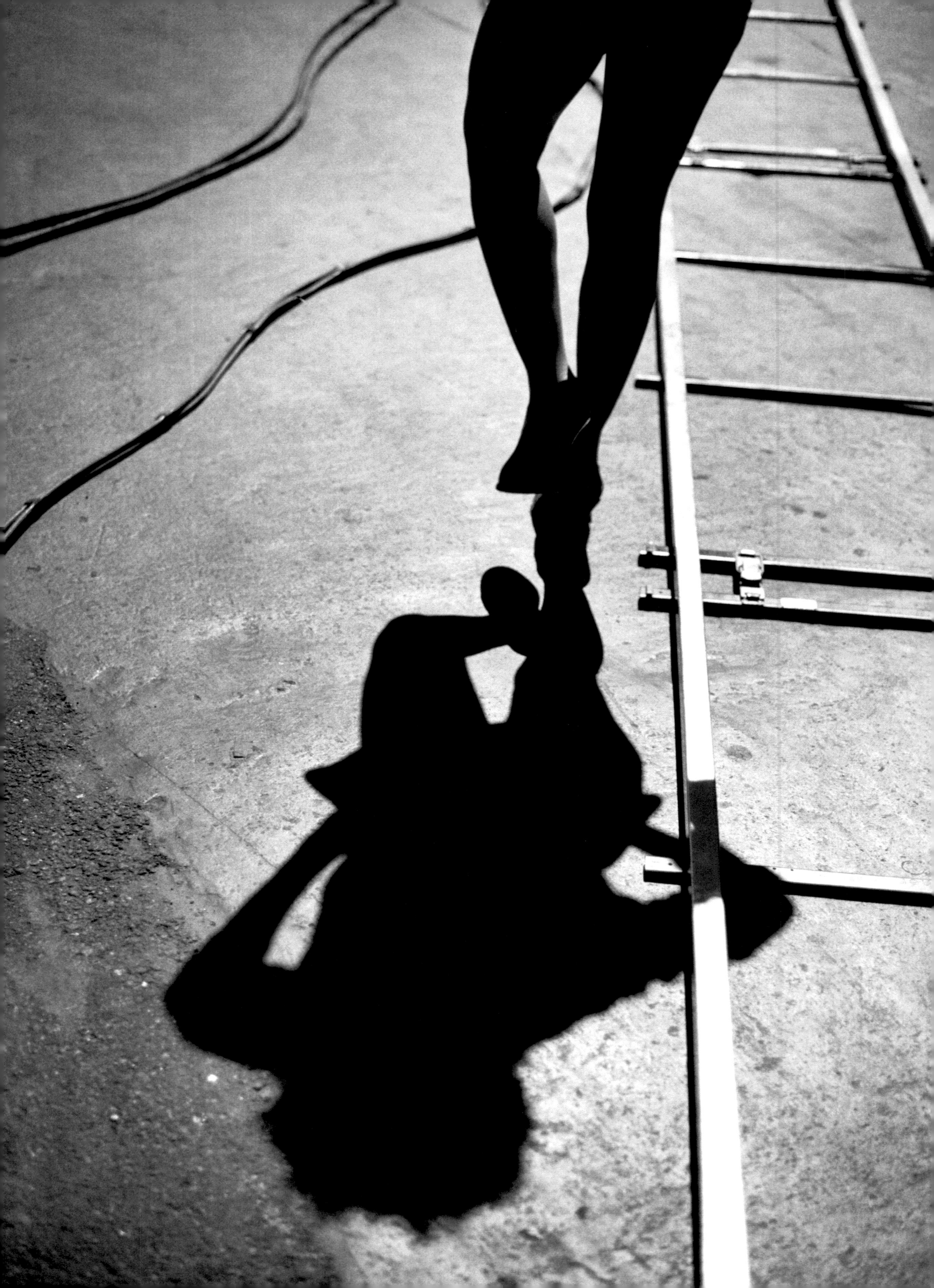

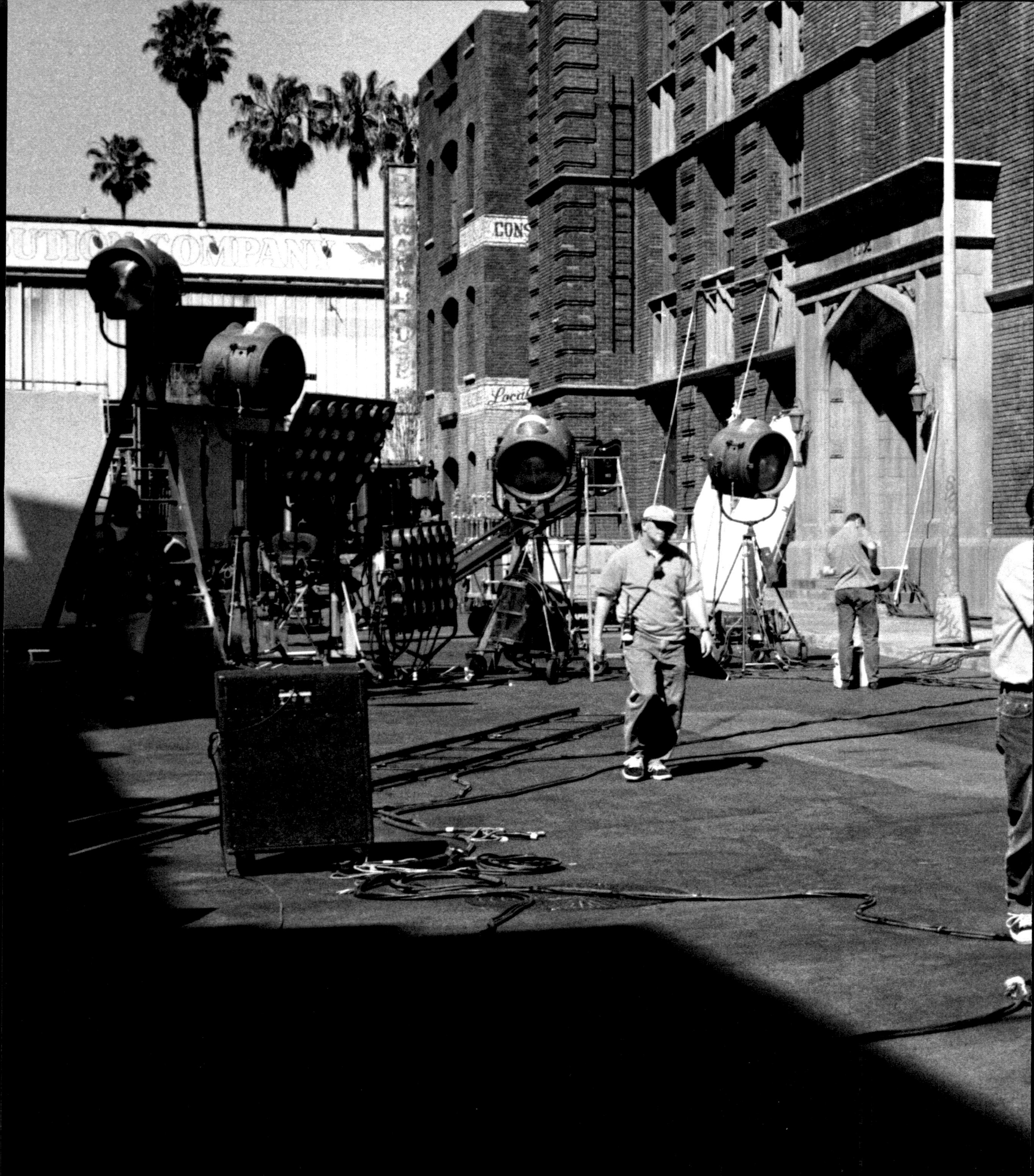
COMPANY
CONS

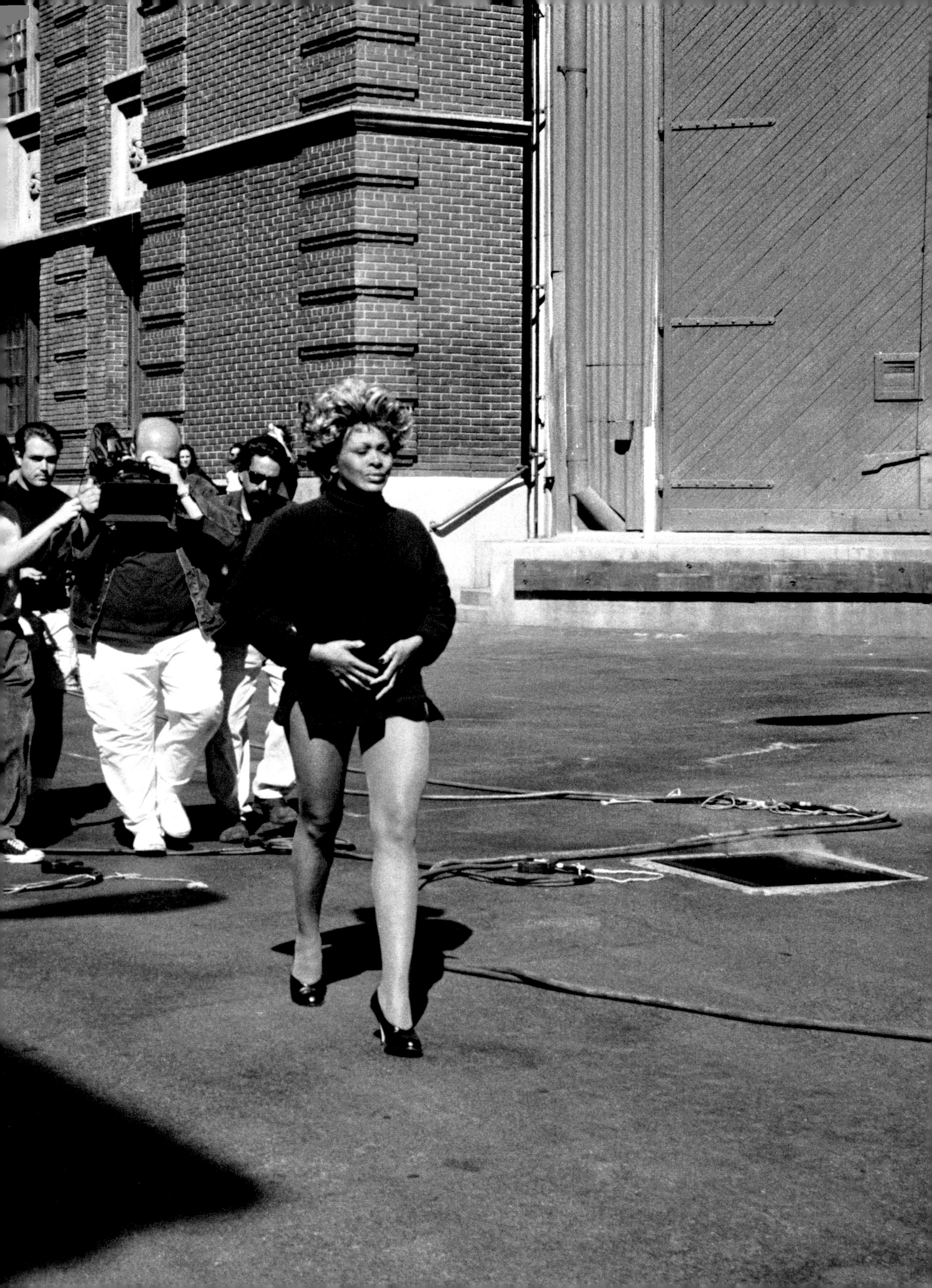

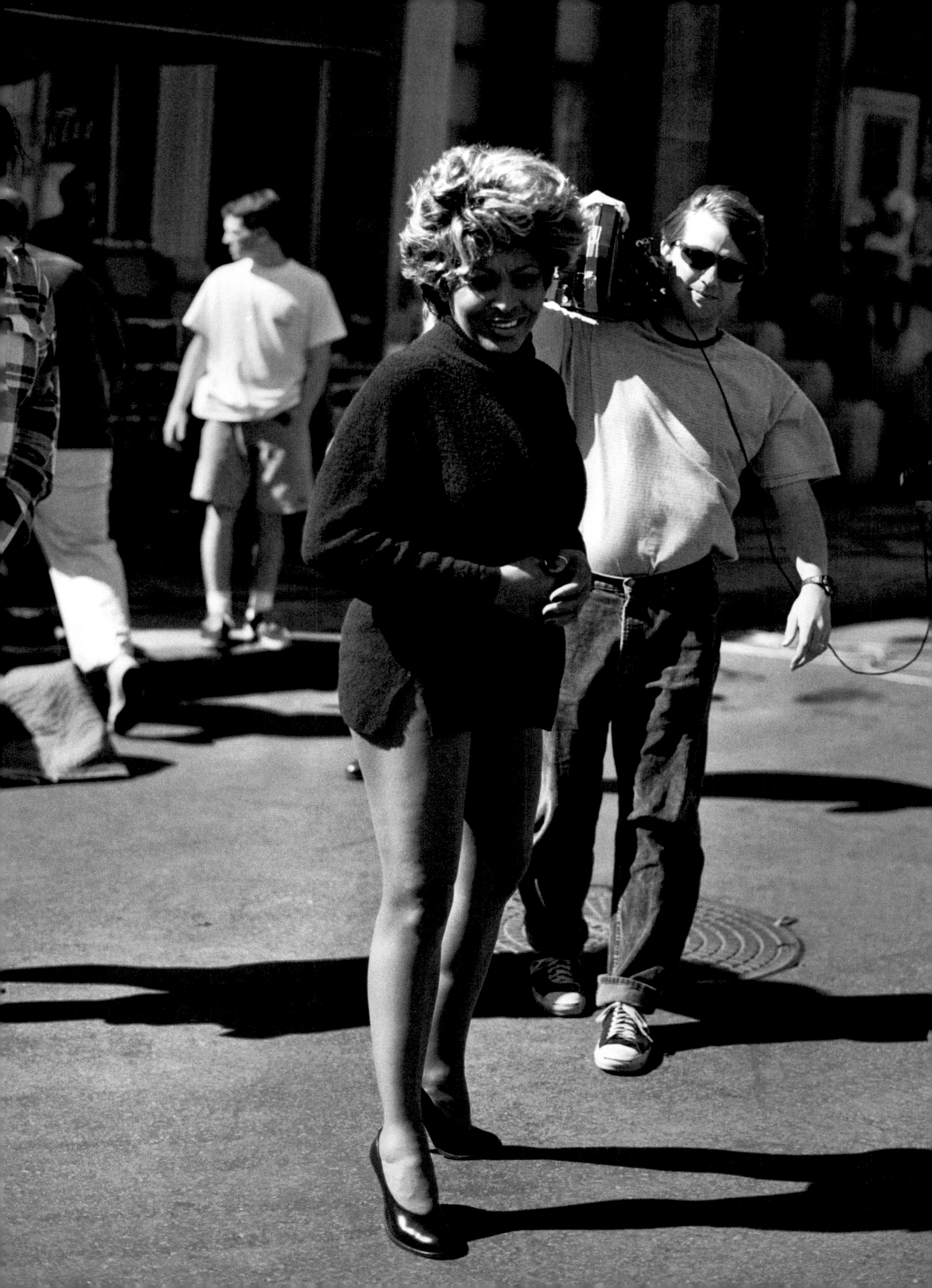

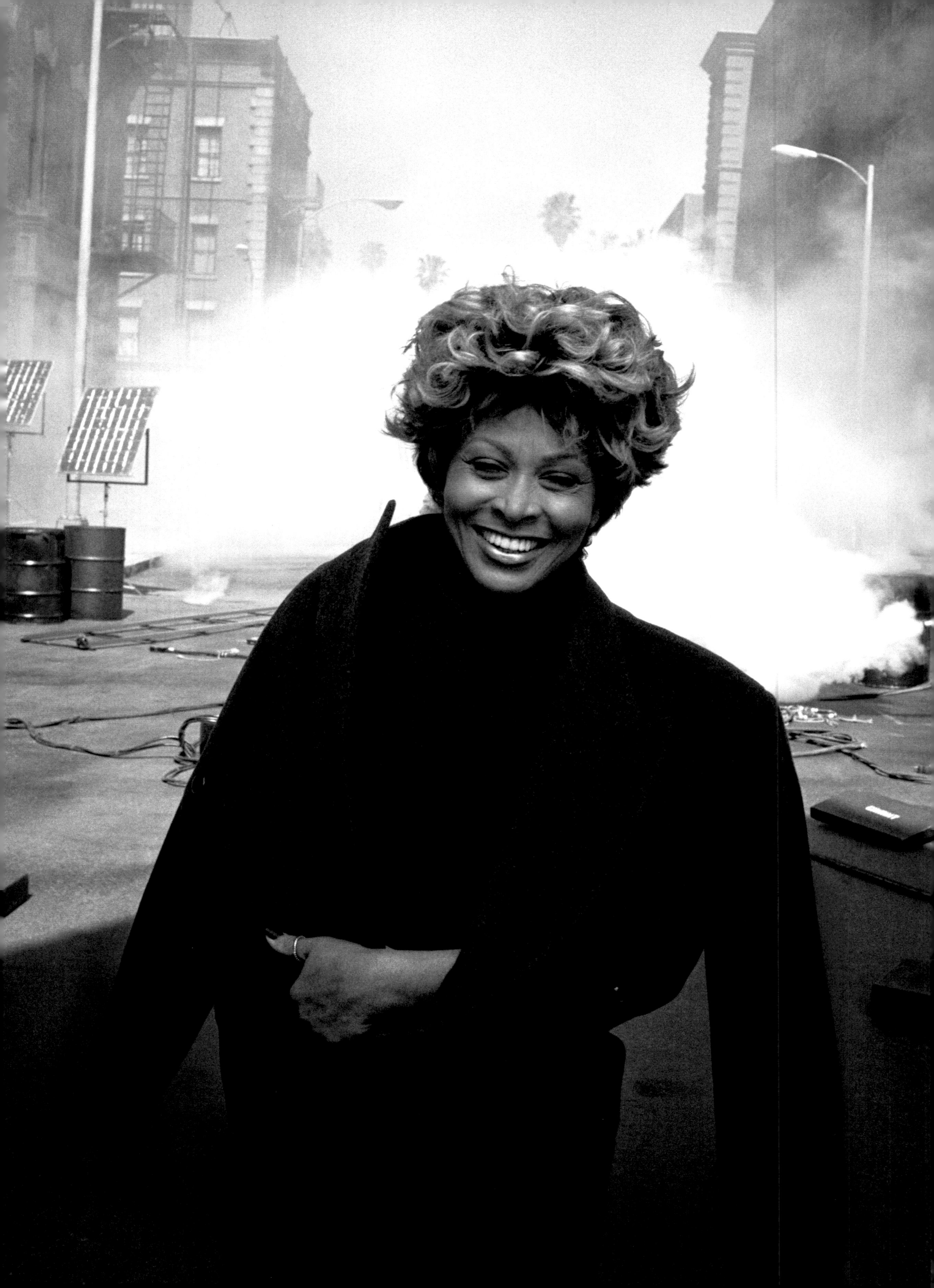

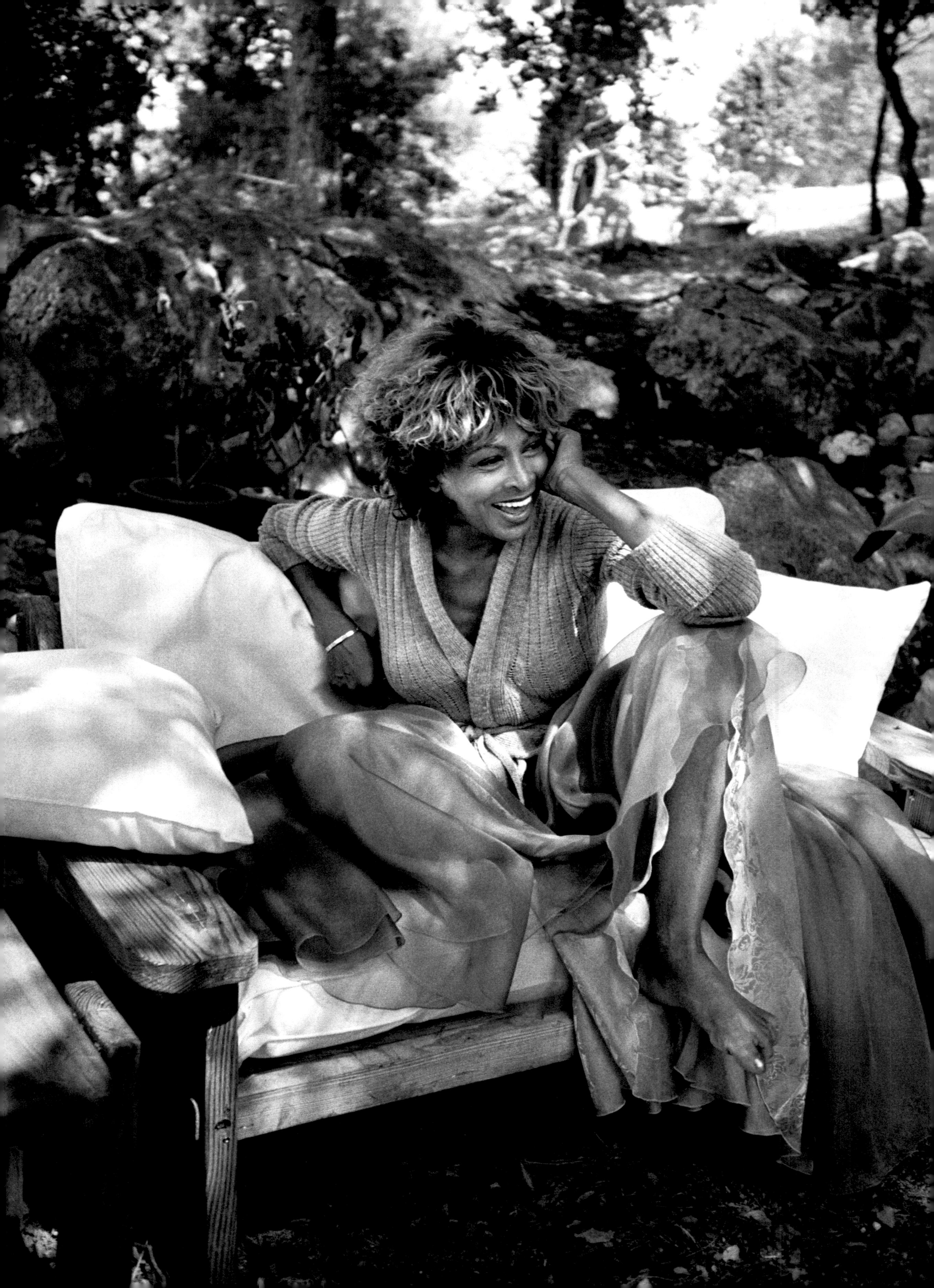

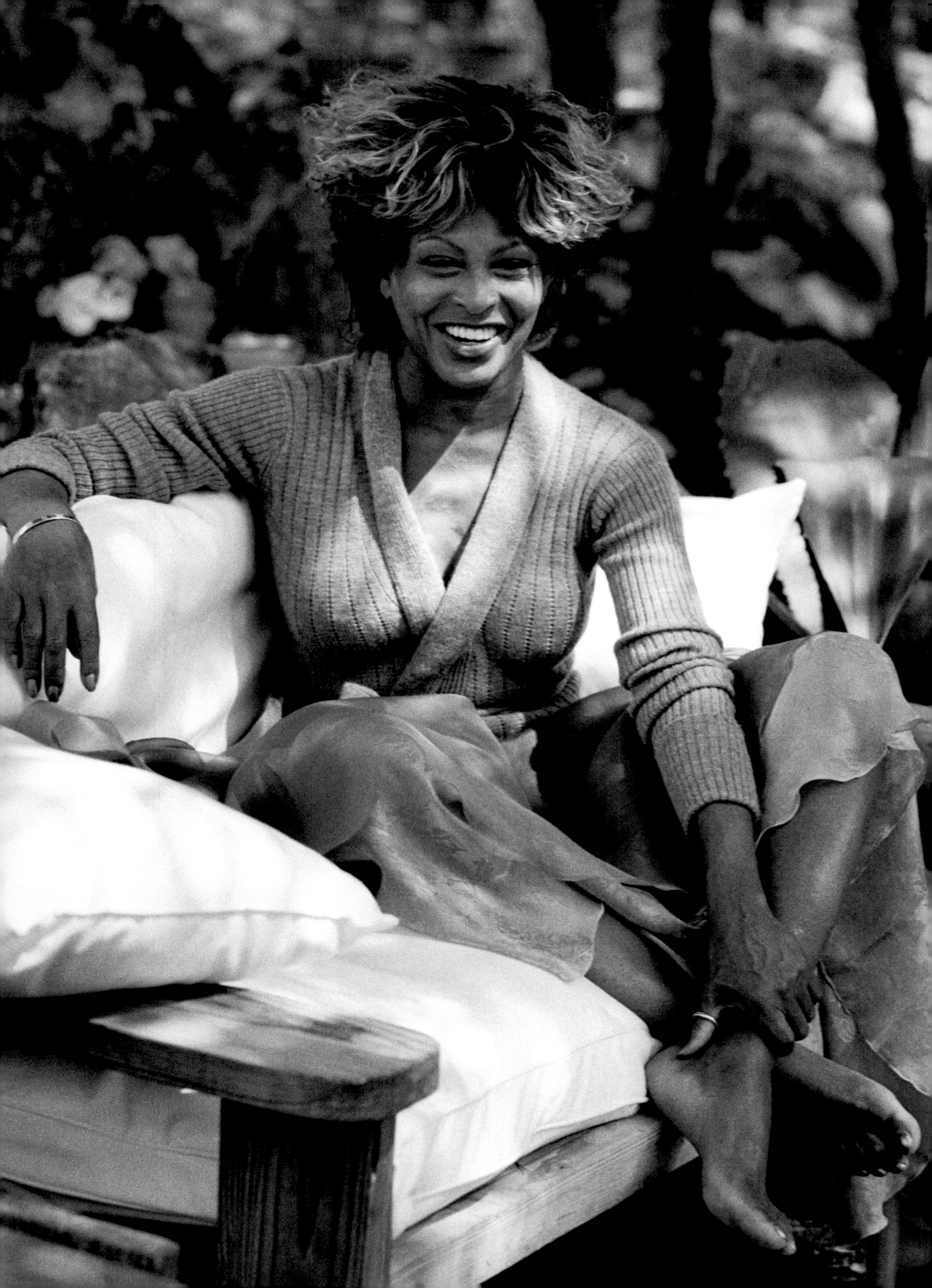

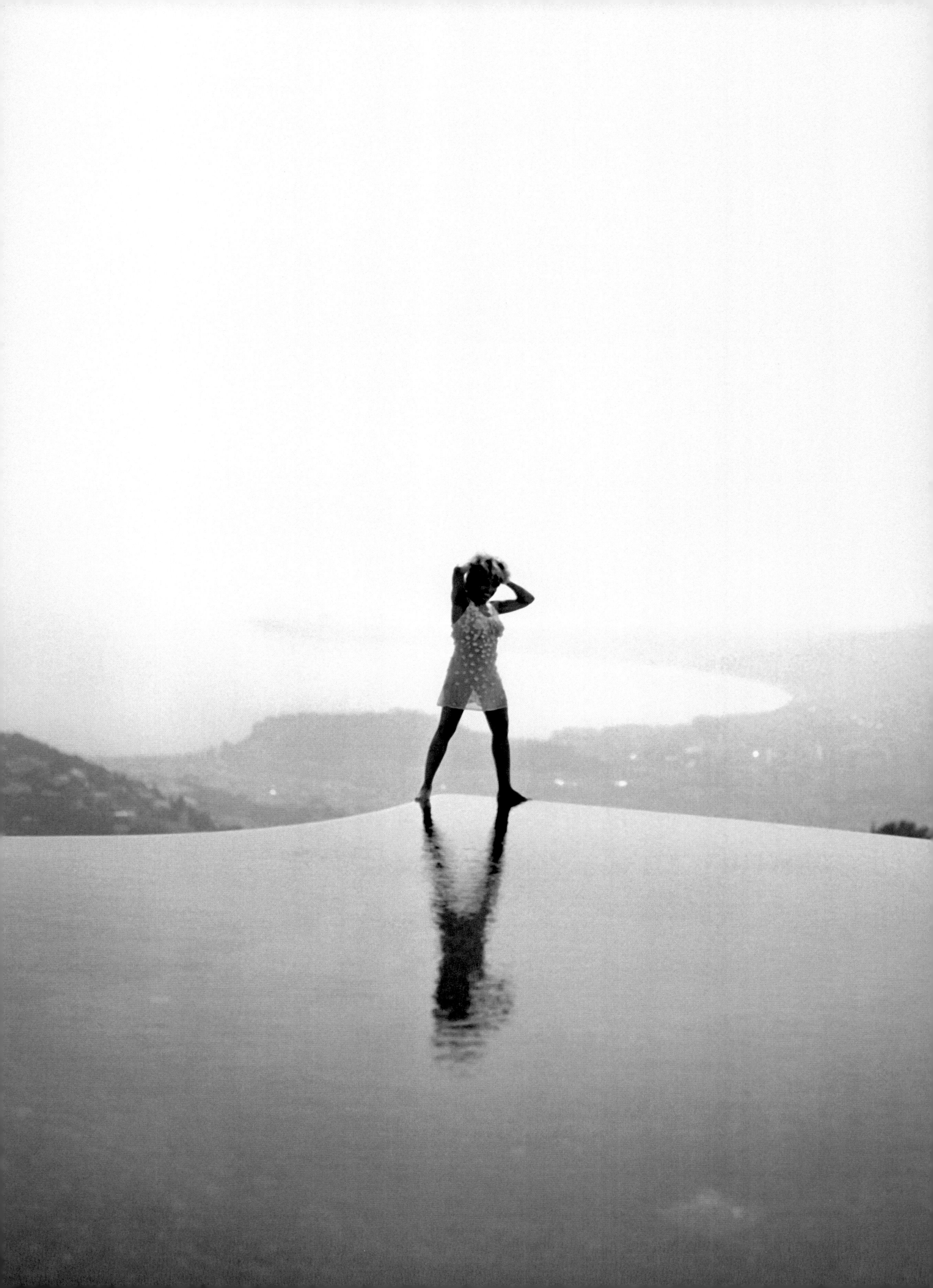

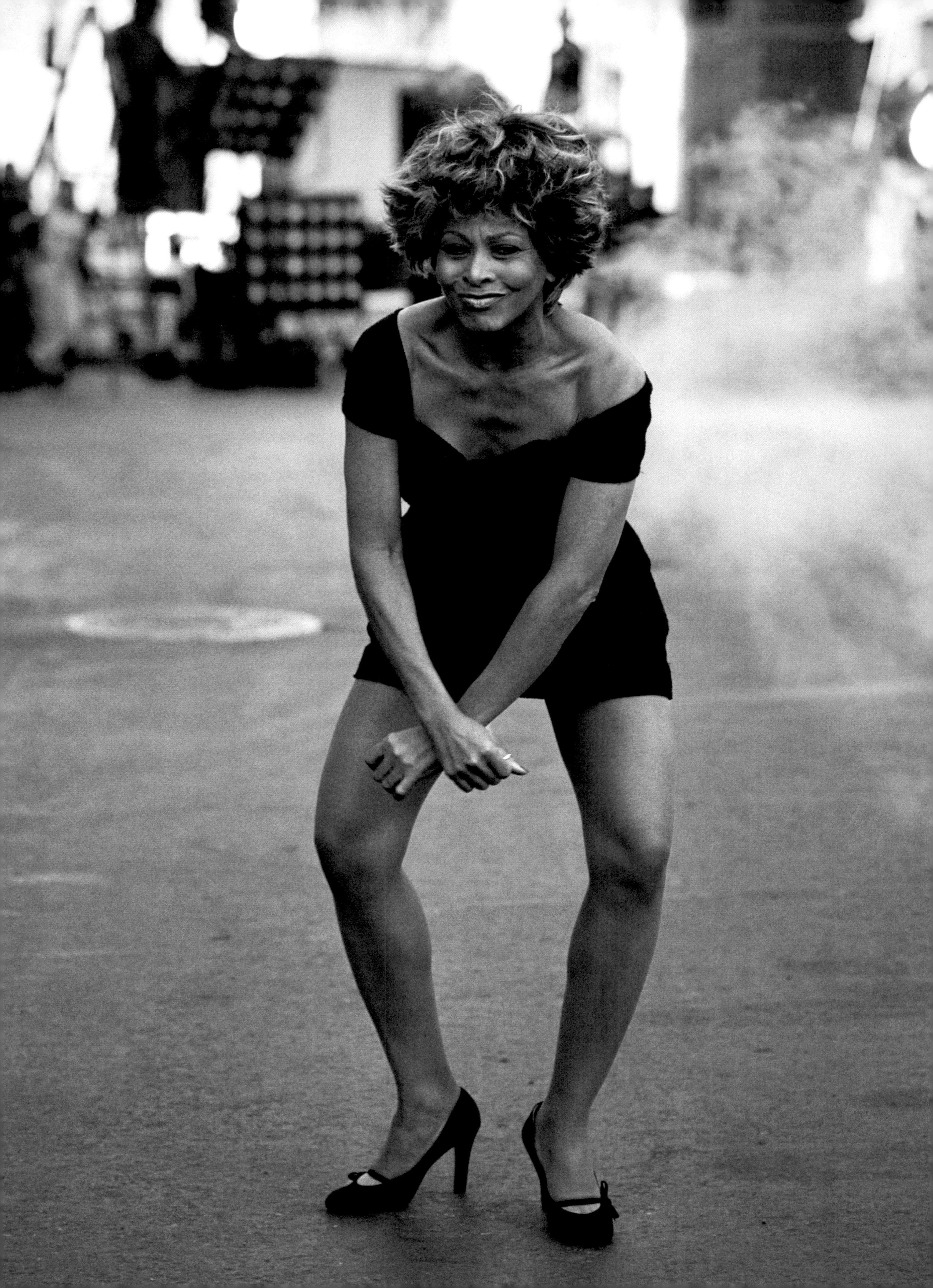

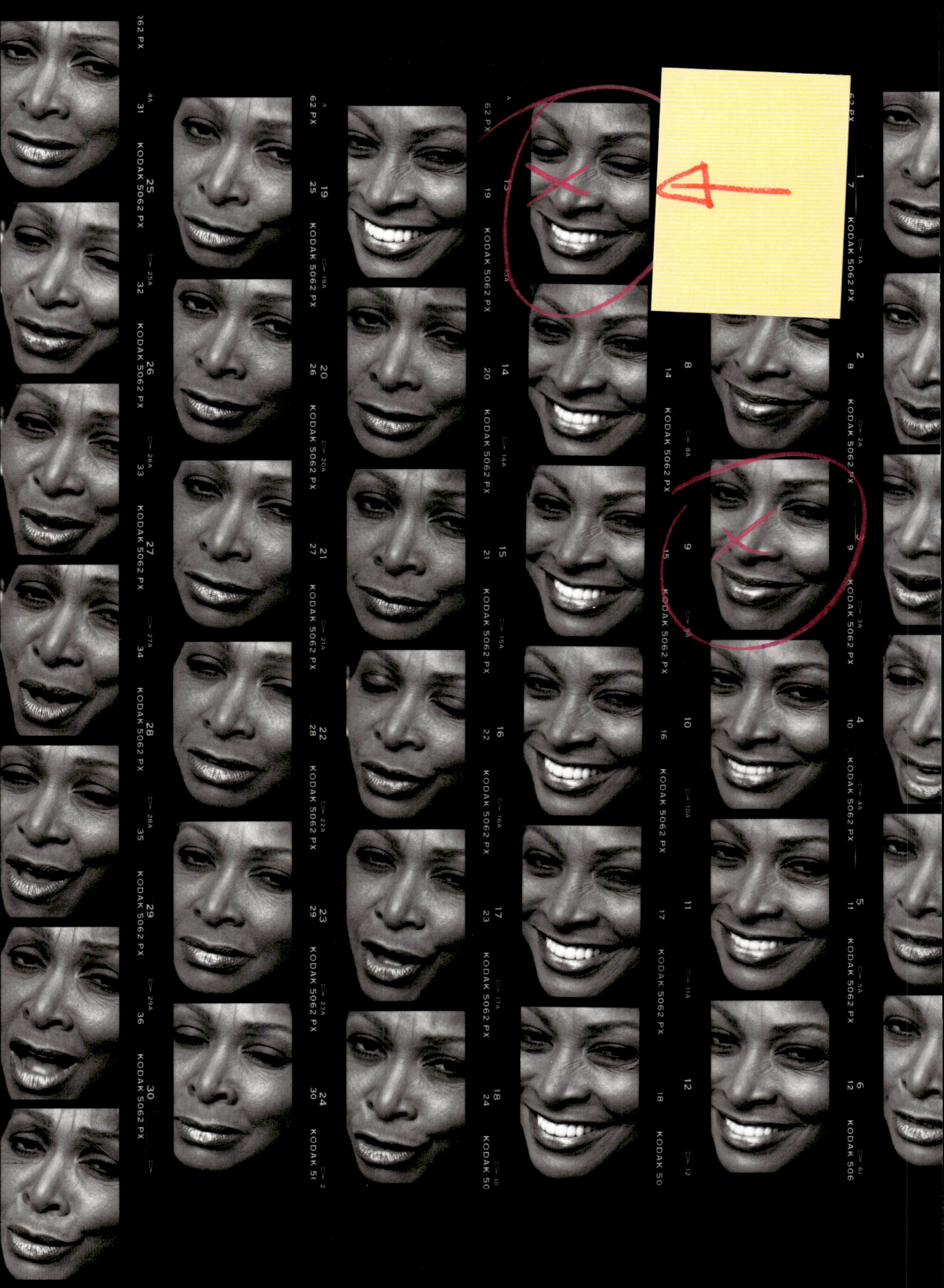
KODAK 5062 PX

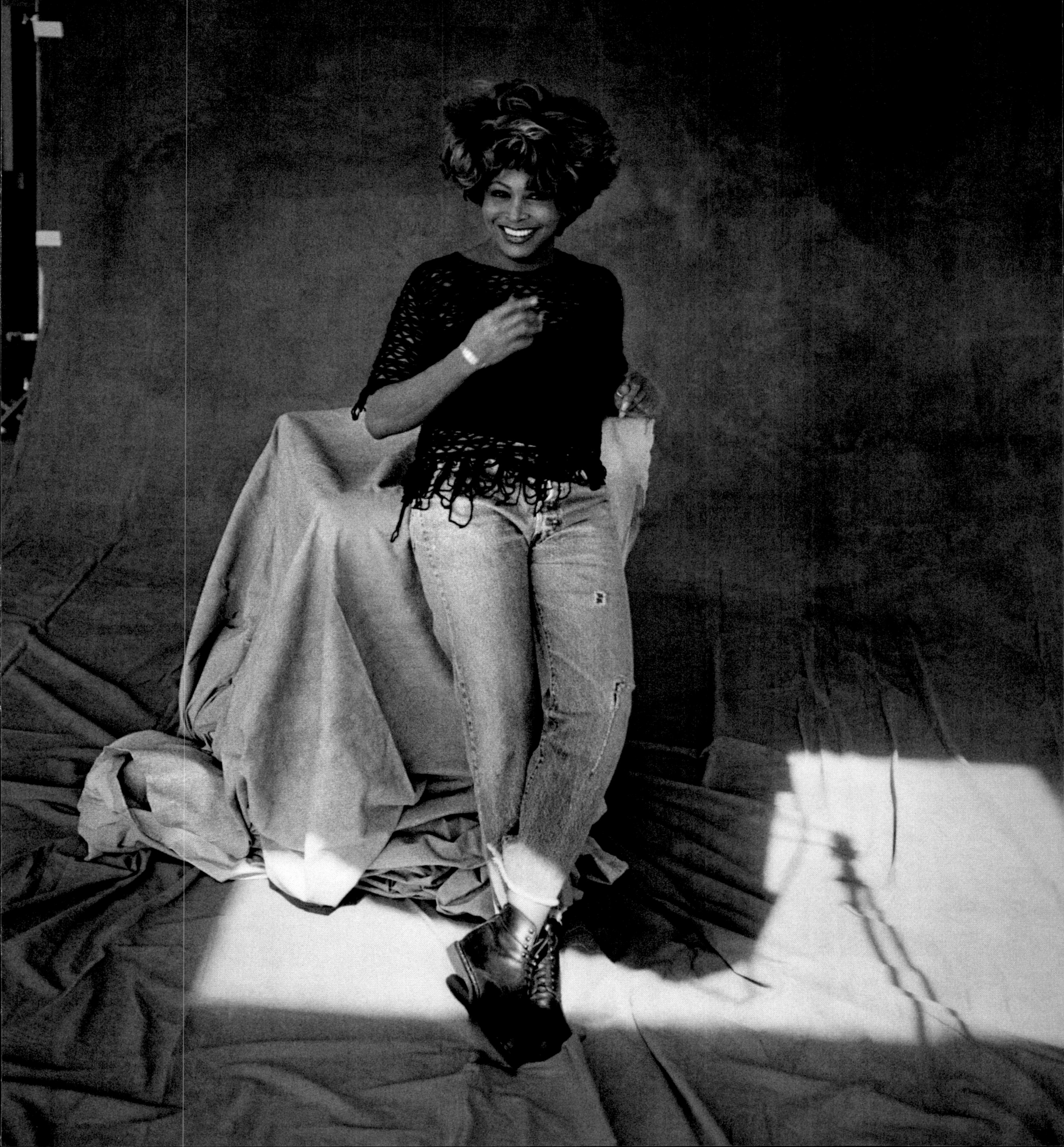

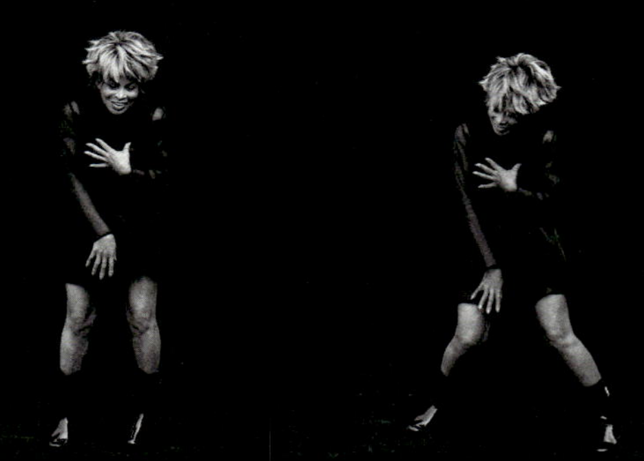

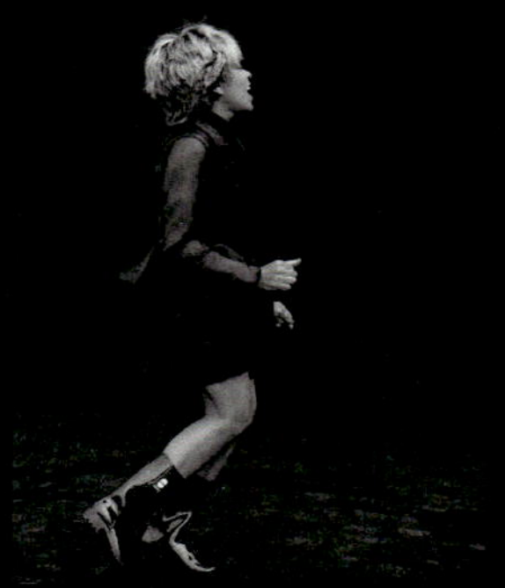

Villefranche, France
1995

Villefranche, France
1995

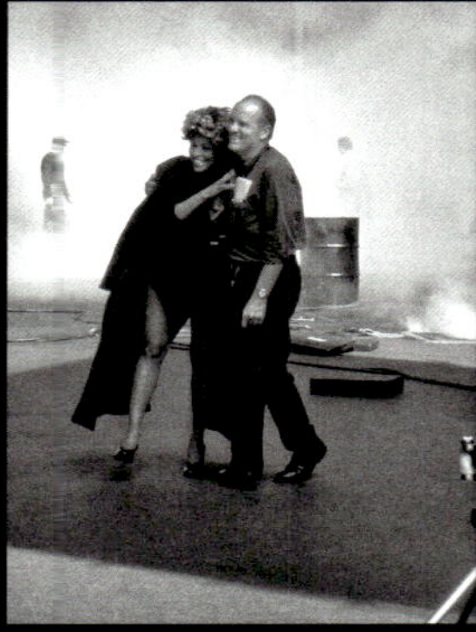

Tina with Peter
Paramount Studios, Hollywood, CA, 1996

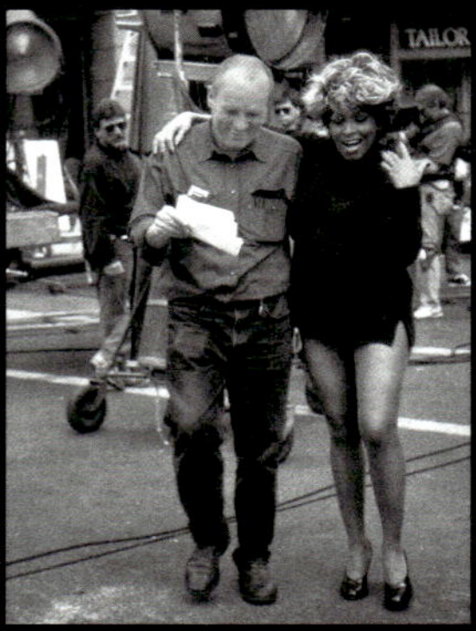

Tina with Peter
Paramount Studios, Hollywood, CA, 1996

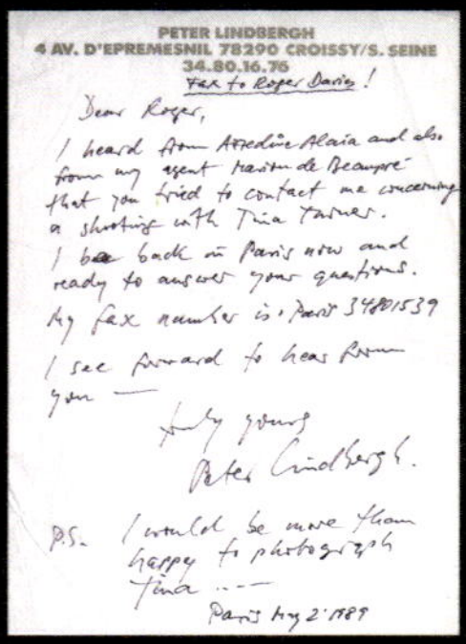

PETER LINDBERGH
4 AV. D'EPREMESNIL 78290 CROISSY/S. SEINE
34.80.16.76
Fax to Roger Davies!

Dear Roger,

I heard from Azzedine Alaia and also from my agent Marion de Beaupré that you tried to contact me concerning a shooting with Tina Turner.

I be back in Paris now and ready to answer your questions.

My fax number is: Paris 34801539

I see forward to hear from you —

truly yours
Peter Lindbergh.

P.S. I would be more than happy to photograph Tina ...

Paris May 2' 1989

Letter from Peter to Roger Davies
Paris, May 2, 1989

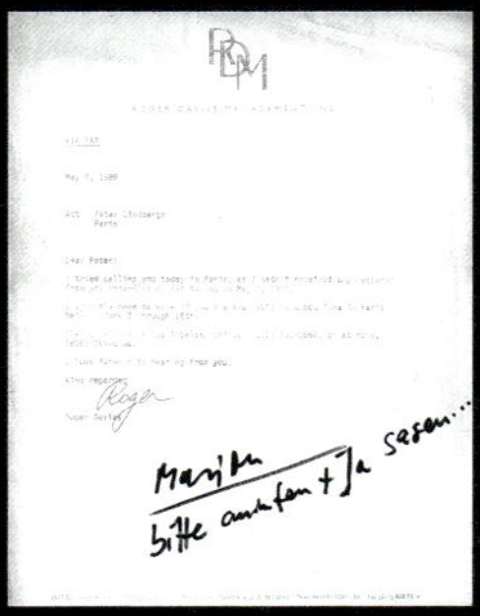

RDM

Att Peter Lindbergh
Paris

Dear Peter:

Roger
Roger Davies

Marika
bitte anrufen + Ja sagen...

Letter from Roger Davies to Peter
Los Angeles, May 9, 1989

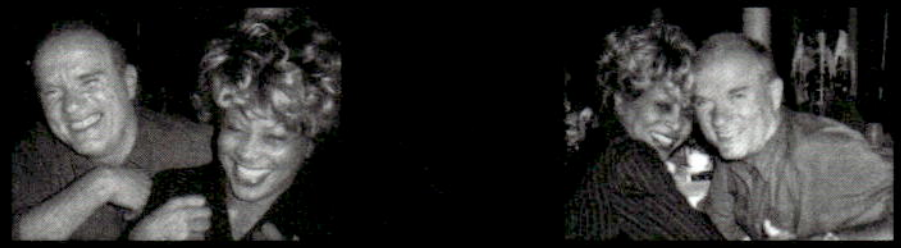

Tina with Peter
Los Angeles, 1996

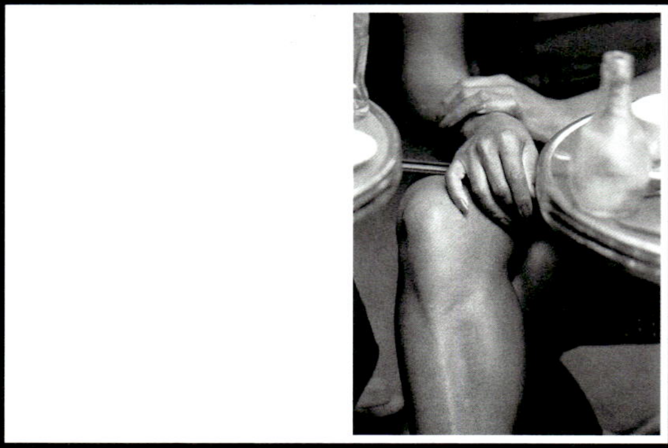

Café de Flore
Paris, 1989

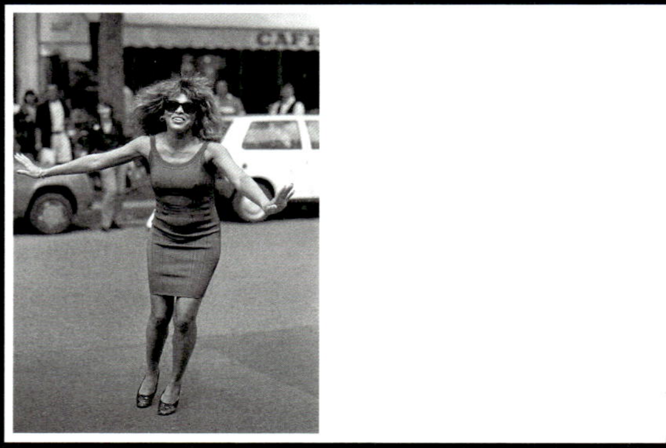

In front of Café de Flore
Paris, 1989

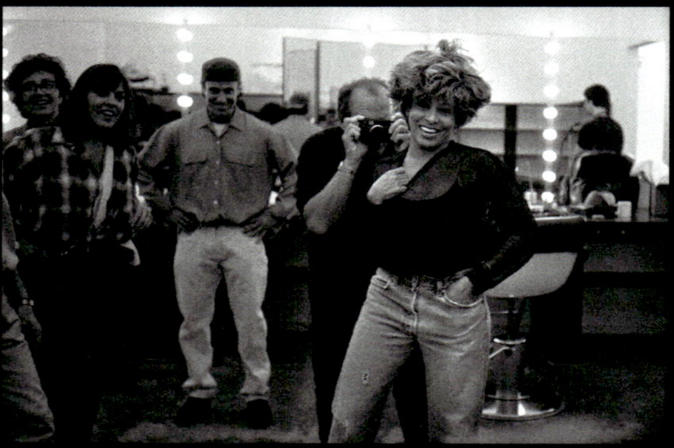

Los Angeles
1993

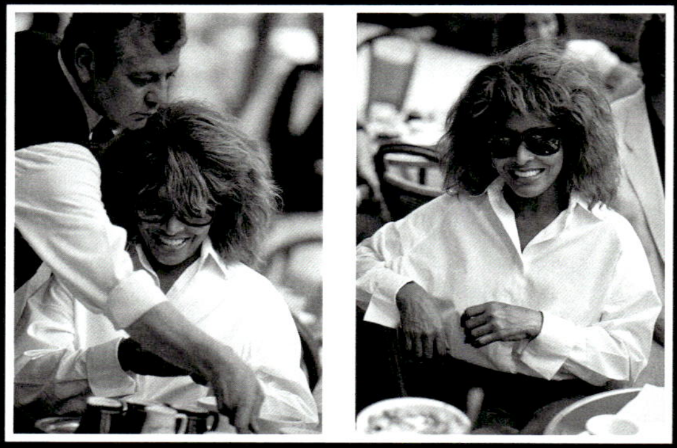

Café de Flore
Paris, 1989

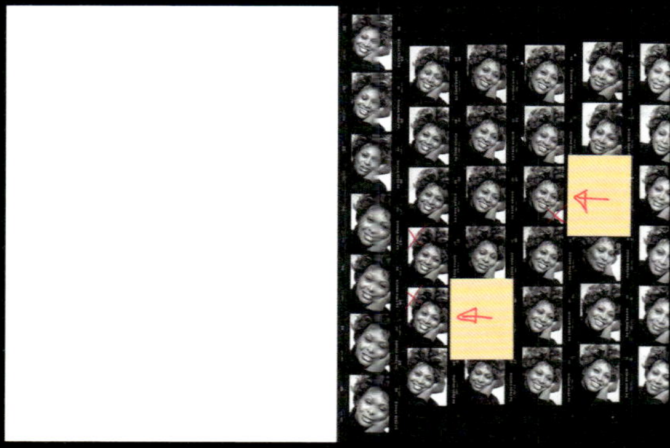

Contact sheet
Los Angeles, 1996

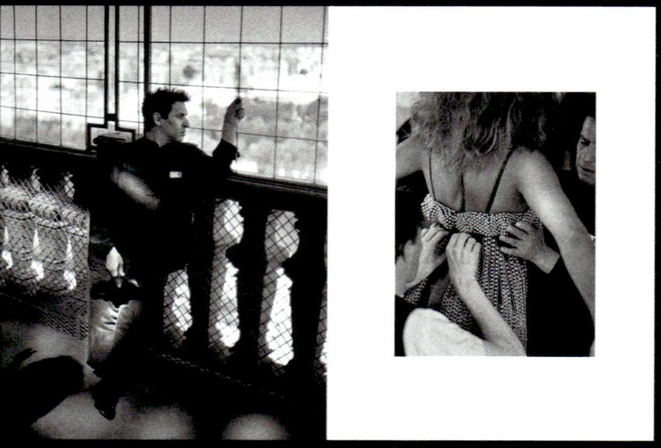

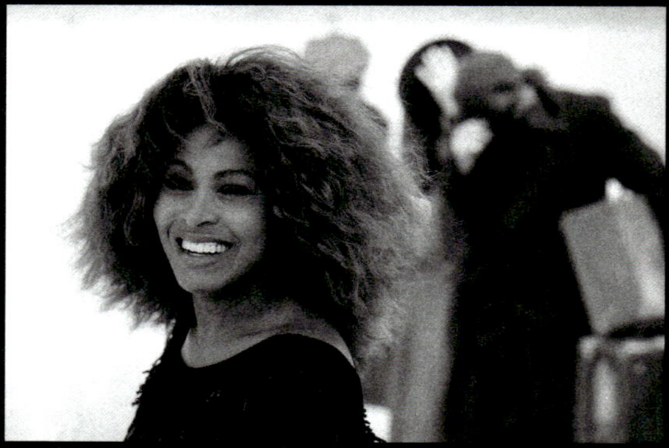

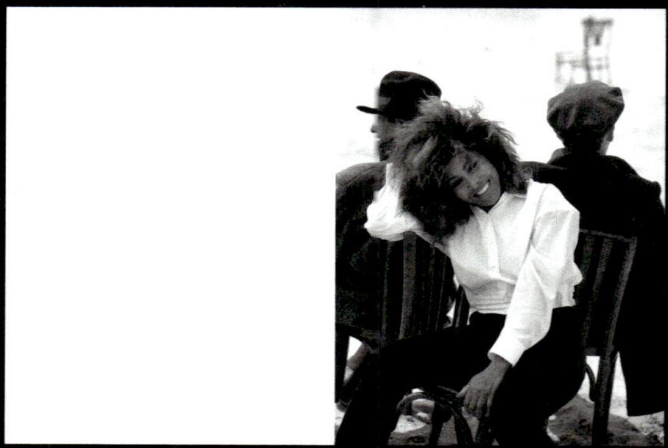

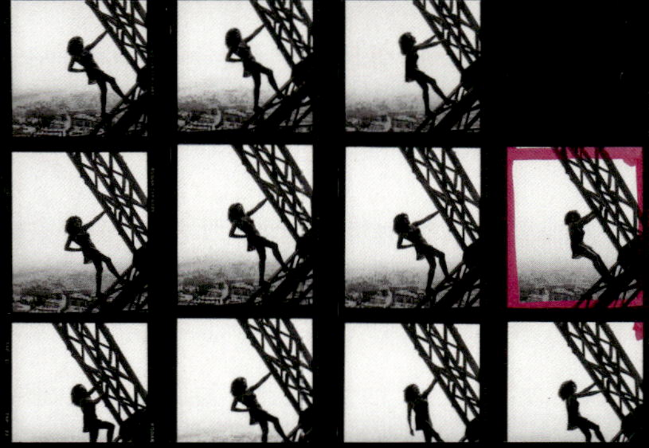

Contact sheet
Eiffel Tower, Paris, 1989

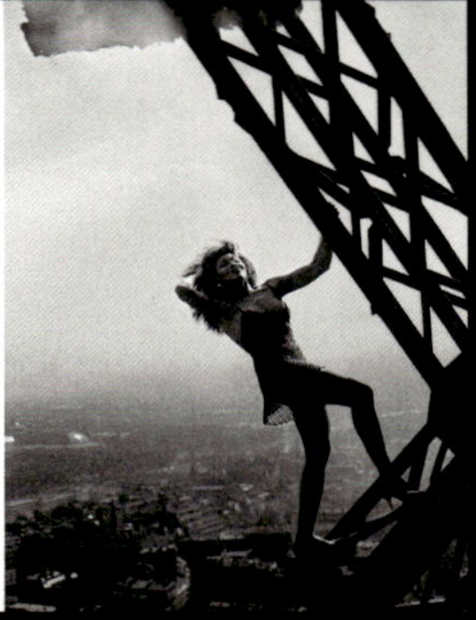

Eiffel Tower
Paris, 1989

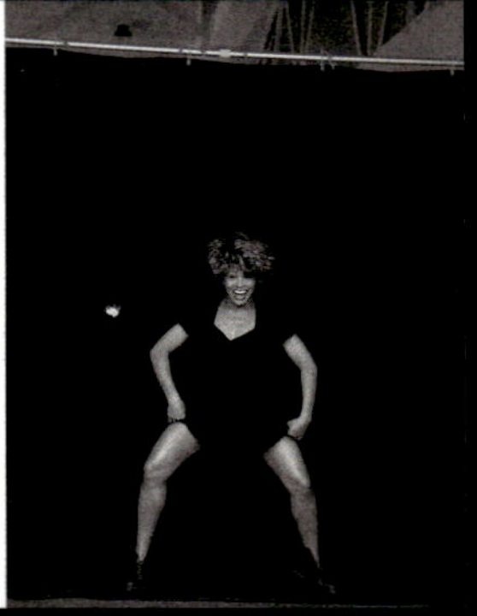

Los Angeles
1993

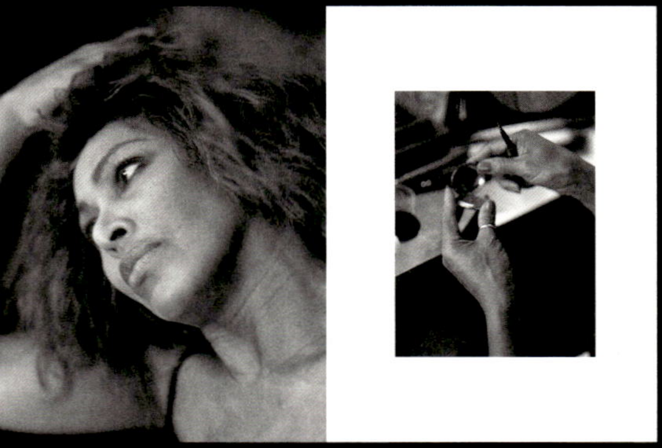

Paris
1989

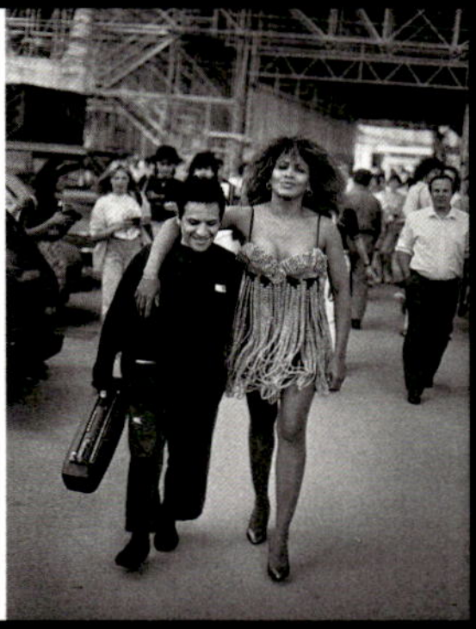

Tina with Azzedine Alaïa
Eiffel Tower, Paris, 1989

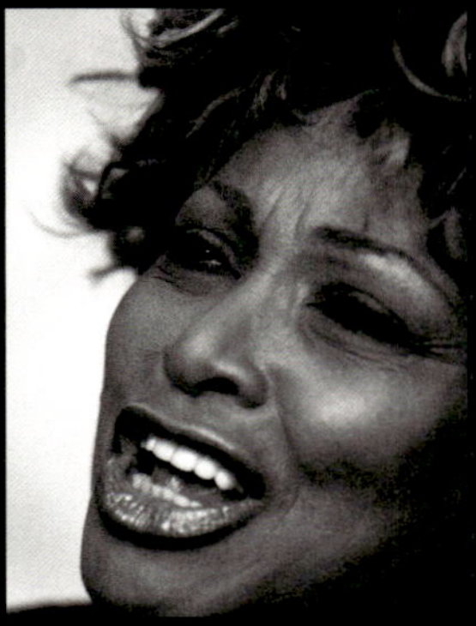

Los Angeles
1996

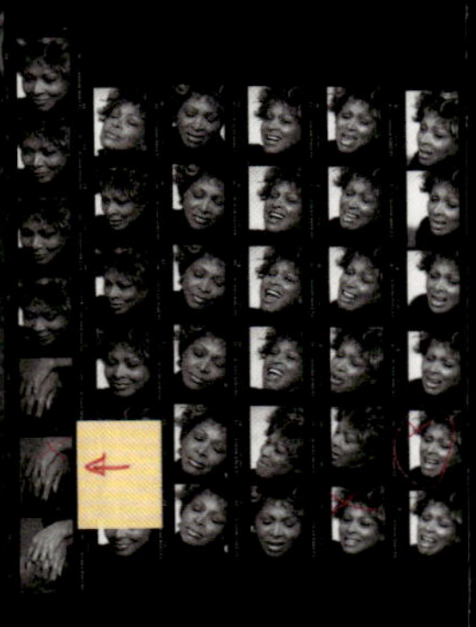

Contact sheet
Los Angeles, 1996

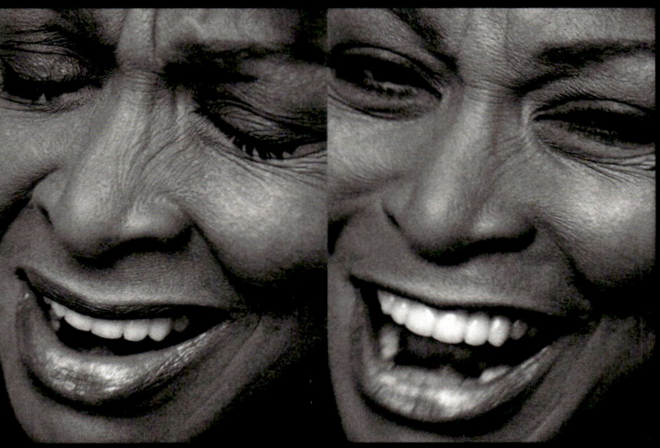

Los Angeles
1996

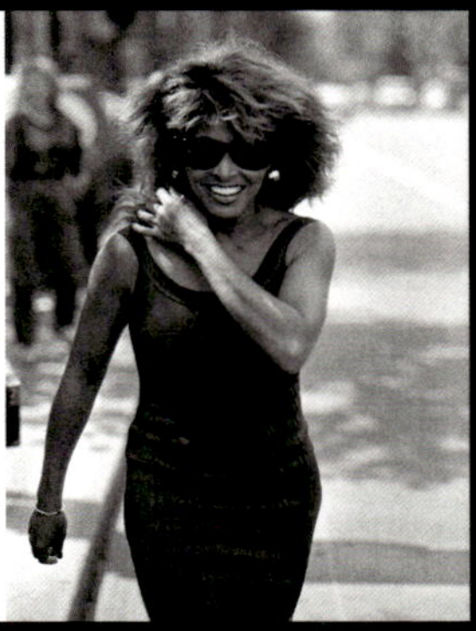

Paris
1989

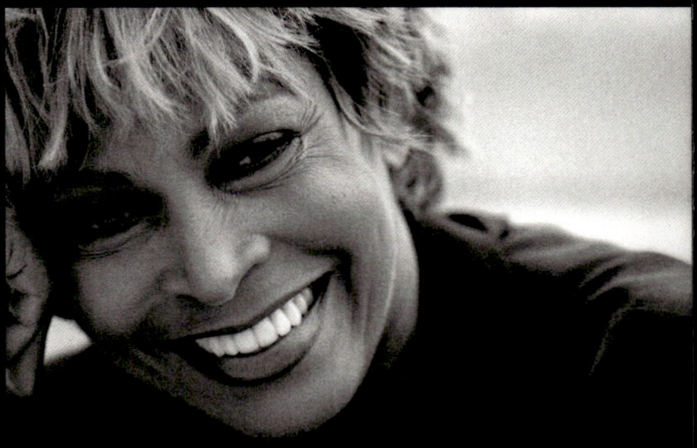

Villefranche, France
1995

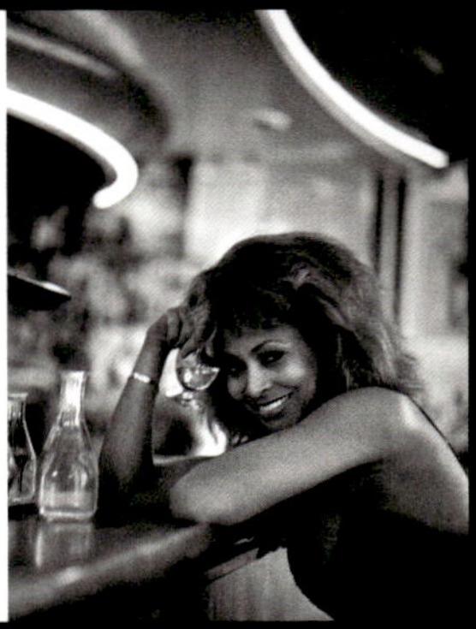

Paris
1989

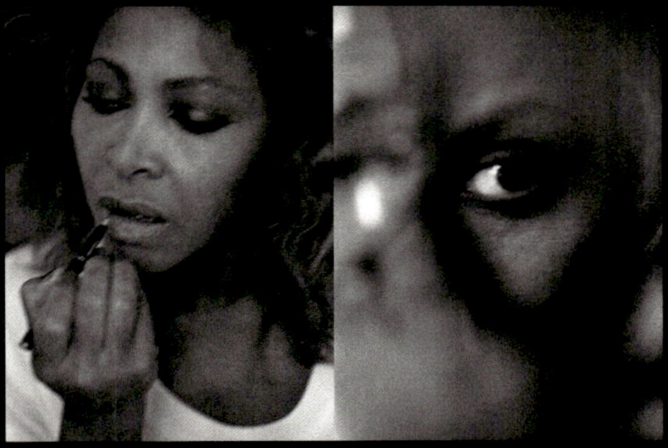

Deauville, France
1989

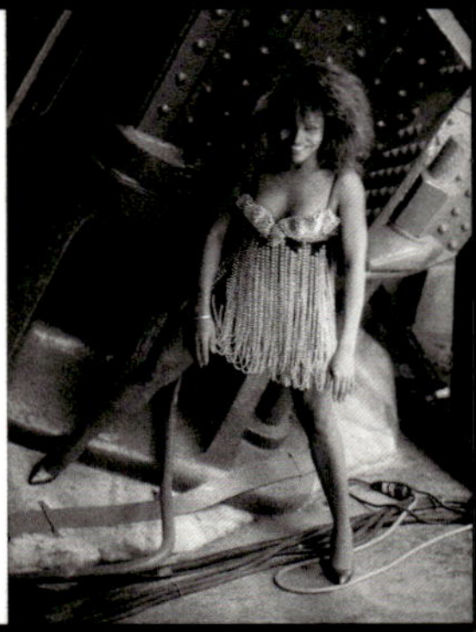

Eiffel Tower
Paris, 1989

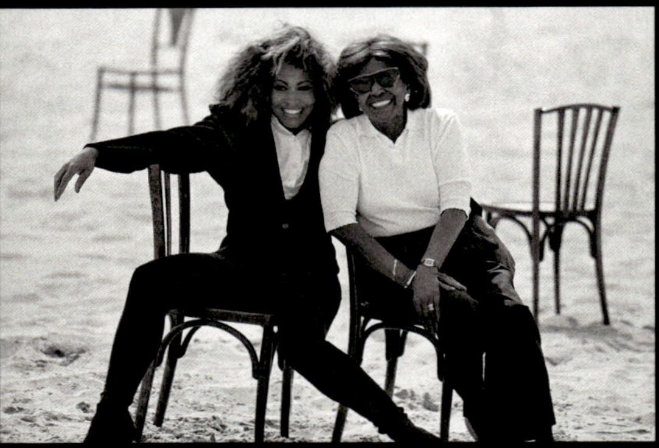

Tina with her mother
Deauville, France, 1989

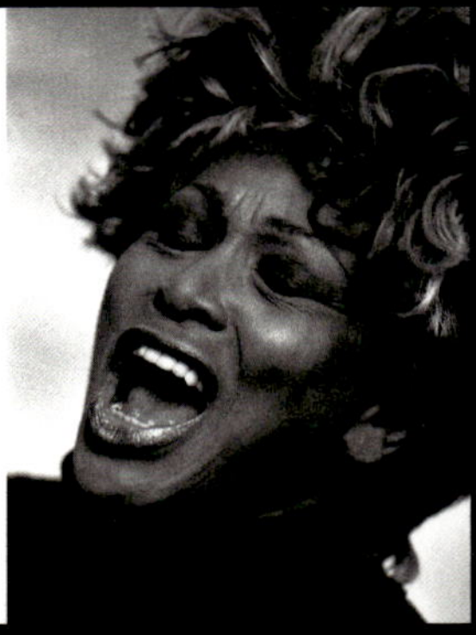

Los Angeles
1996

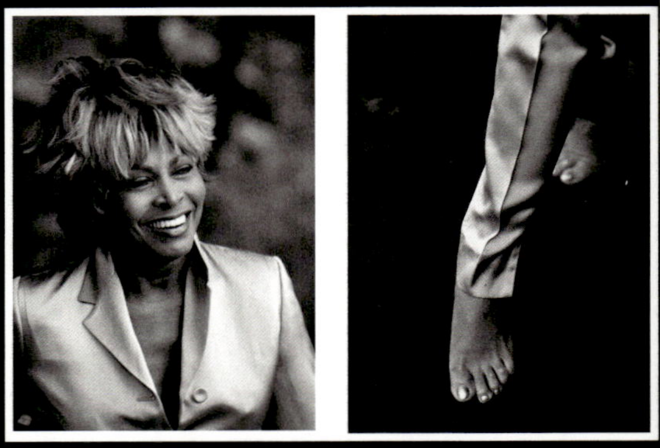

Villefranche, France
1995

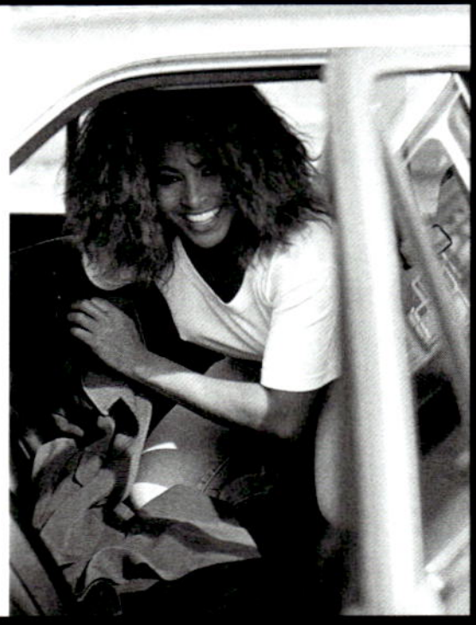

Deauville, France
1989

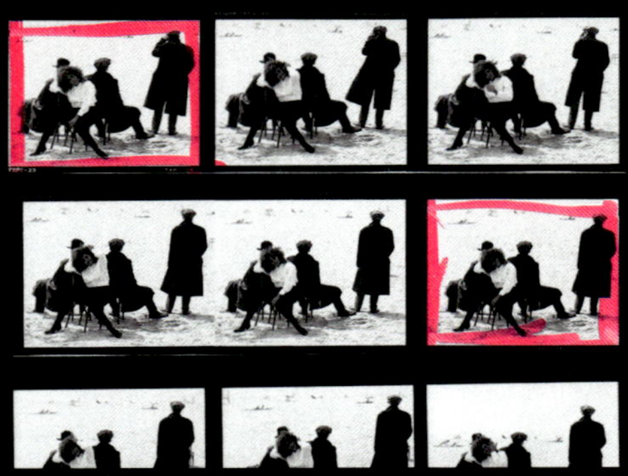

Contact sheet
Deauville, France, 1989

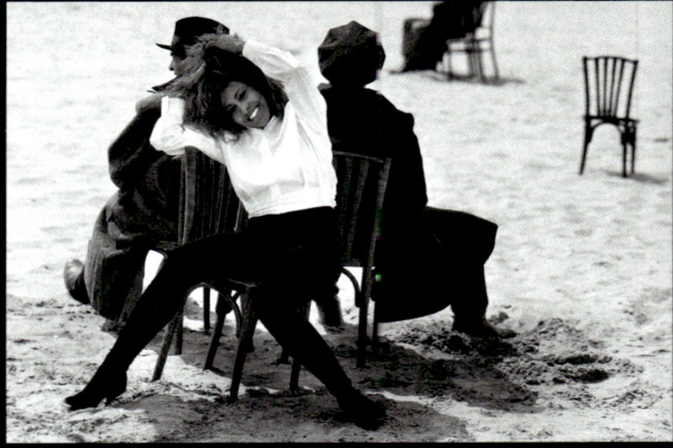

Deauville, France
1989

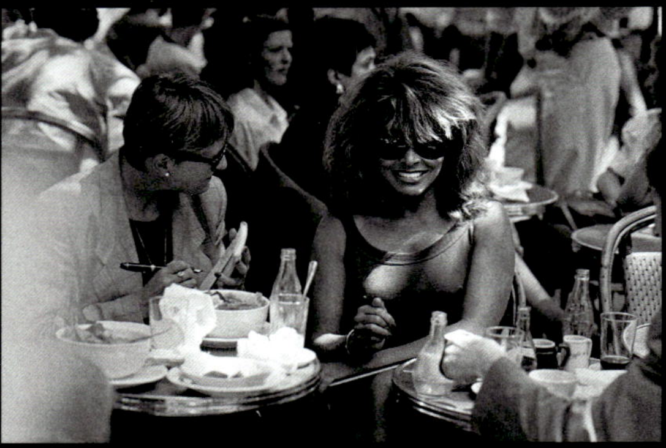

Café de Flore
Paris, 1989

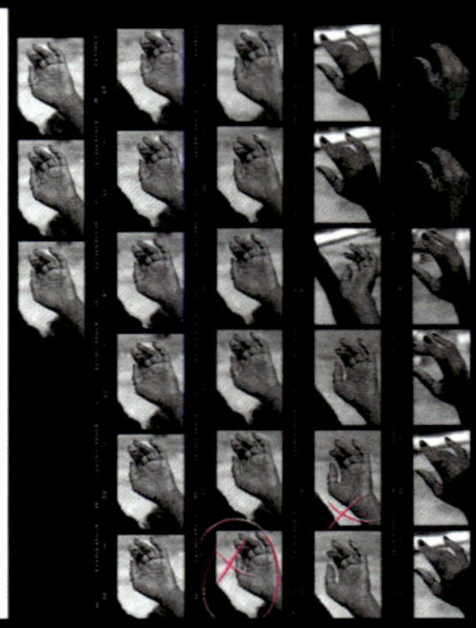

Contact sheet
Los Angeles, 1996

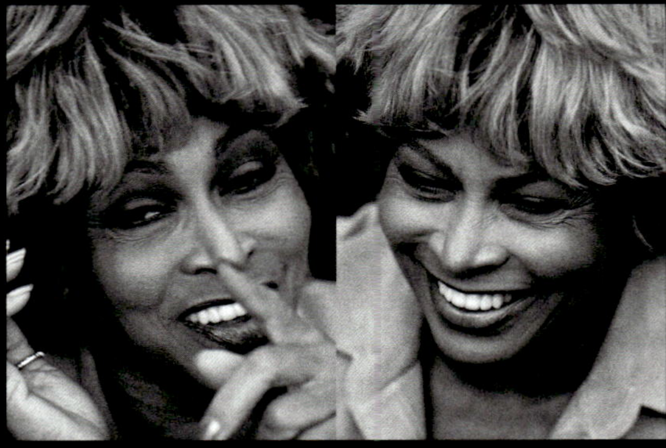

Villefranche, France
1995

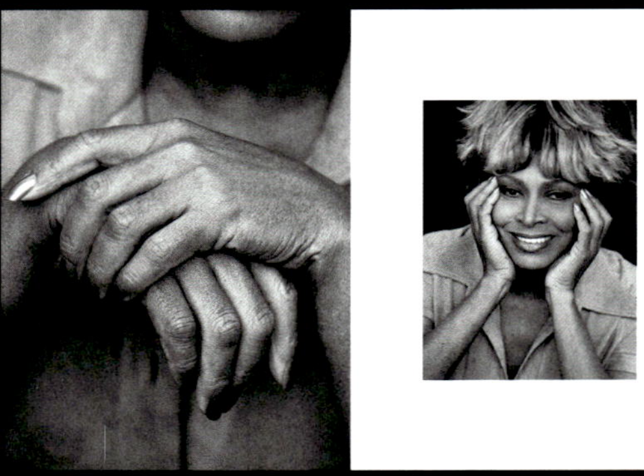

Villefranche, France
1995

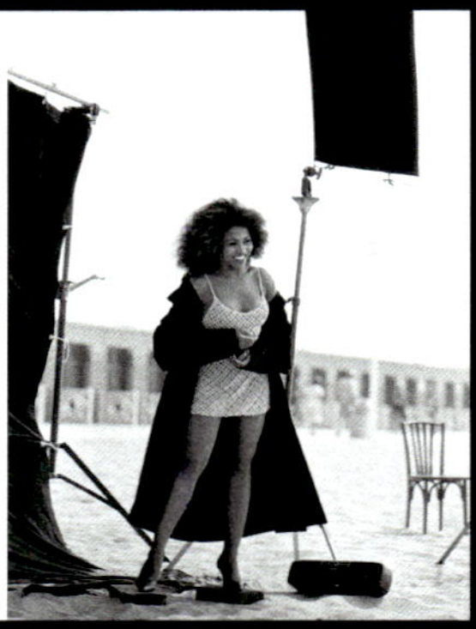

Deauville, France
1989

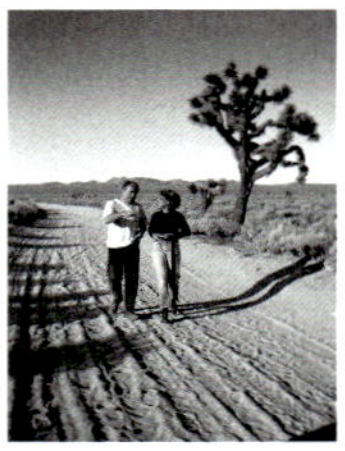

Tina with Peter
Mojave Desert, CA, USA, 1993

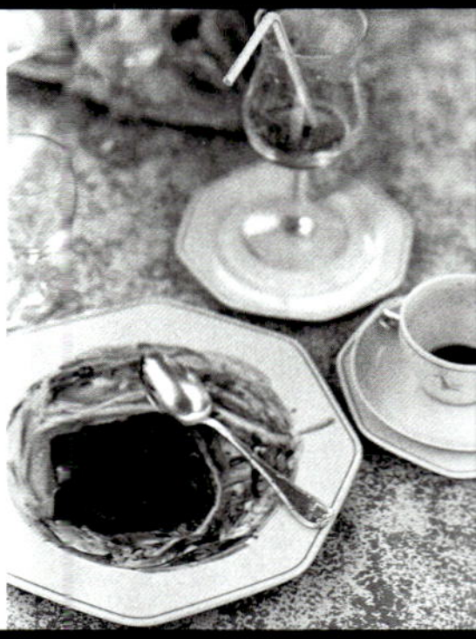

Deauville, France
1989

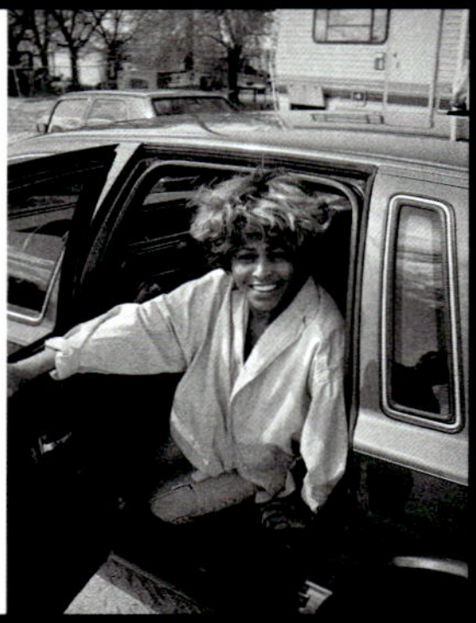

Mojave Desert
California, USA, 1993

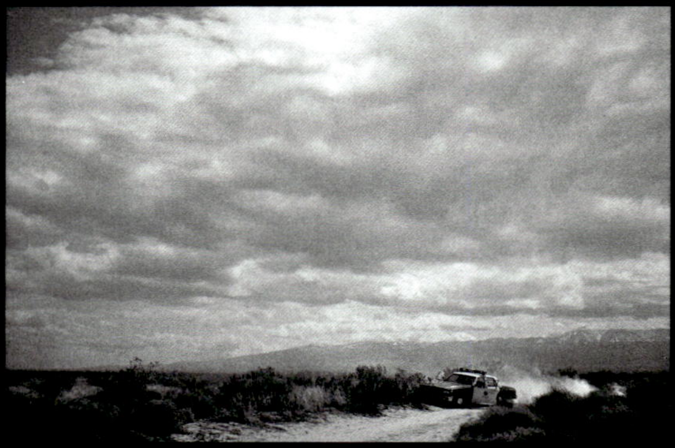

Mojave Desert
California, USA, 1993

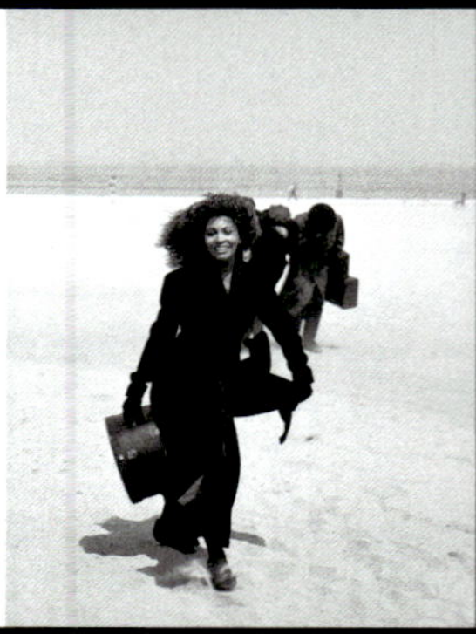

Deauville, France
1989

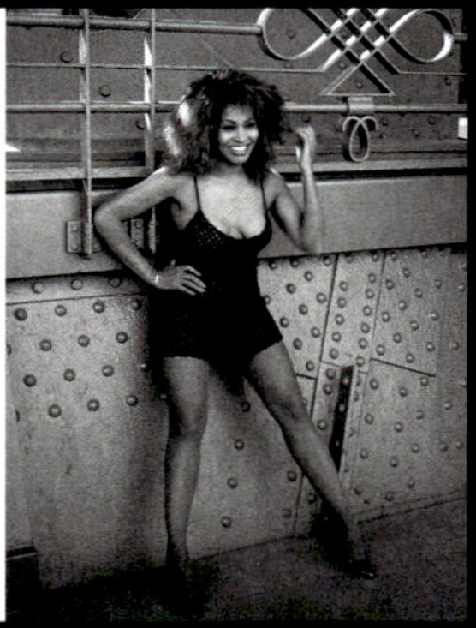

Eiffel Tower
Paris, 1989

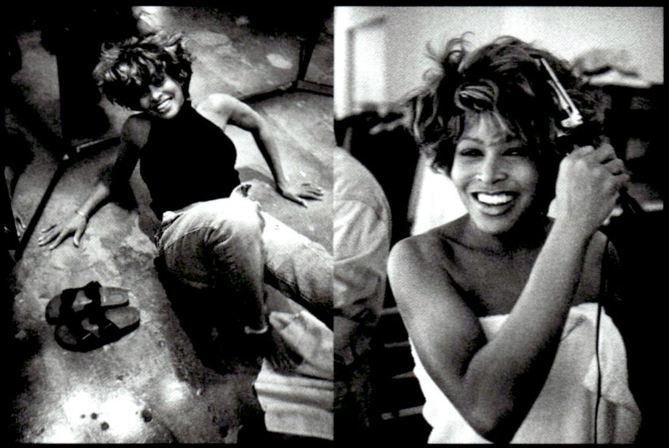

Los Angeles
1993

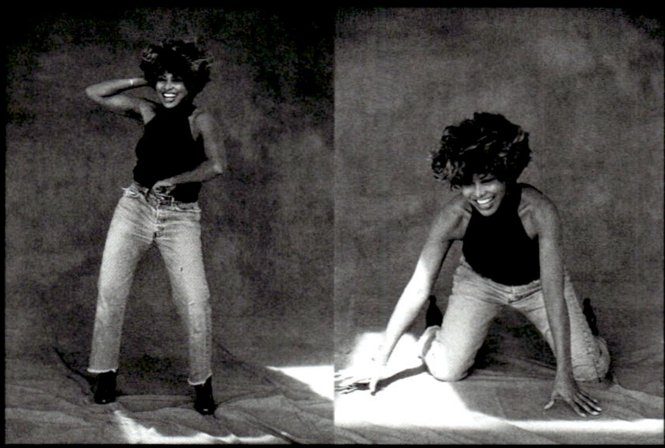

Los Angeles
1993

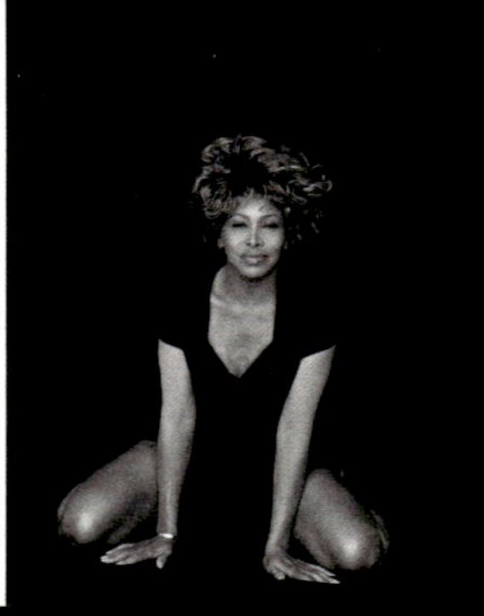
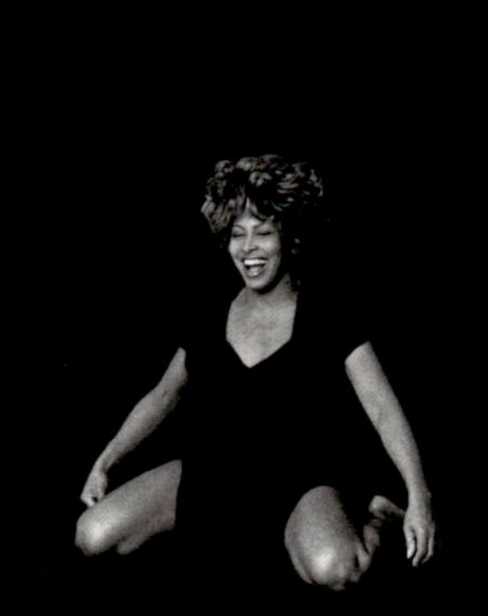
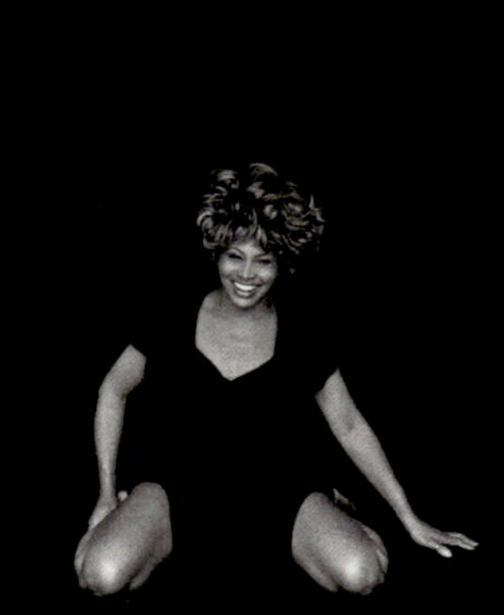
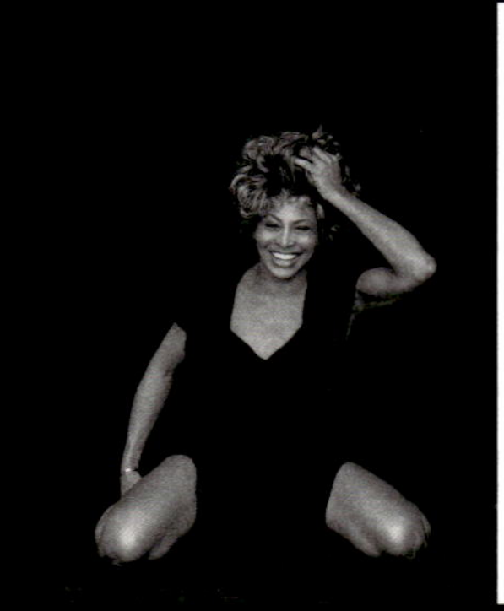

Los Angeles
1993

Los Angeles
1993

Los Angeles
1993

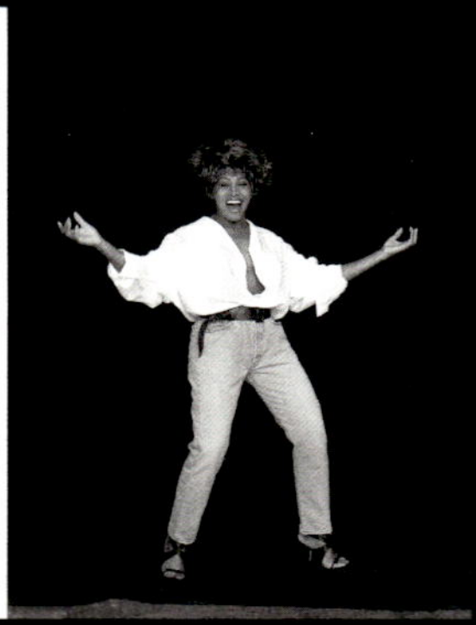

Los Angeles
1993

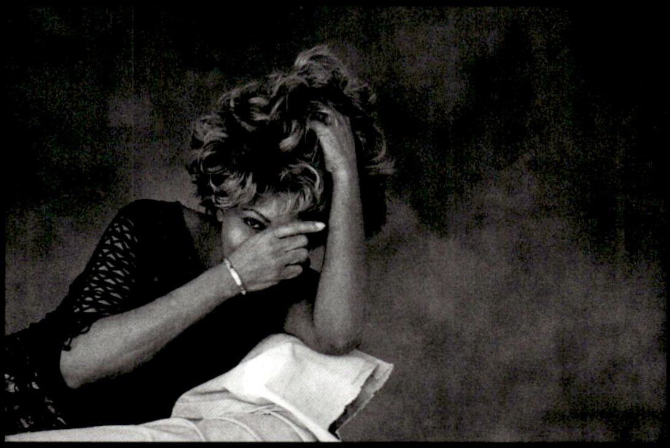

Los Angeles
1993

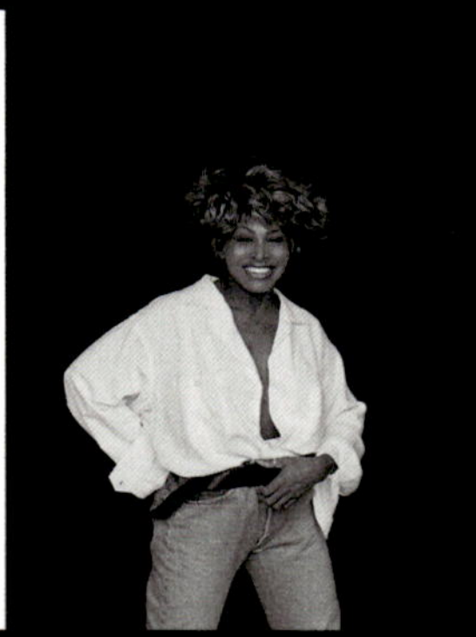

Los Angeles, USA
1993

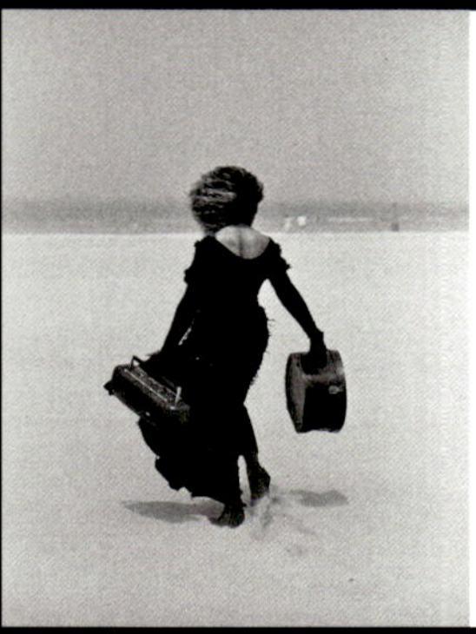

Deauville, France
1989

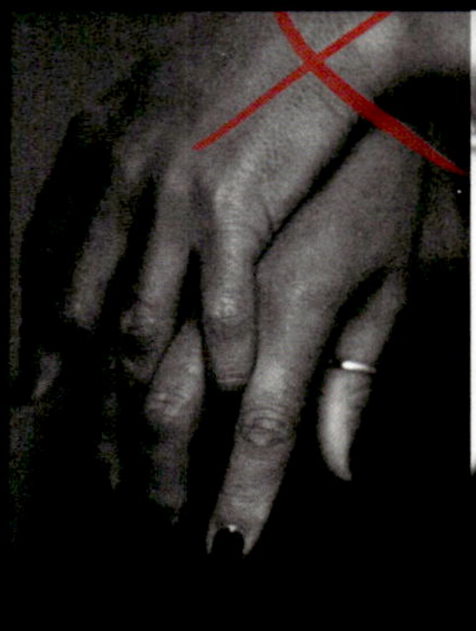
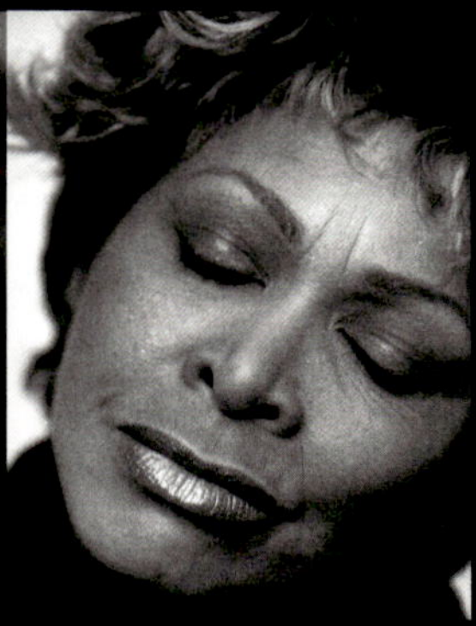

Los Angeles
1996

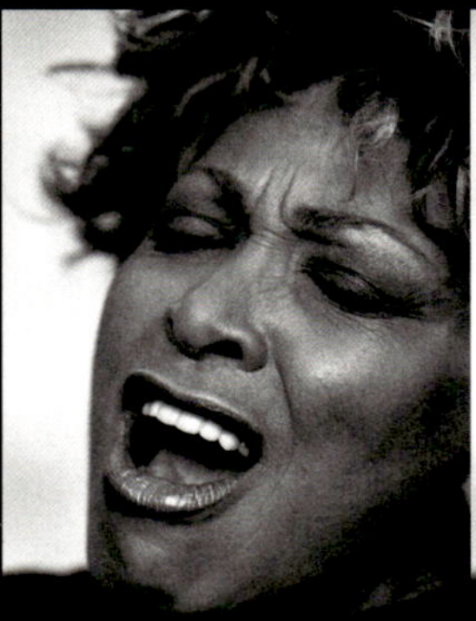
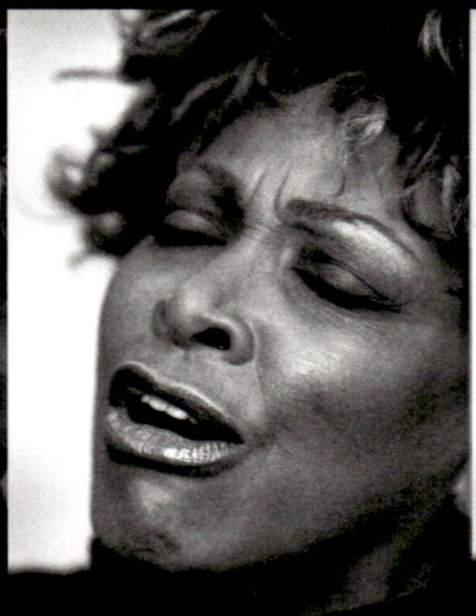
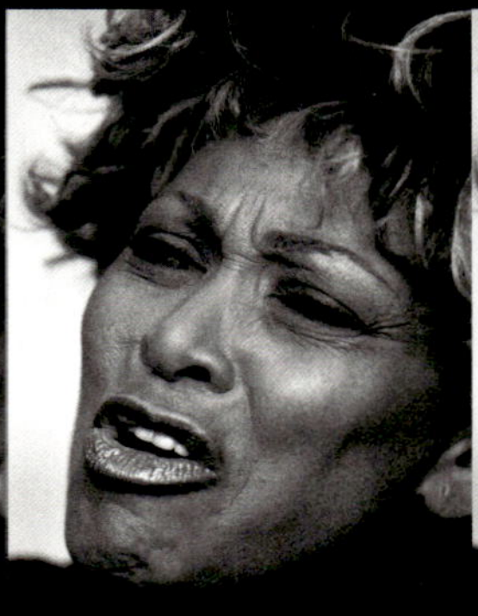
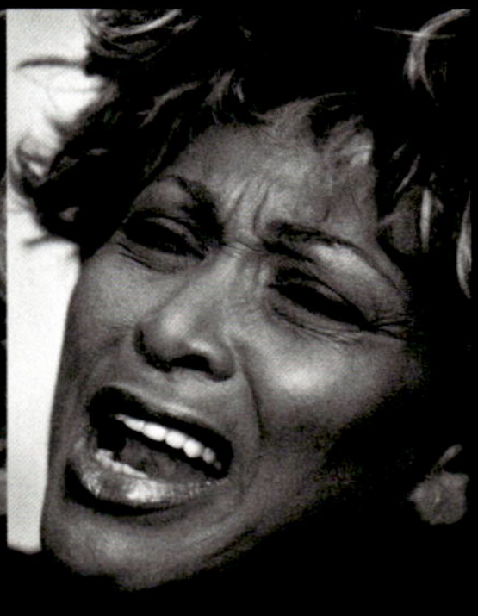

Los Angeles
1996

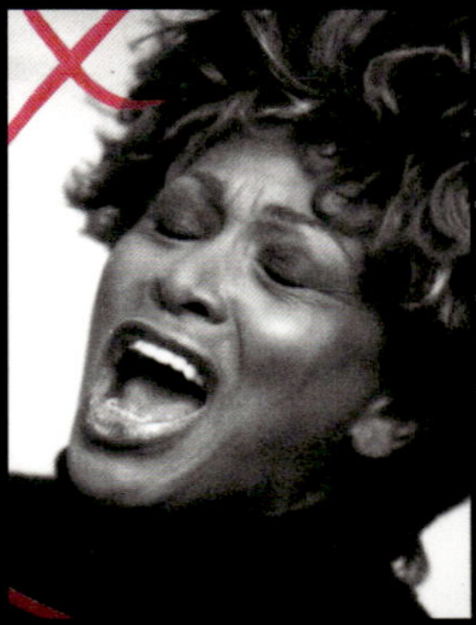
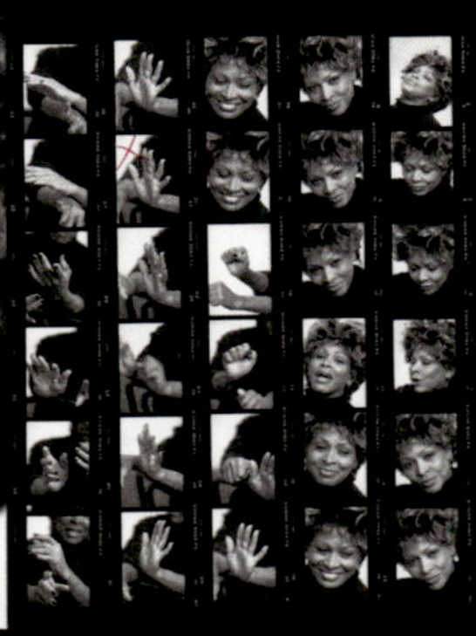

Los Angeles
1996

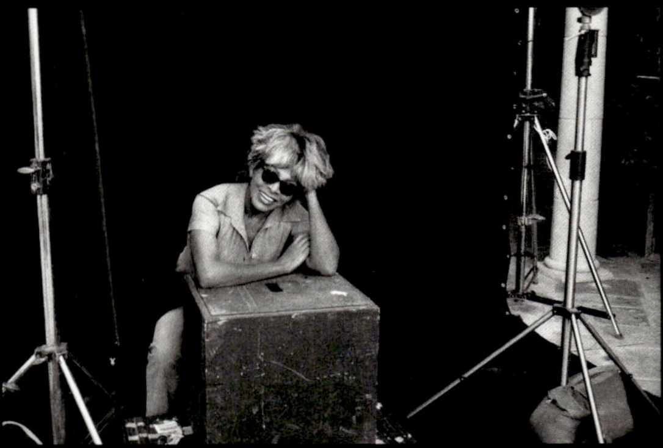

Villefranche, France
1995

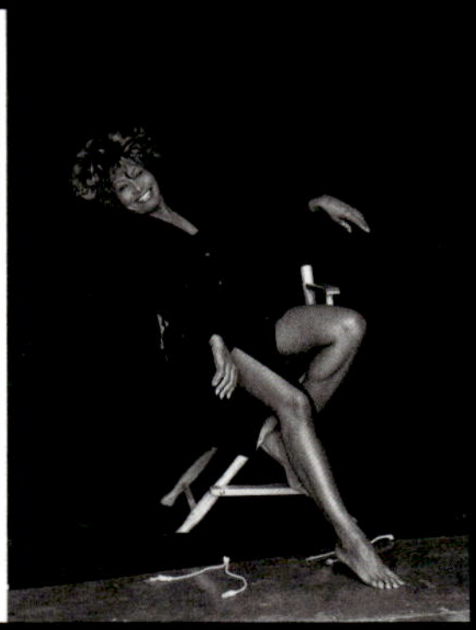

Los Angeles
1993

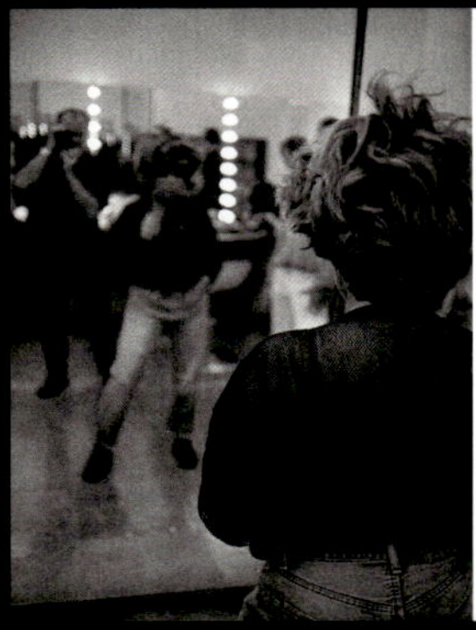

Los Angeles
1993

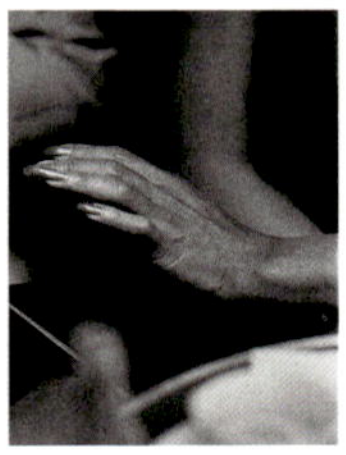

Paris
1989

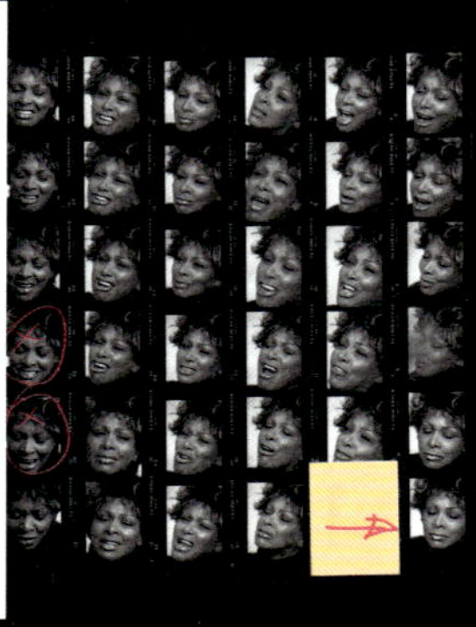

Contact sheet
Los Angeles, 1996

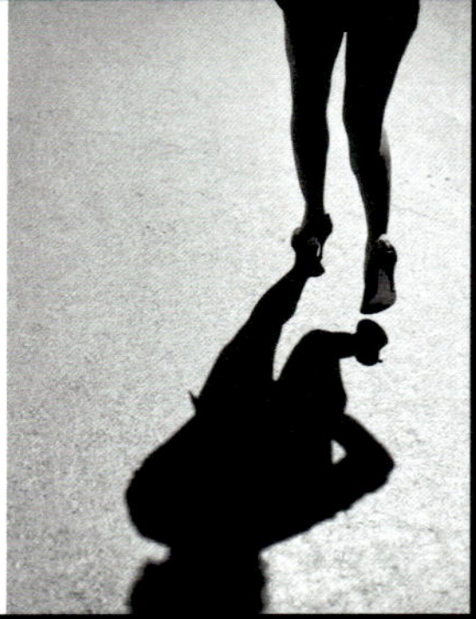

Paramount Studios
Hollywood, CA, 1996

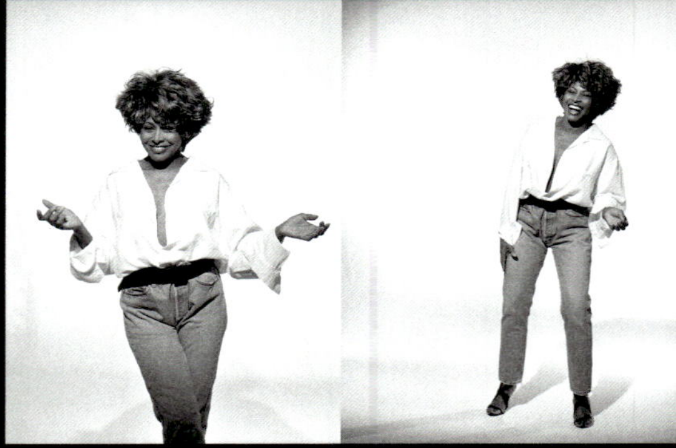

Los Angeles
1993

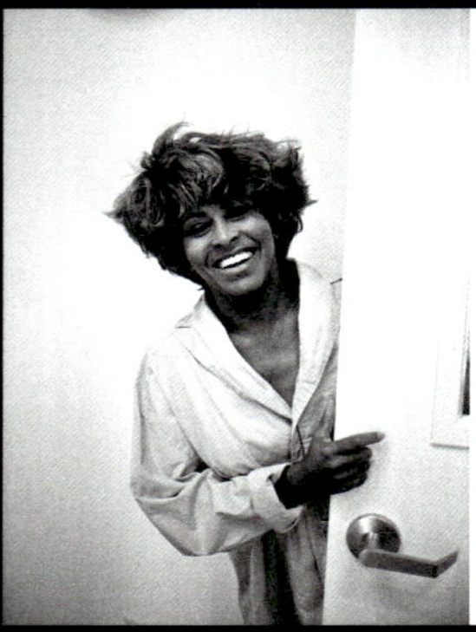

Los Angeles
1993

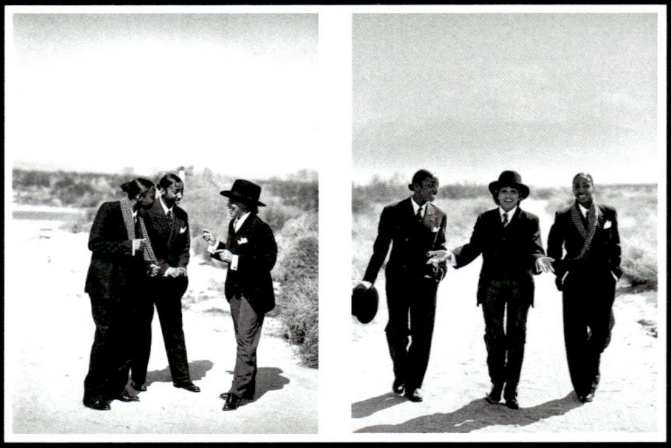

Tina with Nicole and Nikita Blount
Mojave Desert, CA, USA, 1993

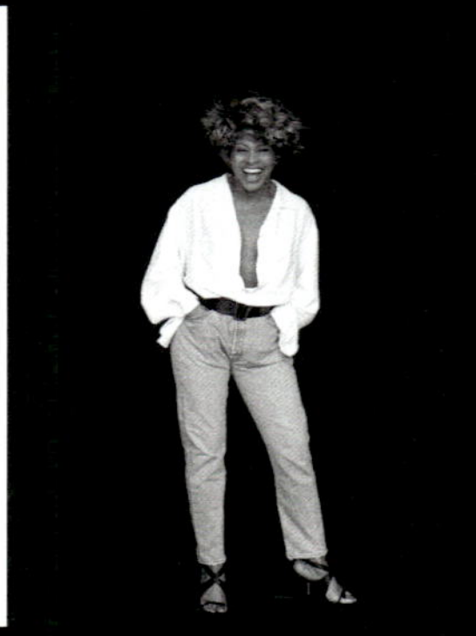

Los Angeles
1993

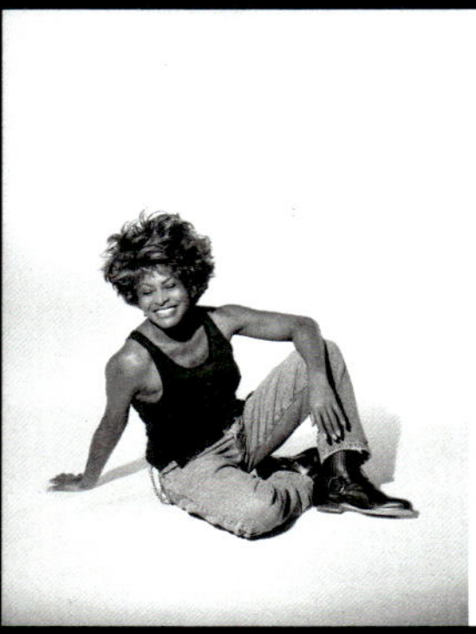

Los Angeles
1993

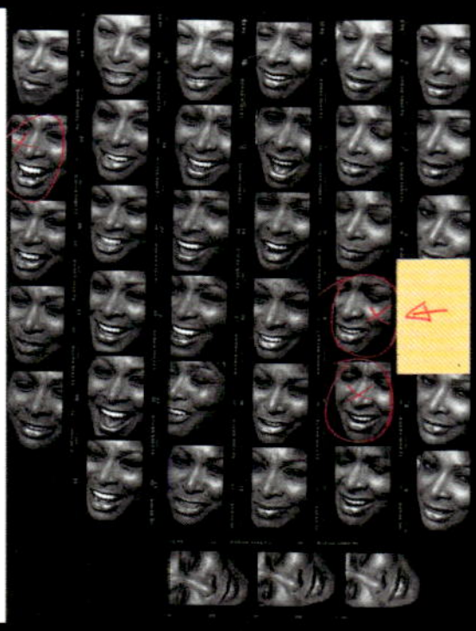

Contact sheet
Los Angeles, 1996

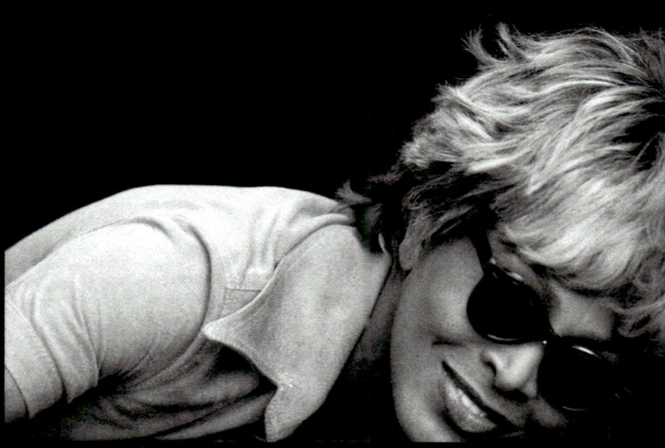

Villefranche, France
1995

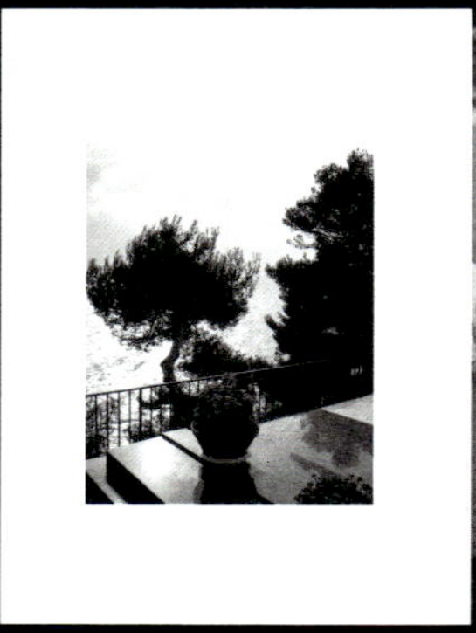
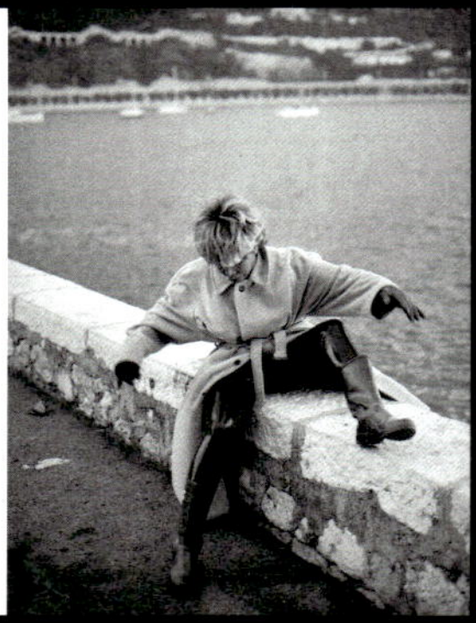

Villefranche, France
1995

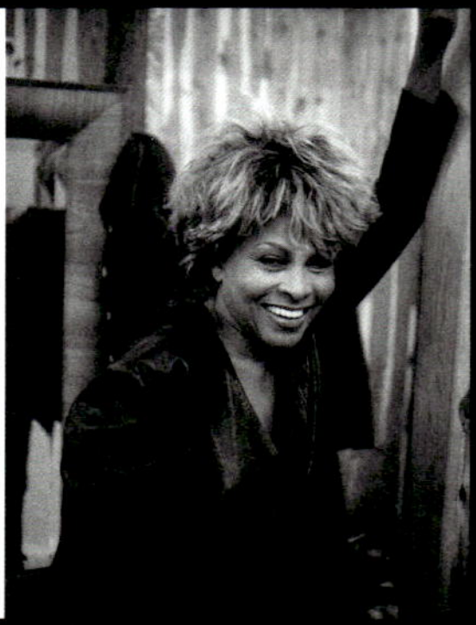

Villefranche, France
1995

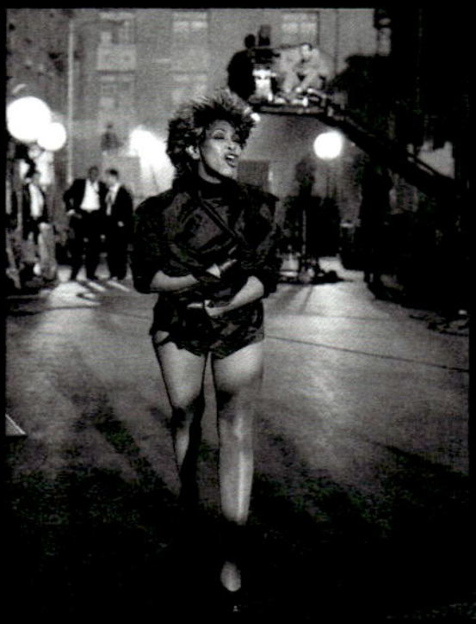

Paramount Studios
Hollywood, CA, 1996

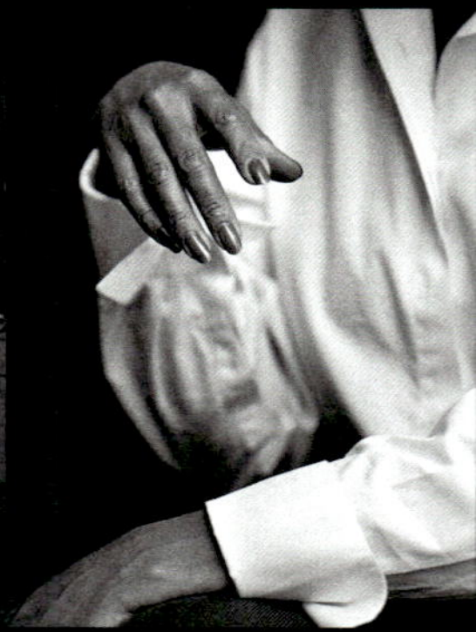

Deauville, France
1989

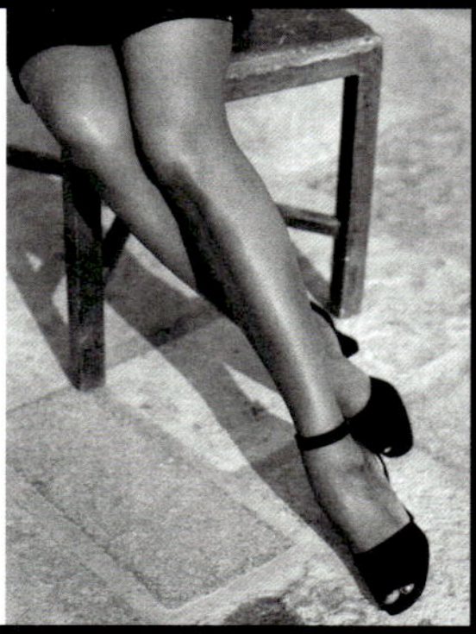

Nice, France
1996

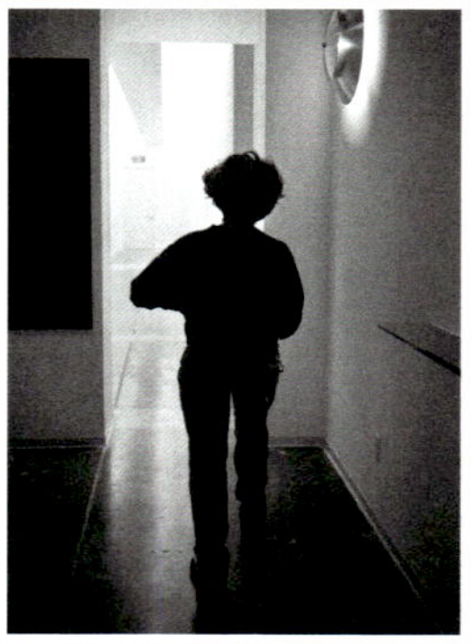

Los Angeles
1993

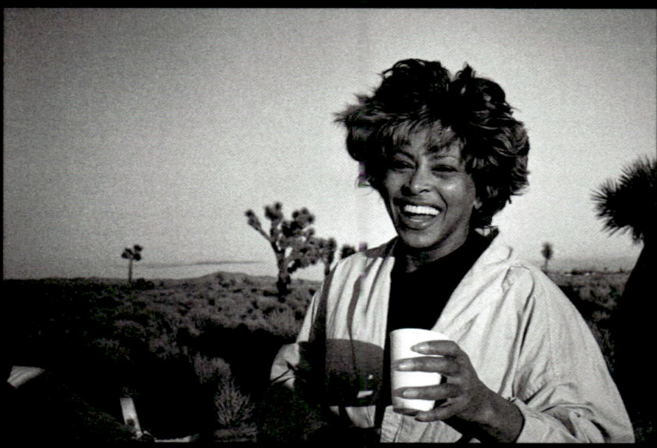

Mojave Desert
California, USA, 1993

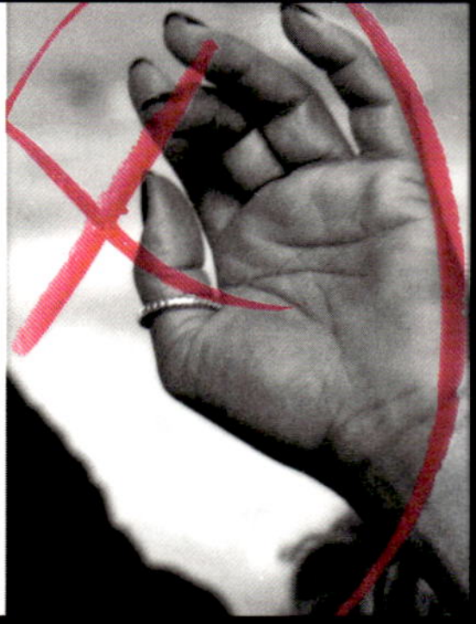

Los Angeles
1996

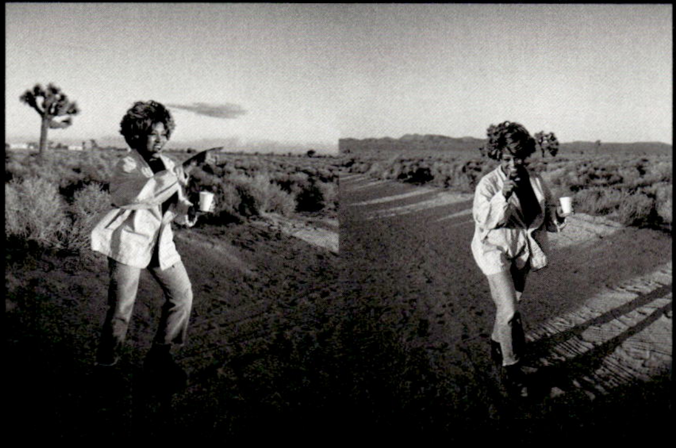

Mojave Desert
California, USA, 1993

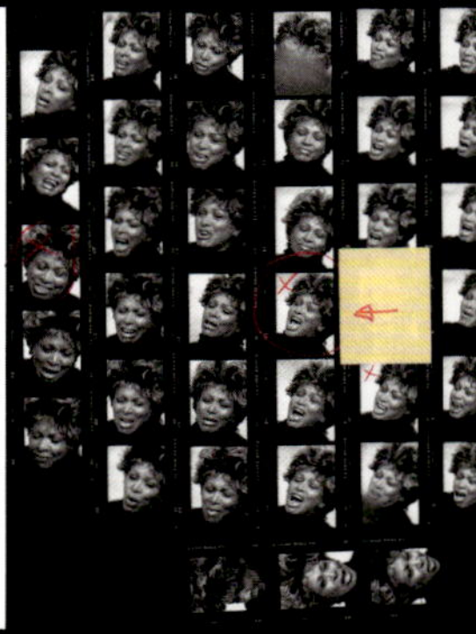

Contact sheet
Los Angeles, 1996

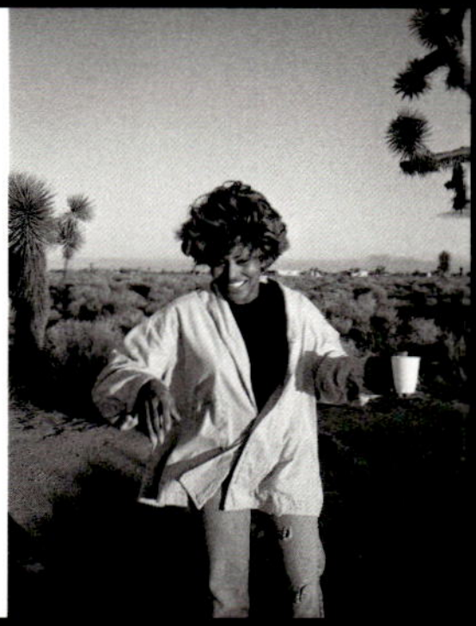

Mojave Desert
California, USA, 1993

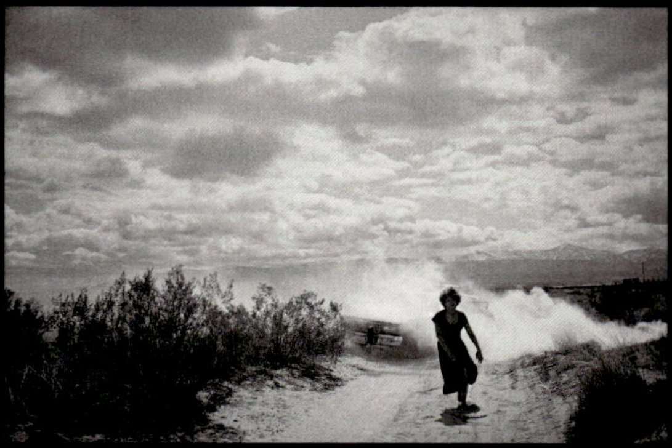

Mojave Desert
California, USA, 1993

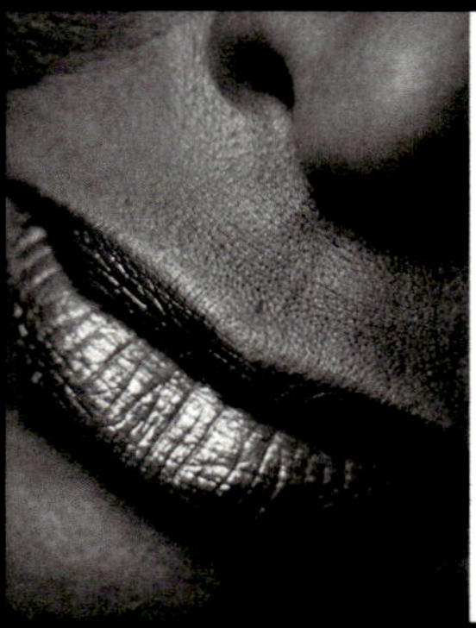

Los Angeles
1996

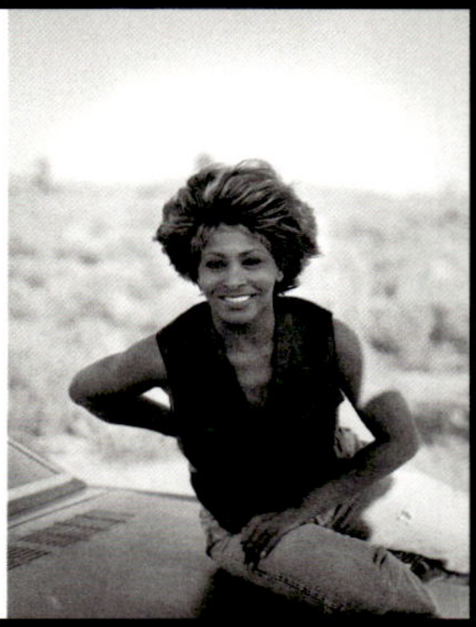

Mojave Desert
California, USA, 1993

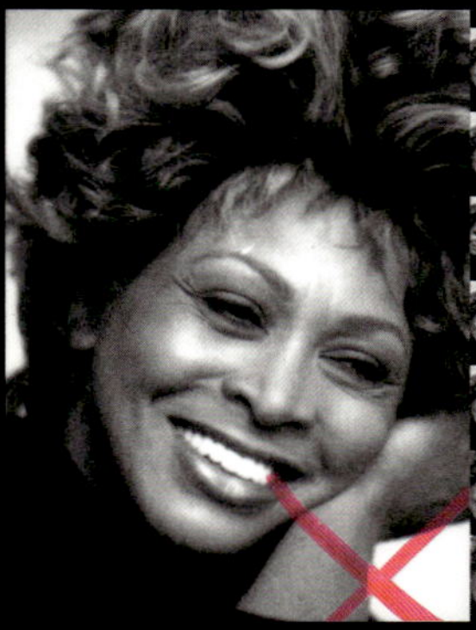

Los Angeles
1996

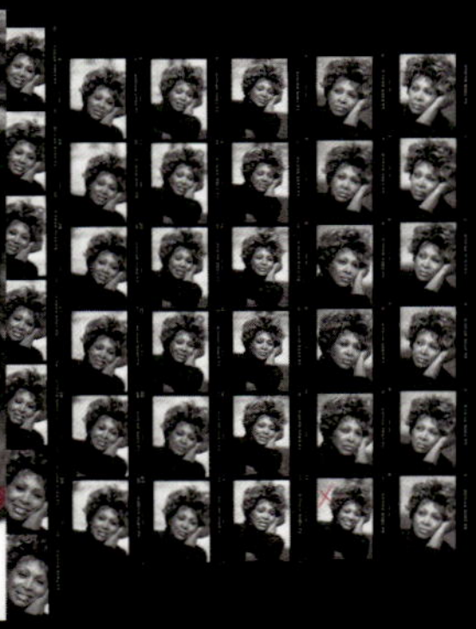

Contact sheet
Los Angeles, 1996

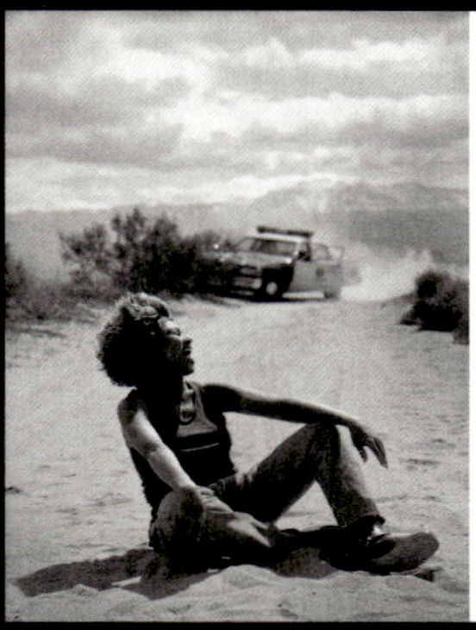

Mojave Desert
California, USA, 1993

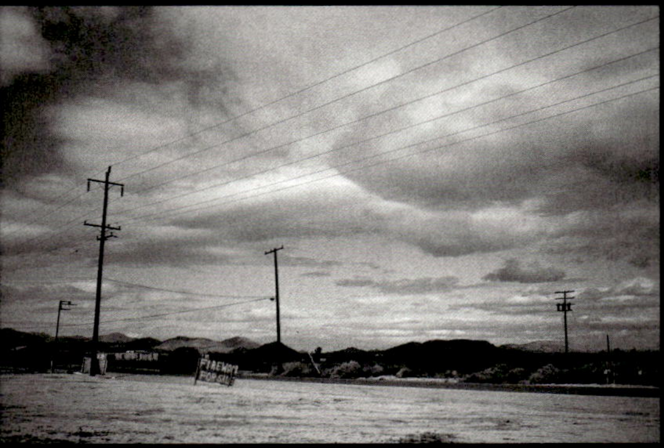

Mojave Desert
California, USA, 1993

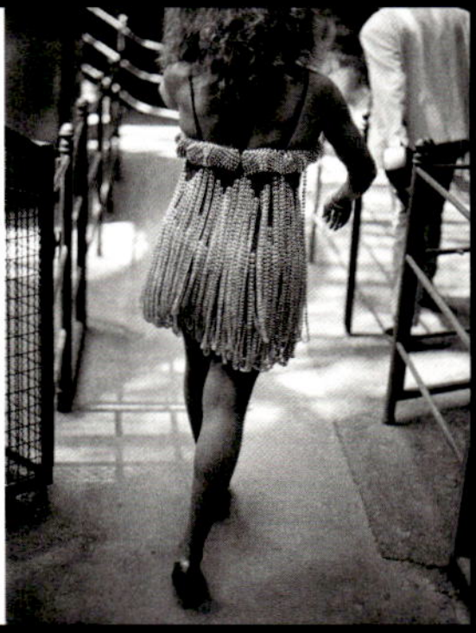

Eiffel Tower
Paris, 1989

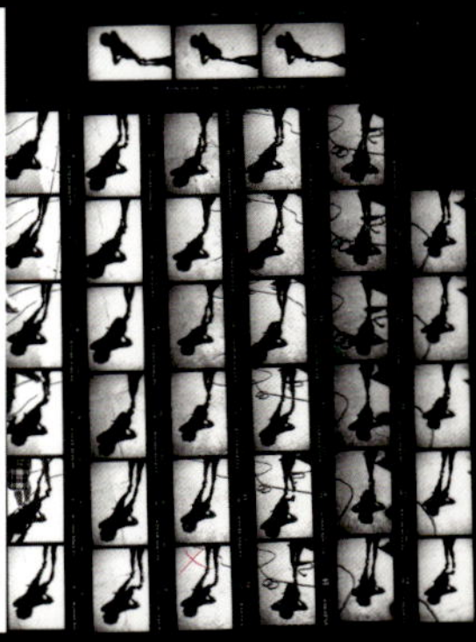

Contact sheet
Paramount Studios, Hollywood, CA, 1996

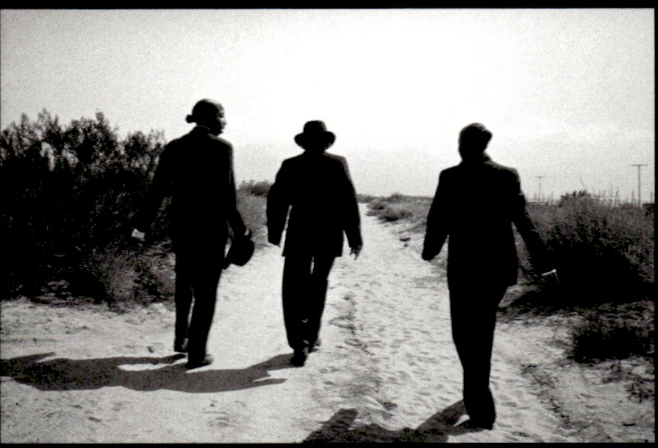

Tina with Nicole and Nikita Blount
Mojave Desert, CA, USA, 1993

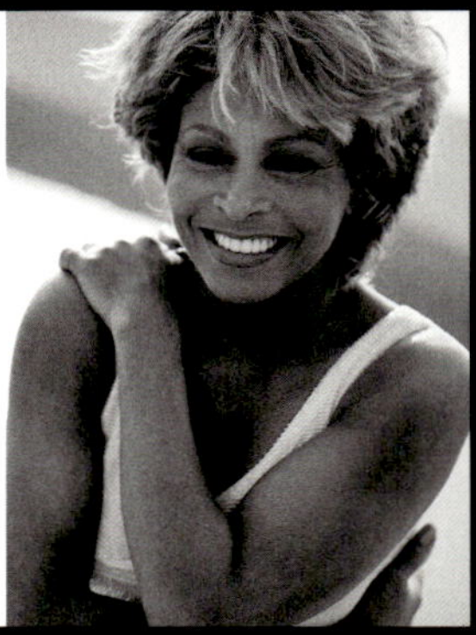

Nice, France
1996

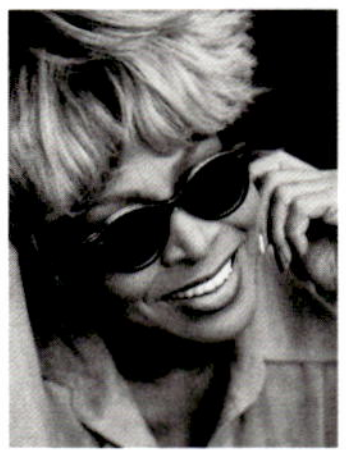

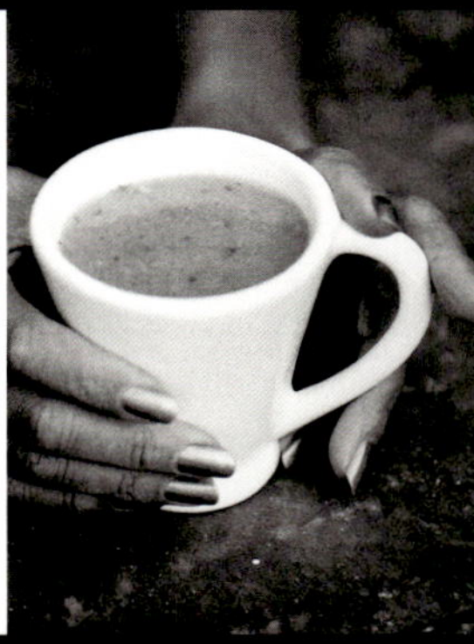

Villefranche, France
1995

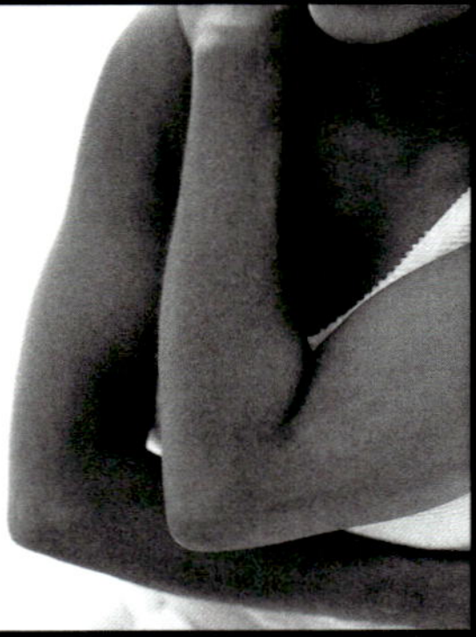

Nice, France
1996

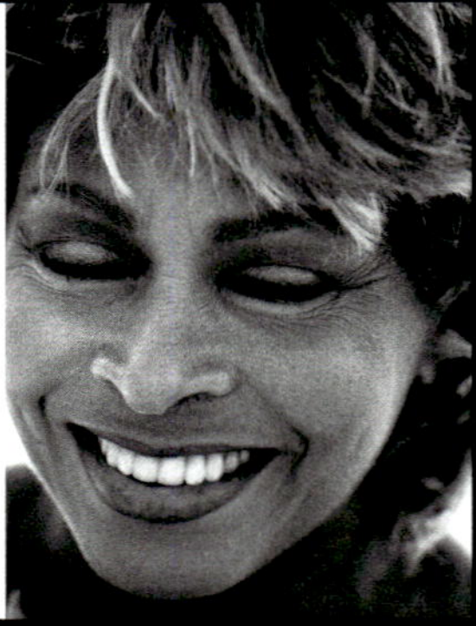

Villefranche, France
1995

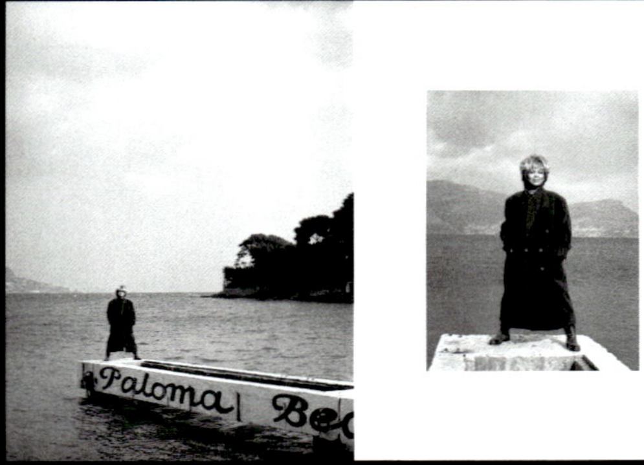

Villefranche, France
1995

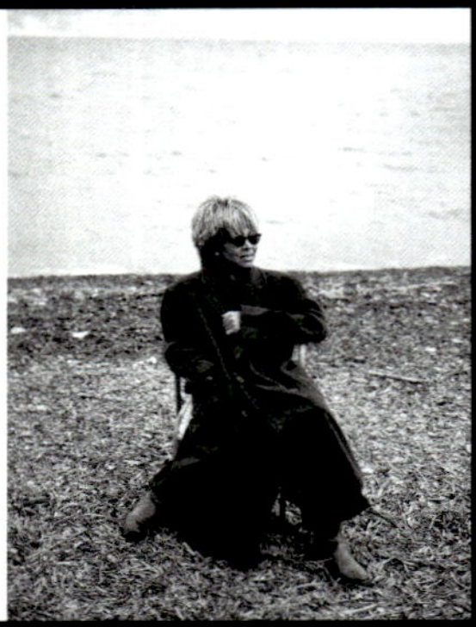

Villefranche, France
1995

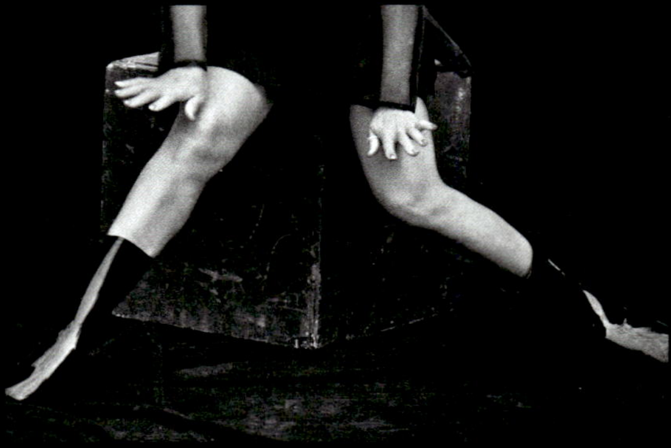

Villefranche, France
1995

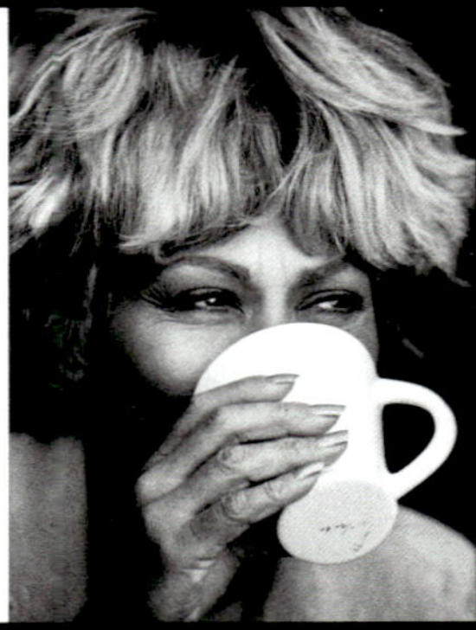

Villefranche, France
1995

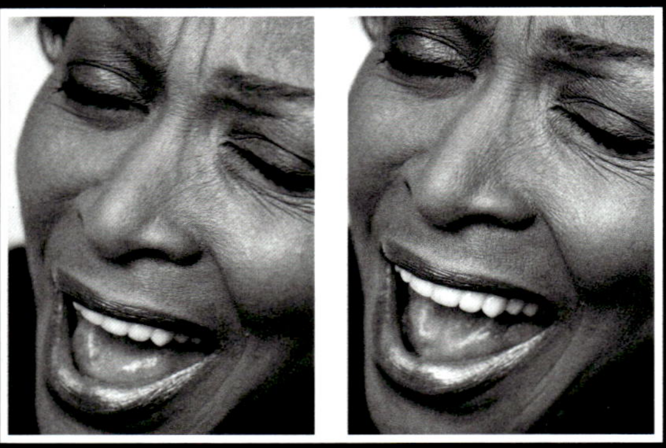

Los Angeles
1996

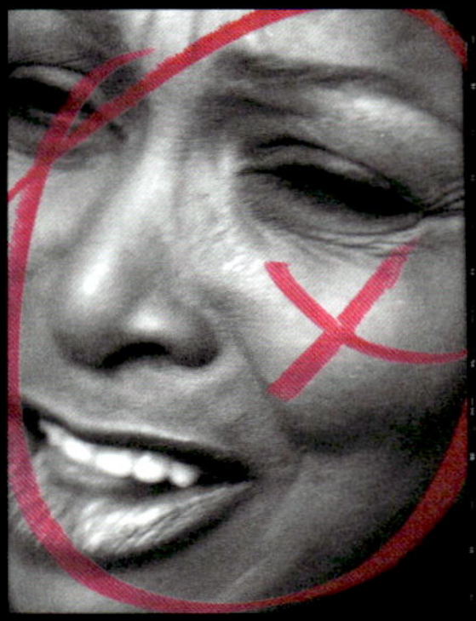

Los Angeles
1996

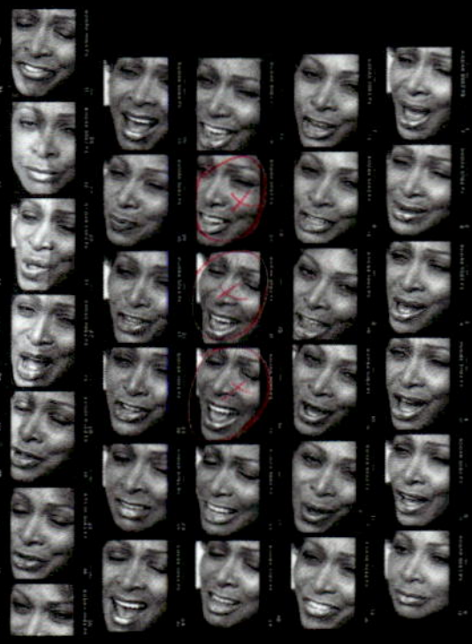

Contact sheet
Los Angeles, 1996

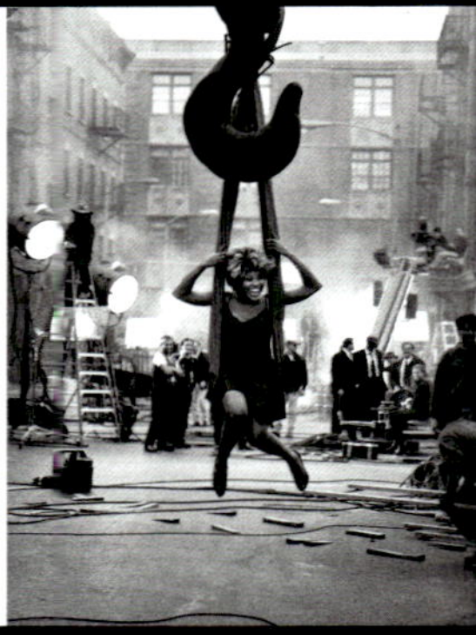

Paramount Studios
Hollywood, CA, 1996

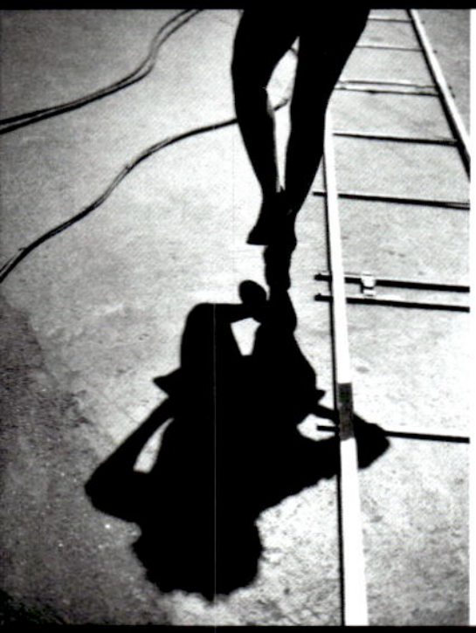

Paramount Studios
Hollywood, CA, 1996

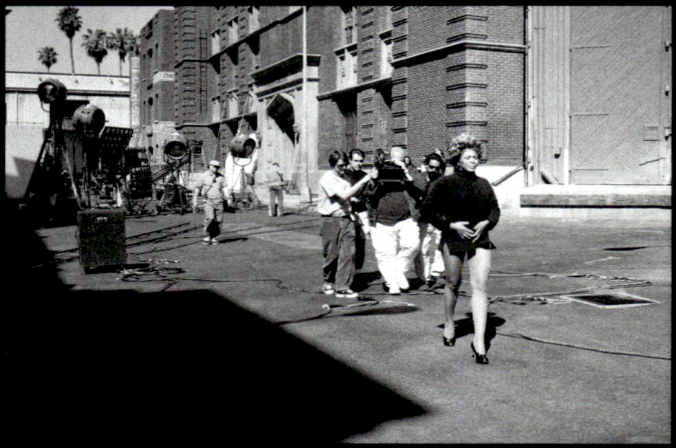

Paramount Studios
Hollywood, CA, 1996

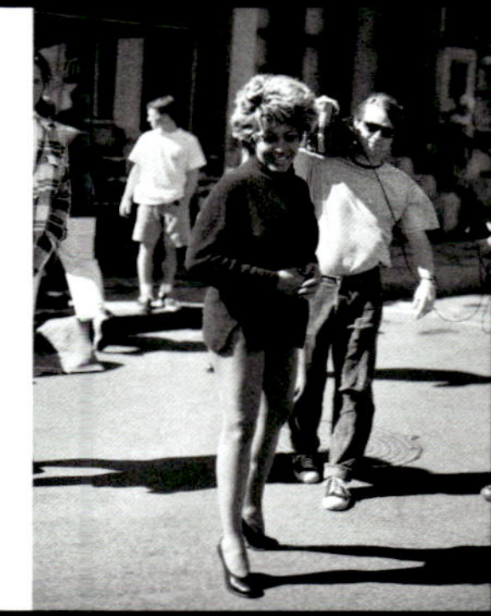

Paramount Studios
Hollywood, CA, 1996

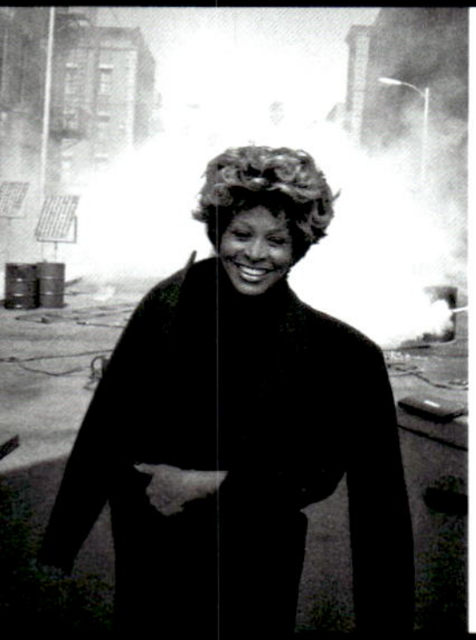

Paramount Studios
Hollywood, CA, 1996

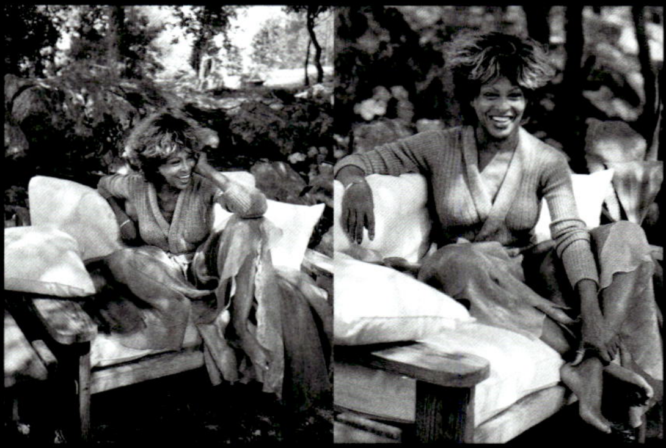

Nice, France
1996

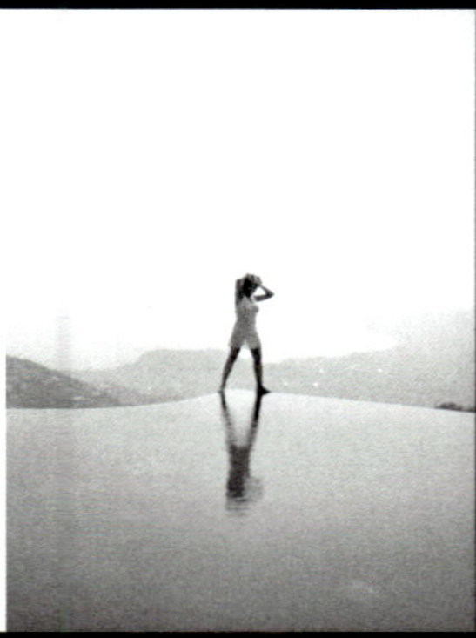

Nice, France
1996

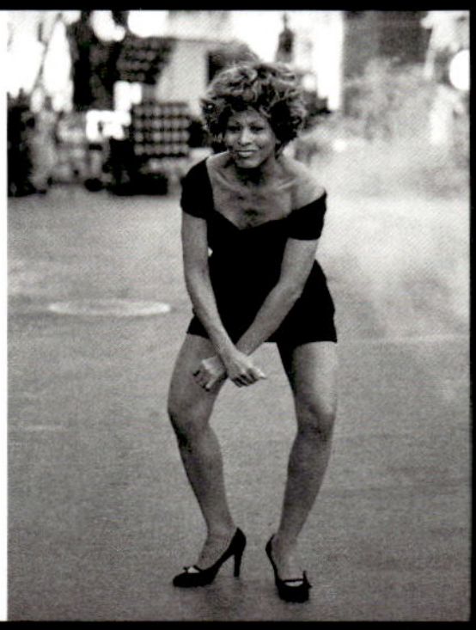

Paramount Studios
Hollywood, CA, 1996

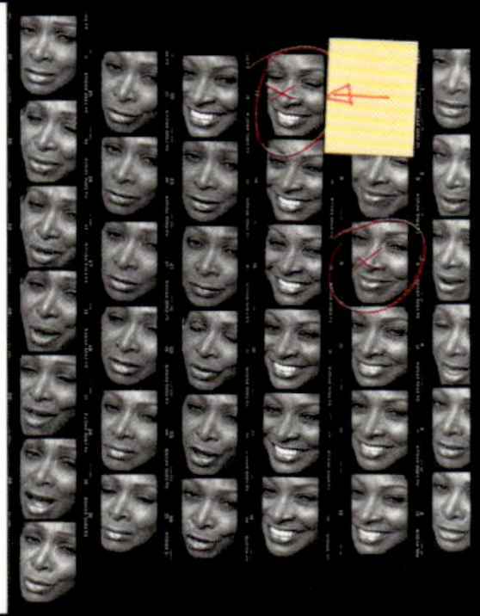

Contact sheet
Los Angeles, 1996

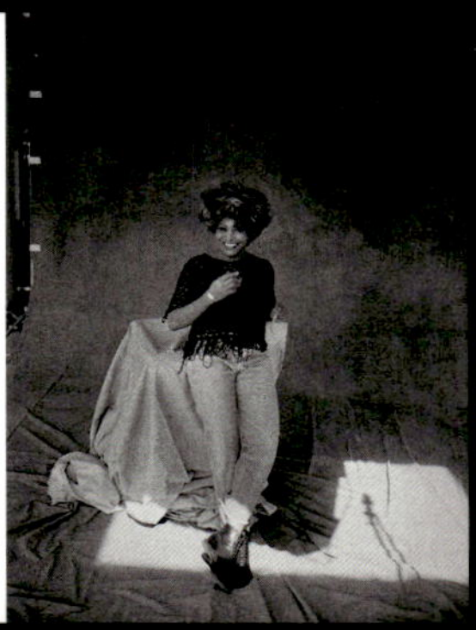

Los Angeles
1993

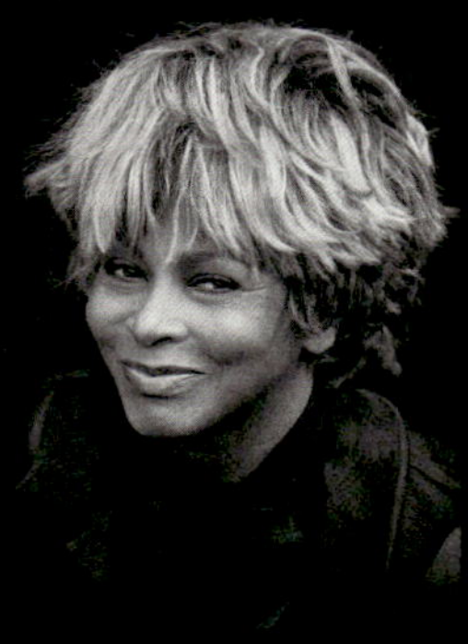

Villefranche, France
1995

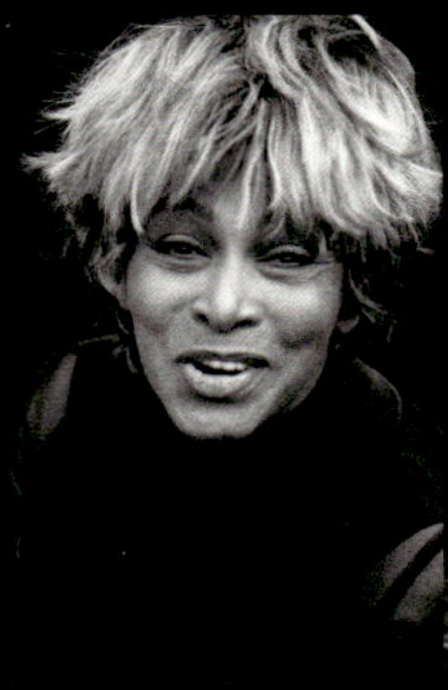

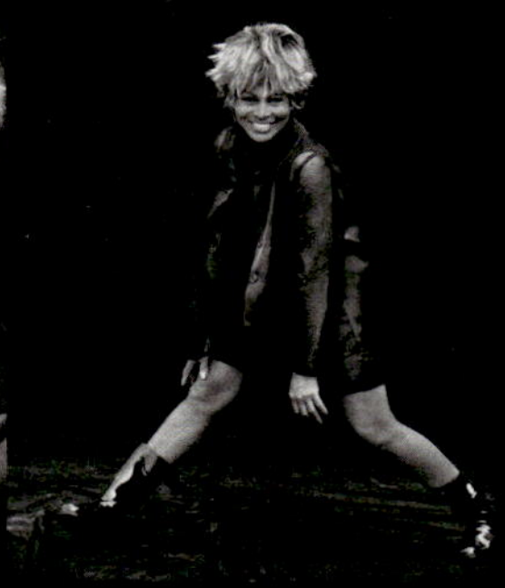

Villefranche, France
1995

COVER
Los Angeles, 1993

BACK COVER
Eiffel Tower, Paris, 1989

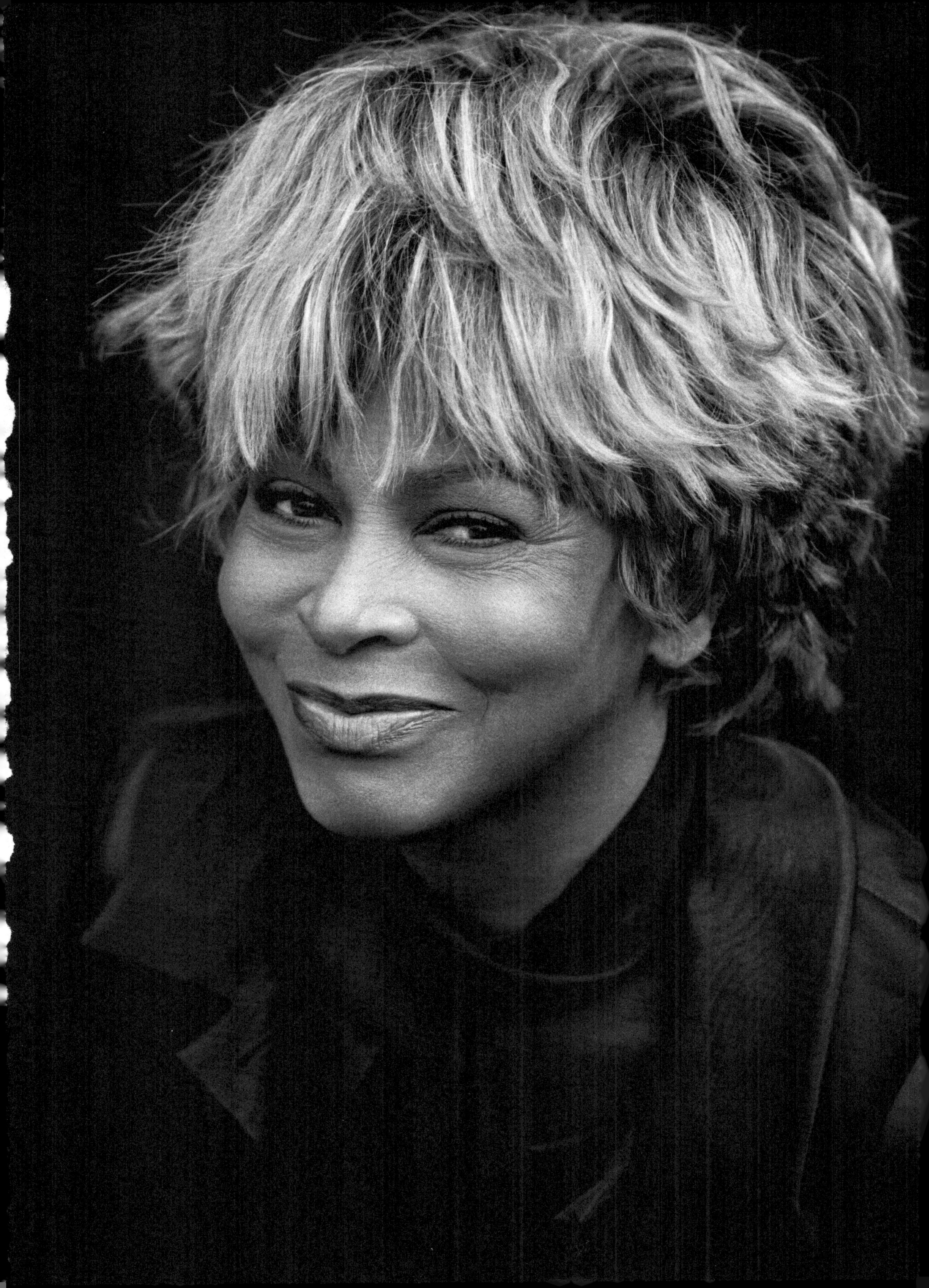

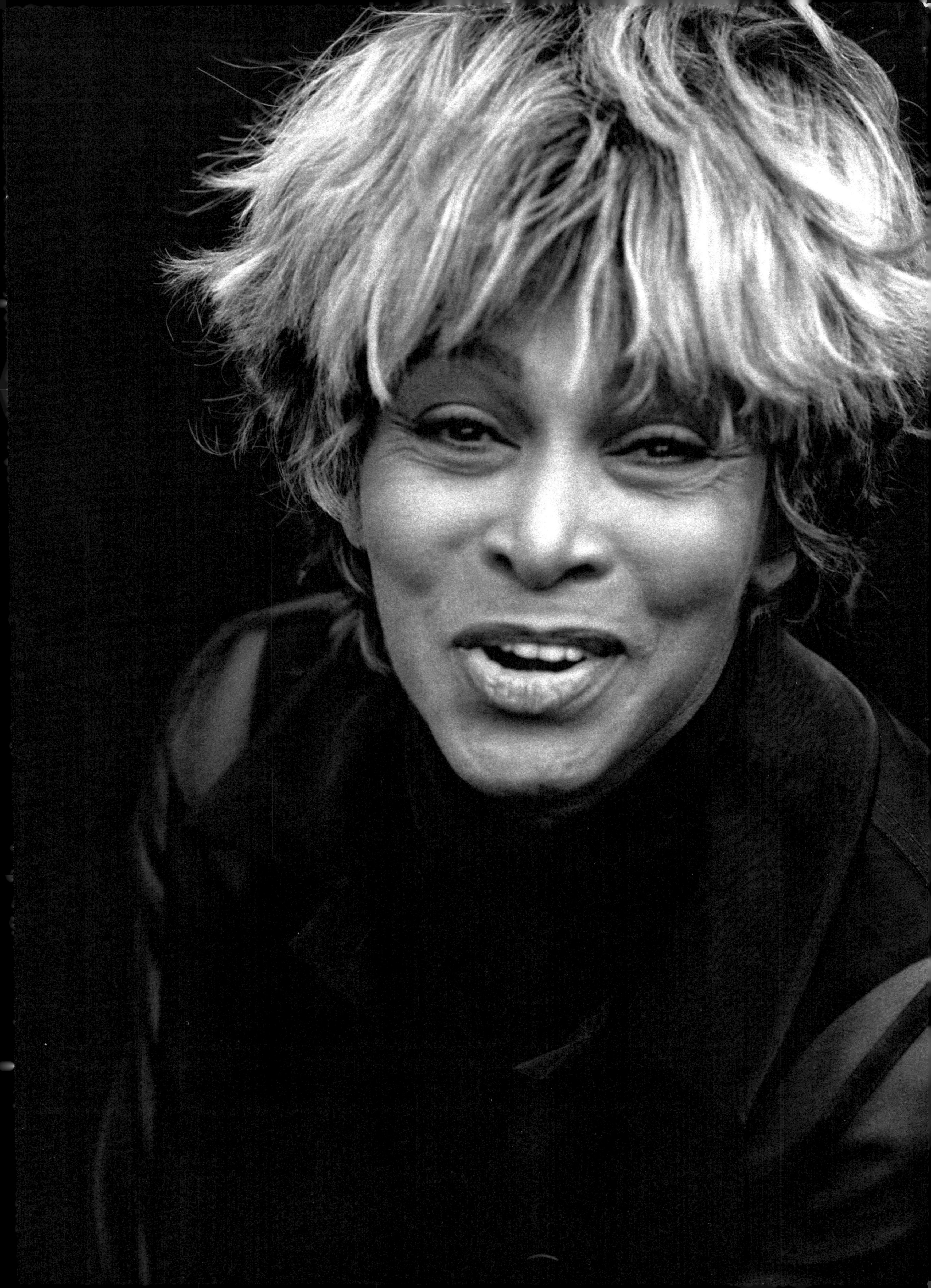